FLORAL PASSION

ALBERT VAN DER MEY

THIES BOGNER

JOHN VAN KOOTEN

INTRODUCTION

Flowers can truly enrich people's lives. This overwhelming conviction kindled and flamed into the roaring inspiration for **Floral Passion**.

As we entered the new millennium, North Americans were moving at break-neck speed to achieve social and financial success. But this has come at a price: the resulting changes in lifestyle have produced health-shattering levels of stress and anxiety beyond anything experienced before.

Changes are needed, and changes have begun. Invariably, in times of conflict and despair, humans have recognized the need to return to the natural world around them to get re-grounded with our core values. While nature itself doesn't replace or eliminate stress, it does bring a peaceful balance that is refreshing and welcome.

Floral Passion is a major catalyst for renewed balance in our lives. By bringing nature into our lives and homes, **Floral Passion** brings a new perspective. **Floral Passion** doesn't suggest we abandon our current ways; rather, it helps us to learn how to progress from just surviving to fully enjoying life. Quantity of life is giving way to a focus on the quality of life . . . and flowers can play a role in this transformation.

People need and love heroes. **Floral Passion** showcases the 'icons' of the floral industry: dynamic, forward-looking men and women who shaped their own lives and set the stage to change the world through flowers.

Floral Passion is a market-driven wakeup call to the power and benefits of flowers.

Just as doctors prescribe medicine to help us get better, **Floral Passion** is the prescription for a healthy, fulfilling, self-actualizing lifestyle through flowers.

Flowers offer countless inexpensive options for creative home decor.

Flowers can improve health and increase lifespan.

Flowers bring serenity and peace to a frenetic world.

Floral Passion is more than a book. It is a defining moment in our quest for the ultimate goal: an improved quality of life.

John Van Kooten
Publisher

— Debbie Zimmerman: "A unique presentation on a remarkable industry."

In Floral Passion, author Albert van der Mey, publisher John Van Kooten and photographer Thies Bogner focus on Niagara as one of the most significant areas of floral production in North America, due in large part to the blending of skills and know-how from the Old World and the pioneering spirit of the New World.

Earnest development of Niagara's rich agricultural resources can be traced to the granting of land parcels to the United Empire Loyalists who settled in the Niagara Peninsula following the Revolutionary War in 1776. Greenhouse development started later through the efforts of Mennonites who came to Niagara. However, the flower-growing industry, now the largest contributor to Niagara's agricultural economy, enjoyed significant growth with the immigration of growers from the Netherlands following the Second World War.

The Region of Niagara, rich in both history and tradition, provides a credible and exciting context for Floral Passion. The book unlocks not only many of the secrets of the producers but also the power of flowers to heighten our senses, strengthen our ability to cope with sad times and enhance our level of enjoyment in good times. Flowers influence every one of our life's events, adding beauty, serenity, quiet calm, a sense of success and gratitude for family and friends and solace in special moments.

Niagara boasts over 200 greenhouse operations dedicated to floral crops, cut flowers, potted foliage and flowers, bedding plants and nursery stock. Floral Passion is a testament to Niagara's floriculture producers who contribute over 30 per cent of Ontario's floral production. Ontario is North America's third largest producer in the greenhouse and floral industry.

In Holland, the Garden Capital of the World, the link between a burgeoning tourism industry and the horticulture and floriculture industry is well known and continually promoted to the advantage of both. Each year at the world-famous Keukenhof flower gardens and at many other attractions and events, including the Floriade exhibition held every 10 years, millions come from around the world not only to view the beauty of flowers but to conduct industry demonstrations, conferences and technology seminars.

The horticulture and floriculture industry in Ontario is taking bold steps to catch up in this global trend. Encouraged by their friends in the grape and wine industry and by their success stories here and in other countries, growers, suppliers and industry associations are exploring the partnership opportunities with leaders in Niagara's tourism industry.

Floral Passion is an enjoyable read made richer by its vibrant photography and human stories based on vision and achievement.

It is a pleasure to write the Foreword for Floral Passion, a unique presentation on a remarkable industry which not only supports the economy but also family life, teamwork, persistence and environmental sensitivity.

Debbie Zimmerman
Chair, Regional Municipality of Niagara

3

CONTENTS

FLORAL PASSION

Floral Passion

We could have called this book Niagara's Big Secret.

Just ask someone to name the main things for which Ontario's alluring Niagara Peninsula is known and the answer is likely to include the Niagara Falls, the fun places, the historic sites and other attractions, the parklands along the Niagara River, the vineyards and the wineries, the fruit orchards, the Welland Canal, the places of fine dining and lodging, Niagara-on-the-Lake with its Shaw Festival and flower-lined main street, and so on.

But don't expect greenhouses to be mentioned.

It's still a little-known fact, especially among non-residents, that the glass and plastic-covered structures dotting the landscape constitute one of the biggest income generators in the area, surpassing even the grape and wine sector.

A primary aim of Floral Passion is to increase public awareness of Niagara's blossoming floricultural industry whose gorgeous flowers and plants bring so much pleasure and contentment to millions of Canadians and Americans throughout the year.

And we want to introduce you to many of the enterprising and resourceful people who make it all happen.

By featuring the Niagara Peninsula, we do not intend to ignore the fact that flowers and plants are produced commercially throughout Ontario and in other areas of Canada, as well as the United States. Everyone involved in the business of growing happiness deserves a big salute. In many ways, the story of Niagara's growers can be applied to all.

Niagara is a natural choice because it allows us to focus on a large number of greenhouses concentrated in a compact geographical area. Furthermore, the name is easily recognizable by people around the world. It's a perfect setting for a gripping tale of beauty and romance.

Then there's the Big Secret: the hugeness of Niagara's output of flowers and plants. It accounts for 35 per cent of Ontario's total greenhouse flower production. In fact, Niagara is North America's third largest producer of floricultural products, following California and Florida.

The Agricultural Census of 2001 recorded 215 flower growers in the Regional Municipality of Niagara, which makes up most of the Peninsula, and placed the farmgate value of their production at $232 million.

— The Niagara Peninsula lies between Lake Erie and Lake Ontario and extends 55 miles from Hamilton in the west to the Niagara River. Its backbone is a wooded cuesta ridge called the Niagara Escarpment. The Regional Municipality of Niagara, which makes up most of the Peninsula, consists of 12 municipalities: Town of Fort Erie, Town of Grimsby, Town of Lincoln, City of Niagara Falls, Town of Niagara-on-the-Lake, Town of Pelham, City of Port Colborne, City of St. Catharines, City of Thorold, Township of Wainfleet, City of Welland and Township of West Lincoln. Within many of these municipalities, there are villages that have retained their charm. We refer to many of them in the book to make it easier for readers to locate specific properties.

Floral Passion

PREFACE

Add to that the value of the flowers grown in the other political areas of the Peninsula – the City of Hamilton in the northeast, including Stoney Creek, and Haldimand County, including Dunnville, in the southeast – as well as the earnings of the support businesses – greenhouse construction, seed supply, mechanical services, trucking, etc. – and the total income is probably approaching $1 billion a year.

It's also significant that the wonderful world of flowers provides more than 3,000 jobs for Niagara residents.

We did not set out to interview every grower in the Peninsula. Had we done so, a book twice as thick as this one would have been necessary to carry all the material. But we did end up talking with a large number of producers, big and small, and their stories and accompanying photographs make up a large segment of the book.

We also cover wholesalers, nursery operators, greenhouse vegetable growers (many flower growers began their career with vegetables) and suppliers to the horticultural industry. There's also a chapter on some of the key people and institutions that assist the greenhouse operators in invaluable ways. Another chapter is devoted to the values that have made many of the growers so successful in their personal and business lives.

We even went to the Netherlands, the country of origin of many of Niagara's growers, to find out why it's often referred to as the Garden Centre of the World. But our main focus, of course, is on Niagara which one day may be appreciated as much for its flowers as for all its other treasures. We feature the efforts that have already gained one community, Niagara-on-the-Lake, an international reputation for its beautiful displays on public and private properties.

There's much more for you to discover in Floral Passion.

So enjoy!

CHAPTER ONE
PIONEERING SPIRIT

'My father's interest switched to greenhouses in 1925. He grew tomato plants for all the neighbours around him. Then he expanded quite a bit, adding annual flowers.'
– Robert Martin

George and Mary Ellen Jeffery struggled to make ends meet after the general collapse of the stock market in 1929 and the onset of the Great Depression.

They grew celery on their little farm on Vine Street in St. Catharines and took it to the public market. Although it was of good quality, there were few buyers. In those dark days, when even pennies were scarce, most people opted to do without such luxuries as celery.

The Depression had begun in the United States, spreading quickly to Canada and other industrial countries. U.S. President Franklin D. Roosevelt assessed the damage in his first inaugural address: "The withered leaves of industrial enterprise lie on every side; farmers find no markets for their produce; the saving of many years in thousands of families are gone. More important, a host of unemployed citizens face the grim problem of existence, and an equally great number toil with little return."

'He was so determined to make a success of himself that he worked seven days a week. But he paid the price. He was in the hospital three times for malnutrition.'

With hardly any income, it was only a matter of time before George and Mary Ellen lost their farm and livelihood. This turn of events, and the difficulties in caring for their children and themselves, affected them profoundly. The stresses of everyday life, compounded by the trauma of losing a child shortly after birth, caused Mary Ellen to become senile, an affliction she carried until her death in 1999 at age 93.

The story that their grandson, Jim Jeffery, relates is a deeply personal one. It's mostly about his grandparents, both of English stock, and his parents, all of whom shaped his character, his life and his business, Jeffery's Greenhouses Inc. on Lakeshore Road West in St. Catharines, one of the largest flower-growing operations in the Niagara Peninsula. His admiration and appreciation are clearly evident.

"My grandmother lived a healthy life, although she was not mentally healthy," he says. "She passed away in February and the previous fall she was still planting in the

— Members of the Jeffery family – Jim, Jimmy, Sandy, Kim, Barb and her husband Rodd Gibson – pose with two striking features: a revolutionary spraying device and a handy cart for moving around the greenhouses.

greenhouses. She had the solace of working."

When his grandfather lost the farm, he also lost his enthusiasm for work. It was actually his eldest son, George, a teenager then, who sparked him on. Jim, George's son, says his Dad was "an aggressive young man who got someone else to sign for him to buy a 12-acre farm with a house at what is now Charles Daley Park in St. Catharines. He grew vegetables and so on. My grandfather looked after the work horses."

The younger George took the produce to the market in St. Catharines and to the local co-op. He managed to earn enough money to look after the needs of his parents and five siblings, the care of the horses and the yearly mortgage payments of $99. Largely through his efforts, the family was able to weather the storm.

"My Dad basically ran the farm during the day. In the evenings, he drove a little pickup truck to Cayuga and the south end of the Peninsula and bought eggs from farmers. He stayed up three nights a week to candle them, looking for imperfections, and then took them to the market along with his other stuff. He was so determined to make a success of himself that he worked seven days a week. But he paid the price. He was in the hospital three times for malnutrition. He just didn't eat enough while he was doing all these things. Twice he was found in the ditch with his pickup truck, the victim of exhaustion. Because of the way his parents were, he raised his brothers and sisters. They all looked up to him. I remember an aunt telling me that my Dad took her out to buy a dress. He also brought home the groceries."

George married his sweetheart, Annie Emma, in 1942. Since they wanted a place of their own, and the house was already occupied, they lived for a year in two small makeshift rooms in a 15-foot end section of a tall cold frame used for starting spring vegetables. The housing problem was solved when they bought a 15-acre farm on Lakeshore Road. There they grew vegetables and harvested peaches, pears and plums. This mixture, plus the vegetables from the other farm, gave them a good variety of products for their stand at the market. Three of George's brothers worked with them for a number of years, but then went in different directions.

— George and Mary Ellen Jeffery relax at their small farm in 1910.

Judy, the first child of George and Annie, was born in 1944. Jim arrived in 1947.

"I remember when I was four or five hanging on to my grandfather's leg as we were going from farm to farm on a wagon. He looked after the horses and brought equipment from one farm to the other."

Jim's family had a Friday night ritual of buying groceries for both themselves and the grandparents. On one of those evenings in 1951, while on the way to deliver the purchases, their pickup truck was involved in a collision and Annie and her two children were thrown from the vehicle. The mother, 33 years old, was seriously injured. For the rest of her life, she would be totally blind and deaf in one ear.

"It's a miracle that she survived," says Jim. "For a time, no one expected her to live. But she was very strong-willed. My father, too, was confident that she would make it, even though he was getting bad reports from the doctors, because he pretty well finished building a new house for

her while she stayed in a Toronto hospital for a year. We had a housekeeper for awhile. One morning, Mom got up and told her: 'I don't need any more help. Thank you very much.' She was on her own after that. And it wasn't too many years later that was also cooking, baking, doing the laundry and ironing. Later on, when we had the greenhouse operation going, she always made a lunch for us. She lived a happy life and passed away just before her 80th birthday."

In 1960, another tragic event occurred. A long-time employee who lived alone in the help house on the property fell asleep while smoking. A next-door neighbour saw smoke coming from the house when she woke up early in the morning. Her son and Jim, his friend, ran to the house to see what was going on, groped their way through the smoke and mess, located the man and pulled him outside. He was dead.

"It was a very traumatic experience," says Jim. "It took me a number of years to get over it." He and his friend received a letter of commendation from the local police department for their rescue attempt.

Two years later, a fire started in one of the two large packing barns on the property.

"Some neighbours had company over on a Sunday and the kids were playing with matches," says Jim. "The fire quickly spread to the other barn. Our remaining horse – the other one had died of old age – was in one of the barns, but it was led to safety. Both buildings were destroyed. My father took it very hard. It seemed like everything he had worked for was suddenly gone. The next morning, he was in the kitchen, sobbed for a few hours, got up and went outside. It was the first time I had seen him cry. It was a sad thing. But he got back on his feet quickly and built a new barn and added a number of greenhouses, using steel bought from the scrapyard at six cents a pound."

The spectacular fire attracted a large number of onlookers. When all the excitement died down, the Jefferys discovered to their dismay that some of the tools they had salvaged from the burning barns and placed outside had been stolen. A further check revealed that thieves had been busy in the cabbage patch as well.

After the first farm was expropriated by the provincial government for Charles Daley Park, all the operations and living accommodations were consolidated at the Lakeshore Road property. In addition to his own vegetable production, Jim's father began growing tomato plants for other farmers. At one point, before competition from Georgia and the Carolinas made significant inroads, this business amounted to four million plants a year. He filled the off-season by buying old houses, renovating them and securing tenants.

After finishing high school, Jim had visions of being a dentist. But he had different thoughts while working on the farm in the summer months: he should be helping his father and preparing himself to eventually carry on the business. So he cancelled his planned studies at the University of Toronto, worked at a transformer factory for a period when there wasn't much to do at home and then, at the urging of his father, signed a 50-50 partnership.

"That was his continued way of saying: 'You're doing this. No fooling around.' In fact, after we came home from the lawyer's office, he never bought or sold anything anymore. He was always there to consult with, but rarely stayed until the final decision was made. I pretty well ran the place at age 18."

At that time, the Jeffery farm grew mainly staked tomatoes, hothouse tomatoes and seedless cucumbers. The gradual change to flowers began in 1965. The first crop consisted of bedding plants – 1,200 boxes in total – which were retailed on the street and also sold at the wholesale market at the Ontario Food Terminal in Toronto.

"We took down more of our orchard to expand the greenhouses," says Jim. "I was convinced that I

— Jim Jeffery, shown in 1967: "I pretty well ran the place at age 18."

wanted to be a greenhouse grower, not a fruit farmer. It was an economic decision. I thought at the time that a fruit farmer needed at least 50 acres to be successful. We started with pansies at the beginning of April and followed through with other bedding plants. In the summer, we had hothouse and field tomatoes and cucumbers. We were still at the food terminal in early November. It was a good place to be because it allowed us to think differently about the company, consider who our customers are, who we would like our customers to be and what products we should grow. We also learned a lot from watching the other vendors at the market – how they changed their crops, for example."

Jeffery's Greenhouses did retail flower sales for 15 years. Then the firm decided to be a wholesale grower only, a status that remains in effect. Under the direction of Jim's daughter, Barbara, the sales manager, it deals directly with its customers at certain times of year and with brokers at other times.

"Seventy-five per cent of the sales are our own," she says.

— A scene from 1944: a harvest is under way on the Jeffery farm.

"We supply a good part of the Ontario market. Only 15 per cent of our sales are in the United States. We're known for our bedding plants."

The greenhouse area on the Lakeshore Road property grew to 430,000 square feet. In 1997, the firm purchased two adjoining 25-acre farms on Fourth Avenue in Jordan Station to accommodate further greenhouse expansion as well as the loading and shipping docks. At last count, 200,000 square feet were under glass.

"We're growing fast," says Jim, "but we're not growing as fast as our customers are asking us for our product, which is a wonderful thing. We still need to buy from other growers to fill our orders. We are growing at a speed we can handle with our infrastructure and our staff. We are adding on an acre at a time."

One of the farms had been a grapery; the other a grazing area for sheep. Many of the vines were removed for the excavation of a three-quarter-million-gallon retention pond. But three acres of grapes at the front of the property were saved to create a nice entrance. A neighbouring farmer looks after the pruning and harvesting.

Barbara and her husband, Rodd Gibson, live on the property. She's worked for the firm since she was a teen, not always with full enthusiasm.

"Everytime we had a day off school, we had to go into the greenhouses," she says, somewhat pitiably.

Her father laughs. He can remember experiencing the same feeling when, as a child, he had to work in the cabbage patch and was paid $2 for a nine to 10-hour shift.

Rodd, educated in accounting, looks after the trucking end, dispatching from 15 to 20 owned and rented vehicles a day during the busy periods. He is also technical adviser in the seed area and handles the purchasing.

Kim, the other daughter, is administrative co-ordinator. She worked in the greenhouses at first and then served as shipping manager. Jimmy, the son, is involved in trucking and dispatching and his wife, Amy, works in the greenhouses. Besides the family members, there are 65 full-time employees. The number on the payroll doubles in the spring.

Jim's wife, Sandy, was already doing the books of the business at age 18. After their marriage in 1967, she also worked in the greenhouses, seeding and planting, as well looking after all the financial work for her husband's parents. By that time, George's eyesight was deteriorating. He lived until December, 1989. Sandy continued her work for the firm, first as office manager and then as human resources manager, until her retirement in 1998.

"Sandy was and still is my inspiration in my mission to build a prosperous, happy family business," says Jim. "She has always been there for me on the good and bad days to help resolve challenges and plan for the future."

He also talks fondly of his sister, Judy, and her husband, Norm Riches, who teamed up with him and Sandy for a number of years to run and manage the company. They are now retired.

As he looks into his crystal ball, Jim sees a number of challenges, such as getting the selling prices that his company needs to counter ever-increasing costs. But he also sees a bright future.

"The growth will continue," he says, "because the demand is there."

— This is the Jeffery greenhouse complex on Lakeshore Road West in St. Catharines. The firm also has a plant on Fourth Avenue in Jordan Station.

"I know some people are complaining about greenhouses, but . . . "

Rob Haynes, whose family has 100,000 square feet of greenhouse area in Jordan Station, pauses, shakes his head and then continues:

"We look upon the greenhouse industry as a saviour of our land. We're the oldest farm in the region and one of the oldest farms in English Canada that is still intact. We've been good caretakers of this land. Not too many families have kept their property in agriculture like we have. We live along the urban boundary and have been able to protect our land from urban development."

When the Free Trade Agreement between Canada and the United States went into effect in 1989, he explains, the easing of tariffs on imported products adversely affected the fruit industry in which his operation, Don Haynes and Sons Farm, was heavily involved. Faced with either continuing solely as fruit farmers and watching their losses pile up or diversifying into flower production, an industry that welcomed an open border, the family opted for the latter. As a result, they were able to keep their heads above water and move on to much better times.

'Our strong point is family. It is the most important thing.'

The Haynes enterprise on Haynes Road now has three divisions: the farm on which 80 acres of grapes are grown strictly for the juice trade, the B & R Haynes greenhouse operation and its wholesale and shipping arm and a manufacturing facility called JGS Sales which produces plastic sleeves for flower growers throughout Ontario and beyond. Employment is provided for 80 to 150 people, depending on the time of year, as well as 13 family members. The current holdings exist of 160 acres of owned land, of which the greenhouses occupy only two acres, and 25 acres of rented land.

The farm dates back to 1784 when the Niagara area was a wilderness inhabited by a sprinkling of settlers, mostly Mennonites who had travelled north following the American Revolution. These people, Anabaptists, had sought refuge in North America from the persecution that

had beleaguered their sect in Europe ever since its founding after the Protestant Reformation. Among the settlers was four-year-old Lewis Hienz – the name Hayes evolved from that – whose family had come to Niagara from either Albany, New York, or Pennsylvania. He, like all the other newcomers, received a grant of 200 acres of Crown land from the British government.

When he was old enough, Lewis built a log cabin and began clearing his land. He had sheep at first and later cattle as well. In 1827, the second generation built a two-storey brick house on the farm, now the home of Rob, his wife, Jan, and their children, Bruce, Megan and Jason. "Pieces of brick are still turning up at the back of the farm where they made the bricks," says Rob. In the early 1960s, the family began switching over to the production of grapes and tender fruit such as sweet cherries and peaches.

"My grandfather, Bruce, started the grapes," says Rob. "He wanted to grow them earlier but his mother was against it. Grapes were associated with wine and that was a no-no as far as she was concerned. Our grapes are used for juice. That's only because, with all our other operations, we don't have time to look after wine grapes. Besides, I don't know whether the market is going to be there for them."

The first Haynes greenhouse was used for producing flowers for the family's garden centre at a nearby crossroads. It was the beginning of a period of growth that has not stopped. In addition to its own greenhouses, the firm contracts a million square feet of greenhouse space. Under this arrangement, Haynes supplies the cuttings for spring garden plants, has others do the growing and then ships the mature products to its customers in an area stretching from Chicago to New York City. In the spring, up to 10 loaded tractor-trailers are dispatched daily from the property.

Haynes also grows close to half a million garden mums a year on 20 acres of land. According to Rob, it's the largest

— Don Haynes takes time out from his farm work to pose with his sons, Doug, Rob and Brian.

producer of that product in the country. This is a great achievement, especially since the first crop 10 years ago was a total failure because "we didn't know what we were doing."

The family unit is the heart and soul of the business. Rob's grandmother, Grace, was very involved until her death in 2001. His parents, Don and Charlotte, are still very active. His two brothers, Brian and Doug, are in charge of divisions. Even the younger set, the eighth generation, pitches in enthusiastically. All the important decisions are made by the family gathered around two tables pushed together in the board room.

"After the trade deal was signed," says Rob, "I didn't know whether we would survive another year. Those times were severe for us. Sure, we were fortunate to be at the right place at the right time to get into what we do now. But we couldn't have done anything without the determination of the family to work hard to get us through the problems. Our strong point is family. It is the most important thing."

— A worker at the Haynes greenhouse operation lifts a hanging basket off its perch. It is ready to be packaged and shipped.

Leo Martin's heart sank a mile when he awoke in the middle of the night just before Christmas in 1939 and spotted flames licking inside his greenhouses a short distance away.

He ran outside. But there was little he could do as the fire, fed by the wooden benches and frames, engulfed the structures and quickly reduced them and their contents to rubble and ashes.

Despair was evident in Leo's face as he observed the mess in daylight.

Later on, an aunt pulled him aside and said: "The world hasn't come to an end. You are a smart man and you may have many years left. You can do it."

These words of encouragement brought about a determination to rebuild and get plants ready for the spring orders.

'There's no choice: you either have to grow or you die.'

Sometimes good things emerge from adversity. With the fire – it likely started in the chimney of the coal-fired heating system – it was community spirit. Neighbours offered to help with hammer and saw. So did members of Niagara's sizeable Mennonite community, to which the Martin family belonged. Even 12 people connected with the provincial Department of Agriculture pitched in.

Before long, Martin Farms on Martin Road in Vineland Station, a forerunner of the region's greenhouse industry, was back in business.

The operation is still there. It's much bigger now, with 110,000 square feet of greenhouse area for the production of vegetable and flower plants, hanging baskets and poinsettias, as well as a propagation business. And part of the property near the QEW has taken on a new look; it's a golf driving range. But one thing has not changed: the Martin family is still in charge.

Leo began his farming career shortly after his marriage in 1913. With the help of his father, who had left teaching at the Rittenhouse elementary school in the area to work with the soil, he acquired 20 acres of land near Lake Ontario and began growing vegetables. And soon after, he built a house for himself and his wife and the family they were planning.

"My father's interest switched to greenhouses in 1925," says Robert, the eldest of two sons, who was born in 1922. "He grew tomato plants for all the neighbours around him. Then he expanded quite a bit, adding annual flowers: marigolds, petunias and alyssum. That's all the choice there was in those days."

In the 1930s, Martin Farms became the second largest employer in the area, the first being the Horticultural Experiment Station near Vineland. Since many of the daily tasks had to be done by hand, up to 40 workers were required during peak periods. Leo and his family made

— Three generations of growers: Robert Martin, his son, Bob, and Bob's son, Charlie.

14

— Robert Martin's interests go beyond flowers. Take walking canes, for instance.
He has dozens of them collected from all over the world.

Caring For Flowers

• Rinse the stems in flowing water and remove any foliage that will be below the water line.

• This will help remove any bacteria and prevent foiliage from beginning to decay under water.

• Prepare a clean vase with fresh water and flower food. Roses would benefit from warm water at body temperature (37 degrees C, 98 degrees F).

• Clean containers and fresh water will prevent bacteria growth. Flower food has main ingredients:

1. Carbohydrates: sugar = energy for flowers.
2. Biocide prevents growth of micro-organisms which clog stems.
3. Acid slows bacteria growth by lowering pH.
4. Hydrator: helps flowers to take in water easier.

• There is no substitute for flower food.

• Cut about 2.5 cm or one inch diagonally off the stems under water with a sharp blade.

• During the time the stems were out of water, they probably sucked up a little air. Cutting a piece off the stem prevents an air bubble from travelling up the stem and blocking water intake. It takes about two seconds after the stem is cut for it to start taking up water again. If the end of the stem rests on the bottom of the vase, it may impede water uptake. A diagonal cut ensures the stem will be able to drink. Dull knives and scissors crush stem tissues.

• Keep the water clean by changing it every other day or so. Check water levels. Make sure you add fresh water with flower food.

• If the water gets dirty or if a stem end is cut out of water, the rest of the flower will not get the water and food that it needs.

• Display flowers away from heat or direct sunlight. For a longer life, store in a cool place at night.

• Heat speeds up the maturation process of flowers. Cooler temperatures slow it down. Try placing them in a cooler back room or basement before you go to bed. Low temperatures above freezing are great.

• Remove dead blooms and do not display flowers next to fruit.

• Ethylene gas also speeds up the maturation process of flowers. Damaged blooms and ripening fruit release significant amounts of ethylene.

Courtesy of Rose-A-Lea Gardens Ltd., Mount Brydges, Ontario

extra efforts to establish a good relationship with the hired help.

"Through the years, we've tried to treat employees as people," says Robert, who made the greenhouses his life after returning home from service with the Royal Canadian Air Force during the Second World War. "My father, for example, used to take a number of employees to Toronto twice a year in his truck. That was in the days when hardly anyone had a car. He gave each one a dollar to spend. A large bunch of bananas hung in the back of the truck and they could grab one if they were hungry."

Such kindness continues to this day. The firm invites all its staff, including seasonal workers from Mexico, to an enjoyable barbecue on the lakeshore at the end of each spring. It's a way of saying thank you for contributing to another successful year.

Bob, one of five children of Robert and Ruth, says the greenhouse operation which he now runs has done very well with niche marketing, without brokers, but believes that success can be maintained only by constantly looking ahead and being willing to change. He adds: "There's no choice: you either have to grow or you die."

Although the graduate of the University of Guelph, with a degree in economics, is preoccupied with the present and the future, his thoughts sometimes wander back to the days when life on the farm was difficult. He wasn't around yet when the big fire broke out. But he can recall the period of his childhood when coal was still a necessary commodity.

"I remember my father getting up during the night to shovel coal into the boilers, which were made from two old threshing machines with the wheels removed, to keep the greenhouses and house warm enough. You can imagine the joy when we finally switched to oil and all those night trips were unnecessary."

— This tunnel system under the Queen Elizabeth Way provides Schenck Farms and Greenhouses Co. Ltd. with convenient access to its land on the Lake Ontario side.

Louis Schenck can't avoid breaking into chuckles as he relates a bit of family history about his great-grandfather, also named Louis, taking on the provincial government.

At six feet, three inches and 240 pounds, and with a temperament to match his size, great-grandpa wasn't shy when it came to pursuing matters that directly affected him. This was the case in 1936 when construction was about to begin on what is now the Queen Elizabeth Way, a major highway that would sever his 200-acre fruit and vegetable farm just west of St. Catharines.

"He kept asking some officials from the Department of Highways: 'What about the planning for my tunnel?', but no one knew anything about a tunnel," says Louis. "So he went to Toronto, sat in the minister's office and suggested he wasn't going to leave until he got his tunnel. The minister informed him that he could have Mr. Schenck thrown out. But Mr. Schenck suggested that he probably wouldn't do that. So they just sat there and stared at each other for awhile. In the end, Mr. Schenck got his tunnel."

'So he went to Toronto, sat in the minister's office and suggested he wasn't going to leave until he got his tunnel.'

The passageway, consisting of a number of tunnels, continues to provide Schenck Farms and Greenhouses Co. Ltd. with convenient access to its land on the Lake Ontario side of the highway where it has peach trees and a newly-planted vineyard.

There were new hassles in 1978 when Highway 406 was built, cutting through the eastern portion of the farm, and more tunnels were needed.

"The government expropriated about 25 acres and then graciously extended our tunnel system," says Louis, who now runs the company along with John, John Jr., Bob, Bill and Joe, all members of the Schenck family.

Great-grandfather's strong will was passed on to his offspring, including the father of Louis, named Louis Joseph. In the late 1950s, he and his partner, brother John, observed injury to peach trees in their orchard near the highway.

Floral Passion

Convinced that this was caused by de-icing salt, Louis Joseph brought the matter to the attention of the authorities and demanded compensation. But the government was of different mind. In the years that followed, a number of officials visited the Schenck farm but offered only sympathy.

Louis Sr. became enraged over the inaction and the continuing damage – some trees were killed outright and others were significantly injured – and took the matter to court. With an apple grower from the Aylmer area, who suffered a similar plight, he fought a long legal battle, winning his argument but then having to go to court again because of an appeal. The case finally ended up in the Supreme Court of Canada.

In 1987, the highest judicial body in the land handed down its ruling. It upheld a decision of the Ontario Court of Appeal which had in turn affirmed a Supreme Court of Ontario trial judgment, finding the government legally liable for the creation of a "nuisance" through the use of road salt. The two plaintiffs were entitled to compensation for losses dating back to 1971. And the government was ordered to pay most of their legal costs.

"It took a few more years before the exact losses were established," says Louis. "The cheque came in 1992."

His great-grandfather, who would have been proud of the persistence and ultimate victory, was of German descent. He was the son of a ship's carpenter who had come to Canada in 1858 from Alsace-Lorraine, an area along the boundary of France and Germany, to work at the Welland Canal, the man-made waterway connecting Lake Ontario to Lake Erie. His own interests were connected with the soil.

In 1882, at age 20, Louis I became a fruit and vegetable grower. Within a few years, he was producing large quantities for the Ontario Pure Food Company. He went into the canning business for himself in a small way in 1891 in Grantham Township, now part of St. Catharines. Six years later, he moved to the city, established a company called L. M. Schenck & Co. and erected a factory and warehouse for processing vegetables, tomatoes and fruit, including apples, all under the brand name of Globe.

An early label for peaches, elaborate in design, reads: "These goods are packed on the farm where grown.

Nothing but the choicest peaches are used and canned immediately, every care being taken to put them up in a clean and wholesome manner. The purchaser can rely that they are equalled by few and surpassed by none."

The operation was sold in 1903 to the newly-formed Canadian Canners Ltd. and Louis I stayed on as manager, a post he would hold for more than 30 years. He was an ambitious man, eager to grasp at other opportunities that might lead to further advancement. And so, in 1907, he began purchasing land where the present farm is located. He would eventually end up with more than 200 acres, all used for fruit and vegetable production.

The first greenhouses on the farm were built in the early 1920s, replacing a number of hothouses. The new structures were used for growing vegetable transplants. After a few years, there was a cluster of them, presenting an impressive sight.

After visiting the farm in the spring of 1936, a writer for the Family Herald and Weekly recorded: "As the main farm buildings came into view, the big group of greenhouses caught the eye, and it was not hard to see that Mr. Schenck was proud of them. All told, 42,000 feet were under glass, with one house alone measuring 392 feet by 50, and two others covering 200 by 40. The tall brick smokestack which towered over the big boiler room would have done credit to many a city manufacturing plant and gave a hint of the size and extent of the business carried on at this ultra-modern food-producing plant."

One 200 by 40-foot greenhouse, built in 1927, is still in use today.

"We've reskinned it with new glass, put in new benches and improved the heating, but the structure itself is original," says Louis. "We use it for begonia stock production. We also have a greenhouse that goes back to 1934. It still has the original bars and glass."

— Junior Farmerettes are at work on the Schenck farm during the Second World War.

— The Schenck operation is run by Joe, John Jr., Louis, Bob, John and Bill, all members of the Schenck family.

Of course, the Schenck operation also has facilities dating from more recent times, including a row of Dutch-made Venlo houses erected in 1985. Altogether, it has more than 200,000 square feet of covered growing space for a variety of flower products, including begonias, kalanchoes and geranium cuttings. It employs from 40 to 80 workers, depending on the season, and deals with brokers, wholesalers, JVK in St. Catharines and Oglevee in Connellsville, Pennsylvania.

The gradual shift away from vegetable production was initiated by the great-grandfather's son, also named Louis, who had started working full-time on the farm in the late 1920s after graduating from the four-year degree program at the Ontario Agricultural College in Guelph and serving an apprenticeship in the canning business.

"My grandfather liked growing flowers in the greenhouses," says Louis. "In the early 1950s, he started with geraniums because he wanted some around his house and couldn't find any. That's one of our major crops now. He was often at odds with his father who still preferred outdoor farming and thought the greenhouses should be just for transplants. My great-grandfather liked to eat and you can't eat flowers."

Louis I died in 1954 at age 92. The following year, grandpa suffered a heart attack and his sons, Louis III and John, took over the helm. Hothouse tomatoes were a big item for a number of years until they were squeezed out by an increasing focus on flowers, mostly cut mums initially.

No tears were shed when the tomatoes became history. Louis remembers his father telling him of the time when tomatoes were scarce and farmers raised their prices. When representatives from a large wholesale firm came around to buy whatever was available, they weren't too pleased to hear about the increase. But the prices were raised again, and then again, provoking an angry response.

Says Louis: "The company said: 'Hey, we clean up your tomatoes and all you guys do is raise the price. We're not very happy about that. We're not going to buy another Ontario tomato, period.' And they didn't for three years. So here's my father stuck with the crop. He had to go from store to store in town to peddle his tomatoes."

Life on the Schenck farm has seldom been dull. In the Second World War, when few men were around to do farm labour, young women pitched in. The Junior Farmerettes, as they were called, planted, weeded and harvested, and, through their banter and laughter, provided a gaiety that was so welcome in those dark years. After the war, the farm got reliable help by sponsoring a number of immigrant families, mostly from Germany and the Netherlands.

Even a Japanese snow monkey showed up once. It was spotted by one of the greenhouse workers.

"Come and see what's going on!" she reported excitedly to the office. "There's a monkey on top of the greenhouse!"

Sure enough, she wasn't dreaming. There indeed was a monkey. A number of them had escaped from their owner on Gregory Road.

Louis believes his company faces a solid future.

"A lot of people look at us as being very conservative, not really changing too much," he says. "But there have been a lot of changes here through the years with both inside and outside crops. We work extremely hard to make sure something works and when it doesn't make sense any more, as with strawberries, sweet cherries and sour cherries, we stop and move on to something else. This is still a family business and we have families to support – there's another generation behind us – and we continue to work hard and do the best we can to make a living. Sure, we'll have good years and we'll have bad years. But we try to position ourselves so that we can be in reasonable shape when the bad ones come along."

CHAPTER TWO
IN THE NEW LAND

'When you see flowers, your day is brightened. It's like sunshine.'
– Marinus Koole

When Marinus Koole celebrated 25 years of business in 1977 with parties and an open house, a booklet produced for the occasion stated alongside a colourful picture of cut roses: "After all these years, we still marvel at the beauty of it all!"

More than a quarter century later, his appreciation of the magnificence of flowers and their power to lift one's spirits has not diminished.

"When you see flowers," he says, "your day is brightened. It's like sunshine."

This enduring love affair of one of the pioneer flower producers in the Peninsula explains to a great extent why his business, Creekside Gardens Ltd. in Jordan Station, has been so successful over the years. When someone like Marinus takes great pleasure out of work and personally enjoys what is being produced, aims are usually set higher and no problem is allowed to stand in the way for long.

Born in 1922 near Middelburg, in the Dutch province of Zeeland, Marinus developed a fondness for flowers at an early age. But he had no experience in growing them when he arrived in Canada in 1948. Everything he learned about the trade in subsequent years was self-taught.

The seeds for his emigration were sown in 1944 by the Allied bombers that breached the dikes near where he lived in a bold attempt to dislodge the German occupying force. Sea water covered the land, presenting a desolate, disheartening picture. The future looked bleak too.

"I said to my girlfriend: 'I'm going to emigrate. There's nothing here except water.' I was so serious about it that I took private English lessons for three years. In the meantime, the land was made dry again. But when my father attempted to grow vegetables and grains on his mixed farm, only to see everything die because of the salt that remained in the soil, I said: 'I'm definitely leaving for Canada'."

Marinus married his fiancee, Elizabeth, and signed up for emigration. They were expecting a baby when the paper work had been completed and all was set for the boat trip across the ocean. But their doctor advised them to wait until the baby was born because of a diagnosed

— Rows of hanging baskets present an impressive sight at Creekside Gardens Ltd.

problem. After she arrived, little Maria developed a vitamin deficiency and lost blood, and her father donated a litre of his to nurse her to stable health. He bade farewell to his parents and eight brothers when she was eight weeks old.

Canada and the Netherlands had agreed on a settlement scheme that allowed thousands of Dutch agricultural workers, married and single, to emigrate. Farmers across Canada, including the Niagara Peninsula, needed them to help replenish the labour pool that had been badly drained during the Second World War. Many people were anxious to leave Holland for a number of reasons, including fear of another war in Europe, severe economic difficulties, limited job opportunities, congestion and an uncertain future for the young.

Upon arrival in Hamilton, Marinus found out that the immigration authorities had changed his placement from St. Catharines to Grimsby. He went to a 100-acre fruit farm where he was provided with accommodation and a job that paid $75 a month. Before long, he was made a foreman, but decided to leave when he didn't get the raise he had requested. He worked in landscaping for awhile. Then, in 1951, he took a big leap into the unknown by purchasing his current farm on Fairlane Road with the help of a private loan of $4,500 from his lawyer.

"It was 10 acres with peach trees and a little house," he says. "It was in a good location and abutted 16 Mile Creek, a source of fresh irrigation water. I began growing gladioli and sold these door to door and at the local market. I asked 50 cents for a bunch of 10. The following year, I built a greenhouse of 2,000 square feet and grew cut mums. Then along came Deny de Jong, a grower in Beamsville, who said: 'I'll sell them for you if you give me 20 per cent.' I told him: 'I grow them myself and I'll sell them myself.' But it was easier said than done because flowers weren't in big demand in those days."

While he worked on developing the customer base for his flowers, he continued to harvest his trees and also planted strawberries. He even grew tomatoes in a second greenhouse that he built. As more markets were opened up for flowers in the following years, he added potted mums, carnations and seasonal plants such as Easter lilies and poinsettias to his product list. The first roses were planted in 1960. Creekside was well on the way to becoming a giant.

— Marinus Koole with his son, Arie, Creekside's General Manager.

By 1977, when the company celebrated its 25th anniversary, roses – 25 varieties of them – covered the biggest area of the seven-acre greenhouse complex. While cut and potted flowers made up the bulk of the production, Marinus and his staff were involved in another venture as well: importing foliage plants, palms and tropicals from the Ivory Coast, Belgium, Colombia, Holland, Jamaica, California and Puerto Rico.

'Whenever I asked my wife what she wanted for her birthday, she said: 'The business comes first'.'

In the ensuing years, the phenomenal growth continued. Branches were established in Montreal, Ottawa and London. At one time, Marinus had 18 delivery trucks on the road.

All the company's operations are now consolidated at the Jordan Station property. The production in the 250,000-square-foot range and outdoor areas is under the helm of Arie, one of Marinus's seven children from two marriages – he married another Elizabeth after his first wife died in 1971. The crops include poinsettias, hydrangeas, Easter lilies, fall garden mums, zinnias, impatiens, begonias, geraniums, patio planters and hanging baskets. The company still does a lot of its own selling.

Reflecting on his early years in Niagara, Marinus says he and his wife lived frugally. If anything was left over after expenses were paid, it usually was pumped into the business.

"Whenever I asked my wife what she wanted for her birthday, she said: 'The business comes first.' When my father was here in 1955, he asked: 'Can't you get a pump to get water out of the cistern?' I said: 'As soon as I have the money for it. I'm not going into debt for that.' I got a pump the next year. In the same year, my wife and I went for a visit to Holland and I finally got to buy myself another coat and she a new dress."

His knowledge of English helped him tremendously as he strived to line up customers for his products. It also prompted the Christian Reformed Church, to which he

— Some of Creekside's colourful blooms.

belonged, to appoint him as an immigration fieldman. For four years, he spent a great part of his spare time finding jobs and accommodation for many newcomers to Niagara and acting as an ombudsman to sort out problems and difficulties. He also served in many Christian organizations and helped to build churches and schools.

"When I look back," he says, "I find that the early immigration years were the best time of my life. We always enjoyed what we were doing. We never had a day when we were homesick. And we always thanked God for His blessings."

SIMPLE BEGINNINGS

Life was a struggle for John and Cornelia Vander Knuyff and their two young sons after moving to a 50-acre farm near Lowbanks in 1957.

They had bought it for $10,000, with a $3,000 downpayment, and there was little money left on which to subsist until John could start growing vegetables and generate some income.

> *'On Sundays, we had a treat: sandwiches with brown sugar and a few raisins mixed in.'*

"That first winter, we lived on $300, and I lost 16 pounds," says Cornelia.

Her son, Arie, then 13 years old, remembers: "We had nothing but brown sugar for our sandwiches. On Sundays, we had a treat: sandwiches with brown sugar and a few raisins mixed in."

John had no implements at first. He did have a wheel, which he had brought with him to the farm, and managed

— Arie Vander Knuyff remembers clearly the tough times his family experienced after moving to Canada in 1952.

— Springtime beauty.

to shape a wheelbarrow. His biggest job was constructing a little greenhouse from window sash donated by caring acquaintances.

In the spring, he grew lettuce plants inside for later transfer to the fields. Other vegetables were also planted outside. The harvested crops were sold to wholesalers in Burlington and whatever was left in the fields was offered for sale to passing motorists.

Although money was finally coming in, not much was left after the bills were paid and the needs of the family were looked after. This would be the situation for a number of years. John once looked after 10 sows, and later many piglets as well, figuring that the local bank would be more likely to lend him money for seed if he presented himself as a pig farmer instead of solely as a vegetable grower. When he wanted to build larger greenhouses, he unloaded grain from boats in Port Colborne and used his earnings to buy the two-by-fours needed for the job.

In 1980, the focus of Vander Knuyff Greenhouses switched to the growing of flowers, including begonias, impatiens, marigolds and petunias, which were sold at the wholesale market in Toronto. It turned out to be a profitable move. The present operation, with a greenhouse area of 85,000 square feet, remains basically unchanged, producing bedding plants, hanging baskets and plugs, as well as seedless cucumbers.

When he lived in the Netherlands, John helped his father operate a large water windmill at Hoek van Holland, just as their ancestors had done for more than two centuries. They grew vegetables on an adjacent field. But everything ground to a halt during the Second World War when German troops moved into the strategically-located landmark.

After the war, when the small country struggled to recover, John and Cornelia decided to head for greener pastures in Canada. They and their sons, Arie and Les, left their home in 's-Gravenzande in the spring of 1952, sailed on the

— John Vander Knuyff offers his products at the wholesale market at the Ontario Food Terminal in Toronto.

centres, including one in the U.S. But most of the business is done through wholesalers.

Although her life has not been a bed of roses, Cornelia, who lives on the property, retains many fond memories. A painting of the windmill which her husband once operated hangs on her living room wall.

"When we were visiting Holland, Michigan, we toured the tall windmill, De Zwaan, which is one of the big attractions there," she says. "We stood among a group of tourists listening to a guide explain how the windmill worked. People started asking questions and my husband answered in detail. He knew more about windmills than the guide. When it was time for us to leave, I said: 'Sorry, my husband has to go.' They all looked surprised. They must have thought that he was a guide too."

Waterman to Halifax and travelled by train to Maitland, a village near Brockville, where Cornelia's sister lived. John soon found a job on a vegetable farm near Burlington. He worked there five years and then purchased his own farm.

In the early 1960s, he began growing box plants as a sideline.

"Nobody bought them," recalls Cornelia. "I once went to the market in Dunnville with petunias. People asked me: 'What kind of flower is that?' Canadians didn't buy flowers in those days except for special occasions. But my husband always said: 'Someday they will start to buy them.' He lived long enough to see this come about."

Arie and his wife, Tjilske, are in charge now, assisted by his brother, Jim, who was born in 1962. Tragically, Les and his daughter died in an auto accident in 1985. Some of the products are still sold at a double stall at the Toronto wholesale market. Deliveries are also made to garden

— John Vander Knuyff's original greenhouse.

Peter Ravensbergen was a tulip man.

He cultivated the colourful species in the village of Rijnsburg, a horticultural beehive in the Netherlands, solely for bulb production. So when he emigrated to Canada in June, 1951, with his wife Sophia and seven children, he had a good idea of how he wanted to continue to earn his bread and butter.

"We boarded a train in Halifax and got out at a station in a rural area near Orangeville where my father was supposed to work for a dairy farmer, our sponsor," says Gerrit, the eldest son, then 10 years old. "But he didn't like the looks of the cows and got out of the arrangement somehow. After three days on the farm, he moved us to Fenwick and began work at Prudhomme's, a large nursery."

Peter's desire to re-enter the tulip business was strengthened by his observation that a great potential existed for a home-grown bulb market in Ontario. By the fall, he had already received a shipment of tulip bulbs from an acquaintance in Holland. These he planted on a small piece of rented land.

It was the beginning of a pursuit, first part-time and later full-time, that would develop into P. Ravensbergen and Sons Ltd., a bustling flower operation near Smithville with close to 38 acres of land, 180,000 square feet of greenhouse

— Four members of the Ravensbergen family – Peter, Jacob, Gerrit and William – with some of their current products in the loading area.

area and a staff of 30, including many family members. It produces a variety of potted plants and bedding plants as well as hanging baskets.

After 11 months in Fenwick, the Ravensbergen family moved to the Smithville area. Peter worked at various jobs, including the railroad, and then was hired by National Steel Car in Hamilton. He did piece work, leaving him plenty of time to make an extra dollar here and there. Of course, his beloved tulips were not forgotten amid all this activity.

'We've built up our own market and are not ready to let it go. We want the freedom to determine whether to dump the crop or sell it. '

"In the winter of '53, he started forcing bulbs in pint-sized raspberry boxes which were placed on a rack behind the wood stove in the kitchen of our old farmhouse," says Gerrit. "There were four in a box. Then he started going door to door in St. Catharines, trying to peddle 50 to 60 boxes a week. I don't recall exactly, but I believe he got a quarter for a box. One Saturday, he took three of us kids and some extra boxes along. By the end of the day, we had made $35. That was a lot of money. He was conscious of being shabbily dressed on Sundays, so he stopped in Smithville and bought himself a suit."

Determined to start his own business, Peter bought eight acres of land west of Smithville in 1956. The soil was clay, as hard as rock in places, but this not deter him from making a start the following year on putting up some necessary structures. With the kind permission of his boss in the pipe division at National Steel Car, where he continued to work as a maintenance person, he gathered all the excess lumber he could find and hauled it home in his new station wagon.

"With pick and axe, we dug out the footings for a 20 by 27-foot barn that would be used for heating and storage," recalls Gerrit. "Then he built a greenhouse, 20 feet by 50 feet, bending the scrap piping himself. He couldn't finish it that year because the bank wouldn't give him $200 to put the glass on. So it sat idle. He got enough money the

— The colourful tulip fields of Peter Ravensbergen Sr. This venture ended in 1968.

next year to finish the job. But he didn't have enough stuff to fill the whole greenhouse, so he used only half of it by partitioning it off. Then there was a downdraft from the coal stove that blew through the greenhouse and wrecked all the tulips. It was one disaster after another."

Peter plodded on. When he came home from the factory, he went straight to his tulip field and planted more bulbs. The family would sit down to eat only when Dad had run out of daylight. The beds, which presented a colourful sight when in bloom, would gradually cover three acres.

"It was the same story with digging up the bulbs," says Gerrit. "We didn't have supper until it was dark. It took us a whole month to dig everything up with a little trowel. When this work had to be done, nothing stood in the way. Even later on, in 1965, my wedding day had to be scheduled so that it wouldn't interfere with the tulips."

In 1959, Peter felt confident enough in his fledgling business to quit his full-time job. Besides tulips, he also had a patch of gladioli. His income that summer totalled only $700. But he was not discouraged – at least, he didn't show it – and he continued on, reassured by his deep Christian belief that the Lord would take care of everything. This is still the faith and trust of his sons.

The end to the tulip undertaking came in 1968. A shipment of bulbs from Holland, where growers were struggling with a mould problem, infected Peter's entire crop. The tulip man wanted to start anew, but his four sons in the business – Gerrit, Rolie, Jacob and Peter – were of a different mind. They won the argument and began growing potted chrysanthemums. This went well. Dominion, a grocery chain with about 40 outlets, which had marketed the tulips in the winter and the gladioli in the summer, now added the mums to its stock. From then on, the story of P. Ravensbergen and Sons Ltd. is one of growth and expansion.

Gerrit began his full-time working career for a raspberry grower. He next worked for four years at Westbrook Greenhouses in Grimsby run by Bill Vermeer – "he taught me how to work" – and returned to the family business in 1963. He eventually became one of the persons in charge. Two brothers, Rolie and Jacob, are still involved – brother Peter died in 1986 – and three of his six children – Peter, William and Alex – also hold key positions. Rolie, the main grower until 10 years ago, does all the welding on the premises. Jacob took over the flower shop sales in Toronto and Guelph from brother Peter in 1985.

— Hibiscus: raw beauty at the Ravensbergen firm.

Gerrit credits his wife, Tina, for standing by his side during the days when everyone had to work long and hard to complete all the tasks and get the crops ready for the next challenge: sales. He remembers a playpen standing in the boiler room and a young son crawling under the benches in a snowsuit and getting so muddied that he needed a quick dunking in the tub before everyone could sit down for lunch.

The brothers are proud of their innovative efforts to use specially-moulded troughs for recirculating water used to moisten the geranium crop. They had become "sick and tired of standing there for days, hand-watering all the little pots."

Gerrit talks fondly of the market at the Ontario Food Terminal in Toronto, his home away from home, where a big portion of the crop is sold. Accompanied by his son, Peter, he still goes there twice a week, leaving at 1:30 a.m. and returning at noon. About one-third of his load is sold before the market officially opens at 6:30.

"I started going there when I worked on the raspberry farm," he says. "I really enjoy it. I'm not much of a social

person – I don't do a lot of partying or visiting – but I would miss it if I didn't go there anymore. I've dealt with some of the people there for 35 years or more."

Besides the business and social aspects, there's another reason for the attachment to the market: the freedom to dispose of flowers as the brothers wish.

"Our father left Holland because he was tired of all the restrictions and the permits that were needed. The horror stories that he told convinced us that he had made the right move. So, here in Canada, we've built up our own market and are not ready to let it go. We want the freedom to determine whether to dump the crop or sell it."

Sometimes, when looking back, the brothers are amazed at how rapidly the greenhouse industry has evolved. There was a time when growers could sell seconds, at a reduced rate, but now everything is quality oriented. The growing has become more sophisticated and intensified, resulting in higher production per square foot. Improvements have been made in irrigation and other processes. The packaging is better. The shipping is expedited. And on and on the list goes. As for the future of the industry, they see many more bright lights, provided the border stays open for Ontario-grown products and the exchange rate on the dollar remains in favour of the growers and brokers.

But Gerrit has no kind words for tulips, even though they played such an important role in the establishment of his family business.

"They just turn me off. Mom and a sister or two would sit here peeling bulbs every day except Sunday from early in the morning until late at night. We had them nicely out of the ground, dried, cleaned, sifted and sized, when we had to put them back in again. And all we did was pick out a few boxes of big ones that could be forced in winter. I thought it was such a senseless job."

— Peter Ravensbergen at work on his first greenhouse.

On most mornings, before break of dawn, the first order of business at Colonial Florists Ltd. on Broadway Avenue in St. Catharines is a half-hour meeting of the key personnel to talk shop, letting the left hand know what the right is doing and perhaps even solving some problems in the process.

In actuality, it's a gathering of two families – Jim and Clemens van der Zalm and their children – who together operate one of Niagara's most respected greenhouse businesses, specializing in the production of geraniums, New Guinea impatiens and other flowers under 240,000 square feet of glass.

'We bought a welding outfit and started to weld, although we had no welding experience. We just didn't feel like paying $2 an hour for a welder.'

"Each one has his or her own responsibility," says Ron, one of Jim's sons, who looks after sales, shipping, including driving a truck to market, and odd jobs such as maintenance welding. "It's a great team. Our personalities fit well into each other."

The business was once run with two other brothers of Jim and Clemens: Ted and Arnold. Ted left in 1976 to devote all his attention to the Colonial Flower Shop on Ontario Street, a business he had acquired shortly after emigrating from the Netherlands in 1953. Arnold died in 1980 when his truck was in a collision with a tractor-trailer on the QEW while on the way to Toronto with a load of product. Jim was just ahead of him with another truck when the tragedy happened. Arnold left a wife and four children.

The van der Zalm clan in St. Catharines originated in Loosduinen, just south of The Hague, where the brothers' parents ran a greenhouse vegetable operation. One of their sons, John, had emigrated already in 1949. Their other children, Ted, Barbara, Clemens, Jim and Arnold, followed at different periods, leaving them with one married daughter and two sons in the Netherlands.

"John told us that there was a future for us in Canada," says Jim, a second cousin of Bill van der Zalm, former premier of British Columbia. "I was working in a

greenhouse at the time and could see no future for me in Holland. So Clemens, Arnold and I went to Canada in 1960. John had arranged a job for me at Dofasco, where he worked. Arnold went to General Motors."

Before long, Jim, Arnold and Clemens teamed up with Ted and built 10,000 square feet of greenhouses at the floral place.

"We built three of them ourselves with used material," Jim recalls. "We bought a welding outfit and started to weld, although we had no welding experience. We just didn't feel like paying $2 an hour for a welder. We started growing things that were not available here, such as asparagus greens to go with roses. That went well. Then we went into spring crops."

One day, a wicked storm tilted one of the houses. With the insurance settlement, a $55,000 loan from a friend's bank – their own bank had turned them down – and a $7,500 farm improvement loan, they purchased a 19-acre peach farm near Lake Ontario and the Welland Canal and put up 27,000 square feet of greenhouses. They grew English cucumbers – "you couldn't give them away" – and tomatoes – "the prices were way too low." Eventually, like many others in the growing business, they switched to flower production.

When the brothers decided to focus on geraniums, the fortunes of Colonial Florists began to rise. "The market was wide open for us then," says Jim. The firm quickly gained an excellent reputation for its propagation of geraniums and its finished product. After many years, this has only been strengthened.

— Here are the main principals of Colonial Florists Ltd., all surnamed van der Zalm: first row, Rob, Jim Sr., Clemens and Paul; above, Jim Jr. and Ron.

THE PROPAGATORS

"Propagating is the bigger part of our business," says Ron. "We do it for 150 growers. We grow one million cuttings for ourselves and 3.5 million for others. In the spring, we rent six trucks to deliver everything."

The methods of geranium propagation have changed considerably over the years. Instead of being rooted in soil, a process that invariably resulted in many losses, the cuttings are now grown in oasis cubes set in specially-moulded troughs. All watering is done automatically below the leaves, lessening the onset of disease and the percentage of loss.

Besides geraniums and impatiens, Colonial Florists produces a variety of other products for wholesale distribution, including dracaenas, begonias, poinsettias, cyclamen, fuchsias and others.

All this production is not being carried out without a few concerns. The biggest one relates to heating costs. Since propagation requires the thermostat to be turned up, these are high enough. But when the price of natural gas doubles, as it has in recent years, they become worrisome. The company has seen its yearly heating bill rise from just under $200,000 to nearly $400,000.

The next biggest anxiety concerns the availability of skilled labour. It's sometimes difficult to find qualified people to replace ones who left for greener pastures, either to start their own business or fill a job that's more lucrative than the one they had. Unlike in earlier years, there's no immigrant pool from which greenhouse owners can draw experienced workers.

But Jim and Clemens, who employ 30 people from November to May, have no worries with the managerial positions. These are filled by their children, all well educated in their field. Three of the five children of Jim and Mary are at Colonial Florist: Jackie, Jim Jr. and Ron. Clemens and his wife, Alida, also have three children in the business: Paul, Jennifer and Rob.

One of the buildings on their property is used for storage for the Warehouse of Hope, a charitable organization founded by Ted's son, Ted Jr., a former missionary in Tanzania. His group collects used clothing and other donated goods for distribution to needy people in Third World countries.

— *A stunning view inside one of the greenhouses of Colonial Florists Ltd. in St. Catharines, a producer of geraniums, impatiens and other flowers.*

— Orchids are so exquisite in their delicate colours, so pleasing in their fragrances and so graceful in many of their forms that they are the favourites of flower lovers around the world.

Tamara Alkema's eyes sparkle as she enthusiastically discusses a major new project launched by her family's business, Alkema Greenhouses in Grimsby, a long-time producer of quality geraniums, geranium cuttings and a wide variety of annuals.

Thousands of orchid plants are being delicately nurtured in a year-long process. If all goes according to plan, and a solid market is found for the showy, fragrant – and costly – flowers, the firm will be well placed to face the future with an added identity and continued growth.

"We all recognized the need to find a unique product that would set us apart from others," says Tamara, who left her job as a nursery school teacher to become the firm's office manager. "We hope that orchids will fill this need. This program represents a challenge for us since orchids are a high-end product and very different from the crops we now grow. It requires learning new growing techniques, marketing the product effectively, finding new customers such as florist shops, and so on."

Challenge often generates excitement, which explains the upbeat feeling exuded by Tamara and other members of her

family involved in the business, including father Clarence, the President, mother Lina, brother Henry, the Production Manager, brother Brian, the Distribution Manager, sister Elaine, who loves working in the greenhouses, and brother-in-law Paul Vanderlaan, the Sales Manager.

'We have become more aware of individual strengths and how each one of us can contribute to the success of the business.'

"We have come through a time of refocusing in the past few years," says Tamara. "We have become more aware of individual strengths and how each one of us can contribute to the success of the business. I think that the positive spirit is the result of much hard work at developing a common vision, respecting our uniqueness as individuals and building team spirit."

In the greenhouse section where the orchid plants are growing nicely in carefully-controlled conditions, Clarence

pauses to praise his children for embracing an idea first suggested by a relative in the Netherlands and eagerly implementing the necessary steps to grow and market a new product. A broad smile creases his face. Obviously, he is satisfied that he and Lina have done the right things, such as instilling proper values, and that one day their business will be left in knowledgeable and dedicated hands.

Alkema Greenhouses, which now has 120,000 square feet of covered growing area and a workforce of 17, rising to as high as 25 in peak periods, was established in Burlington in 1961 by Clarence and his father, Hendrik, who had come to Canada in the spring of 1952 with his wife and six children and a dream to have his own greenhouse business someday. Hendrik's father, Klaas, had been a part-time vegetable grower while working full-time at a lime-making kiln in Harlingen, a town in the northern Dutch province of Friesland. So when the place became obsolete and his job disappeared, just as he feared would happen, he became a full-time grower on land once occupied by a brickyard. Retirement came along and the operation was taken over by Hendrik, a grocer, who enjoyed working in the fields, and another son.

Alas, the vegetable market soured and income was meagre. In an effort to improve their status, the brothers turned to the production of flowers, mainly tulips, chrysanthemums and geraniums. This worked to some extent, but it soon became obvious that the concern was not large enough to adequately support two families with six children each. It was in 1950 when Hendrik started talking openly about emigration.

Clarence was 13 years old when he stepped onto Canadian soil in Halifax. He had been reluctant to leave behind his friends, relatives and familiar surroundings and settle in a faraway land whose language and customs he did not know. A train transported the family to Prince Edward County in southeastern Ontario where Dad would work on a dairy farm. They moved to the Hamilton area the following year after a job had been found in construction.

When Hendrik set up his own business in 1961, finally realizing his dream, Clarence was working at Roseland Greenhouses. Like his father, he was fond of working with the soil, especially among colourful blooms. Both worked in their new business on a part-time basis, producing geraniums and bedding plants, transporting the products in an old truck to the market in Toronto – "we were stopped by the police once because it was burning so much oil" – and learning a lot about the ins and outs of such things as growing methods, disease control, greenhouse operation, marketing and dealing with people. In 1966, Clarence became the first full-time member. In 1962, he had married Lina, a 1952 arrival from Ens, in a reclaimed area of the Netherlands known as the Noordoostpolder, and they were raising a family that would grow to six children. Hendrik became full-time in 1968.

The business was relocated to Grimsby in 1972 after the Burlington property was sold for development. The strong possibility of such an eventuality had prevented the needed expansion of the greenhouse area, then totalling 12,000 square feet, to handle product growth. In Grimsby, there was more elbow room. The greenhouse area there began at 28,000 square feet and grew whenever new products were added to supply an expanding market throughout Ontario and beyond.

"Everything went according to the program we had in mind," says Clarence, who had taken over the helm from his father. "Mind you, it wasn't easy. One of my sons once commented how 'dirt poor' we had been. It's true that almost every penny we made was put back into the business. For example, we had to forgo a lot of things, including downpayment on a house, when a new heating system was needed for the greenhouses."

There are vivid memories of a near misfortune when a severe ice storm brought down power lines, cutting off the electrical supply to the greenhouses. There was no backup generator then. But a hydro worker who happened to stop by came to the rescue with some spare equipment he had in his truck. In 1998, an early spring brought havoc. Garden centre operators and others faced with a sudden demand for flowers caused the phone to ring incessantly. But the stock was not ready yet. This shortened the season for Alkema Greenhouses, with resulting losses. Rather than crying over spilt milk, Clarence discerned an opportunity to thoroughly review his entire operation. He ended up making many changes, including the addition of job descriptions.

Taking advantage of occasional adversity – "when there's a problem, we find a solution" – is one of traits that has led to Clarence's success. There are others, of course, such as hard work, learning from others, eager to test new ideas, keeping up with the latest technology, insisting on quality, and so on. But when he is asked about this subject, he

— Clarence Alkerma, President of Alkema Greenhouses, is second from right. The others are Paul Vanderlaan, Sales Manager; Brian Alkema, Distribution Manager, and Henry Alkema, Production Manager.

points to honesty and integrity, engendered by his deep Christian beliefs, as leading values that guide him in his work and association with others.

"When I was very young, my parents bought a children's story Bible and I was fascinated by it. I tried to pull my mother off her work and get her to read me stories out that book. When an aunt or uncle came over, I asked them: 'Please, read me a story.' My parents sent me to the Christian school and there, too, the Bible was very important. We learned from it that the Lord doesn't want you to do something dishonest or wrong, so you stay away from that and treat everyone correctly. And later on, when you have a job, you do your work correctly and you work all the time – no idle time. I think we were also taught that we were supposed to get ahead in life and make progress and in that way please the Lord because that's why He put us on Earth. He just didn't make us and then leave us; He wants us to be His co-workers. Together, the Lord and His children are building a new world, and that world can only be reached when you live as correctly as you can."

He pauses for a moment, as if deep in thought, before continuing: "When you're a child and you see your mother's change lying on the table, you may be thinking of buying candies, ice cream and different things. But then you decide not to take it because you're afraid that the Lord will see it and hold it against you. Later in life, if you're in business, you will realize that you're not here just to make money. I knew, Lina knew and the children knew that we would not be happy if money were everything. So business is done by listening to the customer, giving him exactly what he needs and delivering it at the proper time and for the price that is agreed upon. It works."

Even if the orchid program becomes a huge success, the Alkema family probably will still be widely known as "the geranium people." It's a deserving reputation that began with the quality demanded and delivered by Hendrik. "I didn't realize until after Dad died in 1988 that he was one of the geranium pioneers in Canada," says Clarence. "Landscapers and others came back to us time and time again because they liked our healthy plants with clearly distinguishable leaf markings and bright flower colour. He started propagating and selling cuttings too."

When he became the boss, Clarence made every effort to uphold the good name. He told an interviewer in 1982: "We're one of the few growers in Ontario to renew geranium stock every year to get cuttings as virus-free as possible."

A lesser known fact is that Alkema Greenhouses also has a role in setting world standards for rainwater. It became involved when Clarence's brother, Harry, a scientist at the Canada Centre for Inland Water in Burlington, needed a large roof from which to collect runoff for use in tests aimed at increasing water quality. Plastic pipe connects a number of barrels placed in a row behind one of the greenhouses.

The achievements and the recognition have made an impact on the younger set. As they face excellent prospects for a bright future, the one who started it all is not forgotten. As Tamara explains: "The fact the business carries our name always reminds us of the legacy that has been given us by our grandfather – a respect for others, producing high quality product, honesty in all dealings."

Flowers In Your Medicine Cabinet

By Dr. Scott Taylor

- Did you ever think that flowers could give you an instant attitude adjustment?

- When your son or daughter, at the first sign of spring, picks the flowers from your budding garden or the dandelions from the lawn, there follows an instant smile and a loving hug.

- Whether weeds or flowers, you didn't throw them out. You put them in water and a vase for your whole family to enjoy.

- A recent behavioural study conducted at Rutgers University in New Jersey shows that nature provides us with a simple way to alter and improve our emotional health: flowers.

- Flowers in our presence increase feelings of life satisfaction, trigger happy emotions and affect our social behaviour in a positive manner – far beyond what was previously believed.

  (I've just gone and brought a fresh-cut bouquet of flowers to my den/office before I continue writing.)

- Dr. Jeannette Haviland-Jones, Professor of Psychology at Rutgers and head researcher in the behavioural study, says this study "challenges established scientific beliefs about how people can manage their day-to-day needs in a healthy and natural way."

- The findings show that flowers are a healthful and natural moderator of moods.

- People of all age groups demonstrated extraordinary delight and gratitude. They were seen to be less depressed, anxious and agitated after receiving flowers and demonstrated a greater sense of life satisfaction and enjoyment.

- I would like to think that we should be bringing home flowers most days from our offices. The presence of flowers makes an intimate connection and leads to increased contact with family and friends.

- Some scientific research is now showing that flowers help senior citizens cope with the challenges of aging. Forget the fountain of youth. It may be growing plants and flowers right in our own gardens. Maybe it is our innate sense of this why our aging population and baby boomers are heading out into the garden more and more.

- Science has shown that flowers can decrease depression, refresh recent memory and encourage companionship.

- No wonder flowers are so wonderful on Valentine's Day!

- Knowing the effects that flowers have on lives and our communities, I cannot help but think how ingesting the beneficial fruits and vegetables of Mother Nature has a huge beneficial effect on our health too. Studies show us repeatedly the effects they can have on heart and cardiovascular health, energy, pain, etc.

- I have observed from my own gardening and lawn experience that there are benefits for the time and effort spent tending to plants and grass. Water and organic nutrients help build a healthy, vibrant plant that requires less pesticides and spray. This is like our body's health. The more we do for it through a healthy lifestyle of food and drink, the less medicinal intervention we may need.

- It comes down to doing more for our plants instead of doing more to them. This allows stronger plants, better able to adapt to the environmental challenges that they face.

- Next time you think about what's for dinner, don't think about the meat first. Focus on which vegetables you are going to prepare. Then, for dessert . . . how about fruit?

- I can't think that more and more of our lives should not be indulged in gardening therapy and/or flower therapy around our homes. Get healthy, get happy and get flowers around more in and out of your home!

Dr. Scott Taylor is a chiropractor in Welland, Ontario.

A few years ago, a woman hired by Peter Glasbergen of Fenwick called the day before she was to start work and asked: "You use pesticides, don't you?"

"Eh, yes," the greenhouse grower replied. But before he could explain that only soft sprays were used in the constant battle against thrips, spidermite and aphids, and that the emphasis was on biological control, she said: "Well, forget about me. I'm not coming in."

Presumably, she had just read a newspaper story on the use of pesticides inside and outside greenhouses and the associated health risks. Such reports, plus the publicity surrounding the government's steps to tighten the screws on lawn sprays, result in anxiety among the public. Indeed, another woman hired for the job at Glasbergen Greenhouses Ltd. on Foss Road also quit before starting work after a second story on the subject appeared a week later.

'The banks have learned their lesson over the years.'

Peter doesn't fault people for being concerned, but he believes the greenhouse industry has become the victim of misconceptions. Instead of being insensitive polluters, growers carefully control the use of pesticides and chemicals in greenhouses and employ systems that prevent residue from entering the outside environment. Furthermore, many growers have turned to biological methods – the release of ladybugs, for example – to help control destructive insects.

"I can remember my father saying: 'In Holland, we never sprayed and had very few problems. Once the spraying cycle starts, you kill one bug that destroys another. And before you know it, the whole cycle has been broken'."

Peter's parents, Piet and Geertje, and their six children – another one was born later – emigrated in 1952 from Rijnsburg, the Netherlands. Dad had worked in greenhouses in the flower-growing region. Later, with a carrier-cycle laden with colourful blooms, he had gone door to door on fixed routes to earn a living as a seller. His sponsor was Prudhomme's, a large nursery with property near Fenwick, and that's where he and his family stayed

for a year. He made only $25 a week, which was hardly enough to feed and clothe eight people and look after other expenses, including the support of his church. So he found a better-paying job at Atlas Steel in Welland and moved into a dilapidated house on a 10-acre farm in Fenwick which he rented. The dwelling was fixed up. But the job at Atlas disappeared after a year when he refused to work on Sundays as the company required. At that point, he decided to go on his own by making use of his rented land.

"My mother was expecting then," says Peter. "She had saved up $30 for diapers. Well, my father took the money because he needed it to put up a little greenhouse, 10 feet by 30 feet. He started with bedding plants, then statice and gladioli and gradually a little bit of everything. Tomatoes, cucumbers and egg plants were grown outside. He took most of his stuff to the markets in Welland and Port Colborne. He continued to do that until shortly before he passed away in 1993 at age 77."

In the early days, Piet also wholesaled to garden centres. As business increased, he enlarged his greenhouse area to 7,000 square feet. Soon there was enough work for his three sons: first Peter and his older brother, John, and later Andy, the youngest. The brothers continue to run the operation, producing potted mums, cut mums, geraniums, sunflowers and hanging baskets in greenhouses that now cover 125,000 square feet. In the summer and after school, they are ably assisted by 11 young members of the three families.

Not everything has gone smoothly over the years. Like other newcomers, Piet ran into ignorant bank managers who just didn't understand how someone could make a living out of a small greenhouse. He once applied for a loan to buy a generator, but was flatly turned down. Another time, he went to the bank with a plan to replace his original greenhouse with better facilities, including a boiler, but it was rejected. He did put up new structures after securing private funding.

"The banks have learned their lesson over the years," says Peter. "The one I deal with now has an agricultural branch staffed by people who know our business and understand our problems."

He has bitter memories of the time in 1989 when the

— Brothers John, Andy and Peter Glasbergen at their greenhouse range in Fenwick.

value of the Canadian dollar dropped steeply just when he had purchased a new greenhouse from Holland. While the structure was being erected that winter, a windstorm sent the roof crashing to the ground. "That greenhouse cost us a bundle," he says. "I took it very hard." To add insult to injury, the bottom fell out of the cut mum business in the spring.

The brothers are greatly concerned about rising energy costs. To lessen the blow, they've taken steps to improve efficiency and reduce loss of heat.

"Half our range is hot water and the other half is steam," explains Peter. "We had consultants in to test every steam trap and they found that 30 per cent were no good. We also put check valves on each boiler so that there can never be a back pressure and resultant energy loss when you're running only one them in the summer. There's also a new system of feeding the boilers with water. We've insulated our heating pipes, put in energy curtains, and so on. When added up, all these steps make quite a difference."

Now the brothers, like many others in the industry, are hoping that the price of energy will not skyrocket as in recent years. If it does rise again dramatically, there could be trouble ahead for some growers. But if it remains stable, even at the high level, says Peter, "we could be facing an exciting future because of the great potential for growth. Only 10 to 11 per cent of North Americans buy flowers on a regular basis. Even if that figure were doubled, what we produce now would be just a drop in the bucket."

Curiosity brought Peter Koornneef to attend the auction in 1968 of the two old greenhouses that the Ontario Department of Highways had purchased from him and his brother, John, to make room for a section of the South Service Road along the QEW.

"Nobody wanted to buy them," he recalls. "I knew some people who would probably be interested in certain parts, so I gave an offer of $10. It was accepted. I then did some phoning around and sold everything in bits and pieces – $750 for a boiler, that type of thing."

The auction was held a month after the Koornneef brothers had moved their business from the DeWitt Road property to a new site on Highway 8 in Winona which they had purchased the year before in anticipation of the service road going ahead.

For Peter, the unexpected windfall was a personal highlight of a long career in growing that began in his teenage years when he worked for his father, Adriaan, a market gardener in Pijnacker, a small community near the Dutch city of Delft, and ended in 1995 when he sold his share of the ownership of A. Koornneef and Sons Ltd. to his sons, Dave and Steve.

The business, with 125,000 square feet of greenhouse area, is a major producer of standard chrysanthemums, cutting 700,000 stems a year. It also grows snapdragons, bedding plants, geraniums and hanging baskets, all sold through wholesalers.

'Whenever I'm in a grocery store in Florida, I walk to the produce department and see flowers from Ontario. This always amazes me.'

Adriaan and his wife, Ann, emigrated in 1949 with six of their eight children. Their eldest son, Arie, had gone to Canada two years earlier. When others were making noises about joining him, the parents felt it would be best for family unity to move everyone across the ocean. Dad was 55.

"When we were on the boat, we found out that our sponsor in Burlington didn't need us anymore because his

— Dave and Steve Koornneef among a splendid crop of commercial mums in their greenhouses in Winona.

crop was already in," says Peter, who was 16 then. "So after we arrived, the family was spread around. Then my father got word from an immigration fieldman that there was a job on a certain farm. But when he got there, he found out that the farm had just been sold. It wasn't a great beginning."

Adriaan landed a job at E. D. Smith, a producer of jams and tomato products. He soon discovered that factory work was not to his liking, having spent much of his life growing vegetables in cold frames and fields. After a year and a half, he quit the job and joined the staff of a greenhouse operation in Stoney Creek. Now he was more content.

The children, who held jobs of their own, chipped in to help their parents buy a four-and-a-half-acre fruit farm with a house on DeWitt Road in Fruitland in early 1951.

With money left behind in Holland – emigrants could take only a handful of dollars out of the country – a greenhouse was purchased by an acquaintance the following year and shipped to Canada. It was only 3,000 square feet.

"We started growing mums in the fall and snaps in the spring," says Peter. "Why mums? There was a fellow in the Peninsula, Deny de Jong, who was very persuasive. He wanted to sell mum cuttings and talked my father into trying them. These were bunched mums, not the big commercial ones we grow today. Everything went well and we soon added bedding plants."

He and two younger brothers once loaded a panel truck with sweet peas, a crop that was over-abundant, and then drove to the local general hospital. He offered the flowers for sale at the front gate and the others set up shop at the side one. Business was brisk until the police showed up, in response to a complaint from a floral shop, and told them to leave because they were on public property. The public markets in the area provided a more acceptable setting.

After their father's death in 1964, Peter and John continued the operation in partnership. Business grew and expansions took place. Then came the plan for the service road and the talk about expropriation, prompting the brothers to acquire the Highway 8 property. They began in 1968 with 30,000 square feet of glass and added 15,000 square feet of plastic in the winter. There was no looking back.

When Peter and John retired in 1995, the business was left in the hands of Dave and Steve, both of whom had worked in it since their boyhood.

Peter still follows developments in the flower industry with great interest. He's optimistic about what lies ahead.

"Since we started our business in the early '50s, the flower industry has grown tremendously and is now very vibrant," he says. "We have learned to export to the United States. We have such huge markets there – the eastern seaboard, the area south of Lake Erie, right up to Chicago. Some stuff is even going to Florida. Whenever I'm in a grocery store in Florida, I walk to the produce department and see flowers from Ontario. This always amazes me. As long as the dollar stays below 80 cents, we will have a tremendous market south of the border. And keep in mind that our market here in Canada has also grown by leaps and bounds."

— Delicate beauty at A. Koornneef and Sons Ltd.

Greenhouse Flower, Potted Plant, Cuttings And Bedding Plant Production By Variety, 2001

	Ontario	Canada
Cut flowers		
Chrysanthemums (Standard)	3,936,000	4,090,100
(Sprays)	18,069,000	26,244,000
Gerbera	9,570,000	11,826,000
Iris	6,734,000	9,218,100
Roses (Except sweetheart)	18,947,000	38,555,000
(Sweetheart)	12,101,000	13,304,000
Snapdragons	8,200,000	10,045,000
Tulips	17,719,000	35,276,000
Alstroemeria	12,886,000	24,524,000
Lilies	13,852,000	20,829,000
Other	13,928,000	29,218,000
Potted plants (finished)		
Azaleas	2,236,000	3,051,100
Chrysanthemums	14,444,000	16,689,000
Geraniums	10,830,000	26,737,000
Lilies	4,284,000	5,006,800
Poinsettias	7,759,000	12,398,000
Tropical, foliage and green plants	8,190,000	13,786,200
Hanging pots (foliage)	1,157,000	2,010,400
(spring)	3,892,000	6,902,100
Other	70,401,000	10,230,000
Cuttings and other propagating material		
Chrysanthemums	12,173,000	19,388,000
Geraniums	8,903,000	19,493,400
Poinsettias	6,646,000	10,246,000
Seedlings and other	205,122,000	647,043,400
Bedding plants		
Ornamental bedding plants	198,428,000	492,495,000
Vegetable plants	370,080,000	489,582,000

Source: Statistics Canada

33

CHAPTER THREE
MAKING IT HAPPEN

'You have to remember that you are just one person, a small part of the business, and you have to find people who are as excited about the business as you are.'

– Bill Vermeer

'WE DO WHAT WORKS'

When Bill Vermeer is asked to name his favourite flower, he responds: "I see beauty in every flower, but a SOLD one is best."

This should come as no big surprise to anyone who is familiar with the name Westbrook. Bill has nurtured and guided this company through 45 years of phenomenal growth to make it one of the leaders in the horticultural business in the Niagara Peninsula. With its three divisions – Greenhouses, Floral and Systems – Westbrook is involved from growing and producing potted plants, marketing and distributing to building greenhouse structures.

"If you're asking, was this all by my own design, the answer is no," says Bill, the President, in his office at Westbrook's two-storey marketing and distribution centre on Hunter Road in Grimsby. "I took the opportunities when they arrived. I must have made a few decisions that were right."

> *'I took the opportunities when they arrived. I must have made a few decisions that were right.'*

During the last three decades, the astute businessman set aside hands-on greenhouse work so that he could concentrate on the growth of his business. However, he remains a grower at heart.

"I was always interested in growing plants, especially the ones that I liked," he says. "It didn't matter whether it was a tomato or a flower."

The greenhouse business has been his life. He was born in De Lier, in the vast greenhouse area of western Holland known as Westland. All his relatives from both sides of the family were involved in growing in some way. His grandfather, after whom he was named, owned a very large greenhouse range. An enlarged photograph from the early 1900s, showing family members at the greenhouses, hangs in a prominent spot in the lobby at Westbrook.

"My grandfather had been a very prominent greenhouse grower who was ahead of his time," says Bill. "My father had greenhouses too, strictly for vegetables, and I remember as an eight-year-old boy walking through his greenhouses and thoroughly enjoying everything around me. I couldn't get enough of this. The discussion at our house usually centred on either greenhouse growing or the church."

At age 18, he spoke to his father, Cornelius, and mentioned his desire and dream to go to Canada. "He was not very supportive of my idea to leave Holland. Then finally, after a year and a half, he said: 'Why don't we all go?' " So in 1952, Cornelius and his wife, Trinette, and eight of their nine children became immigrants. Annie, who was already married, remained in Holland.

On March 4, 1952, a cold day, the Vermeer family arrived in Grimsby. Cornelius and the older sons started working in greenhouses immediately. Bill's first employer was H. C. Jeffery who grew flowers and dabbled in real estate.

"At the time, Mr. Jeffery was also involved in building houses and needed some labourers," says Bill. "The greenhouse we all worked in was only 30,000 square feet and there wasn't much work, so I decided to change jobs. I could make more money in construction. To this day, when Mary and I drive by a house in St. Catharines or Hamilton that I was involved in constructing, I can still envision myself laying those bricks."

But he hadn't come to Canada to be a construction worker for the rest of his life. So he searched for an opportunity to return to greenhouse work which, after all, was in his blood. Besides, he had to think seriously about his future now that he was married to Mieke (Mary), the girl who had stolen his heart.

— A night-time view of the Westbrook plant in Beamsville where mini-roses are produced.

— The division heads: Peter (PJ) Vermeer, Manager of Westbrook Floral Ltd.; Chuck Vermeer, Production Manager of Westbrook Greenhouses Ltd., and Archie Vermeer, Manager of Westbrook Greenhouse Systems Ltd.

involvement as a partner in Lakeshore lasted nine years.

"Now I have this," he says, referring to the enormous Westbrook business. "It is sold to my children and I am basically an investor now."

He and Mary have 11 children, nine of whom are shareholders of the company and involved in the business, each with his or her own area of responsibility.

The eldest son, Chuck, is Production Manager of Westbrook Greenhouses Ltd., overseeing the growing at three locations: Plant I on Main Street West in Grimsby, Plant II on Lincoln Avenue in Beamsville and Plant III on Ontario Street in Beamsville. The total range measures 1,200,000 square feet.

In the early days, cut mums and carnations were the staple items. Then imports came along and production was switched to potted plants. A wide variety of plants are now produced, based on weekly production schedules, and this production is increased quite substantially during the peak periods leading up to Mother's Day, Valentine's Day, Easter and Christmas.

"Before I left Holland, I was engaged to Mieke VanderWel, and she joined me in Canada," he says. "We were married on January 24, 1953."

Shortly thereafter, he was approached after a Sunday morning church service by John van Staalduinen who had a greenhouse business in Stoney Creek.

"He mentioned that he had heard I was very interested in working in greenhouses. He knew an individual that I should get in contact with – Deny de Jong, who lived in Beamsville and was quite involved in the greenhouse business at that time."

Deny, a Dutchman in his mid-50s who had moved to Niagara from South Africa in 1950, was a main proponent of flower production in the region. Bill and Deny became partners in 1958. In the early 1970s, Deny returned to South Africa. Bill purchased the remaining shares of the operations in both Grimsby and Beamsville and retained the original name Westbrook, derived from a stream that flows down the escarpment on the west side of Grimsby.

Bill was off and running. He soon involved himself in other business ventures as well. With a friend, Jake Koornneef, he built up a greenhouse business in Delray Beach, Florida. "Jake decided to move to Florida," he says, "so I sold him my interest in that business." In the early 1970s, he bought another greenhouse operation in Newark, New York. Five years later, he expanded his holdings even further, buying a place in Utica, New York. Both acquisitions involved partnerships with former employees, Gerry de Wit in Newark and Gerry, Tony Nederhand and Jan Barense in Utica.

"These businesses grew into very big operations," says Bill. "At one time, we employed 300 people steady at the two places. We were one of the biggest operations in the eastern United States. I sold both businesses a few years ago. Since my children were not involved with them, I took the opportunity to let those businesses go."

Back in 1970, Bill was also part of a handful of growers who founded Lakeshore Produce, a wholesale company that sold their products and developed new markets. His

The fourth child, Peter, popularly known as PJ, is Manager of Westbrook Floral Ltd., the division responsible for sourcing, marketing and distributing flowers and floral supplies. It also manufactures dish gardens and cut flower bouquets. To augment Westbrook's production, it buys a large volume of flowers from local growers and from the various markets around the globe. Distribution is done throughout Canada and the United States with a fleet of 55 trucks.

Archie, the middle son, is Manager of Westbrook Greenhouse Systems Ltd. which manufactures greenhouse structures, benches and material handling systems. Its 40,000-square-foot plant is located next door to the marketing and distribution centre.

"From the '70s to the '80s, we developed greenhouses that we wanted for ourselves," says Bill. "At first, we didn't sell them, but then we had people say: 'Make an exception and build one for us.' Well, we built one, and it grew from there. Today we have many of the processes done by robots. It's unbelievable how times change."

— This is the dish garden production area at Westbrook's marketing and distribution centre in Grimsby.

His other children at Westbrook are Janet McLeod, Production Co-ordinator; Bill Jr., Manager of Plant I; Walter, Switchboard Operator; Lisa Heuving, Sales Manager; Terry, Logistics Manager; Ian, Manager of Plant II, and David, Shipping Centre Manager. Bill and Mary's eldest daughter, Ann Yarascavitch, is a teacher's aide at a Catholic school in Whitby.

Bill attributes the involvement of his children to the strong family unit that he and Mary cemented over the years.

"We had a lot of fun together, especially with such a big group," he says. "They all fitted in nicely. The kids always got along with each other right from the start, and we always tried to have dinner together. One rule was that we never talked negatively about the business or about any person. It didn't occur to us to talk negatively because the business and the employees were our livelihood."

Within the divisions, Westbrook employs over 400 full-time and part-time people. Once a month, under the helm of Rej Picard, the Chief Executive Officer, the shareholders meet to discuss developments in each division and their short-range and long-range plans.

"The kids always try to improve on things," says Bill, "and every day the company grows bigger and they keep on expanding it. You know, we are pretty simple people who do what works. If something doesn't work, we have no problem dropping it. We are progressive in our thinking and we have no hangups."

He has received a number of honours for his significant role in making the Ontario flower industry a thriving concern and contributing to the economic welfare of his community. The latest came in October, 2002, when the Brock University, Faculty of Business Lifetime Achievement Award was bestowed on him at a gala dinner in Niagara Falls of the Niagara Entrepreneur of the Year Awards.

As Bill reflects on his many years in the greenhouse business and his tenure as President and long-time director of Flowers Canada (Ontario) Inc., some interesting comments emerge:

On the key to success: "I invested only in horticulture because that was my hobby and that's what I liked doing. I

— Bill Vermeer accepts an award from the Brandee Elliott Foundation in 2002 for his contributions to the well-being of fellow citizens.

never bought land for an investment or anything like that. If you can manage your own money, that's the nicest way of investing. I always had the most enjoyment out of that. The bottom line for me was that I enjoyed what I was doing."

On human resources: "I was very successful in working with people and partners. You have to remember that you are just one person, a small part of the business, and you have to find people who are as excited about the business as you are. I always tell my children that you only know a person if you are married to them or if you have worked with them."

On finances: "Sure, money was a problem at first. It was very hard to convince the banks to lend me money. I remember the difficulties we had when we were asking for a $3,000 overdraft loan. It took nearly 15 years before the banks fully trusted us. Now it's a lot easier. I hear that people can already get money to start in this industry if they say they've worked in greenhouses somewhere."

On work: "My wife did the bookkeeping for the first 10 years. And if I was not finished with work at three

o'clock on Saturdays, she would come to the greenhouse with the small children and help out. I stopped working with my hands 30 years ago. But there was nothing in the greenhouses that someone else did that I hadn't done myself. I could easily correct and guide people – from building greenhouses to welding heating pipes to selling or whatever it took to make the business successful."

On selling: "I remember we had a salesman who sometimes came to me and would mention how hard it was to sell flowers. I would go on the phone and usually was able to sell everything. But I had an advantage: I could lower the price a bit if I needed to. In anything you do, you must be able to sell yourself. If you can't, it won't work."

On the future: "As a farming industry, we will encounter many, many more changes in the next decades. The future will definitely be interesting and challenging. We look forward to this."

— A protective Canada goose keeps a wary eye on visitors to Westbrook's main office.

– *The roof of one of Westbrook's greenhouses has been opened to let in the fresh air and sunshine. This Skyline design is manufactured by Westbrook Greenhouse Systems Ltd.*

When Robert Bierhuizen describes himself as "a kind of forerunner," it's not an idle boast.

Fifteen years ago, a decade or so before the consumer market was ready to accept flowers that went beyond the traditional varieties, the owner of Sunrise Greenhouses Ltd. in Vineland Station was already "fiddling around" with cyclamen, Persian violets and some other flowers that subsequently became very popular.

And long before natural gas prices went through the roof, causing consternation among growers, he formed a company, Energrow Services, that purchased natural gas directly from producers, resulting in significant savings for its nine members. It became the embryo of a much larger group with identical aims, F&V Energby Co-op, which he helped to establish for Flowers Canada (Ontario) Inc.

The list of Robert's innovative efforts goes on and on. It shows that, never satisfied with the status quo, he always is eager to apply new ideas stemming from research and to search himself for new ways to assist and improve his own business and the industry as a whole. This leadership role was recognized in 2000 when Flowers Canada (Ontario) selected him for its prestigious Grower Award.

Robert's grasp of the complexities of greenhouse growing and the appreciation of his colleagues is remarkable when one considers that he wasn't brought up in the field. He lived in Rotterdam, a large city in the Netherlands, where his father was in the newspaper industry as head of the dispatch department of NRC Handelsblad. No one in his family was involved in greenhouse work.

"I was introduced to greenhouses through a friend's father who had a little greenhouse in his backyard," he says. "As kids, we were always puttering around in it. That's where my interest in greenhouses began. Later on, I got a real kick out of picking tomatoes after school in greenhouses in the Berkel-Rodenrijs area just outside Rotterdam."

He went to horticultural school for four years, did very well and advanced to a higher level for three more years of study. When his education was completed, it was time to serve in the Dutch armed forces. His training as an air force helicopter pilot came to an abrupt end when tests determined that he was colour blind, so he was steered

— Robert and Francis Bierhuizen amid brilliance in their Sunrise Greenhouses on Second Avenue in Vineland Station.

to other areas. Twenty-four months later, he was a civilian again and looking for work.

He tried his hand briefly at a few jobs – working in Rotterdam's landscaping department and giving weekly radio reports on crop prices and related matters – before starting a business venture with a friend in Berkel-Rodenrijs. They rented a gardening centre, branched out into landscaping and also purchased a neighbour's greenhouse for tomato and lettuce production.

"We did this for five years," he says. "Everything went well. Then the friend, who had married in the meantime, went to Canada to visit with relatives. When he came back, he said Canada was the place where we should go. There was lots of room and there weren't so many regulations. I told him I would go the following year, take a look and make up my mind."

In August, 1976, Robert visited his friend's family in Huntingdon, near Montreal, and travelled on to Banff, Alberta. On the way back, he passed through the Niagara region, saw a number of greenhouses near the highway and decided to stop at a few addresses he had been given in Holland. He talked with Bill Vermeer of Westbrook Greenhouses and Andy Olsthoorn of Lakeshore, both of whom encouraged him to move to Canada. Back in Holland, he told his friend that they should sell their business and head overseas. The friend, however, didn't want to proceed so quickly and advised him to go first.

In October, Robert encountered Andy who was on business in Holland. Then things started happening quickly. In December, Robert married Francis, whom he had met only a month before his initial trip to Canada, and they emigrated in January. Robert immediately began work at Westland, Andy's new greenhouse operation in

Jordan Station. He had his foot in the door.

Through partnerships, he became involved in running Olsthoorn Greenhouses in St. Catharines and Hunter Road Greenhouses in Niagara-on-the-Lake. He even became an owner of the latter. In time, he divested his interests in the two operations and began concentrating fully on the development of a 12-acre property on Second Avenue in Vineland Station which he had purchased in 1989.

"We went through some difficult times," he recalls. "We had ordered new greenhouses from Holland to bring this place up to speed – it had old greenhouses of about 30,000 square feet – on the understanding that 60 per cent could be financed. Then, while the greenhouses were on the boat, the bank manager came down and said he was sorry to inform us that it was not 60 per cent, but 40 per cent. This was at a time when the economy was in a severe downturn. Well, we managed to struggle through that. It never came to our minds to quit."

*'We can learn so much
from each other.'*

Sunrise Greenhouses, now with 150,000 square feet of covered growing area, plus rented property, produces potted plants, including mini-roses, Easter lilies, chrysanthemums, caladiums and campanula, for the wholesale market. About 20,000 square feet of the greenhouse space and most of the outdoor area is used by a new venture, formed in partnership with Alex Pijl and called The Arbory, for growing small nursery stock such as patio tree roses, miniature weeping pussy willows and heathers.

Robert believes it's important to add to the product mix because consumers in North America are now catching up to the Europeans and demanding something new each year. And the partnership concept works well, he says, because "We can learn so much from each other."

As she leads visitors through the growing areas, all computer-monitored and controlled, Francis stops at an ebb-and-flood bench, slightly bowed upwards in the middle, which her husband helped develop. The design ensures that the bench will completely drain dry, thus preventing algae growth.

Sunrise has another unusual feature: a basement holding 15 water tanks, the fertigation units and other services such as heating and irrigation lines. This means everything is out of the way, permitting more efficient use of the above-ground space.

Francis, the mother of three children – Rodney and Angela, both highly-skilled rowers, and Chandra, whose passion is horse-back riding – looks after the firm's financial affairs. The working relationship with her husband is "very close." But when it comes to finding ways to improve things in the day-to-day operation and looking ahead at what might be coming, Robert usually stands alone.

He was given the Grower Award mainly for his commitment to innovation by implementing measures based on research done in Ontario and funded by the Ontario Ministry of Agriculture, Food and Rural Affairs, Agriculture and Agri-Food Canada, the University of Guelph, the Cecil Delworth Foundation and Flowers Canada (Ontario).

He was one of the first growers to utilize blackout to help control the height of his Easter lily crop, thus requiring less use of chemical growth retardants. He also quickly adopted the technique of interrupted cooling of his lilies, based on only one year's research results, because of the improved plant quality.

He was among the leaders in adopting a structured pest monitoring program and being willing to explore the potential of biological control strategies as a means of reducing his reliance on conventional pesticides. Moreover, he was the first grower in Ontario to screen a portion of his production area where he had forced ventilation to reduce the movement of many pests, including thrips, into the greenhouse and show that it had a real benefit.

In the environmental area, he was one of the first smaller growers to convert a portion of his operation to a recirculating subirrigation system and utilize the European A/B system for crop fertilization based on specific crop target values. He also installed HID lights to improve the quality of his winter-grown mini-roses. With these lights,

energy curtains can be kept closed on cold days to lower heating demands without affecting the light requirements of the plants.

Energy conservation remains at the top of Robert's concerns. Besides his work to get lower gas prices for the industry through a co-operative arrangement, he has taken other steps to lower his own heating bill. Energy curtains cover his entire range and his boiler efficiency is maximized with a condenser unit to recapture heat from flue emissions. Unquestionably, more steps are on the way.

At last word, Robert was studying a computer program that incorporates weather forecasting with crop production modelling to ensure the best energy use and plant quality. For instance, it may be possible to grow a little cooler if warmer and sunny days are coming. He was also involved in researching a new heat storage system that would allow boilers to operate independently of the current heat load. As well, the 24-hour load would be averaged to cut down gas consumption during peak demand.

Little wonder that Robert, with his knowledge, drive and foresight, is in great demand to be a member of organizations and committees dealing with matters related to his industry and the Peninsula.

— Sprinklers provide needed nourishment for the small nursery stock, including heathers, growing outdoors at Sunrise Greenhouses.

THE LEARNING NEVER STOPS

Greenhouse grower Ted Oorsprong has a fondness for machinery, readily admitting that "my favourite thing is the mechanical side of the farm."

There's evidence of this penchant throughout the premises of Northend Gardens (1991) Inc., the Jordan Station company that he and his wife, Carrie, own and operate. The place is technically advanced, employing the latest devices available from the Netherlands. In addition, a few pieces of imported material-handling equipment are on display – well, they're actually for rent or sale – in the large warehouse adjoining the greenhouse range of 200,000 square feet.

'There's always something new we can try. That's what makes this job so interesting.'

But there's more to Ted's average day than working with nuts and bolts, installing mechanical contrivances and offering labour-saving machinery such as scissor-lifts to other growers. He's the person in charge of a fast-growing operation that specializes in custom plug production and also produces a variety of potted seasonal products, annuals and hanging baskets. As such, he is actively involved in all sides of the business.

Northend Gardens was the name of a popular garden centre set up in St. Catharines in 1961 by Ted's parents, John and Leonie. They initially produced only vegetables in some small greenhouses that were built on their three-acre property acquired in 1960. Flowers entered the picture after it was decided to open the retail centre.

John, who had emigrated in 1954 from Honselersdijk, in the Westland region of the Netherlands, worked long and hard to build up his business. Then misfortune struck. In 1963, he developed a lung problem while steaming for a crop of tomatoes and died of pneumonia at age 33. His wife was left with the burdensome responsibility of carrying on the operation while looking after her five young children, including three-year-old Ted.

Leonie, a native of Belgium, then met Gerard Kraan,

formerly of the Dutch village of Ter Aar, and they soon were married.

"I worked at General Motors during the day," he says, "and at night I was in the greenhouse. It was tough, but there was no choice because I had to support the family."

In the ensuing years, sheer dedication and hard work by both Leonie and Gerard resulted in a steady growth in the volume of business at Northend Gardens. In the mid-1980s, it became obvious that more growing space was necessary to ensure continuing advancement. The range at that time covered 50,000 square feet. But the property was landlocked, surrounded by new residential development, which precluded further expansion. A new location was needed.

"I always liked the Jordan area," says Ted, then in charge of the business. "We looked around, bought a 15-acre piece of land on 15th Street in 1988, put up some greenhouses and relocated in 1990. Carrie and I couldn't afford a house, so we moved into the barn. It wasn't until 1998 that our house was built."

With all the elbow room, it didn't take long for Northend Gardens to become a sizeable operation. For 10 years, it produced mainly cut flowers and bedding plants. Then it moved heavily into plug production, with 60 per cent of the output going to other farms. Seed sales jumped from $20,000 in 1999 to $500,000 two years later.

A big portion of the other crops goes to Northend Floral Inc. in St. Catharines, a wholesale firm that grows and distributes patio and aquatic plants and specializes in marketing annuals and perennials. It is operated by Ted's younger sister, Linda, and her husband, Stephen Bouw. Linda had already started selling her brother's products in 1989 while she worked at a flower shop in Toronto.

Carrie, who has two children, Jon and Austin, is involved in the business.

"I didn't know much about flower growing," she says, "but I enjoyed it right away."

She now spends much of her time at a computer screen, doing administrative work and sharing her husband's

— Ted and Carrie Oorsprong share time in the greenhouse with their children, Austin and Jon.

enthusiasm for all the technical wonders that have eased the strain of greenhouse work.

"I'm a big fan of computers," says Ted. "The one that controls our greenhouses is there every day, 24 hours a day, seven days a week. It takes away a lot of the worry."

While running his business, renting, leasing and selling equipment, being involved in partnership with some other growers in an offshoot export company called Intergrow Export and promoting his industry, he continues to keep his ears and eyes open for new ideas to further improve efficiency and growing and, of course, to boost income.

"I never got past Grade 12," he says, "but I never stopped learning. I'm learning whenever I read trade publications, visit Holland, attend shows in Ohio or talk with colleagues in Niagara. There's always something new we can try. That's what makes this job so interesting."

— *Work, ranging from filling pots to watering plants, is in full swing at Northend Gardens. At the end of the day, the Oorsprong family relaxes at their covered, year-round swimming pool.*

The breathtaking view beyond the barn and greenhouses of Northend Floral Inc. on 4th Avenue in St. Catharines looks like something lifted from the Hollywood hills: a huge pond, some three acres in size, in a valley-like setting and a gorgeous house and swimming pool on a higher level, all against a backdrop of trees.

Stephen Bouw refers to the three-million-gallon pond and its island as "our little project." Actually, it's the initial stage of an ambitious plan that may take him and his wife, Linda, 10 years to fully complete.

"My dream is to create a natural setting, a spot where people can sit along the water, relax and enjoy the scenery," enthuses Linda. "But it will be strictly for our personal and company use. The pond will be a display area for the aquatic plants we produce. We also plan to use it as an educational source for people who deal in plants but don't know too much about them. I envisage holding seminars here, with the participants sitting in a specially-built area on the slope overlooking the pond."

The little lake, fed by rainwater and seepage, serves as a water source for fire protection and standby use in the greenhouse operation. But more exciting, especially for Linda and Stephen, will be its function as the centrepiece of a private botanical garden and a showpiece for Northend Floral.

Linda, effervescent and knowledgeable, is a born salesperson. Her abilities in this field became apparent at an early age when she helped out at Northend Gardens, her family's garden centre in St. Catharines. She eventually became in charge of the sales there while her brother, Ted Oorsprong, looked after the growing. Selling continues to be her responsibility at the wholesale firm she and her husband own jointly.

"I enjoy sales," she says. "It gives me an opportunity to meet so many interesting people. I look upon them as partners. I get a lot of satisfaction from helping them by offering a great variety of patio and water plants. I'm delighted when I see a store doing extremely well because that means I am doing well."

She met Stephen, also from St. Catharines, while both were students at The Niagara Parks Botanical Gardens and School of Horticulture near the Falls. He graduated from the three-year program in 1985 and she in 1986. He went on to major in business at Cornell University in Ithaca, New York, and she found a sales position with Sheldrik's, a dried flower business in Toronto, adhering to her view that "it's important for any child to work somewhere else first and then come back." They were married in 1987. Stephen later became a manager of the Toronto Parks Department.

While working at the flower shop, Linda also began selling products grown by her brother who had moved to a larger location on 15th Street in Jordan Station. A few years later, in 1994, they formed Northend Floral as a separate company to serve as the selling arm of his business.

Stephen and Linda moved into their new house on the outskirts of St. Catharines in 1996. He then commuted to his job in Toronto. One day, while Linda was planting in her garden, her young son, Eric, suggested they sit somewhere. When they found a spot, he said: "Mom, I think we should build a barn and work here so Dad doesn't have to go to Toronto all the time."

The advice was followed. Stephen bought Ted's shares in Northend Floral and then built a 10,000-square-foot distribution and administration building and an adjoining greenhouse area of 18,000 square feet on his 22-acre property. Now the family – Mom, Dad, Eric and Danielle – could enjoy a bit more togetherness.

'My dream is to create a natural setting, a spot where people can sit along the water, relax and enjoy the scenery.'

In addition to being a main seller for Ted, Northend Floral handles products grown under contract by up to 20 other growers. The greenhouse production space exceeds 200,000 square feet. A large segment of the total output is made up of a wide assortment of patio plants in the company's exclusive Patio Plant line. But in the last few years, aquatic plants have made inroads, and they soon will account for 40 per cent of total sales to major chain stores and independents in Canada and the United States. Northend Floral's own greenhouses are used solely for growing 240 varieties of these plants.

"Backyard ponds have become quite popular," says Linda. "They're the in thing with home gardeners. We saw a gap in the water plant business and took steps to fill it."

She and Stephen are busy bees, leading a rapidly-expanding company and looking after a backyard project of their own. As far as she is concerned, they have enough on their plates for now.

"Our goal for the next five years," she says, "is to get back to some family life."

— Stephen and Linda Bouw are the owners of Northend Floral Inc. which grows and distributes patio plants, aquatic plants and a variety of flowers.

— *This three-acre pond in a valley-like setting will be used as a display area for the stunning water garden plants produced by Northend Floral.*

CHAPTER FOUR

ROUGH MOMENTS

*Explosions. Fires. Storms. Tragedies. At times, life was not easy for some of Niagara's growers.
But they persevered, and overcame, and moved on to better times.
Tanis Cole, one of those growers, shows some of the gorgeous blooms that are now
produced at Midway Farm Market and Greenhouses.*

Pauline Valk describes 1993 as "the year from hell."

It's one she and her husband, John, would like to forget. But they can't.

First, one of their greenhouses on Livingstone Avenue in Grimsby caught on fire, injuring their son, Sean, who was burned by plastic. Then their other son, Rodney, who was in hospital at the time of the fire, died of abdominal cancer at the age of 19. Before the year was over, the family struggled to cope with a crop failure.

"We were definitely down," says Pauline. "But we received great support and encouragement, especially from other greenhouse people. They came around and asked: 'What can we do for you?' and 'What do you need?' We realized more than ever that the greenhouse industry is a closely-knit community and that we are fortunate to belong to it."

'We realized more than ever that the greenhouse industry is a closely-knit community and that we are fortunate to belong to it.'

— The poinsettia trees growing at Valk Greenhouses Ltd. in Grimsby are nearly as tall as John Valk and his son, Sean.

Rodney, who thoroughly enjoyed greenhouse work, had been looking forward to entering the family business, Valk Greenhouses Ltd., on a full-time basis after his schooling. His untimely death touched the hearts of many. The greenhouse industry set up a scholarship in his name at the University of Guelph. The Valk family also donated a scholarship in his memory at Grimsby Secondary School.

Rodney's grandfather, Harry, the founder of the business, was born in Amsterdam, the Netherlands, where his father was a tailor. The family later moved to Roden, in the province of Groningen. Harry went to agricultural school and then became a grower, producing mostly vegetables. He married Maria and became the father of two children, Gerda and John. Then, like so many others, he was infected by the emigration bug. The family headed for Canada in 1952.

"We arrived on a dairy farm in Troy, a small place near Brantford," says John, six at the time. "My father got $100

a month and a little house. We've torn down better sheds than that. The outhouse was at the front of the place."

In 1959, the family moved to Grimsby where Harry had bought a 9.5-acre fruit farm for $17,500. In addition to looking after the cherry, peach and pear trees, he worked as a spray painter and spot welder and raised laying hens. Intending to get into tomato production as well, he soon bought a used greenhouse for $100 and erected and repaired it for an additional $3,000.

During his high school years, John worked part-time at the nearby R. Jordan Greenhouses Ltd. operation and developed an abiding interest in flower growing. After finishing Grade 12 in 1964, he began working full-time for his father who had a crop of tomatoes in his 4,000-square-foot greenhouse. Father and son formed a partnership and the focus was gradually changed to potted plants, particularly hydrangeas.

"We started with 1,000 pots of hydrangeas in the backyard," says John. "They became our specialty. We still grow a large number of them, in addition to geraniums, poinsettias, fuchsias, impatiens and cuttings, all for the wholesale market."

When John married English-born Pauline in 1969, he obtained a provincial government loan of $40,000, with interest at five per cent, which enabled him to build a new house for his parents and new greenhouses. From then on, the business continued to expand.

In 1986, John, sick and tired of being at the mercy of the elements, pioneered a new system for curing hydrangeas that involved the construction of a dual-purpose greenhouse designed by Westbrook Greenhouse Systems Ltd. At the end of summer, the plants were transferred to the facility from the outdoors where they normally would have stayed until the end of December in all kinds of weather. The curved canopy of double poly could be rolled

— The Valk family: Pauline, John, Sean, his wife, Janet, and their children, Logan and Ethan.

up, giving John total control over the curing conditions. In the spring, after the transfer of the hydrangeas to the glass range, the new greenhouse could be used for normal production.

After the first year, John described the results as "phenomenal." By eliminating the exposure of his hydrangeas to excessively cold or wet periods, he had been able to increase the yield significantly.

Now he and Sean have another step in mind: bring in new environmental-control equipment that would allow year-round production of hydrangeas.

"You either specialize or get phased out," says John. "The margin is getting smaller and we have to make up for this on volume and efficiency."

Once on the outskirts of town, Valk Greenhouses Ltd. is now surrounded by residential development. It has 130,000 square feet of covered growing area plus support buildings.

"We're always building or updating something," says Sean.

He started in the business full-time in 1995 after graduating from the University of Guelph with a degree in horticultural science and business. His wife, Janet, mother of two children, is a great support, working in the office and also in the greenhouses when required. The workforce ranges from 15 to 40, depending on the season.

Pauline is the firm's Secretary-Treasurer. She and John also have a daughter, Nadine, now a resident of Ottawa. John has been very active in the industry, serving as President of Flowers Canada (Ontario) Inc. in 1986-87 and President of F&V Energby Co-op in 1988-92.

The Valk family has added a touching tribute to both Harry and Rodney in the firm's new office building. Portraits of the man who had worked until he was past 80 and the grandson who had wanted to follow in his footsteps hang prominently in the entranceway. And under each photo is their favourite hand tool, reminders of their contribution to the growth and success of the business.

The unforgettable blizzard of Friday, January 24, 1977, struck almost without warning.

Louis Wierenga was at his new greenhouse business on Balfour Street near Fenwick, looking after the hydrangeas that had been transferred from his old place in Port Dalhousie, when the temperature suddenly plummeted, the sky darkened and swirling winds began to whip up the falling snow. He decided to close up shop and head for home.

The storm grew in intensity while he was on his way to Port Dalhousie, where his family was still living. The road was treacherous, almost impassable, and the snow was being blown around in a blinding frenzy. He soon became stranded, like thousands of others that day, and sought shelter in a nearby farmhouse. He spent the night there, and much of the next day, unaware of what was happening in the greenhouses that were sprouting his livelihood.

One can imagine his shock and utter dismay upon learning that all his cuttings and hanging baskets in four greenhouses were ruined after a switch controlling his lone boiler froze and shut off the heat. To make matters worse, one of the houses began to cave in from the heavy accumulation of snow on the roof. There was no insurance to cover the losses.

'I was in the greenhouses in the morning, in the afternoon and in the evening. It was difficult because I had to look after my family too.'

"He was devastated," recalls his wife, Miep. "He was ready to give up. When Monday morning came, he didn't want to start work. He told the girls who were working for us to go home. Then he pulled himself together and the next day he called them back. We cleaned up the mess and put in a new crop, but he remained depressed for a long time."

When the blizzard struck, the eldest son, Lloyd, was taking one of his sisters to Calvin College in Grand Rapids, Michigan, after her Christmas break.

— Wierenga Greenhouses Ltd. near Fenwick specializes in assorted foliage plants and hanging baskets.

"I got a call over there not to come home too quick," he says. When he finally did get home, he couldn't believe his eyes. "The amount of snow was overwhelming. I could walk from a snowbank right onto the top of a greenhouse."

In July, a month after moving to their new place near Fenwick, the Wierenga family received visitors from Holland: Miep's mother and youngest brother. It was a happy occasion. Then tragedy struck. While swimming in a pond on the property, the brother, 33 years old and single, collapsed and drowned.

Miep would have to cope with one more severe blow before year's end. In November, her husband became seriously ill. The diagnosis: bone cancer. She was spending more and more of her time in the greenhouses, doing her husband's work. He died in early February at the age of 47.

Now it was up to the grief-stricken mother of seven children to continue running the business, Wierenga Greenhouses Ltd., along with Lloyd, then 20, who became a partner.

"I was in the greenhouses in the morning, in the afternoon and in the evening," she says. "It was difficult because I had to look after my family too. But I did what I had to do. It came to a point, though, that all the responsibilities and work were too much for me and we took on a grower-manager. He stayed three years."

— Pete and Lloyd Wierenga in their striking office building.

Another son, Pete, came on board in 1982 at age 17. He later took over his mother's part of the ownership. Under the helm of Lloyd and Pete, the business moved ahead and eventually entered good times with a specialty: tropical plants.

Louis was born in Bierum, in the Dutch province of Groningen. He worked as a labourer in greenhouses there and later in Aalsmeer, emigrated in 1954 with his bride, Miep, formerly of The Hague, and settled in Toronto. He first worked for a landscaper, then joined the staff of the city's parks department and also set up his own part-time landscaping business.

"He was used to working 60 hours a week," says Miep. "With the city, he had a 40-hour work week, so he did landscaping on the side. That business grew. Then he quit the parks department and started on his own. He always wanted to have his own greenhouse, so this was a step in that direction."

In 1963, the Wierenga family – there were five children then – moved to a two-acre property with a small greenhouse in Port Dalhousie. Louis continued with landscaping, under the name of Multifloral Landscaping, while his wife did most of the greenhouse work, tending to bedding plants for use in the landscaping business as well as retail sale. Louis became a full-time grower in 1969.

"It was tough in those days for a small operation like ours," says Miep. "We had to find our own customers. If someone couldn't pay, we were out of luck. Things began to improve in the early 1970s when the Ontario Flower Co-op set up its auction. At least, we could bring our product somewhere and get a paycheque every week."

The business grew steadily. Miep even got a salary after it was incorporated in 1975. The greenhouse area was gradually expanded to 17,000 square feet. But when Louis wanted to add on more, the municipality, cognizant of abutting residential development, said no. It was time to move on.

Louis and Miep purchased a nine-acre property near Fenwick in December, 1976. It included 30,000 square feet of greenhouses set up for tomato production. Benches had to be put in place first. Then the cuttings had to be moved from Port Dalhousie. This work was well under way when the blizzard struck.

Lloyd and Pete rebuilt and modernized their greenhouses in 1985, adding acrylic roofs for increased strength and energy conservation. An energy curtain, which doubles as shading, was installed the following year. The first greenhouse expansion was 6,000 square feet. The total area is now 73,000 square feet.

Over the years, the brothers tried different crops, including cut flowers. They took over someone's iris production, but phased this out because of poor demand and lack of a cooler. They now grow 30 varieties of tropicals. Their clients include other growers, distributors, independent garden centres and mass retailers throughout Ontario, Quebec and the northeastern United States. There are 32 people on the payroll – the equivalent of 15 full-timers – including Lloyd's wife, Anita, who looks after the books, and Pete's wife, Lorraine, who handles production management and order processing.

First-time visitors are impressed with the size of the new office building and its handsome interior.

"When it was designed," says Pete, "we kept the future in mind."

— A truck is ready to be loaded with a shipment of plants.

On a mid-November evening in 1963, Cornelis and Mary Vander Hoeven were startled by an enormous explosion outside their house on Stewart Road east of St. Catharines.

"It's the boiler!" Mary knew right away what had happened.

Her husband rushed out the door and got the shock of his life. All that was left of the concrete-block boiler room that had stood 100 feet from the house were two chimneys and a pile of rubble.

The force of the blast had lifted the outside shell of the coal-fired boiler, a large, heavy piece of steel, and deposited it in a field 200 feet away. One concrete block had slammed into a neighbour's basement wall. Fortunately, there were no injuries. But the damage was severe. One quarter of the glass of the greenhouse lay shattered among the cyclamen and potted mums, which quickly became a total loss.

'I was stunned. I just sat in the house for two days, not knowing what to do.'

The explosion, presumably resulting from an electrical problem, happened just when Cornelis was in the process of becoming a full-time greenhouse grower. He was adding 10,000 square feet to the 15,000-square-foot greenhouse that he had built while he worked for General Motors in St. Catharines.

"I was stunned," he recalls. "I just sat in the house for two days, not knowing what to do. I wasn't insured for boiler explosion. Finally, I said I should do something and started phoning around to get a new boiler and new glass and arrange for a new boiler room to be built. A friend offered to put all the junk in his truck and that was a huge help for me."

By Christmas, the business was up and running again. But it took awhile for Cornelis and Mary to get over the loss of $20,000, a colossal amount in those days. They used the $41 they had received for their scrap to buy Christmas presents for their children, including newly-born twins, Andy and Peter.

— Cornelis Vander Hoeven and his twin sons, Andy and Peter, at their greenhouses in St. Catharines.

The two sons are now the owners of Vander Hoeven Greenhouses Ltd., producing potted plants and bedding plants in 140,000 square feet of covered space – greenhouses, cold frames and A frames – on Linwell Road East in St. Catharines. The business has been there since 1968. Most of the products go to wholesalers and the rest directly to garden centres.

Cornelis and Mary emigrated from the Netherlands six weeks after their marriage in 1951. He was from Wateringen and she from Den Hoorn, both near The Hague. A friend in Canada had told him: "It's beautiful there." No more convincing had been needed.

The couple landed on a fruit farm near Niagara-on-the-Lake and moved into a small house that had a woodstove but lacked washroom facilities and running water. They had to crawl over an electric fence to get to an outside toilet.

Cornelis didn't mind the hard work. In Holland, he had

toiled in tomatoes since age 13 – "I was too wild to stay in school." But he figured that his labour was worth more than the $80 a month he was being paid, especially after Mary had a miscarriage and the medical bills started piling up. His request for a $10-a-month raise was granted only after he had agreed to clean up all the soot from the woodstove that had accumulated through the house.

He next went to work on a vegetable farm where the accommodation was not as primitive. But he wanted to get a place of his own as soon as possible. In 1953, after working at General Motors for a year, he bought a lot in St. Catharines for $475 and built his own home for $4,500. He was pleased with the progress he was making in the new land. Mary, however, was smitten by homesickness and longed to be with her family.

"After 1956, my wife wanted to go to Holland, but I didn't feel like it," he says. "I told her: 'You go there and stay as long as you want.' It was the only way for her to get over

— An old cement mixer is put to good use as a soil mixer at Vander Hoeven Greenhouses.

His five daughters, who disliked working among the tomatoes, were tickled pink when the flowers started to appear. He and Mary also had three sons – the eldest died of leukemia in 1969 – so there were plenty of hands available at their beck and call. Five of their children are now involved in greenhouse work, including Andy and Peter who took over the family operation in 1984 when they were 21 years old.

The parents live on the opposite side of the Welland Canal, within eyesight of the greenhouses. Hardly a day goes by when Cornelis doesn't drop by. After all, he has a woodshop on the premises in which he crafts wonderful creations for his grandchildren.

The Peninsula In 1936

To most people, the term Niagara Fruit Belt brings to mind the Niagara Peninsula and its well-known ability to produce peaches, grapes and other fruits.

What is less familiar to most Canadians is the fact that this narrow, 40-mile strip of land bordering the south shore of Lake Ontario can also qualify as one of the most bountiful market gardens in Canada, if not on the continent.

Its climate is tempered by the lake on the north and protected by the rugged Niagara Escarpment on the south. This land of favoured soil produces every year an almost unbelievable tonnage of fresh human food and is one of the most intensively cultivated sections in Canada.

Motor tourists who use the fine highway – which provides a traffic backbone for the Fruit Belt – in the thousands every year inevitably note the peach orchards and vineyards which dot the countryside as they pass.

To the agriculturally-minded motorist, another feature is quite obvious, and that is the dozens of greenhouses which dot the landscape. These indicate the extent of the vegetable production which hundreds of Niagara fruit growers have found fits in so well with their orchard and small fruit practices.

From the April 29, 1936 issue of Family Herald and Weekly Star

her feeling. She went with one of the children. The other two were looked after by acquaintenances. Well, she came back after four months and said she had decided not to return to Holland to live."

With the family reunited, Cornelis bought a two-acre property with a house on Stewart Road, built a greenhouse and began growing tomatoes and potted mums while continuing to hold his job at GM. His goal was to become a full-time greenhouse grower.

"If I had to work all my life in a factory," he says, "I would have gone back to Holland myself."

Five years after the boiler explosion, the Vander Hoevens were told to leave. Their land was expropriated by the St. Lawrence Seaway Authority which needed some 2,000 acres for a new canal from Lake Ontario to Thorold. The project was never undertaken.

"They paid me in July and I had to get out in August," says Cornelis. "I asked for an extension because I didn't want to lose my tomato customers. But no way."

The family moved to their new property of nearly seven acres on Linwell Road East. It took a month to clean up the place before construction of a 17,000-square-foot greenhouse could begin. While he was building, Cornelis fell through glass and badly cut his arm. Naturally, he had to halt work for awhile. When all was finally done, a tomato crop was planted.

The gradual switch to flowers began in the early 1970s.

"I was playing cards one day with a friend who mentioned that he had an order for geranium cuttings but no room to grow them," says Cornelis. "I was asked to put them in an aisle in my greenhouses. I said OK. A year later, I had two houses with flowers. Then I gradually changed over completely. 1984 was the last year I grew tomatoes."

AFTER THE FIRE

On a hot August day in 1990, Bill Cole was about to start picking peaches on his parents' farm on Fourth Avenue in Jordan Station when one of the workers shouted: "There's smoke coming from the barn!"

Indeed, white smoke was billowing from the three-storey frame structure which he had left only five minutes earlier. It was being used for cold storage of fruit and also held all the farm's equipment and supplies such as baskets and even bales of straw.

"I raced to it and managed to pull out an orchard sprayer," says Bill, now Manager and part-owner of the business, Midway Farm Market and Greenhouses. "But that was it. Everything else was destroyed."

Flames had quickly engulfed the building, as well as a sport utility vehicle parked next to it, sending a large plume of black smoke into the air. The cause was traced to an electrical fault.

"It was traumatic," says Bill. "In a matter of minutes, we went from having everything we needed for our work to not having anything, not even a shovel. The loss was only partly covered by insurance. We built a new barn and replaced the equipment, but it took us a long time to get over the experience."

'The credit union singled me out as an up-and-coming entrepreneur in the growing business.'

Good things are happening now at Midway. The focus has shifted almost completely to production of flowers and plants for both retail and wholesale use – seven acres of sweet cherries are still left – and business continues on the upswing. In fact, it's going so great that the 30,000-square-foot greenhouse range has been expanded by 58,000 square feet.

"Retail sales at the front of our place were growing every year and we needed more space for this area of our business," says Bill. "We also went in production of cuttings, which required extra room. The expansion was a

— Flames engulf the packing barn at Midway Farm Market and Greenhouses in Jordan Station in 1990.

major investment for us. It was the only way for us to keep up with the demand and move ahead."

Born in 1968, he was raised on the Cole family farm in Port Dalhousie, a well-known fruit and vegetable and pick-your-own strawberry operation. The property was originally given to the family of Laura Secord, Canadian heroine in the War of 1812, with whom his great-grandfather was related by marriage. She had made her way through the U.S. lines to warn the British of a U.S. attack, thus bringing the British victory in the battle of Beaver Dam. The farm ended up in the possession of the Cole family where it remained until it was sold for subdivision development in the mid-1970s.

Bill's parents, Herb and Tanis, then purchased a 35-acre fruit and vegetable farm in Jordan Station. They had two small poly houses in which hothouse tomatoes and some flowers were grown. These products were sold at their roadside stand, along with onions, squash, apples and other produce.

The son joined the partnership after graduating from the two-year horticultural program at the University of Guelph in 1991. A small greenhouse of 7,200 square feet was built for bedding plants. As sales picked up, this was soon expanded. The main focus shifted from fruit to a wide assortment of plants for both retail and wholesale use, including annuals, perennials, ivies, herbs and hanging baskets.

"The fruit is not entirely forgotten," says Bill. "We have three stands at the St. Jacobs market in Waterloo. This is a tourist attraction. Thousands of people shop there on Thursdays and Saturdays. We take our cherries there as well as fall mums and apples. Whatever is left at the end of the season is donated to community homes and worthy causes."

His mother, being of Ukrainian background, raised him and his brother, Herb Jr., with her traditions. He is married to Barbara and they have three children, Robert, Chantel and Owen. He's also a member of the Niagara Credit Union – "one of our biggest supporters" – which financed the recent expansion.

"The credit union singled me out as an up-and-coming entrepreneur in the growing business," he says, proudly displaying a framed poster with a family picture and a brief history of the business that the financial institution printed in his honour.

– Tanis Cole and her son, Bill, with some of the beautiful flowers and plants they grow in their greenhouses on Fourth Avenue.

— *A dazzling closeup of a potted mum.*

A RUDE WELCOME

Mother Nature gave Tom Valstar a harsh welcome when he was about to launch his career as a greenhouse grower in the summer of 1972.

A twister struck just after he had taken over Scott Street Greenhouses Ltd. in Niagara-on-the-Lake from his brother-in-law, Dick Vanderende, who was setting up a new business on Lakeshore Road. When the roaring winds abated, 2,200 panes of glass lay shattered on the dirt floor.

"We hadn't even moved into the house yet," recalls Gord, Tom's son, then 15 years old. "My uncle called: 'Close all the windows! There's a storm coming!' I heard glass breaking and dashed for the house. I was pelted by huge hailstones and that hurt. But I was more concerned about damage. I was shocked when I saw the mess. A bank of trees had been uprooted. And there was glass all over the place. Luckily, we didn't have a crop in yet."

'It's fascinating how automation has changed things.'

Two years later, a neighbour's barn caught on fire, generating tremendous heat that again cracked a large number of panes in the greenhouses.

"This was our welcome into the industry," says Gord, who took over from his parents in 1997. "We were wondering what was going to happen next."

What happened was a steady growth in the Scott Street operation, the purchase in 1979 of a second location, on Tanbark Road in St. Davids, the later consolidation of everything at the new place and continued expansion. The business now has 202,000 square feet of greenhouses for producing poinsettias, geraniums, mums, Easter lilies, hanging baskets, assorted bedding plants and various cuttings.

Tom was 18 years old when he emigrated with his parents and eight siblings from De Lier, the Netherlands, in 1951. He arrived on a farm near Sudbury and later found work in a nickle mine. After moving to St. Catharines, he hooked up with an acquaintance from his hometown and headed to the West to work on a pipeline. Upon his return, he did

— Gord and Wilma Valstar and their sons, Steven and Mark, at Scott Street Greenhouses in St. Davids.

a few odd jobs before becoming involved in trenching. He next went into trucking, initially with a dump truck, and stayed in this work for 15 years.

In 1972, he and his wife, Riet, whom he had married in 1954 – they had gone to the same school in Holland – decided to enter the greenhouse business. After all, many of their close friends were already in this field. They purchased the property on Scott Street, with a greenhouse area of 30,000 square feet, and were ready to get started with a tomato crop when the twister struck. After the cleanup and repair, the business was up and running.

"In the winter, we grew mums for Mother's Day," says Gord, who began working full-time at age 15. "After that, we had poinsettias. We soon expanded by 20,000 square feet. Our new location in St. Davids had 30,000 square feet of greenhouses when we moved there in '79 and we put on 45,000 square feet that year. We operated both properties for a number of years and then decided to put everything under one roof. The one on Scott Street was sold to Simon van Spronsen in 1987 and he named it Willy's. We kept our business name, Scott Street Greenhouses."

His wife, Wilma, was an experienced greenhouse worker before their marriage in 1979. She is still at his side, performing jobs that range from office duties to work among the plants. One of their two sons, Steven, is one of the 15 full-time workers. Mark attends school.

"Our place is never empty," says Gord. His firm does its own shipping of all its spring products and lets wholesalers handle the seasonal ones. Further expansion probably hinges on whether the sons are interested in staying with the business. But further modernization is certain.

"It's fascinating how automation has changed things," he says. "For example, when I first started, we mixed soil with a shovel. Then we used a rototiller, a cement mixer and a tractor with a front-end loader. Now we buy the soil pre-mixed, done by machines. Modernization is an ongoing thing, involving all facets of the business."

John van der Zalm acknowledges that he likely wouldn't be in business today as co-owner of European Planters Inc. if some kind and understanding people hadn't come along when he was down, badly needing a helping hand.

In 1985, shortly after setting up a venture in St. Catharines that made tropical dish gardens, he lost sight in one eye when an artery behind the eye burst due to exertion from rowing, a sport in which he excelled. This didn't stop him from continuing his work and driving his 10 routes to flower shops throughout southern Ontario. But then a more serious situation confronted him.

"One day, when I was returning home from making a delivery, I developed a problem with my other eye," he says. "I became virtually blind. Of course, I couldn't do any work, which was devastating. But an unemployed friend, my brother, Jim, and my parents kept things together. Fortunately, the problem with my good eye cleared up rather quickly. When I was working again, some greenhouse people stopped by so that I could go with them to the auction and sell my products. All this support was extremely helpful. Within a year, Jim had joined me full-time."

'We soon had planters everywhere, even in the washroom, and concluded that we needed a bigger place.'

After the brothers had moved their expanded operation to a new greenhouse on Irvine Road in Niagara-on-the-Lake in 1996, hoping to catapult it forward with seasonal crops, another dose of misfortune hit. Their first two crops, poinsettias and hydrangeas, were total failures. Already reeling from costs that far exceeded their expectations, they now began to wonder about the future of their business.

"We were left in a vulnerable situation," says Jim. "We were very straightforward with suppliers and others that were owed money. Well, they gave us an opportunity to continue on, allowing us extra time, interest-free, to pay off the debts. After I had come up with a plan, they did not have to call us once for money. Everything worked out well, thanks to their support. We're not vulnerable any longer."

Jim was born in 1958 and John in 1960, both in St. Catharines. Their father, Ted, acquired the Colonial Flower Shop on Ontario Street after his arrival from the Netherlands in 1953. With a number of brothers, he also became involved in running a greenhouse operation on Broadway Avenue called Colonial Florists Ltd. He married Mary Hendriks, whose family was also involved in greenhouse work in Niagara.

"We grew up in the greenhouses on Broadway," recalls Jim. "As kids, we learned a lot about growing. On the weekends, we had to get up at 6:30 because there was work to be done. And in the summer holidays, we had to work too. A holiday for us meant going to the beach at Port Dalhousie."

Jim eventually began working full-time in the greenhouses. John went to the flower shop. When his younger brother, Don, also joined the staff, he decided to leave. "There was not enough challenge left for me," says John. "Business had levelled off after it had been brought to a certain plateau." Don and his father continue to operate the shop.

John soon became involved in another pursuit. His parents had returned from a trip to Holland in 1983 with an idea to make tropical dish gardens. He was extremely interested. Before long, he had connected with suppliers of ceramic and brass containers from Holland and of stoneware from Germany, rented a 1,800-square-foot warehouse in St. Catharines and launched his production under the name European Planters.

"I had no idea where I was going with this," he says. "I was on the road all day and made the planters at night. It was only after Jim came on board that business really began to pick up. It's amazing what happens when you have someone in the office answering the telephone. We soon had planters everywhere, even in the washroom, and concluded that we needed a bigger place."

The brothers leased a piece of land wedged between Colonial Florists Ltd. on Broadway and built a 6,000-square-foot facility. They also launched a side business, bringing in finished product from Florida. For the first trip, they used their van. Then a tractor-trailer was purchased. Before long, more space was needed, but the location was

— Jim and John van der Zalm offer dish gardens, tropicals, hanging baskets and an assortment of flowers.

not suited to accommodate an expansion and easy truck access.

"We then merged the two businesses under one holding company and decided to move," says John. "In 1996, we bought five acres on Irvine Road and put up 27,000 square feet of greenhouses with a 150,000-gallon cistern underneath because there was no municipal water supply. The first year, we had no water. So a neighbour, who was drawing water from the lake for irrigation, came to our rescue. We had decided to dabble in seasonal crops. But that got off to a terrible start with two crop failures, very traumatic experiences."

The business rebounded. The brothers still offer ceramic and wicker dish gardens and assorted tropicals. And among the flowers they produce are poinsettias and hydrangeas, the products that caused them so much misery at the outset, as well as geraniums and impatiens hangers.

"The future looks more promising now then when we started the project," says John.

This is good news for any budding greenhouse growers in both families. John and Karen have four children and Jim and Catherine have eight.

PETER'S DELIGHT

Harry Voogt and his son, Peter, had just finished glazing the roof of their new greenhouse in Virgil in August, 1986, when a wicked storm struck, pounding the neighbourhood with hailstones the size of golf balls.

"I stood here and watched it," recalls Peter. "Those stones were big. They ruined all the peaches on either side of us and put a few dents in my truck. But worst of all for us, they smashed a lot of the glass of the roof we had been working on. The sound was sickening."

Harry adds: "It was a mess. The broken glass inside was the worst part. Fortunately, we didn't have a crop in yet."

The shards were quickly cleaned up, the roof was repaired and glazed and tomatoes were planted. When the picking began, tomatoes were scarce and father and son had no problem getting rid of theirs. In fact, buyers at the Ontario Food Terminal in Toronto were literally fighting over them and offering high bids. In the Voogt family, there was an upbeat mood.

'It was a mess. The broken glass inside was the worst part. Fortunately, we didn't have a crop in yet.'

Voogt Greenhouses Inc. eased out of tomatoes and soon began growing flowers exclusively, much to the delight of Peter. He had preferred flowers over vegetables ever since he graduated from the two-year horticultural program at Ridgetown College near Chatham. His range of 80,000 square feet – Dad is no longer directly involved – now produces 60,000 poinsettias annually, as well as hydrangeas, potted roses, hanging baskets, geraniums, impatiens and other bedding plants.

Harry, born in De Lier, the Netherlands, was 11 years old when he emigrated to Canada in 1948 with his parents, Peter and Nellie, and four siblings. The family went to their sponsor in Manitoba, stayed a few weeks and then headed for Ontario even before their crate with furniture had arrived. They ended up on an apple farm near Queenston.

In addition to working on the farm, Harry's father bought apples and sold them to the immigrant community. Three

years later, he was the owner of a 30-acre grape and peach farm near Niagara Falls. He took his next big step in the late 1950s, buying 10 acres of land in St. Davids and building a 30,000-square-foot greenhouse for tomato production. Other vegetables were grown outdoors.

Harry had started working for his father after quitting school at age 16. His pay consisted of some pocket money and the privilege of using the family car. Real income came his way when he worked for Ontario Hydro at the Niagara Falls tunnel project. After three years, he started on his own, selling apples and potatoes at the public markets in Port Colborne, Welland and Niagara Falls and trucking vegetables to wholesalers, mostly in Ottawa and Montreal. He married JoAnn in 1962, continued his trucking and then bought a 10-acre field in St. Davids on which he built a house and later a greenhouse. Like his father, he grew tomatoes and other vegetables which he sold at his stand at the wholesale market in Toronto.

"We did very well with tomatoes," he says. "But after many years, the work became too much for me. I sold the farm in the mid-1980s, severing off two acres for a new

house and a hobby greenhouse of 15,000 square feet. I grew tomatoes and took them to Toronto. I was thinking of retiring. But Peter didn't know what to do, so we decided to start from scratch somewhere else. We bought three acres of peach land in Virgil, removed the trees and built a greenhouse of 40,000 square feet. We started with tomatoes. But we also put in a crop of poinsettias, just to keep Peter happy."

Peter, born in 1964, had worked for a few flower growers after graduating from college to get some experience under his belt. At one place, a rose operation in Vineland, he worked four months without pay, although he was permitted to hang baskets in unoccupied space and pocket the money from the sales. Now he is in full charge of the Voogt operation, running a successful business with the help of his brother, Brian, his wife, Heather, and a number of employees.

"When we moved into flowers, I had to do a little hustling," he says. "We managed to build up a good customer base. Now our focus is on delivering an excellent product, year after year."

— Peter and Brian Voogt with the transport truck that delivers their products to wholesale customers.

TASTY TULIPS

When the Netherlands was liberated from German occupation on May 5, 1945, Queen Wilhelmina told her weary subjects:

"The firing squad, the prison, the torture camp have disappeared. Gone is the unspeakable oppression by the persecutor, who for five years has tormented you. Gone is the horror of famine."

Holland, normally a land of plenty, saw thousands of its citizens wither away to mere skeletons and drop dead in the streets after the advance by the Allied armies was stopped in the fall of 1944 and the food supply to most of the country was cut off.

During the horrible months that followed – the Dutch refer to them as the Hunger Winter – many people were reduced to eating tulip bulbs, sugarbeets and other food substitutes to fend off starvation. The bulbs were roasted on the stove like chestnuts.

"They did not taste so bad, but easily led to indigestion," Walter E. Maas writes in his book The Netherlands At War: 1940-1945.

The mere thought of eating tulip bulbs is probably repugnant to most people. Although there's nothing poisonous about them, and devouring specially-prepared ones can be enjoyable, they can trigger an allergic reaction in some people. So it's best to avoid them.

But to food connoisseurs like Daryle Nagara, chef at Vancouver's Farmont Waterfront Hotel, the edible petals of the tulip are a gastronomical delight.

"The flower tastes a little like crisp iceberg lettuce and snow peas, with a nice peppery finish," he says.

He grows 2,000 tulips in his rooftop organic garden at The Waterfront and uses the blooms in some of his spring menu offerings. For example, there's a crisp and colourful salad prepared with the following ingredients:

4 cups mesclun salad mix
16 edible tulip petals

Vinaigrette:
1 teaspoon chopped parsley
1 clove garlic, minced
1 teaspoon bee pollen
2 tablespoons honey
1/4 cup white-wine vinegar
1/4 cup extra virgin olive oil
Salt and freshly ground pepper
1/3 cup grated Asiago cheese

Toss the mesclun salad mix and tulip petals with enough vinaigrette to lightly coat. Arrange the tulip petals and mixed greens in the cheese baskets and serve at once.

Combine parsley, garlic, bee pollen (available at most health food stores), honey, vinegar and olive oil, whisking together to combine and emulsify. Season vinaigrette to taste with salt and pepper. Sprinkle with cheese. Makes four servings.

Try this delightful offering with assorted dips, courtesy of **Kristyna Kelley**, The Waterfront's Food and Beverage Co-ordinator:

Tempura Fried Emperor Tulips
With Hindashi Tenju, Apple and Chinin Wine Jelly and Tamarind Glaze

Tempura Batter
1 egg yolk
2 cups ice cold water
1/8 teaspoon baking soda
1 2/3 cups flour

Hindashi Tenju
1 cup mirin
1/4 cup Japanese Soya sauce
1 cup dashi (2 1/2 quarts water,
3-inch-square kombo,
1 cup dried bonito)
1/2 teaspoon salt

Apple and Chinon Wine Jelly
1 cup grilled hoo doo ranch apples
1 cup sugar
1/4 cup cider vinegar
2 cups chinon wine
2 ounces pectin
2 teaspoons lemon juice

Tamarind Glaze
4 ounces grated fresh coconut
1 onion
1 teaspoon chopped coriander leaves
3/4-inch piece of ginger
1/2 tablespoon cumin powder
2 garlic cloves
1 teaspoon sugar
3 tablespoons tamarind
1 teaspoon ketchup
6 stoned dates
2 teaspoons lime juice
1/2 teaspoon salt

Grind all ingredients.

Dip the tulip petals into the tempura batter. Fry until golden in vegetable oil until crisp and light brown. Season lightly with salt. Place tulips on attractive platter and serve with the three assorted dips. Garnish using fresh tulips.

CHAPTER FIVE

COMING UP ROSES

'When people are coming in, it's important to have a neat place. A good image is essential in business.'

– Otto Bulk

Rose grower Otto Bulk wanted something eye-catching to welcome and impress visitors to the new sales offices at his vast greenhouse complex near Dunnville.

"When people are coming in, it's important to have a neat place," he explains. "A good image is essential in business."

When his fourth plant and the adjoining sales offices were being designed, he included a solarium with exotic plants and cascading water, intending to add a touch of grandeur to a place that, in many eyes, was already something to behold. "Wow!" became a frequently-heard exclamation. Some wedding parties even requested to have their picture taken in the splendid setting.

Otto's company, Rosa Flora Growers Ltd., is the largest grower of hybrid tea and sweetheart roses in Canada, annually yielding 10 million of them in 50 varieties. In addition, he and his staff of 150, including part-timers, grow from four to five million snapdragons, a million gerbera, half a million stephanotis, 2.5 million alstroemeria and some other crops. His greenhouse area for producing this huge output totals 850,000 square feet.

'Instead of workers going to the roses, they let the roses come to them. We now use our space to the fullest.'

— A solarium with exotic plants and cascading water is one of the features at Rosa Flora Growers Ltd. near Dunnville.

Roses have always been a part of Otto's life. His father, Frank, grew them in his greenhouses in Aalsmeer, the Netherlands. Naturally, the six children in the family were required to lend a hand. Otto, born in 1950, went to work among the roses full-time after graduating from horticultural school. Although he enjoyed the work, and his future in the family business seemed secure, his thoughts often wandered to faraway Canada where two of his brothers lived. Jake had emigrated in 1965 and Frank had followed two years later.

"Frank worked for Marinus Koole at Creekside," he says. "He was to stay there nine months under a work experience program, come back to Holland and then I would go. But that never happened. He decided to stay in Canada."

Jake established his own business, Rose-A-Lea Gardens

Ltd., in Mount Brydges, near London. With cut roses as the principal product, it grew by leaps and bounds. His current holdings include the rose operation in Princeton that was formerly owned by Peter van Wees. Frank also established a rose business, initially with a partner on Merritt Road near Beamsville and later on his own on Marshagan Road near Dunnville. It's called Rosalin Gardens Inc.

Otto and his wife, Corine, whom he had married in 1974, went on vacation to Canada. What they saw and heard impressed them greatly. They fell in love with the country and resolved to emigrate as soon as they could sell the business that Otto had taken over from his father.

"We came here in 1977, a half year after selling the operation in Holland to someone from Italy," he says. "I began work at a greenhouse near Brantford, but was laid

off after eight weeks due to a lack of work. When I told my wife, she was understandably very worried. But within 24 hours, without knowing about this situation, Clarence van Staalduinen called me up and said he had a position available for me in his greenhouses in Brantford, and would I be interested. Would I! In the meantime, we bought 30 acres, an open field, on Diltz Road near Dunnville."

His first priority was to build a house – he and Corine had three children then – with a $32,000 loan. It was a bare structure, with unpainted walls, when the family moved in. Construction of a greenhouse was begun in the spring of 1978.

"My focus was not on how large it should be – it was 16,800 square feet – but just on having a place of our own in which we could grow hybrid tea roses. I had heard from

— *This striking entrance to Rosa Flora's fourth plant leads to the solarium.*

my brothers that roses were a good thing here. My father came over from Holland and looked on with a critical eye. When I rented a rototiller and started working the soil, he shook his head and said: 'That's no good. It won't grow.' But everything grew well. In the first year, I had fantastic roses. Bill Snoei of Bayview Flowers in Jordan Station was my first customer. I also went to the wholesale market in Toronto. Business was good and we were happy. I did the growing and selling and Corine kept the books. The following year, we already increased in size."

The growth never stopped. More land was acquired from neighbours and more growing space was built. Rosa Flora, with its handsome buildings, acrylic greenhouses and neatly landscaped properties on both sides of Diltz Road, now presents an imposing sight to visitors and passing motorists.

"We've grown big on purpose," says Otto, with a twinkle in his eyes. "Corine and I have six children and hopefully they will become involved."

They may have to wait awhile. Only one of the six is involved full-time: Arielle DeBoer, Rosa Flora's Human Resources Co-ordinator. The others are Frank, a network administrator at Dordt College in Sioux Center, Iowa, who plans to attend university to attain a Master's degree; Margaret, who is continuing her university studies in Ontario toward achieving a doctorate degree in sociology; Esther, who is employed full-time in the area of child and youth work; Joshua, who is majoring in political sciences at Dordt, and Sarah, who plans to attend the social sciences program of Mohawk College.

One of Rosa Flora's exceptional features, besides the solarium, is the co-generating station that has been producing electricity and carbon dioxide for all the company's needs since 1992.

"We were always thinking of how we could run the lights cheaper," says Otto. "When Ontario Hydro thought it was running short of power, it set up a co-generating program and we got in on it just in time. The excess power we produce is sold to Ontario Hydro. Heat is a byproduct of the process and we use it to full advantage for our greenhouses. Our boilers are fired by natural gas."

— Otto and Corine Bulk and three daughters, Arielle, Sarah and Esther, visit one of the greenhouses.

His entire range has high-pressure sodium lights for use during periods of minimum sunlight. Canadians, he says, have been the leaders in this field. Growers from Holland travelled to Canada just to have a look at what is being done with the lights. They came also when word reached them that Otto had developed a unique system for increasing his growing space without adding on greenhouses – a system that has been adopted since by other growers.

"I had been thinking of how to increase production per square metre," he says, "and Ed Feenstra, the General Manager, and I finally came up with a motorized rolling table system that effectively cut out the pathways. Instead of workers going to the roses, they let the roses come to them. We now use our space to the fullest."

All is not rosy in the rose business, however. The competition from Ecuador has become intensive. That country, with its year-round warm climate, can produce roses that are cheaper and better, with larger buds. Ontario-grown carnations disappeared because of imports and roses could be in serious trouble for the same reason. That's why Otto, for one, is not putting all his eggs in one basket and also grows a number of other flower products in large volumes.

"We do have one big advantage," he says. "When an order for roses is called in from the States, for example, we can deliver them the next morning with one of our own trucks. Our customers appreciate this excellent service."

By the way, Otto has three more brothers in Canada. Hans owns Eurosa Gardens, a producer of cut flowers in Brentwood Bay, British Columbia. Paul, the youngest family member, works for a wholesaler in Vancouver, and Peter, who lives in Grimsby, has had experience with the technical aspects of growing systems. Elly, the remaining sibling in the Netherlands, is a teacher.

To Frank Bulk, the black soil in the Dunnville area looked rich, much like that of the Aalsmeer area of the Netherlands where he grew up. It would be an ideal place to erect a greenhouse and grow roses, his family's specialty.

So, in 1977, he bought 30 acres of land with a rundown house on Marshagan Road and began building a barn, his first structure. Then the spring rain came down in torrents. When it finally stopped, water blanketed the fields, including the construction area.

"I couldn't even get to the barn," Frank recalls. "It was quite a shock to see all that water. It turned out that we were living in marshland where rainwater and snowmelt couldn't drain away. We later learned that malaria was quite common around here in the early days because of all the mosquitoes. They didn't tell us that when we bought the property. In retrospect, the name of the road should have given us a clue."

He went ahead with the greenhouse, ignoring comments from people in the area that "this guy must have a hole in his head to build in such a low area." In true Dutch style, he built an earthen dike about two feet high around three sides of the greenhouse site, leaving the road to complete the protection. Since then, the wall has done its job in keeping out the water.

As for the black soil, Frank found that it was deficient in some key nutrients, creating an annoyance and an expense. But that's not a big problem anymore because his business, Rosalin Gardens Inc., grows its sweetheart and tea roses hydroponically in the 45,000-square-foot range.

'I couldn't even get to the barn. It was quite a shock to see all that water.'

Frank followed his brother, Jake, to Canada in 1967 when he was 17 years old. As per prior arrangement under a program that allowed young Dutch farmers to gain work experience abroad, he began a nine-month work period for Marinus Koole of Creekside Gardens in Jordan Station whose production then included roses. Since his father was a rose grower in Aalsmeer, he was no stranger to this work.

— Frank Bulk grows roses at his Rosalin Gardens Inc. operation near Dunnville.

"When the time was up," he says, "I asked for a nine-month extension. I liked it here so much that I didn't really want to go back to Holland. I then was asked to stay permanently. Marinus said he would arrange everything. Well, he came up with my immigration papers and made me foreman of his rose operation."

In 1973, Frank and a partner, Martin Boerefijn, purchased a greenhouse concern on Merritt Road near Beamsville – it's now called Cedarway Floral Inc. – and began their own rose production. The partnership split in 1977 and Frank and his wife, Els, headed for the Dunnville area to start their very own rose business.

The roses produced at Rosalin Gardens were sold initially to wholesalers. When two of the Bulk children, Alex and Derrick, joined the firm full-time, direct selling was instituted. They deliver roses to flower shops throughout Ontario. The other two children, Janna and Aliska, work in the greenhouses.

For 10 years, Els had her hands full looking after no fewer than 75 purebred Suffolk sheep on the property. These were used for showing and for wool and meat production. The venture ended when the work became too demanding.

"But she's hasn't slowed down," says Frank. "Besides doing the bookkeeping and helping out among the roses, she's still the farmer in the family. We grow soybeans and corn, and she looks after that."

HE'S AMAZED

When Peter Bulk picked a site near Welland in 1982 to set up a rose-growing business, he had no idea that the historic community along the Welland Canal promoted itself as the Rose City.

"It was a surprise to learn that the city was known for its roses," he says. "I couldn't have selected a more appropriate place."

Welland's Chippawa Rose Garden features over 50 rose beds and 1,500 blooms. Each June, when the flowers are at their peak, the city celebrates its month-long Rose Festival with many cultural, sporting and general interest events and activities. The Rose City title was officially adopted in October, 1921.

Peter's business, Peter Bulk Greenhouses Ltd. on Cataract Road, grows cut roses year-round for the wholesale trade. Although it's not officially part of the festivities, its mere presence strengthens Welland's choice of its Rose City designation.

Born in 1954, Peter was raised on a dairy farm near Aalsmeer, the Netherlands. His father-in-law grew cut roses and he ended up doing the same. He had a small greenhouse operation, made little money and could see nothing bright on the horizon. Relocating to larger premises would require a staggering outlay. So he and Yvonne made up their minds to move to Canada.

'It would have been hard to accomplish all this in Holland.'

"In 1982, we arrived in Dunnville where my cousin, Otto Bulk, had a rose business," he says. "I talked to him and he encouraged me, saying: 'There's lots of room.' I worked a couple of months and then found the property at Welland. It was seven acres with an old house."

He ordered a 17,000-square-foot greenhouse even though he didn't have enough money left to pay for it. "I needed $75,000. I told the greenhouse builder: 'I can't help you until I can start selling some flowers.' He said: 'OK, we'll take a chance on you.' One appreciated help like that and it made us work harder. When we started to cut flowers, we never looked back."

The initial crop consisted of six varieties of sweetheart and tea roses. Now there are 24. The range has increased in size to 125,000 square feet and the land to 41 acres. The family has grown too – there are four children. A beautiful house was built on the property in 1997.

"I'm amazed at how well we've done," Peter says while watching some of his eight full-timers processing roses for packing. "It would have been hard to accomplish all this in Holland. Canada is still a land of opportunities for those who want to work or start up their own business. Some may not agree, but I believe Canada is good for its farmers. With hard work and blessings, success is possible."

— Peter Bulk: "With hard work and blessings, success is possible."

A Beauty

— The Welland Rose

Niagara's Rose City has a stunning rose that it proudly calls its own.

Registered as the City of Welland, it's a hybrid tea whose fragrant flower is a pretty blend of shades of red, orange, yellow and ivory that stands out in sharp contrast to the glossy, dark green leaves.

This beauty, developed by the William Kordes Rose Nurseries in Germany, was officially adopted by Welland's City Council in August, 1991. It is grown and sold by Sheridan Nurseries of Georgetown, Ontario.

The initial purchase of 65 bushes was made by the Welland Parks Department and planted in the spring of 1992 in a specially-prepared circular bed in Merritt Park.

The rose, which flowers continuously from spring until frost, has since become a highly popular addition to many home gardens in the city. Total sales are now in excess of 2,400 bushes.

— *The stunningly beautiful roses grown at Peter Bulk Greenhouses Ltd.*
touch the hearts of thousands of people.

POSITIVENESS

Scott Lindeboom was still bubbling with excitement a few weeks after returning from an annual four-day floral trade show in Amsterdam, the Netherlands, where he and a large contingent of other Niagara growers kept their eyes and ears open for all that's new and promising.

"You have to go to events like that to find out the latest of what's going on in the business and what's available. For me, it was worthwhile. I saw a few varieties of roses that looked very interesting."

'Lindy's Flowers has always been a family-run business, with everyone pitching in with the workload and having a good time at it.'

As the operator of Lindy's Flowers on Highway 3 near Dunnville, a grower of cut roses, he remains immensely interested in varieties with large heads that can challenge the competition from Central America.

Scott's parents, John and Wilma, are the owners. John runs a wholesale route, servicing flower shops in midwestern Ontario and the Bruce Peninsula with a wide variety of local and imported flowers and particularly his home-grown roses. Wilma does the bookkeeping and fills in wherever necessary.

— Scott Lindeboom and his brother, Ben, work on a greenhouse expansion at Lindy's Flowers near Dunnville.

— Monique Lindeboom admires the beauty around her.

John and Wilma, both born to parents originally from Holland, bought their property – 10 acres with a house and a cornfield – in 1980, two years after Scott was born. John previously worked for his father-in-law in a wholesale business, selling flowers to various floral shops in Toronto. He later rented some greenhouses in Listowel to grow bedding plants. After one year, he moved to the Dunnville area, built 10,000 square feet of greenhouses and put in a crop of mums. In 1985, due to back problems, he switched to roses.

Over the years, expansions have increased the green-house area for rose production to 75,000 square feet. The most recent building program, including 25,000 square feet of greenhouse, a new warehouse and a 3,000-square-foot tropical plant greenhouse, was completed in the summer of 2002.

Scott began full-time greenhouse work after graduating from the two-year horticultural program of Niagara College. He is assisted by his sister, Monique, who tends to the tropical plants, makes planter baskets and fills out flower orders for the wholesale route. Dan, a brother, works at another rose operation in the Dunnville area as a maintenance manager. Ben, the youngest brother, is in high school and wants to become an electrician.

"Lindy's Flowers has always been a family-run business, with everyone pitching in with the workload and having a good time at it," says Scott.

— Henry Westerveld and his son, Bradley, among the roses.

Henry Westerveld points to two solid reasons why he wanted to specialize in cut roses when establishing Pine Ridge Gardens Inc. on Diltz Road near Dunnville in 1990.

"I always liked roses," he says, "and I always wanted my own business in farming."

With the help of his father and an understanding banker, he bought a 30-acre site, marked by a grove of pine trees, put up 20,000 square feet of greenhouses and began growing sweethearts and tea roses.

"Everything went according to expectations," he says. "We sold to wholesalers and at the auction in Mississauga and the demand kept going up. We soon had to expand. Now we're at 147,000 square feet. Things have worked out very well for us. We feel that we've been blessed."

Henry and his wife, Rennie, the parents of three children, live in a handsome house on the property. Mom looks after the firm's books. Dad has his hands full with the roses, grown hydroponically and with the aid of artificial lights, as well as snapdragons and stephanotis. During the busy periods, up to 22 people are employed.

'My heart was in farming. I knew it was ideal for family life.'

Born in 1964, Henry grew up on a Dunnville area dairy farm owned by his Dutch-born parents, Ben and Alice. His first ambition was to become a cash-cropper. Then his mind was set on a career in agricultural banking. He studied two years at Dordt College in Sioux Center, Iowa, and finished his education at the University of Guelph, earning a Bachelor of Science degree in agriculture.

"The banking idea sort of faded away," he says. "My heart was in farming. I knew it was ideal for family life. And when I worked part-time for Rosa Flora, I made up my mind to get a farm of my own – one for flowers. I've never regretted that decision."

His plan at the outset was to eventually build up his range to 40,000 square feet and then stop. A larger size, he figured, would only bring headaches. But the growing export market and the pressure to produce more prompted him to expand.

"I don't want the business running me; I want to run the business," he says. "I want to make sure that there's enough time for the family, the church and other things that are so important in life."

69

— The scenic entranceway to Pine Ridge Gardens Inc.

Floral Passion

One setback after another befell Ron Rempel in 1986 when he attempted to get his new greenhouse on Lakeshore Road in Niagara-on-the-Lake ready for production of cut roses.

In a moment of frustration, he blurted out: "Lord, will this ever get started?"

The trouble began when he was building a 50,000-gallon cistern for the 22,000-square-foot, Venlo-style greenhouse he had purchased during a visit to the Netherlands. After pouring the concrete, he headed for Toronto, pleased with the progress he was making. But upon his return, he discovered to his horror that the whole thing had caved in.

"All the concrete and the reinforcing rod lay eight feet below," he says. "I had to get a backhoe to scrape everything out. It was a real scramble to clean up the mess and start fixing things because I was anxious to get started on my first crop."

Then, when everything seemed to be in place, a summer hailstorm pounded the area, wiping out 55 acres of peaches on his nearby farm and rented property. To make matters worse, ground water and muck filled the cistern to overflowing, causing the floor to buckle. Once again, the cement mixer was running hot.

'We sell a lot of freshly-picked roses to people from town. They can be great gifts.'

"Of course, we were behind when we got everything straightened out," says Ron. "But the first crop was good. You can imagine how relieved I was."

He is of Mennonite stock. His parents, Nick and Elizabeth, were born in southern Russia and emigrated with their father and American-born mother to western Canada in the 1920s. After the Second World War, they moved to the Niagara-on-the-Lake area, having bought a 25-acre fruit farm with mostly peach, cherry and plum trees and a strawberry field. Their son arrived in 1946.

"I grew up on the farm and developed a keen interest in growing, landscaping and so on," says Ron. "After finishing high school, I took a year off to travel the world and then enrolled in the three-year course at the Niagara Parks School of Horticulture. I graduated in 1971 and landed a position with the municipal parks department in Calgary, overseeing the construction of Confederation Park. I came back to Niagara in 1975 and took over the family operation."

He still runs Rempel Fruit Farms, producing tender fruit, grapes and three acres of peonies, flowers that are cut in bud form like roses and sold to wholesalers, ending up in stores as far away as Washington State.

Ron and his wife, Debbie, whom he had married in 1980, bought a 10-acre peach farm in 1984 and built a farm market on it for selling their fruit and vegetables. The greenhouse arrived two years later. After 10 years, the retail outlet was closed and Debbie opened a store on Queen Street in downtown Niagara-on-the-Lake, a quaint shopping area that bustles with tourists in the summer. Rempel's Farm and Flower Market offers frozen yogurt, ice cream, bakery items and even hanging baskets.

When the first roses were cut at Rempel Greenhouses, Ron's excitement was tempered by the realization that he now had to sell them. "Nobody had heard of Rempel's," he says. "It took some time for us to become known. But we kept at it. We made sure our quality stayed good and we didn't panic and sell at inferior prices, and eventually the wholesalers started buying."

With the assistance of three full-timers, two offshore labourers from Jamaica, who also work on the farm, and his father, who still shows up now and then just to keep active, he now grows 15 varieties of hybrid tea roses and a few sweetheart ones, all hydroponically. Nearly half a million stems are cut annually for the wholesale trade. Retail sales for walk-in customers are also available.

"We sell a lot of freshly-picked roses to people from town," says Ron. "They can be great gifts. In fact, a lot of stores give them to their customers as a token of appreciation."

— Ron Rempel: "It took some time for us to become known. But we kept at it."

Chapter Six

Perennial Pleasures

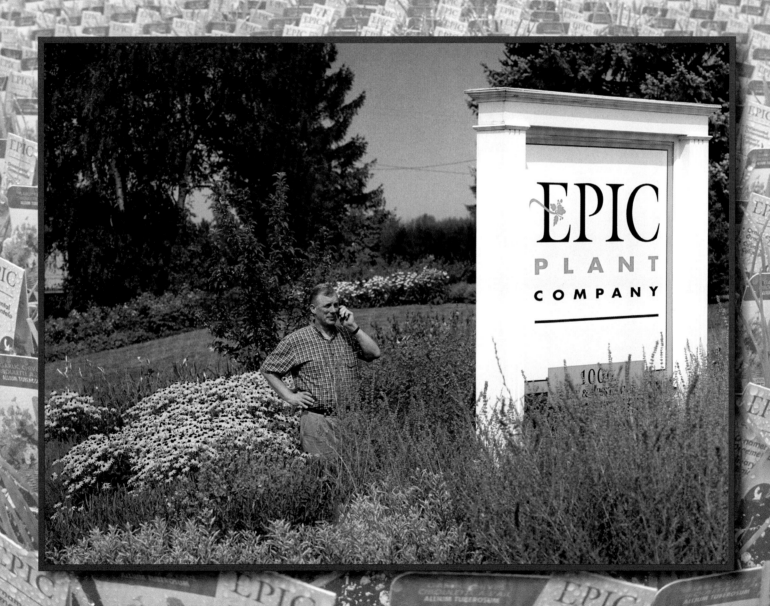

'We want to get people involved in gardening like the Europeans do.'

—Peter Denee

— The Epic Plant Company in Niagara-on-the-Lake is one of Canada's leading producers of perennials, herbs and aquatic plants.

Peter Denee* is a big fan of aggressive and diversified marketing. He has ample proof that it works wonders.

The rapid rise of his Epic Plant Company to its present status as one of Canada's leading producers of perennials, herbs and aquatic plants – it annually grows more than 4.5 million plants in up to 1,500 different varieties – can be attributed in a large degree to his penchant for a strong marketing approach.

"I learned a few things while I was in the retail business," he says. "I understand consumers more than most growers do."

His company, which has a 260,000-square-foot greenhouse complex and outdoor production areas on East and West Line in Niagara-on-the-Lake and has a partnership with two other growers to produce its program, pays particular attention to the tags that identify the plant material.

"We have to provide useful information for the consumer," he says. "We need more than just the name of the product scribbled on popsickle sticks. Ninety-five per cent of our perennials are not in bloom when they leave our place, so promotion is needed to sell them. Our tags have large, full-colour pictures and information about the plants and how to help them along."

The tags, which slide securely into a slot on the container, also list Epic's website, through which e-mails can be sent to the company. "Before this, retail customers couldn't get in contact with the producer. We've come out of hiding. With e-mail, we can respond instantly to inquiries."

In addition to its annual Plant Guide, a 96-page catalogue, the company produces The Epic Gardener, a twice-yearly magazine to which customers can subscribe at no cost. Peter's son, Mark, who manages the office, does most of the writing.

---

*'We need more than just
the name of the product scribbled
on popsickle sticks.'*

As a further marketing tool, Epic, in conjunction with ITML Horticultural Products Inc. in Brantford, has developed a distinctively round container that enables consumers to easily recognize its products.

Peter's interest in horticulture was probably induced by his father, a pharmacist in the Dutch town of Harderwijk, who grew medicinal plants in his garden. The inquisitive son, one of nine children, later studied at the Florens horticultural college in Aalsmeer. In 1969, at age 21, he emigrated to Canada. His instructors had encouraged him to work outside Holland, and thus pick up an extra language, which they deemed a requisite for eventual success.

He began working for $2 an hour at the Dundas cactus operation of Ben Veldhuis. A year later, he was hired by McMaster University in Hamilton as a greenhouse technician in the biology department. He married Mieke, whom he had met before coming to Canada, and they moved to Montreal where he started working in the interior plant maintenance business.

"I enjoyed the work, such as planting in malls, but not the political environment in Quebec," he says. "I couldn't see myself bringing up a family there. After a year, I was back at McMaster. In my spare time, usually in the early afternoon already, I hooked up a trailer to my Volkswagen and looked after lawn maintenance for mainly elderly people."

In 1977, Peter and Mieke bought Hartman Greenhouses, an old, rundown flower operation in Dundas. They struggled to make ends meet. But they plodded on and developed a plan to make things work better. With a government improvement loan obtained through their bank, they took down the greenhouse and built a retail garden centre. The place began to hum. It later developed into a garden gallery called Denee Floral Ltd. and then Denee Garden Gallery.

"What helped us tremendously was a co-operative effort involving two others in the business," says Peter. "We advertised together in the newspaper and we did a lot of other joint marketing. In the process, we learned from each other."

The retail experience provided him with valuable insights into customer service, general business practices and, of course, marketing. He was ready for the next step in his career: to become a wholesale grower of perennials.

Peter had noticed that the perennials displayed in garden centres were mostly small and dormant with uninformative labels. With the popularity of home gardening on the rise, he saw a need to offer consumers something much more appealing. He envisioned producing large, vibrant plants of many varieties, each with a colourful picture tag.

In 1989, he and Mieke sold their garden gallery to Holland Park and turned their attention to a 10-acre peach and pear farm they had purchased in Niagara. The trees were removed and a greenhouse area of 30,000 square feet was built. In the first year of operation, 300 different items were produced.

The original name of the business, Park Perennials, was later changed to Epic Plant Company to reflect the fact that other products such as herbs, water plants, clematis and ground cover are grown as well.

Peter thought at first that 10 acres were too much. But the dramatic growth of his company, resulting in big expansions of his greenhouse area, soon put space at a premium. With 150 to 200 items being added to the product line each year, it became necessary to arrange with other growers to produce plants. He has partnerships with Jan van het Riet, the foreman at his nursery, who started his own operation, Van Treat, on Line 1 near Niagara-on-the-Lake, and Paul Lucas of VP Perennials near Simcoe.

— Peter Denee and his son, Mark, display a few of the 1,500 different varieties of plants they produce.

Springtime is the busy period at Epic. That's when the year-round staff of 35, including two of the four Denee children – Mark and his brother, Ryan, who works in greenhouse production – swells to as high as 110. It's also when the one truck used for year-round duty is assisted by a fleet of as many as 35 rented vehicles for delivery throughout southern Ontario and other regions within a radius of about 1,000 miles. "We have to hire the drivers," says Peter. "It's like starting up a trucking company every year."

He foresees even further growth. "We see ourselves providing a complete package to the retail market. We want people to get involved in gardening like the Europeans do. If we get 10 per cent of North Americans to become plant lovers, we will need a lot more greenhouses."

* During the production of this book, we learned of Peter Denee's untimely death after a short battle with cancer.

73

— Keith Wilson, Valleybrook's Production Manager, has a lot to keep track of during a regular day at work.

When John Schroeder wanted to expand his flourishing perennial business in Abbotsford, British Columbia, to the east, he didn't hesitate in selecting the Niagara Peninsula as the location for a sister operation.

"There were three main reasons: the climate, the market and U.S. access," he says. "The winters there are warmer than almost anywhere in Ontario. Greater Toronto and the Golden Horseshoe represents three times the population of B.C. And the U.S. is just a short drive down the QEW."

But finding suitable and available property in the preferred area of the Peninsula – Vineland – was not as easy a matter. In fact, after a year of looking, John's real estate agent could steer him only in the direction of Niagara-on-the-Lake, an area he had resisted moving to because of the extra 20 minutes of travelling time to the highway.

Valleybrook Gardens (Ontario) Ltd. has been located on a 30-acre property on Line 4 in Niagara-on-the-Lake since 1993. It's in an unsheltered location, exposed to constant wind, which requires his staff to closely monitor the plant moisture levels throughout the year. But it's a place where a lot of exciting things are happening, all contributing to the tremendous growth that has made Valleybrook a well-known and respected name in the perennial business in Canada.

Together with his wife, Kelly, John oversees production of just under five million plants annually at his location in Niagara and on his 25-acre site in Abbotsford.

"Plants have been my life," he says. "They've always fascinated me. When I was a kid, I pulled flowers apart to see what was inside."

His rural upbringing undoubtedly contributed to this affection.

He was raised among plants on his family's mixed farm near Abbotsford. His parents, Mennonites of German extraction, had purchased the property four years after emigrating from Poland in 1949.

John, born in 1956 and one of five children, was in his third year at the University of British Columbia, specializing in ornamental horticulture, when he laid the foundation for what was to become Valleybrook.

"I had just finished a summer job with the provincial Ministry of Agriculture in Cloverdale where I learned that ornamental heathers were in short supply," he recalls. "At the university, I had to do a propagation experiment as part of my studies. I then started thinking that this was a good opportunity. I could use the university greenhouse to experiment with heather plants."

He ended up getting 5,000 heather cuttings from the university's Botanical Garden. With fellow student Dennis Haak, he cultivated them into small plants and sold them. "We thought it was really cool. You take this cutting which costs you nothing, you grow some roots on it, put it in a pot and suddenly you've got thousands of dollars." The university later bought $3,000 worth of plants for a large landscape project.

After graduating with a Bachelor of Arts degree in agriculture, John rented a five-acre property from his father and started growing perennials, the ground-cover kind. His plan was to gradually move into other nursery stock. "I really didn't want to do perennials," he says. "I couldn't get excited about them. But I did so well that I could see a great market. It's been perennials all the way."

> *'Gardening with perennials has suddenly become a passion for a whole generation of people that, for the most part, weren't even gardening just a few short years ago.'*

He bought the property in 1983 and acquired another five acres in 1988. In the meantime, he set his sights on the potentially lucrative market in the east.

"I flew to Ontario in '85 to attend trade shows and then started going there once a year to investigate the market and the area," he says. "I liked what I saw and heard. By '87, I was already looking for property."

John Valleau, one of staffers, went to Ontario in 1988 and rented some land at an existing Niagara nursery to distribute Valleybrook's B.C.-grown perennials. For two years, he worked on developing the branch business before leasing a larger site in Fonthill and beginning production in earnest. The land at Niagara-on-the-Lake was purchased a few years later.

With 254,000 square feet of covered growing area, including a facility with a removable roof, and lots of space outdoors, the Niagara business produces over 1,500 varieties of container perennials, ornamental grasses, hardy ferns and ground covers. It is managed by Phil Goodfellow.

Each plant bears the brand name Heritage Perennials. It comes with a distinctive tag that has a colour photograph of the plant in full bloom and contact adddresses on the front and cultivation tips on the back. The unique bright blue container displays the slogan "The best perennials come out of the blue."

Another effective marketing tool is the company's Perennial Gardening Guide, a full-colour book that offers authoritive tips on planting, growing, controlling pests and other related subjects, as well an illustrated description of the various Valleybrook products. The author is John Valleau, the Corporate Horticulturist in Niagara. In the introduction, he writes:

"Gardening with perennials has suddenly become a passion for a whole generation of people that, for the most part, weren't even gardening just a few short years ago. It's all part of that nesting thing we keep hearing about: baby boomers with more leisure time, two incomes and the need to make their surrounding beautiful. But what I really see happening lately is so much more than middle-aged couples with pretty yards. People of all ages, all over North America, are taking these yards and turning them into the wonderful, personal spaces that we call gardens."

John Schroeder foresaw this trend when he and Kelly, whom he married in 1978 while in university, started Valleybrook. Indeed, they quickly discovered that demand for their products would not be a problem. Their biggest challenge involved finding the continuous financing that was needed to sustain growth.

"One of the unique things in this business," says John, "is that it takes cash all the time for land and greenhouses and you are producing a product that you sell only a few months of the year."

A lot of cash was needed in 1989 after a severe cold spell, followed by blasts of Arctic air, destroyed 70 per cent of his stock in Abbotsford. To protect himself against a repeat experience, he built more greenhouses, including heated ones, and provided more blanket coverage for his outside plants. The covered growing space there now amounts to 170,000 square feet.

"I'm a very optimistic and positive person, but that year was the lowest point I think I ever had in the business. You walk outside and look at your field full of plants and you see that they're all dead."

John also started an operation in Maryland but closed it after three years after deciding that the consumer base in the northeastern U.S. could be served just as well from the Ontario location.

Emphasis is placed on the careful selection of product.

"Obviously, we keep up with what's new and being promoted in the media," says John, "but we won't grow a new plant just because it's new. It truly has to offer something better or different than existing cultivars."

— A gardener's delight.

CHAPTER SEVEN

GROWING AND SELLING

'Our business has developed to the point where I sit down with growers and do long-term planning for a whole year of production exclusively for us.'

— Rob vanStaalduinen

A GIANT

Andy Olsthoorn of Lakeshore Produce was anxious.

It was just before Easter in 1974, the busiest time of year for people in the flower business, and all his trucks on the way to making deliveries in the United States were stopped at the border, unable to proceed, because of the desire of American officialdom to require Product of Canada stickers on the potted plants in place of the identical wording that was printed on the plastic sleeves.

It would be impossible to comply with this unexpected rule without incurring huge costs and possibly disastrous delays. Nor could Lakeshore and other wholesalers, who were equally affected, dispose of all the pots in Canada, where their customers were already well looked after. Andy knew that he had to act quickly.

"Lakeshore was building their business in those days because I remember we had tractor-trailer loads of flowers for that Easter," says Rita, his wife. "Andy flew to Ottawa first but couldn't get anywhere. Then he heard that a certain senator in the States was closely involved with what was happening at the border. So he flew to Washington, went to the senator's office and requested to see him. The senator refused. Andy then stayed in the office and wouldn't leave until he could speak to him. The senator finally agreed. After Andy told him what was happening and what the results could be, he picked up the phone, talked to the border people and told them to make sure all the trucks got through. Well, the flowers got to their destinations after a delay of two or three days. Everyone was smiling when Andy arrived home. We held a big celebration for him."

'He never stopped selling after that. His greenhouse days were over.'

At six feet, four inches, Andy struck an imposing figure. His mere presence in a room could draw attention. And when he embraced an idea, or a cause, he would pursue it vigorously. To him, nothing could block ultimate success.

In a tribute published in the Globe and Mail after Andy's sudden death from an abdominal aneurysm in December, 1998, at the age of 68, his daughter, Elizabeth, wrote:

— Hydrangeas present a colourful sight at the huge Lakeshore Inc. greenhouse complex on Fourth Avenue in Jordan Station.

"When he and some Dutch friends started Lakeshore Produce, Andy realized that the U.S. market had huge sales potential for the flower industry. Determined and persistent, he began knocking on the doors of major supermarket buyers. Many times, they said no until they were so sick and tired of Andy that they said yes just to get rid of him. Many of these people became Andy's close friends and some of Lakeshore's biggest customers today."

The super salesman and businessman, who, through his pioneering efforts and subsequent undertakings, contributed immensely to the well-being and growth of Niagara's greenhouse industry, was 20 years old and single when he headed for Canada in 1951 with a few friends. He looked forward to an exciting future in the new land, knowing that more opportunities awaited him there than in Holland. As the youngest in a family of 11 children, he was at the bottom of the totem pole for someday earning a living in his father's greenhouse vegetable and flower business.

He had worked in greenhouses in the Maasdijks-'-Gravenzande area in Westland, Holland's city under glass, where his family lived. He had done some buying and selling too, with notable success, and thought of pursuing this type of work in Canada. But a few hurdles had to be overcome before he could reach this goal.

Andy worked first for his sponsor, a dairy farmer near

Ottawa. With his earnings, he bought a used car. But it was destroyed a few hours later when fire levelled the garage to which it had been taken for repairs. He next took his few belongings, including a pair of wooden shoes, to the Simcoe area where he joined the tobacco harvest. Then there was a succession of other jobs: at a copper-nickel mine near Sudbury and at hydro tunnel projects in Niagara Falls and Kelowna, British Columbia.

At one point, his friends, who had accompanied him on these sojourns, returned to Holland. He stayed, determined to endure the rough conditions and loneliness. Just before leaving for Canada, he had asked his father for a few dollars. The reply: "They don't make dollars in Holland. You will have to earn them in Canada." So he didn't want to go back and be looked upon as a failure. His pals returned after a year and settled in the St. Catharines area. He drove there in his new car and told them that he liked the area and that he would stay there too, but that he would go to Holland first for a holiday. It was during this trip that he went to a local carnival and met Rita Ammerlaan, a 20-year-old from Schipluiden.

"Andy wanted me to go to Canada but my father advised me against it," she recalls. "So we wrote letters for a year. That didn't make me much wiser because Andy's letters weren't exactly exciting. We then decided to give it a try. For me to come to Canada, Andy found a Dutch family where I could work as a housekeeper. In those days, if you came to Canada as a single girl, you had to get married in 35 days. I didn't want to do that, of course, because I hardly knew the guy. I came in September, 1955, stayed with this family for a week and then began working for Canadian people, first at a lawyer's house and later at a parsonage, to learn the language and make some more money."

In this period, Andy was a long-distance truck driver. Previously, he had worked at a logging camp in the bush in Quebec and at the General Motors plant in St. Catharines. He put all his net earnings in the bank and Rita paid for his groceries and other necessities because they wanted to buy something for themselves someday. Andy enjoyed being on the road. But Rita was extremely unhappy.

"He was away for days on end and I wasn't too pleased with that," she says. "In fact, I became sick and tired of just sitting in my room alone most of the time. I said: 'Listen, we either get married or I am going back to Holland.' He said: 'Let's work a little longer and we can save a little more.' But I told him: 'You love this truck driving, but I hate it here. I'm so lonely. I don't know anybody. When I have a day off, I don't know what to do with myself.' Well, we did get married – on September 1, 1956. We rented a little house for $45 a month. I didn't even need a key. If I kicked the door, it opened."

Rita felt comfortable enough with her command of English to work for a department store during the busy Christmas season. She next did piece work in a sweater factory. A year after their marriage, she and Andy used their

— Andy Olsthoorn is shown in 1984 with his sons, Jim and Neil.

savings to buy a small greenhouse operation in Kitchener with a large old house and a small shop for making flower arrangements for weddings, funerals and other occasions. As neither she nor her husband knew anything about flower arranging, the fellow who worked there was kept on staff. This business and the sale of bedding plants from the greenhouse provided a fair income.

But life in Kitchener was not entirely rosy. During her pregnancy, Rita lost one of her twin sons. The surviving one, Neil, is now one of the partners in Lakeshore. Rita and Andy also felt not quite at home in the community and had no close associations there. In fact, they would travel to St. Catharines on most weekends to visit with friends and acquaintances. After a year, they sold their business and moved to Niagara for good.

The new place was in Beamsville. It was a tract of land with a nice bungalow. Andy added three greenhouses with a total area of 10,000 square feet and went into hothouse tomato production. Alas, everything flooded during a deluge. Then he grew snapdragons, and they were beautiful, but no market could be found for them.

"We also had lots of field tomatoes," says Rita. "I took Neil, who was just a baby, to the field every day in his buggy. His legs were tanned a deep brown because he was outside all the time. I would give him his bottle, he would fall asleep again and I would pick more tomatoes."

Andy once told an interviewer that in Beamsville "I finally began doing what I liked best – the Dutch call it handel. I went from store to store, peddling vegetables and fruit." Rita expounds: "The fellow who was looking after our sales at the market brought back our tomatoes night after night and said: 'Andy, there are just too many tomatoes on the market.' Well, Andy became a little sick and tired of that. He bought a little green pickup – second-hand, of course – found a tarp on the garbage belt, which I cut to size, and got peaches from our neighbour to take to the market along with our tomatoes. On the first day, he went out 3:30 in the morning and came back with the biggest smile on his face. He said: 'You know what, I made $25 today. From now on, nobody else has to sell my tomatoes. I am going to do it myself.' He never stopped selling after that. His greenhouse days were over."

— Cala and Easter lilies: exquisite blooms at the Lakeshore operation.

The Beamsville business was sold, the family moved to a rented house on Lakeshore Road and Andy continued buying and selling. Then daughter Wilma was born. Instead of feeling ecstatic, Rita was depressed. She sorely missed her family in Holland, particularly her mother and sisters.

"Andy knew how homesick I was and said I should go to see my family. So I took Neil, who was a year and a half, and Wilma, who was three months, and went to Holland. Once there, I didn't want to go back. I wrote Andy: 'I love you, but I am not going back to Canada.' He said: 'You can't do this. You have the kids.' I said: 'If you love me enough, you'd come here too.' And he did – after five months."

The family lived with Rita's parents. Six sisters and a brother, all unmarried, were still at home. Andy began work for a transport company, delivering goods to Germany and other places in Europe. But he didn't like working for someone else anymore and talked of setting up his own trucking business. When Andy and Rita went to the boss to ask for advice, they were told that Andy needed papers, that he was required to go to school and that the course was tough. "The boss looked at me and said: 'Andy can keep on working for me and you can go to school for him.' What did I know about a transport company? Well, I wanted to stay and Andy made it absolutely clear that he didn't want to go to school, so I took the course. I went to school in Gorkum three days a week for nearly a year and actually did very well."

Instead of starting his own company, however, Andy announced that he wanted to return to Canada. His wife, initially disappointed, finally gave in. She had come to realize that it was not easy to live with her parents again after being married for a number of years. It was difficult also to bring up her young son in a home where he had seven extra mothers. "He was being spoiled. If I said no,

— A bird's-eye view of Lakeshore's complex on Fourth Avenue. The company has another large greenhouse facility in South Carolina.

they all said yes. He walked on the table between the plates and they were still laughing." Furthermore, Rita found that her former girlfriends were married, leading different lives, and that the good times they had together in earlier years could not be re-lived.

Andy went back to the Niagara area to look for some land on which to start up a greenhouse business. Before long, he wrote to Rita that he had purchased 12 acres on Scott Street in St. Catharines and that the house on the property was fine. Two months later, she and her two children were back on Canadian soil.

A number of greenhouses were built for vegetable and flower production. Someone else looked after these, as well as the growing, while Andy pursued the line of work he loved most: the buying and selling of produce and flowers. He and his family would live on Scott Street for 14 years and experience growth in three important areas: three more children, Elizabeth, Jim and Annette, would be born, the greenhouse area would be expanded six times and the buying and selling would develop into a flourishing and profitable business.

Andy developed a close relationship with a number of other greenhouse owners who shared his interests, notably Jake Koornneef, Bill Vermeer and Ton Hanemaayer. Feeling they were stronger together than apart, these men formed Lakeshore Produce in 1965 as a company to market and distribute their goods. They first used a little office on Scott Street and later moved to Hanemaayer's place in St. Catharines. Their largest customer then was Dominion, a grocery chain, which accepted store-to-store delivery

of fruit such as strawberries, peaches and plums and also flowers later in the year.

Around this time, an idea struck Andy while he was thinking of ways to make his greenhouses more productive in the summer: why not grow the long, seedless cucumbers which were popular in Holland but largely unknown here? He did. Then the time arrived to put them in stores. The regional director of produce of Dominion, doubtful about their acceptance by consumers, said: "We'll pay you only if we sell them." The cucumbers that were placed in a store in St. Catharines were quickly snapped up and the director phoned the same day to request more.

Developing the flower market was a slow process. There was a big demand for special occasions, such as Easter and Mother's Day, but for a great part of the year flowers were not a hot sales item. It took a lot of effort on the part of Andy and others to turn this around to the point where they could have truck routes and runs for selling flowers on a weekly basis. Increased availability promoted the products and boosted sales. But the biggest growth factor was the development of the export market to the United States.

Andy's first shipment to the U.S. took place in 1964. His father-in-law, on his first visit from Holland, thought it was ridiculous to go all the way to the States to try to sell flowers. Andy replied: "Well, Dad, I'm just going to try. We'll see where it goes." As a truck filled with potted mums wrapped in newspaper left Scott Street, someone – it could have been Andy – followed in a car and shot an 8-mm film of the trip to the border and the crossing into New York. Unquestionably, it was a memorable event.

— Rita Olsthoorn: "Everyone was smiling when Andy arrived home. We held a big celebration for him."

The mums were delivered to a wholesaler in New York City. When the man refused to pay, Andy hopped on an airplane and straightened out the matter in a jiffy. He then looked around for someone else to deal with and met Gerry Black, another wholesaler, with whom he could do business. Andy displayed a big smile when he returned home. After all, he had his foot in the door to a huge market – 100 million people from Maine to Baltimore. The U.S. duty on imported flowers then was five per cent. It was gradually reduced to zero under the Free Trade Agreement.

As the customer base grew over the years, the partners in Lakeshore could not produce enough vegetables and flowers themselves to meet the demand. They made arrangements with other growers to supply needed products. This, of course, resulted in a big boost for the entire greenhouse industry. The phenomenal growth eventually led to a decision to put the Lakeshore operation, including offices, warehouse, packing area and loading bays, in a new building. It was constructed in 1977 on a 17-acre site along the Queen Elizabeth Way in Jordan Station. One acre was severed for a house for Andy, Rita and their children. A new greenhouse complex was built towards the rear of the property. Called Westland, it was owned by Andy and a partner, Peter van Beurden. Later, Lakeshore also had an operation in Florida that specialized in tropical plants for sale in supermarkets.

As with the wholesale business, Andy preferred to enter into partnerships for his greenhouse operations, leaving him free for buying and selling. This was a mutually beneficial arrangement because the partners knew that they would become full owners someday. Over the years, some of Andy's Lakeshore partners left to pursue interests of their own and others came on board. He eventually bought out his remaining partners before selling the operation to his sons, Neil and Jim, who now run the business with a partner of their own: Jim Dertinger.

Although Andy didn't work in the greenhouses, his sons certainly did. As young boys, they were required to come home straight after school and put in a few hours of labour. "We never got to play sports in school," says Neil, somewhat ruefully. "In the summers, we had to get up at 5 a.m. every day to pick tomatoes. When this was done, we were told to paint the greenhouses. I often wished I would have flunked so that I could have gone to summer school."

— These women seem to be enjoying their work among the lilies.

There was no pay until later years. When money finally entered the picture, it went directly into bank accounts which Andy controlled until the boys were 21.

The greenhouse work turned out to be a good education. Both Neil and Jim joined the Lakeshore company and worked their way up the responsibility ladder. By the mid-1990s, they were at the helm of the ship. Their father then was focusing all his attention on an enterprise he had launched with a number of other businessmen: St. David's Hydroponics Ltd.

Andy and Neil had been selling hydroponically-grown bell peppers imported from Holland. Flying them in and trucking them to market was a costly business and involved a lot of hassle. So it was decided to grow them right in Niagara – in moist, inert material instead of soil. A greenhouse facility was built in St. Davids in 1985. The operation turned out to be such a success that a second plant, including the head office, was constructed in 1996 along the QEW in Vineland Station. "Andy had his heart and soul in that business," says Rita.

When Neil and Jim took over, the Lakeshore Produce name was changed to Lakeshore Inc. But this was a relatively minor decision compared to the ones that were to follow.

In 1996, Lakeshore USA came into being with 300,000 square feet of greenhouse area in Gaffney, South Carolina.

And in the same year, Lakeshore began production in a greenhouse complex of 850,000 square feet on Fourth Avenue in Jordan Station. The emergence of these huge developments signalled a major shift in the company's business strategy: it would concentrate more on its own production in its own facilities and less on buying from others. Potted plants are the staple item at both places.

Even the shipping end in Niagara, now involving 15 trucks, is affected by the new direction. The original Lakeshore building was put up for sale and all the operations, including distribution, were consolidated at the Jordan Station complex.

The company also added a new segment to its business called Floralake. This is a full-fledged cut flower operation that supplies supermarkets with bouquets and arrangements.

"We felt it was a good tie-in for our business because supermarkets were already offering our cuts and pots," says Jim.

Even Andy, who used to spend six months of the year flying to Europe and across Canada and the United States to drum up business, was astounded by the rapidity and scope of the changes. Neil says: "Believe it or not, my father used to tell Jim and I: 'You're going too fast. You've got a good living, so take it easy. You're putting too much pressure on yourself'."

The Lakeshore operation is a large and important component of the local economy. In the busy periods, it provides employment for up to 300 people. Which is why Jim, for one, shakes his head in disgust whenever complaints are voiced about greenhouses taking up space that should be retained for other agricultural uses.

"We have no problems with farmers," he says. "We have problems with people who come to live in the country, in an agricultural area, and they see greenhouses and say: 'What is that? Oh no, I'm in a factory!' They don't see greenhouses as an agricultural instrument. They don't understand that you are taking five acres of property, controlling the environment and producing 50 acres of product that used to be grown outside with diseases, bugs and inefficiencies."

— Rob vanStaalduinen: "Just think how much more we would need to grow to satisfy the demand if North Americans started buying flowers as often as Europeans do."

"Niagara's floriculture industry will see sustained growth for at least another 20 years."

This is not just some wishful thinking on the part of Rob vanStaalduinen, Divisional Vice-President of Ontario Flower Growers Inc., a wholly-owned subsidiary of the 150-member Ontario Flower Growers Co-operative. He's an expert in economics who, through ongoing research into demographic changes and selling trends, has developed an intimate understanding of future demands in the biggest market: the eastern United States.

Besides the data on his computer screen, Rob bases his rosy projections on a number of factors that will continue to greatly influence the development in Niagara. One is the moderate climate between Lake Ontario and Lake Erie, ideal for growing. Another concerns the Dutch – their ideas of growing and specializing and their work habits. Then there's the excellent distribution system.

'They have money to spend, and spend they will on fresh cuts and garden and indoor plants.'

"Look at where we're located," he says, pointing to the Peninsula on a large map that hangs in his office at the Ontario Flower Growers' warehouse on Bartlett Road near Beamsville. "We can load a truck here at five in the afternoon and the driver can be sitting in Chicago at six the next morning waiting to unload. Within 500 miles from us, there's also Milwaukee, Indianapolis, Columbus, Washington, right up to Boston. If we go farther, 1,000 miles out, then there could be second-morning delivery, which is still pretty good, to places such as St. Louis, Nashville, Charlotte and Atlanta. Within two days' drive of here, there are 150 million people living."

In an area with such a huge population, the potential exists for a huge jump in demand, resulting in higher and higher production in Niagara and more and more Ontario transport trucks laden with floral products, all exempt from duties under the Free Trade Agreement, crossing the Peace Bridge and other border points.

There's a cluster of successful greenhouse operations in the Kalamazoo area of Michigan, but their output pales in comparison to Ontario's. American growers tend to be more regional in their marketing, while the Ontario shippers cover the entire eastern half of the U.S.

"We are a huge player in the North American market," says Rob. "We are bigger than any individual state in the

— Transport trucks are being loaded with flowers and plants at the Ontario Flower Growers Inc. warehouse near Beamsville.

Floral Passion

production of flowering potted plants. But there's enough room for everybody."

His confidence that the demand for flowers and plants will continue to increase, perhaps substantially, was expressed in a speech at a conference of greenhouse growers at the University of Guelph. Over the next 20 years, he said, from 80 to 90 million people in the U.S. and Canada will be turning 50. They will have paid off their mortgages. They will have accumulated capital from investments, including the once soaring real estate market. And they will inherit more than $10 trillion from their parents. Besides all that, they hold the best jobs.

"They have money to spend, and spend they will on fresh cuts and garden and indoor plants. They will affect our industry in a profound way."

Rob's family has been involved in flower growing for several generations, beginning in the Netherlands. His grandfather, John, was a grower in Bleiswijk, north of Rotterdam, before emigrating to Canada in 1948 with his wife and children, including five-year-old Ray, Rob's father. The business John started near Stoney Creek was later taken over by Rob's uncle, Brian.

"I started there as a teenager," says Rob, born in Grimsby in 1967. "I worked there for five summers and found that hustling flowers was more exciting than school, although I did manage to get a degree in business administration from Lakehead University in Thunder Bay."

He joined the staff of the co-operative, established in October, 1972, by 63 Ontario growers who felt that the costs of delivery and credit were eroding their net profit and that an alternative marketing system was needed.

The sales operation that was set up in a rented building alongside Highway 401 near Toronto was popularly referred to as "the clock" because it was based on the Dutch system of using a large clock that rotated counter-clockwise after an auctioneer launched the bidding from a higher-than-expected selling price. The price declined until a buyer pressed a button to stop the clock, thus making a purchase.

The auction, located since the fall of 1985 in the co-op's own building at Tomken Road and Midway Boulevard

in Mississauga, close to Pearson International Airport, is still simply called "the clock." But now there are two of them, one for cut flowers and the other for potted plants, operating five days a week. They are computerized.

In 1983, after deciding to broaden its horizons and expand into the export field, the co-op hired Jack Atkin to launch a direct sales business by finding buyers. Rob took over the subsidiary in 1989.

His operation moved from the Mississauga auction building to Niagara in 1997. The volume of business increased immediately. Within two years, the warehouse space had to be doubled to 40,000 square feet.

A fleet of eight trucks, including four tractor-trailers, is on the road five days a week, making deliveries throughout the eastern U.S. as well as Atlantic Canada and Quebec. The staff has grown to 30, including 10 sales representatives.

"When I started, we sold products from our members only," says Rob. "That's changed. We now sell what our customers want. When you're marketing and selling products like we're doing, you need to be more customer-driven. If you're only production-driven or grower-driven, that's going to hold you back. Our business has developed to the point where I sit down with growers and do long-term planning for a whole year of production exclusively for us."

Such planning requires full knowledge of what the customers want. These include mass market retailers, independent garden centres and supermarkets. Of course, it's also necessary to keep abreast of consumer desires and buying trends.

The increased availability of flowers has contributed significantly to the success of the industry.

"If you wanted to buy flowers 25 years ago," says Rob, "you probably had to go to your local florist. Now you can go to almost any gas station or drug store and get them."

With more and more people poised to become regular buyers of flowers and plants that are within easy reach, the prospects for further growth look bright indeed.

As Rob said in his speech to the greenhouse growers: "We all know that the consumption of flowers per capita is much higher in western Europe than it is here in North America – roughly double. I had been told that's because flowers were a part of the people's lives there as they had grown up with them. That may be true, but it is also true that they have a much older population there, and they have had for some time. Just think how much more we would need to grow to satisfy the demand if North Americans started buying flowers as often as Europeans do."

Ornamental Flower And Plant Sales, 2001

	Ontario	Canada
Retail florists	$77,965,000	$154,750,000
Domestic wholesalers	$217,369,000	$302,070,000
Mass market chain stores	$76,369,000	$210,411,000
Other greenhouses	$40,601,000	$75,558,000
Exported	$91,815,000	$141,862,000
Direct sales to the public, including roadside stands and owner-owned retail outlets	$89,027,000	$240,462,000
Government	$2,482,000	$8,691,000
Other channels	$66,292,000	$133,184,000
Total ornamental and plant sales	$661,920,000	$1,266,988,000

Source: Statistics Canada

THE CLOCK

– Here's a peek inside the auction centre of Ontario Flower Growers Co-operative in Mississauga. The flowers and plants taken there by member growers are placed on carts and paraded before representatives of wholesalers and retailers of floral products in the Toronto area and beyond. When the auction of a batch begins, a higher-than-expected price is displayed on one of the two computer-controlled clocks. This price declines until a prospective buyer stops the process, thus making him or her the purchaser. The co-op was established in October, 1972.

— *The assembly area of the auction building is a delightful place to view the colourful variety of flowers produced by Ontario growers.*

The transport trucks of Bayview Flowers Ltd. that rumble along the roads of Ontario and many areas of the United States display the catchy slogan "Our business is blooming."

It's not a gimmick. In fact, the business is blooming to such an extent that the owners sometimes scratch their heads in disbelief.

"It astounds us how our business has been able to grow and the people we have and the growth rate we are running at," says Stuart van Staalduinen. "We often sit back and say this cannot be in our hands. It is just unbelievable to us."

Clare, his brother, adds: "We feel blessed."

Their company operates in four locations – two in Jordan Station, one in Brantford and one in Simcoe – and has a total greenhouse area of 350,000 square feet, as well as outdoor acreage, and an employee roll numbering 160, including part-timers. It produces potted plants, bedding plants, seasonal and holiday crops, cut flowers, including roses, and bouquets, much of which are shipped in its own trucks to customers in Ontario, Illinois, Wisconsin, Michigan, Massachusetts, New York and the District of Columbia.

'It astounds us how our business has been able to grow and the people we have and the growth rate we are running at.'

The customer base is so large and demanding that Bayview cannot grow everything itself. Eighty per cent of what it ships is bought from other producers. At last count, it had 19 trucks, including four tractor-trailers, in its fleet.

"We are more plant handlers than growers now," says Stuart.

The seeds for all the success were sown by his parents, Clarence and Metta, soon after they emigrated from the Netherlands in 1948. Clarence was originally from 's-Gravenzande and Metta from Monster, both in the Westland district. No strangers to greenhouse work, they were determined to start up their own business in the new land.

— Clare van Staalduinen of Bayview Flowers Ltd.:
"We feel blessed."

Clarence began work for a market gardener in Islington, near Toronto. He quit after a few months, fed up with being poorly treated, and moved to another farm where he looked after vegetable garden crops. The owner had a few acres of unused land that he could rent. In his after-hours, he planted thousands of gladiolus bulbs, intending to earn some extra income just from bulb production.

"After the first year, he let some of the gladioli bloom," says Stuart. "With my uncle, who had come over from Holland, he went to flower shops and dealers. But they couldn't get much money for their flowers, so they decided to try their luck by going door to door. They went three days – my father rode a bike with a basket in front – and didn't sell one bunch. On Thursday, when they were ready to give up, a few sales were made. Encouraged, they decided to try one more day. Well, on Friday they sold everything within an hour or two because it was pay day."

In the early 1950s, his parents and their relatives, Pete and Lies Verkade, were in Brantford, operating a small business named Holland Greenhouses. They grew garden plants for sale to the public and later began doing business with retail florists as well. The partnership ended in 1963. Pete stayed with Holland Greenhouses and Clarence launched his own operation on a six-acre parcel he had acquired in Brantford, calling it Clarence van Staalduinen Greenhouses.

Slowly, the business was built up through hard work involving the entire family. Mom often joined her husband

in the greenhouses. Len, the eldest son, came on board to look after sales. The other children – Stuart, Clare and Wilma – helped out after school, on Saturdays and in the summer months.

"We worked from the time we were nine or ten years old," says Stuart. "We were paid a pittance: 50 cents an hour to start. I remember going on strike for $1. Dad split the difference and we worked for 75 cents. But when the boys turned 21, Dad gave each of them 20 per cent of the company. It was his way of saying: 'You've contributed to this all along, so thank you very much. You are now part of it'."

In time, Clarence stopped growing for retailers and went strictly into the wholesale trade. His main crops were six-inch potted mums – these are still being produced in large numbers – snapdragons and carnations. With the sons in mind, the business was expanded in 1982 through the purchase of a greenhouse operation in Simcoe. And in 1987, for basically the same reason, the Bayview greenhouse business on Jordan Road and a branch in North Tonawanda, New York, were acquired from grower Bill Snoei, a former garage mechanic. The U.S. operation was later sold. The company purchased a 23-acre site just down the road from the original Bayview place in 1993 and built its fourth Ontario facility. By this time, all the parts had been consolidated under the Bayview name.

— A pleasant environment for a Bayview sales meeting.

— Ontario-produced flowers and plants are trucked regularly to the United States. Insets: a Bayview truck, part of its cargo and the logistics room.

The shift towards direct selling began in the 1980s.

"We decided to take control of our sales markets," says Stuart. "We felt that if we didn't direct-market ourselves, we'd always be in someone else's hands. We didn't want to lose control of our destiny."

Diversification, besides making good business sense, also would allow Clarence's three sons to use their individual gifts to full potential.

Obviously, the strategy has worked. Stuart and Clare are in charge of a business that is blooming and booming. Len is there too, after having been away from it for awhile to run a venture of his own. All remain deeply touched by the struggles of their parents to get them on the road to success. Clarence died in 1999.

"He worked hard, very hard in the early days," says Stuart. "I can still see him watering his spring plants at eight o'clock at night and then loading them. He had to be up at 4 a.m. to take them to the market. He didn't make much money."

Clare adds: "Dad was a very religious man. If he made money, he would make sure that the needs of the church and the Christian school were looked after first."

As for the future, Stuart says simply: "We are growing our business and trying to grow it in a controlled manner and we'll see where our gifts and the Lord take us."

Floral Passion

— Wholesaler Brian van Staalduinen is upbeat about the future of the flower business.

In a time when Ontario-grown flowers are a huge export item, boosting the pocketbooks of their growers and handlers and brightening the lives of millions of Americans, Brian van Staalduinen is bringing floral products into the province from such warmer climes as Colombia, Ecuador, California and Florida.

His wholesale business, Staalduinen Floral Ltd., picks up roses, cut greens, carnations, tropical foliage plants and gladioluses in Miami, the central gathering point, trucks them to its warehouse in Stoney Creek and then sells and distributes them, along with a wide range of home-grown products, to 500 florists throughout Ontario, Nova Scotia and Prince Edward Island.

"Our carnations come from Colombia," he says. "That country can grow a better product for a cheaper price than you can grow it here. It's the same with roses from Ecuador."

When the value of the Canadian dollar was high, in relation to the Dutch guilder, his firm imported many specialty cut flowers from the Netherlands. But this became an expensive undertaking when the value dropped. More and more growers in Ontario then began producing specialty crops of good quality, enabling Staalduinen and other wholesalers to rely less and less on imports from across the ocean.

Brian's father, John, who founded the family business in 1952, began importing tropical plants from Florida in the early 1960s. Their sales doubled within a year.

"There is a good market for good quality tropical plants," he told an interviewer from the magazine Canadian Florist, Greenhouse and Nursery. "The use of artificials in planting in homes and in public places like restaurants and hotels has not had any ill effects in our sales of real live plants. In fact, we are inclined to think that these plants, good as they are, do actually fill a temporary need for some locations. Real plants often follow when the people get tired of the lifeless plastics."

He had come to Canada in 1948 from the Dutch village of Bleiswijk, north of Rotterdam, with his wife, Mary, and their three children, Brian, Ray and Bill. He worked for a year at Prudhomme's, which had a nursery in Fenwick, and then for Cocks Nursery and Landscaping in Winona before buying a small greenhouse business in Stoney Creek. He grew carnations, snapdragons and cut mums and sold these to floral outlets in Hamilton. Sensing that a wider market could be reached, he imported a greenhouse from Holland and increased his production.

In 1957, John teamed up with Deny de Jong, a grower in Beamsville, to form a wholesale company called Beamsfloral Supply Ltd. At first, this firm largely limited its efforts to selling the products of the two partners. Gradually, flowers produced by other growers were added to broaden the range and ensure a large, steady supply. The partnership ended in 1964 when Deny moved from cut flower production to propagation and no longer was interested in a wholesale distribution arrangement. John continued on as the sole owner of the firm, renaming it Staalduinen Floral Ltd.

By this time, cut roses constituted an important part of John's business. In 1961, he had taken over the rose-growing greenhouses of the E. D. Smith company in Winona. By implementing new methods of growing, replanting the beds with new varieties and selling the flowers through his wholesale firm, he was able to make the concern modestly profitable. When factory expansion forced him to move, he consolidated his greenhouse operations on a site on Highway 8 at Fruitland. This business, Staalduinen Growers Ltd., still produces roses, although most of the greenhouse area of 90,000 square feet is used for growing potted plants.

The firm's facilities on Arvin Avenue in Stoney Creek include offices and a 15,000-square-foot warehouse where Ontario-grown and imported flowers and plant products are stored in temperatures a few degrees above freezing until they are transferred to one of 15 trucks for shipment to the retail outlets that ordered them. Brian, the youngest of John's sons, is the President. There are 35 full-time and five part-time workers, including Brian's entire family: his wife, Gerda, is Office Manager, son Duane is Sales Manager, daughter Wendy, formerly manager of the greenhouses, is in marketing and son Brian is now in charge of the greenhouses, overseeing a staff of six full-time and four part-time workers.

'There's a growing demand for our products. That's because the Martha Stewarts of the world are showing people how to use flowers.'

Brian is upbeat about the future of the flower business.

"In general, I see a very positive industry," he says. "There's a growing demand for our products. That's because the Martha Stewarts of the world are showing people how to use flowers. Also, there's a huge potential market here when you compare our consumption of flowers to that of Europe. One of the reasons Niagara has been so successful is that there are a lot of good growers who picked up on the technology from Holland, Denmark and other progressive countries. In that sense, it's a good, solid industry."

Then he touches on something that lingers in the minds of many people inside and outside the greenhouse community.

"Obviously, the low dollar has helped a lot. If it ever goes back to par, I don't know what would happen to all the stuff that goes to the States. But that's true for every industry."

— *All members of the van Staalduinen family – Wendy, Brian, Duane, Gerda and Brian Jr. – are involved in the operation of Staalduinen Floral Ltd. in Stoney Creek.*

It's More Demanding

With the temperature plunging to minus 30 degrees (C), it was one of those mid-winter nights when greenhouse growers toss and turn in their beds, unable to sleep, constantly worrying about a malfunction in their heating systems and all the unpleasant consequences that they may have to cope with.

On Fairlane Road in Jordan Station, grower Bram Boekestyn's heart began to do double duty when he realized that his boiler had quit. Unbeknownst to him, the wrong type of oil, without winterizer, had been pumped into the system that night. He rushed into the biting cold, took warm water out of the boiler, climbed onto the tanks and poured the water over the lines. The boiler started again.

"I did this from midnight until 5:30 in the morning," he says. "Of course, I was ice, and the tanks were ice, and I fell with the pails in between the tanks and hurt myself, and I stood on top of the tanks and screamed: 'Who wants to buy this from me?' I was beat."

His sons, John, Brian and Ed, are glad that no one came around with a purchase offer. They took over a thriving concern when their father retired in 1994 on his doctor's advice because of a heart valve problem.

'It's way more demanding now than when I was in it, even with all the automation.'

Boekestyn Greenhouses Ltd. has become a major producer of potted holiday crops such as lilies, chrysanthemums and poinsettias. A sister company, Flora Pack Inc., operates as a wholesale seller and shipper for up to 60 growers.

The original Boekestyn property on Fairlane Road was sold a few years ago and all the operations were accommodated in a modern, 235,000-square-foot greenhouse facility on 13th Street in Jordan Station. A 40-acre site at 11th Street and Fourth Avenue, also in Jordan Station, was purchased recently for future expansion.

Bram's roots are embedded in the greenhouse industry. His father grew vegetables and tomatoes in the Dutch village of De Lier and the entire family helped. But when he came to

Canada in 1952 at age 18, following the lead of a number friends in the same age group, he ended up at a ranch in British Columbia. He was back in Holland four months later, a casualty of homesickness.

After serving a compulsory 14-month stint in the Dutch army, Bram was on his way to Canada again. His brother, Bert, had talked him into going to St. Catharines.

Since there were few greenhouses in Niagara then, he had to look for work in another field. He jumped from job to job – "you name it and I've worked there." He earned wages in construction, on a hydro project, in a tobacco field, in a moving van and at a lumber camp. For five years, he drove a transport truck to points in the United States. But he never abandoned the thought of someday having a greenhouse, just like his father, and making a living with the soil.

"I made a start when I bought a piece of land in Jordan Station and began growing tomatoes with one plastic greenhouse," he says. "My wife, Ina, looked after the

tomatoes while I continued with my job. Then I built another greenhouse with an improvement loan of $7,500 which had a condition requiring me to work in it full-time. I continued to grow tomatoes and just got by. We didn't go on holidays. We couldn't even afford a babysitter."

After five years, Bram had to dip into his meagre savings to travel to Holland to see his ailing father. The trip was an eye-opener. Deeply impressed with all the expansion taking place in the Dutch greenhouse industry, he became convinced that he had been too narrow-minded in running his business. Back in Canada, he secured another loan, enabling him to expand again and hire help. Gradually, he switched to flowers.

"It was tough for 10 years," he says, "but then things started to turn around. We got a lot of moral support in those days from Andy Olsthoorn of Lakeshore Produce. He often came back from the States and said, boys, we've got to do this and that. He also ordered some stuff from us."

— Bram Boekestyn on a regular visit to his sons, John, Ed and Brian.

Bram entered the wholesale selling field when he and seven other growers met to discuss their unhappiness with the firm that was handling this work and decided to do it themselves.

"I warned them that this was going to be a big step because how are you going to sell all this stuff. This was in the fall and it was all poinsettias. I said you better be prepared to be stuck with half the crop at least. Well, it sort of went like that. And right away four of them quit. In the end, only two were left: Nick VanGeest of Gregory Greenhouses in St. Catharines and myself."

Flora Pack, formed in 1977, is now wholly owned by the Boekestyn family. With 11 workers, it buys, sells and ships. Most of the products are taken across the border to places as far west as Chicago and as far south as the Carolinas. The operation was located for many years at Gregory Greenhouses, then moved to the Boekestyn's, and plans are in the works to relocate it to an off-site facility.

Although Bram is retired, he can still be seen in the greenhouses on most days, tenderly caring for exotic echeveria plants. He describes this as a hobby. Unquestionably, it's also an excuse to observe what's happening in the ever-changing world of flower production.

"It's way more demanding now than when I was in it, even with all the automation," he says. "For instance, we had four varieties of mums, all requiring the same treatment. Now they have I don't know how many varieties, most of them requiring different treatments and timing. We had to work hard with our hands. Now they have to use their brains more."

As for the future, John, who is in charge of Flora Pack, explains that for the next five years the Boekestyn firm has decided to work with all the assets it now has and do things that will allow it to react to market forces and other factors over which it has no real control.

His deep religious convictions surface, as happens so often with many other growers, when he adds: "No matter what we do, we need to realize at the end of the day that everything was done for the glory of God."

Promoting Flowers

Like their counterparts in Canada, the growers of cut flowers in the United States realize that much needs to be done domestically to boost the per capita consumption of their products.

So they've taken the bull by the horns, aggressively pursuing a promotion campaign aimed at encouraging the everyday use of flowers outside of the traditional gift and holiday occasions.

The goal is to narrow the gap between the per capita buying of fresh cut flowers by consumers in the U.S. and those of Europe and Asia – and thereby dramatically expand the market and bring about the need for higher domestic production.

"We're not re-inventing the wheel," says Stan Pohmer of Minnetonka, Minnesota, Executive Director of the Flower Promotion Organization, an alliance of growers in the U.S. and Colombia. "We're following what others have done very successfully. We know that traditionally people think of cut flowers as a gift for a special event or occasion such as anniversaries, birthdays or births. And flowers do make fantastic gifts to express our emotions and sentiments. But their usefulness and enjoyment can extend far beyond gift giving."

His organization came into being in 1999 after growers in the U.S. and Colombia decided to end 30 years of industry infighting over trade differences and pool their resources to launch a multi-million-dollar consumer marketing campaign, called Flowers Alive With Possibilities, to stimulate incremental flower purchases for their mutual benefit.

"Under our program, flowers are being positioned as home decor accessories rather than gifts," says Stan.

"We offer a unique array of application ideas featuring flowers used throughout the house, delivering fresh, easy and unique home decorating solutions."

Here are a few examples:

Flowers in the bathroom? Why not! A simple plastic tumbler filled with fragrant blossoms makes an attractive air freshener.

You can also add a touch of romance in your bedroom with a few beautiful stems that complement or accent the colour of your linens or wallpaper.

Or make visitors feel extra special with a bright bunch of cut flowers sitting pretty on the guest room nightstand.

For a window treatment, imagine a row of simple vases holding your favourite flowers, instead of the usual curtains.

For artwork, how about hanging a vase of flowers instead of a watercolour?

In the family room, fill an empty fireplace with a big bucket of flowers. Or arrange a variety of containers with cut stems across your fireplace mantle.

For an instant laundry brightener, rinse out an old bleach or detergent bottle, fill it with cut flowers and place it on your washing machine or shelf. It'll help lighten the load on washday.

And don't let your staircase go bare. Create a "stepped" effect with a series of flowers in interesting containers.

91

IT CAN BE DONE

Albert Elmers was expected to be a dairy farmer, like his father was. He was 16 when he quit school in 1976 to start work on the family farm near Wellandport. But his heart wasn't in it, and he told his Dad: "Don't keep the farm for me."

Well, he eventually did become a farmer of sorts, producing flowers instead of milk.

He's co-owner of UFD, or United Floral Distributors, a wholesale company on Canboro Road near Fenwick that deals with 60 growers locally and 20 others in different parts of the world, from Ecuador to the Netherlands. It also has a number of greenhouses for its own production of flowers, including roses.

Albert's partner is Debbie Boverhof, daughter of the late Ton Hanemaayer, a grower in St. Catharines and a notable figure in Niagara's postwar greenhouse industry. Flowers have been her life. In fact, all of the four children of Ton and Maria are involved in the floral business in some capacity.

On the other hand, Albert, one of three children of Bart and Tina, who spent their honeymoon on a boat that took them and other Dutch emigrants to Canada in 1952, had no idea in his teenage years what he wanted to do in life off the farm. "I just wanted to have fun," he says. His mother had died when he was eight.

He first worked at Dofasco in 1979 for 15 months as a millwright apprentice. The wages were good, but he didn't like the atmosphere and Sunday work. So he left this job to become a worker for a trenching business in Smithville.

"I made less money, which was fine, but I couldn't see myself going anywhere," he says. "Then I heard that Oak Hill, a wholesale florist in the area, was hiring. That's where I worked next."

After a year, Albert went on the road as a salesperson, searching out and making contact with potential customers in the United States and getting them on board. He did this work for four years and then decided to start on his own. With his wife, Kathy, he launched a wholesale business called Country Garden in a small, rented warehouse in Fenwick. They hired sales staff and increased their accounts to the point where it became necessary to build larger quarters.

'Our company belongs to one of the fastest growing industries in the area.'

In the meantime, the owners of Oak Hill, John and Barb Donker, sold their business and, with Debbie, started a similar operation called Pinewood Acres. A year later, in 1991, Pinewood and Albert's company merged and United Floral Distributors came into being with five partners: John and Barb, Albert and Kathy, and Debbie, who had been associated with both Oak Hill and Pinewood.

The large partnership didn't work out and John and Barb departed. UFD, with Albert, Kathy and Debbie in charge, moved to its new building at Canboro Road and Victoria Avenue in 1996 and entered a period of rapid growth. The company has 19 trucks servicing flower shops in a large area that encompasses the Toronto region, Ottawa, Detroit, Cleveland, Hartford, Jersey City, Philadelphia and the outskirts of New York City. This large customer base requires a lot of production.

— Albert Elmers and Debbie Boverhof outside the entrance to UFD near Fenwick.

"We don't have contracts with growers, just gentlemen's agreements," says Albert. "We deal with the same people all the time for our products and they fill our needs. We make sure that we get a good price and that they get a good price. It's a win-win situation."

UFD's own greenhouse area now totals 70,000 square feet.

There's more to Albert's life than flowers. He is a fanatic fan of the Toronto Maple Leafs and memorabilia of the hockey club adorns his office. He and Kathy have five children, of whom Jamie and Brett are among the 65 workers on the company's payroll. Debbie and her husband, Rudy, have four children, including Michael and Devlin who work at UFD. Rudy, a long-time dairy farmer, now grows cash crops on 1,500 acres.

Albert looks at the days ahead with confidence.

"Our company belongs to one of the fastest growing industries in the area," he says. "Niagara's growers have a lot of good things going for them, including the climate, and our products are second to none, but the biggest reason for the growth is the exchange. This presents us with the challenge of continuing to build up the industry as a whole so that we can survive even without the exchange. With hands-on people and positive attitudes, this can be done."

— UFD has 19 trucks servicing flower shops in Ontario and the northeastern United States.

CHAPTER EIGHT

THE RIGHT MOVE

'*It was so important for the boys in our village to work, work, work.*
This was our way of life.'
— *Ton Boekestyn*

On a bitterly cold day in January, 1978, Leo Reus became teary-eyed as he surveyed what was left of his newly-erected greenhouses near Fenwick.

He kept thinking: "I'm just starting here and now everything I've done is gone. I have a wife and two kids and what are we going to do now?"

He and his wife, Emmy, recent arrivals from the Netherlands, had placed all their hopes for earning a livelihood in their plastic-covered range of 25,000 square feet. He had put up the structures himself after first building a barn with used lumber obtained from the site of a factory that was being dismantled.

"We had a lot of snow that winter, just like in the winter before," he recalls. "It started piling up on the plastic roofs. Our greenhouses were ready, but we didn't have hydro in them yet – and no heat, of course – because the hydro people were busy looking after problems all over the place. The plastic started to sink down from the heavy snowload. We tried our best to push this off. Finally, we got heat. But this only resulted in more serious difficulties."

Water from the melting snow entered the greenhouses through gaps by the posts, creating a quagmire. Some of these posts were sinking in the mud, and there was concern that the greenhouses would collapse.

For Leo, it seemed like the end of the world. But not for long. "We told each other that we could only go forward," says Emmy. "We didn't give up. We fixed all the broken things and got our business under way."

Their business, Balfour Greenhouses Ltd., now has a greenhouse area so expansive – 330,000 square feet –that Leo and his Operations Manager, son-in-law Duane van Alstine, ride bicycles to get around the place. It is a major producer of a flowering plant called kalanchoe blossfeldiana. In addition, it grows somonas in partnership with a German firm that granted it an exclusive licence for North America. Caladiums and orchids are also produced by the 40 full-time workers.

Leo grew up in a horticultural environment in Grootebroek, near Enkhuizen. His father cultivated potatoes, gladioli and tulips in the 1950s before becoming

— Leo and Emmy Reus, residents of Canada since 1976, now have 330,000 square feet of greenhouse area for their flower-producing business near Fenwick.

a salesman of equipment for growers. After finishing school, Leo entered the bulb field. He and Emmy were involved in that business, growing five hectares of tulip and daffodil bulbs, when they were smitten by the emigration bug.

Leo knew that a huge investment would be necessary if he wanted to advance and succeed in Holland. Moreover, he didn't like the bureaucratic climate there. So he suggested to Emmy that they move to Australia. But she gave him a flat no. "All I knew about Australia was sheep," she explains. "And it was so far away. Canada had a more familiar sound to it and it was a lot closer." They had already been to Canada to visit her aunt.

The couple and their two young children, Marion and

Lucy, arrived in their new homeland in August, 1976. Leo began work at Waterloo Flowers, a greenhouse operation in Breslau, near Kitchener. He would stay there for nearly a year. In the meantime, he kept his eyes open for a suitable piece of land where he could start his own business. While driving through the Fenwick area, he spotted a For Sale sign on a 15-acre property on Balfour Street with a wartime stucco house and some cabbage, kale and shrubs. To Leo, it looked great, and it was in a good location, so he ended up buying it.

When he applied for a bank loan to pay for the greenhouses he wanted to erect, he was turned down because he didn't have a credit record. He had better luck with the Farm Credit Corporation. Then the winter came.

— Duane van Alstine uses a bicycle to move around the greenhouses.

Still fresh in his mind was the famous Blizzard of '77 which had struck just after his boss in Breslau had gone on holidays, leaving him in charge. Now there was more inclement weather, bringing misery and despair.

'I had been so busy building and growing that I hadn't thought about the selling part.'

After all the damage had been repaired, the business of growing could get under way. Begonias in four-inch pots were the first flowers ready to be marketed.

"I suddenly realized I had to sell them," says Leo. "I had no clue how to go about doing this. I had been so busy building and growing that I hadn't thought about the selling part. In Holland, we took our stuff to the auction and that was the end of the story. But here I had to go on the road with my old truck. I went to Toronto, to neighbourhood flower shops and to a few wholesalers. In the end, most of the flowers were sold. But for me, this method of selling was the hardest part of getting into business."

In the early days, Leo and Emmy grew "just about everything under the sun" in the greenhouses and in the fields because they didn't know in what direction they wanted to head. They even had witlof, commonly known as Belgian endive, a favourite among the Dutch immigrant community. A roadside stand at the front of the house, looked after by Emmy, offered bedding plants and vegetables to the passing public.

"There's a story," says Duane, "that they used to look out the window on Sundays and, if they spotted someone there, they'd run over." Laughing, his mother-in-law adds: "Sometimes we told each other: 'Don't run too fast because it's only a small car'."

After a few years, Leo and Emmy went to Florida just to get away from everything for awhile. They toured a greenhouse and were so impressed with the Christmas cacti that were growing there that they bought a large number of cuttings. Their first crop earned them "fantastic money." The second year was excellent too. But then other growers got involved, the market became glutted and the price went down. Kalanchoes eventually became the specialty product at Balfour Greenhouses.

Leo and Emmy still like to get away from it all. In lieu of early retirement, which they realize is impossible for them, they set aside one week every month for travel. Leo also continues his involvement with the local volunteer fire department. A member of the brigade since 1979, he's the district chief now, responsible for the Fenwick area.

"If a call comes through, I go, regardless of what I am doing," he says. "It gives me a good feeling if I can help somebody out."

But most of his time is spent in the greenhouses. These are equipped with state-of-the-art technology and up-to-date conveniences such as rolling benches. In contrast, there's a soil mixer made from the parts of a feedlot mixing machine. Placed out of the way, in a deep pit, the self-made equipment does its job well.

Family members are usually close at hand. Emmy is the office manager. Daughter Marion, who met Duane when he started working for her father, is an administrative worker. The other daughter, Lucy, equipped with a master's degree in business administration, is employed with the Royal Bank Financial Group in Toronto.

Leo believes there is plenty of room for growth in his industry. In fact, he can see "a million opportunities," particularly in the area of marketing. Connected to that is the need for growers to improve their public image.

"For example, instead of polluting the air, as some people say we are doing, we are fighting carbon dioxide gases by taking it from our boilers and reusing it in our greenhouses. Yes, we have some work to do to correct the misinformation."

— A spectacular night-time view of the entrance to Balfour Greenhouses.

A shipment of Dutch tulip bulbs has just arrived at Pioneer Flower Farms Ltd. on Seventh Street in the outskirts of St. Catharines and the owner, Henk Sikking, is busily operating a front-end loader to move them to areas where his workers can begin the processing.

"I check everything that comes in," he says, after finishing his noisy task. Beads of sweat are on his brow. "These bulbs are my bread and butter and I want to make sure that everything's OK. We get 40 containers of bulbs a year, so I do this often."

Forced indoors, the bulbs produce about 15 million cut and potted tulips in 60 varieties, making Henk one of the largest tulip growers in North America. He also turns out a fairly large number of other products on a smaller scale, including daffodils, hyacinths, irises, lilies, poinsettias, amaryllis, mums, violets, geraniums and hanging baskets. His sales gross nearly $8 million a year.

'The future looks super good for the entire industry.'

"We grew with the market," he explains. "Our biggest customers nowadays are chain stores and fruit markets, all with big orders. If we had stayed small, we would have fallen out of it. What the flower shops buy of our product is very little."

Henk hails from Warmond, a village in the western part of the Netherlands, where his father, Johannes, was a bulb grower and forcer for many years. He worked on the farm until it was expropriated by the municipality for housing development in 1962. His next job was with a grower of freesias and roses in Aalsmeer. He found the work among flowers, as opposed to strictly bulbs, thoroughly enjoyable. In 1968, he accepted an offer to manage a farm in Tunisia,

in northern Africa, where roses and gladioli were grown outside.

"It was run by a big corporation owned by 10 German wholesalers," he says. "It was a good place to make money, but it wasn't so great for social life. I stayed there two years and went back to Holland in June, 1970."

Upon his return, he was approached by Jack Vink, a neighbour in Warmond, who had purchased JVK, a St. Catharines-based wholesale supplier for the greenhouse industry.

"He said: 'Why not go to Canada?' Well, he got me interested. I worked on Jack's farm for half a year until I could get my immigration papers. He found a sponsor for me in Lefroy on Lake Simcoe. After I had been there three months, Jack came by and said a neighbour of JVK on Seventh Street wanted to sell his 25-acre fruit farm and that it would be an excellent place to start a greenhouse business."

Henk's father travelled to Canada to offer advice and support and the farm was purchased in April, 1971. In effect, Henk and Jack had become neighbours again. The young man, still single, worked part-time for JVK that winter. In 1972, he erected a 15,000-square-foot greenhouse and began growing potted mums. He put in a tomato crop in the summer and cut mums in the fall. Pioneer Flower Farms and its industrious owner were on the way to gaining a respectable name in the greenhouse business.

In addition to his indoor crops, Henk began growing tulips outside in 1974. He purchased the bulbs from Holland, forced them into bloom and sold the flowers at the flower auction in Mississauga and through a wholesaler, Lakeshore Produce. He gradually switched to total indoor production.

— Henk Sikking displays some of the millions of Dutch tulip bulbs that are kept in cold storage at Pioneer Flower Farms Ltd. in St. Catharines.

The growth of his tulip business is reflected in the size of his ultra-modern greenhouse complex. It now totals 280,000 square feet. There are also two acres of buildings for cold storage of bulbs. Underneath it all is a 400,000-gallon reservoir in which rainwater is collected for irrigation.

A section of the complex resembles a factory floor. It holds a number of large pieces of sophisticated machinery, manufactured in Holland, that enable the production of tulips to be fully automated. But even with the use of the latest equipment, many workers are still needed. The firm employs 25 full-timers and up to 70 part-timers, including 26 from Mexico.

The Sikking family is fully involved too. Henk Jr., the eldest of three children of Henk and Sibylla – she died in May, 2000, after 24 years of marriage – is Manager of the operations, overseeing the growing and staffing. Peter, a student of horticulture at the University of Guelph,

— A view of the large Sikking operation on Seventh Street in St. Catharines.

Floral Passion

— Tulip bulbs are being planted in pots at this fast-moving line at Pioneer Flower Farms. Henk Sikking with some of his tulips: "We grew with the market."

works part-time and Anita helps with the book work while studying accounting at Brock University.

Henk sells 20 per cent of his output at the flower auctions in Mississauga and Montreal. The remainder is exported to the United States through wholesalers. He describes this sales arrangement as ideal for serving significant sections of the markets in the two countries. For the years ahead, he paints a bright picture.

"The future looks super good for the entire industry," he says. "We always hear some doom and gloom when the economy slows down. But all recessions have been good times for us. People continue to buy flowers, perhaps even more. And as far as the value of the dollar is concerned, we should remember that in 1973 our dollar stood higher than the U.S. dollar and we still sold in the States. We have built up a good customer base there. They know we are very strong on quality. So I'm not worrying about a change in the dollar."

In late May, 2000, Tony VanderKaay was relaxing on the patio at the side of his house at Garden City Greenhouses Ltd. in St. Catharines, lazily sipping an after-supper coffee, when a Niagara Airbus pulled into the driveway.

He was puzzled. No one in his family was leaving or returning.

But when people started pouring out of the vehicle, smiling, waving, chattering in Dutch, the mystery was gone. He jumped up and, with his eyes glistening with joy, rushed to greet his surviving brothers, sisters and in-laws from the Netherlands, all 22 of them, who had made a surprise visit for his 35th wedding anniversary.

> *'Canada has been a very good country for us and we are thankful that we made the move.'*

"I was absolutely flabbergasted," he recalls. "My wife, Elizabeth, had arranged everything behind my back – it had taken months – and I had never suspected anything. She had also arranged a full week of activities. We had a great time. You know, this anniversary present was one of the highlights of my life."

Tony is the self-proclaimed black sheep of the family. He sold his greenhouse concern in the Netherlands in 1974 and emigrated with his wife and two young children to distant Canada, leaving many of his kin to wonder why. Over the years, he had been visited by a number of family members. But when the door of the bus opened, it was the first time in a quarter of a century that all the siblings – one brother was deceased – were together. And since most of them were in the greenhouse business themselves, there was lots to talk about and observe.

Tony owns Garden City Greenhouses, a 60,000-square-foot operation that produces an assortment of potted plants, flowering annuals and hanging baskets. He branched out in 1984, buying 50 acres of land with 60,000 square feet of greenhouses on Concession 5 in St. Davids. After a number of expansions, this place is now 240,000 square feet. It was purchased by his son, Ted, and named Garden City Growers Inc. when the company was split into two

— Tony VanderKaay proudly displays some of the beauties he grows at Garden City Greenhouses.

parts in 1998. In the mid-1980s, Tony sold half of the St. Davids property to a small group, of which he was a member, that planned to build facilities for the production of hydroponically-grown peppers. He's still a partner in the enterprise, St. David's Hydroponics Ltd., which has nearly one million square feet under glass in plants in St. Davids and Vineland Station.

He was born in 1938, the ninth in a family of 13. His father, Theodorus, began his own greenhouse operation in Poeldijk, in the Westland district, in 1923. He sold this five years later and, with a younger brother, bought a larger place in De Lier where he grew vegetables and flowers and

also looked after some cows and pigs. Seven of the eight sons of Theodorus and Hendrika would become owners of greenhouse businesses. Of their five daughters, four would marry greenhouse owners.

"That's the way it went in Westland," says Tony. "There weren't too many things a young man could do besides growing. That was the way of life there. If I had been born in Rotterdam or The Hague, I probably would never have become a grower."

At age 13, he went to horticultural school two days a week and worked for his father the other days. He finished his schooling two years later and began working full-time. In 1963, after his engagement to Elizabeth, he became owner of a four-acre property with some old greenhouses, one of two neighbouring businesses which his father had purchased. He and Elizabeth, whom he married two years later, grew lettuce in winter, then tomatoes, endive, freesias, mums and grapes. The eldest of five children, she came from a greenhouse family too and was an experienced and hard-working helper.

The place was fixed up nicely. There were no big problems with the crops, although the prices caused occasional grumbling. The family grew too – Karen was born in 1966 and Ted arrived three years later. But Tony became increasingly troubled. "He felt like he was living in a spider web," says his wife.

"I'm an anti-socialist," Tony explains. "I didn't like all the social laws and paying for everything beforehand. Also, it was difficult to move ahead with all the regulations and restrictions. I heard stories about Canada from friends and acquaintances who were in the greenhouse business there and became very interested. There seemed to be more opportunities there – at least at that time. My father was also pro-America and pro-Canada and probably would have emigrated if he were younger. All the information I received was positive."

In 1972, he sold a little car and used the money to buy round-trip air fare for a first-hand look at Canada, particularly Niagara.

"I liked it very much. It was the place for me. I sold my greenhouses two years later and headed for Canada with my wife and two children. We went to Niagara because we knew some people there, including Andy Olsthoorn, my cousin Ton Hanemaayer and Bram Boekestyn, my wife's cousin."

He had no real desire to take up greenhouse work in the new land.

"In Holland, we saw people doing leisure things, such as boating, while we always had to work, work, work in the greenhouses. When we went to Canada, I thought of trying something else. Maybe I could buy a dump truck and start driving. But when I arrived, I quickly saw that there were plenty of trucks here already."

So he started working in greenhouses after all. He helped here and there and also sold vegetables for someone on the market in St. Catharines. But he hadn't come to Canada to live in rental property and work for a boss. He very much wanted to get a place of his own. He looked around and found something he liked: four acres on Read Road with a small house that Elizabeth dubbed "the chickencoop."

Part of a barn and a greenhouse of 20,000 square feet were built, cactus cuttings were purchased and Garden City Greenhouses was in business. Tony took his plants to the auction clock in Mississauga.

"I did well," he says. "I thought I was in heaven, but heaven was not there yet."

He grew cacti for three years and then changed to geraniums and hanging baskets which he sold at the wholesale market in Toronto. The business grew from there. Another son arrived: Andy, now a student at Brock University. A new house was built for $75,000 and the mortgage was paid off in three years, demonstrating that everything was going well. Indeed, there were no regrets about the move from Holland.

"Mind you, everything didn't always go the way I wanted," says Tony. "And I found that some things were easier in Holland, such as marketing and distances one has to travel. But living here is way more relaxing. That's important to me. Canada has been a very good country for us and we are thankful that we made the move. We are looking with confidence and trust to the future."

99

— Tony VanderKaay's siblings and in-laws from Holland make a surprise visit to St. Catharines in May, 2000.

Floral Passion

Peter Fransen was a mere 10 years old when his father, who was switching from cold frames to greenhouses at his property near Delft, the Netherlands, pointed to a welding machine and said: "Start welding."

For Dad, it was just a way of introducing his son to the adult world – a world that seemed to arrive so quickly in many greenhouse families where work, work, work was the order of the day.

As to be expected, Peter didn't do much in the way of welding. But the introduction must have had some effect because he later chose a machining course, of which welding was a part, when he needed another subject to finish his formal education. Having started school at age three, after the death of his mother, he was considered too young to graduate upon completing studies in electrical work.

'I don't make the prettiest weld. But it doesn't break and it doesn't leak.'

Peter, who owns Marshview Greenhouses Inc. on Pettit Road in Wainfleet, now finds that his training in the two trades sometimes comes in handy.

"I was looking for a welder once when I was putting up an addition and making changes to the heating system," he says. "But it's difficult to get somebody to come in and do a certain job when you need him. The usual response is: 'I'm busy. I'll see you in six weeks.' So I did the work myself. I don't make the prettiest weld, but it doesn't break and it doesn't leak."

Greenhouse operators, he says, wear many hats: they are growers, with full knowledge of what it takes to get their products ready for consumers; they are business people, developing markets and making sure that enough money comes in to keep their operations viable; they are psychologists, knowing how to deal with individual employees, and they are maintenance people, prepared to fix minor problems in all areas.

"That's what makes the job attractive and keeps it interesting."

Peter was 19 years old and single when he came to Niagara in 1968 with a friend. In the summer, he worked for a nursery, hoping to learn the English language. The Dutch owner insisted on speaking Dutch to him, but he always replied in English. He then trained to become an electrician and obtained his Canadian licence. His intention was to work for himself, but rough times in the building trades prompted him to set his sights on other ways to earn a living.

When he met Mary, his future wife, the choice of a future career was obvious. She had grown up in the greenhouse industry; her father, Cornelis Vander Hoeven, had built his first greenhouse in St. Catharines in 1959 when she was five years old. With their common backgrounds, Peter and Mary opted to enter the growing field.

Their first operation was launched in 1974 in partnership with Mary's sister, Paula, and her husband, Frank, on a 50-acre property at Gasline, near Port Colborne. In a greenhouse of 10,000 square feet, they grew bedding plants and then holiday crops for their own retail sales outlet as well as for the wholesale trade. Their greenhouse area was eventually increased to 60,000 square feet.

In 1993, Peter and Mary went on their own, buying nine acres of land, with an option for an additional 10 acres, in Wainfleet. They tore down an old greenhouse on the property, built a new one and began growing for the wholesale market. With expansions, they now have 52,000 square feet for producing cyclamen, their main product, English ivies, holiday crops and spring plants.

Mary chuckles as she recalls the three requisites for a future husband she had set when she was a teen:

"He couldn't be a Dutchman, because they're too stubborn; he couldn't be a greenhouse farmer, because I wanted something else in life, and he couldn't be a hockey fan."

Although she struck out on all three points, the mother of four is as happy as a lark with how her life has evolved. The greenhouse setting, she says, provides "a beautiful way to bring up the children. What could be more important than that?"

— Peter Fransen finds the diversity of his work interesting.

Ton Boekestyn was 11 years old when he bought live chickens from a neighbour and sold them at a profit to other neighbours.

Then he bought ballpoint pens for 50 cents, knocked on doors and offered them for 75 cents.

Every cent he made went to his savings account.

At age 14, he left school and began working for his father, a greenhouse vegetable grower. He was given a choice: either have wages paid out or settle for an allowance with earnings deposited on his behalf in the bank. He picked the latter. After a full day among the tomatoes and cucumbers, he often worked into the evening at another business, bunching carrots and scraping up extra money.

He acquired a moped at age 16, when he could legally ride one, and sold it at a profit. This was the start of a sideline that later included cars and motorcycles as well. He had a fondness, and obviously an ability, for buying and selling and making good money in the process.

'He is always looking. He always sees opportunities.'

At 19, he became owner of a greenhouse operation. His father had bought a three-acre property for him when he was only three and had built 60,000 square feet of greenhouses in two stages. With sufficient funds on hand for a downpayment, his ambitious son, one of nine children, took over the property. Dad kept the mortgage.

"It was so important for the boys in our village to work, work, work," Ton explains at his attractive residence near Virgil. "This was our way of life. We never got compliments from our parents – that just wasn't done – so there was a big desire on our part to prove ourselves."

The community he refers to is De Lier, in Holland's Westland region, where he and a number of other Niagara greenhouse growers were born and raised. Their penchant for working hard and doing business, he believes, has contributed substantially to the success of the floricultural industry here. This is something of which he is immensely proud.

He sold his business and flew to Canada in 1972 at age 31 because he had developed a great dislike for the Dutch income tax system and the bureaucracy and was disappointed in himself for building a new greenhouse and going into debt for half the cost. When he landed in Niagara with his wife, Ria, and their two daughters – a third daughter was born later – he had no intention to resume greenhouse work. But after nine months, he had come to realize that his knowledge in this field could be put to good advantage. He purchased a five-acre farm in Niagara-on-the-Lake, imported 60,000 square feet of greenhouses from Holland and grew cucumbers. In 1980, he expanded, buying 45 acres of land in St. Davids and building 60,000 square feet of greenhouses. By this time, he was fully into flower production, growing potted mums, geraniums, Easter lilies and hydrangeas.

The properties were eventually sold and a new operation, called Virgil Greenhouses Ltd., was launched on a seven-acre site on Hunter Road. Freesias became the sole crop in the 130,000-square-foot range after Ton's younger brother, Pim, a freesia expert, emigrated from Holland in 1989 and joined the business as a partner.

Ton, who also co-founded Flora Pack, a wholesale firm, is easing himself out of greenhouse work, figuring it's time to fully enjoy other things in life. But he doesn't expect to abandon the love for wheeling and dealing that has motivated him since his boyhood.

"He is always looking," says Ria. "He always sees opportunities."

101

— Ton Boekestyn takes advantage of a perfect summer day to do some garden work.

'GO FOR IT'

Pim Boekestyn has sound advice on how to get ahead in business – or life in general, for that matter.

"When I do something, I do it well," he says. "I put all my effort into it. If you believe in something, go for it, and it will succeed."

He's the embodiment of self-confidence. And this explains why it didn't take him long, after arriving in Niagara, to establish himself as a specialist in freesias, producing an exquisite, sought-after product with the aid of sophisticated growing techniques that he developed.

'When I do something, I do it well.'

Freesias are the only flowers he produces in his 130,000-square-foot range at Virgil Greenhouses Ltd. on Hunter Road near Virgil. He now owns the business which was originally founded by his older brother, Ton, who grew potted plants.

Pim, born in 1955, the youngest of nine children in a greenhouse family in De Lier, the Netherlands, was 16 years old when he started custom work in greenhouses for a neighbour. He did this for five years, travelling all over Europe and enjoying the opportunity to observe what others in the industry were doing. Then he headed for North America.

"I first went to Canada," he says. "My brother was here already. I stayed half a year and then went to Florida where I worked in a nursery for three months. After that, I returned to Holland and started selling and delivering for my brother-in-law in Naaldwijk who grew freesias. I bought myself into the company."

After all his travels, Holland seemed terribly crowded – "it was full" – and his thoughts often turned to Canada. He felt a bond because his wife, Evelyn, was originally from Barrie and his brother lived in Niagara. Moreover, he had seen opportunities.

"In 1987, I started thinking about the move," he says. "My idea was to start growing freesias in Canada with a new technique. The following year, I thought: 'If I'm going to do it, I have to do it now. I have money in my pocket and I

— Pim Boekestyn uses special techniques for growing freesias year-round.

know how to grow flowers, so it won't take a lifetime to get started'."

He and Evelyn and their three daughters – a son was born later – arrived in Niagara in 1989. He bought a share of Virgil Greenhouses and planted freesia bulbs, defying skeptics who said the species couldn't be grown here successfully, at least as an exclusive crop, because the summer climate was too warm. The first blooms, a good variety, were snapped up at the wholesale market in Toronto. Now nearly everything is picked up at the door.

"Freesias are popularly used for wedding corsages," says Pim. "They also make a beautiful table display. They're spring flowers, but year-round production is possible with special techniques."

One of his three computers controls a unique underground cooling system. "Initially, nobody here and in Holland had it. I put two things together to make it work." That's all he will reveal. His other systems are for climate control and office use. The latter one has a registry of everything about growing and selling of the last 10 years.

Pim, who likes to project a positive attitude about his business and the industry as a whole, is irritated when he hears some growers constantly complaining.

"That's not the way to move ahead," he says. "I'm often tempted to tell them: 'Well, if you don't like your job, find another one'."

Bert Vrolijk's mind was made up quickly when he visited Canada in 1979 to observe life and work and as certain if there was room for him in the flower industry, his chosen field.

"I was impressed with the amount of open space, the affordable housing, the nice climate and the demand for good greenhouse growers," he says, "and I returned to Holland convinced that I would have a good shot at finding a job here."

Twenty-four years old, single and filled with ambition, Bert emigrated to Canada the following year after responding successfully to a help-wanted advertisement placed by Marinus Koole of Creekside Gardens Ltd. who was looking for a manager. He worked at this greenhouse operation in Jordan Station for five-and-a-half years, in the meantime marrying Marjan, a Dutch-born Californian, and looking out for a place where he could start on his own. He finally found it: a five-acre hobby farm with fruit trees on Honsberger Avenue in Jordan Station.

'In our industry, there are still a lot of great opportunities.'

"It was in a good location, which is an important factor in our business, and it had a good house and excellent soil," says Bert. "But we were not fruit farmers at all, so we pulled out some trees to plant a number of flower varieties such as delphinium and statice. We needed some cash as soon as possible, so we started picking fruit from the remaining trees. Two persons could make $200 in a day. But I was glad when we could start cutting flowers because we could then earn $200 an hour. So all the fruit that was still hanging in the trees was for the birds. I refused to pick sour cherries and so on."

The rest of the trees were removed to make room for more flowers. Some varieties were grown merely as an experiment to determine if there was a market for them. In the fall of 1986, the first greenhouses were built, giving Bert and Marjan 12,000 square feet for indoor production. Their business, Peninsula Flowers Inc., was well on its way to becoming a thriving concern.

Bert was well qualified for the undertaking. He was born in Duivendrecht, near Amsterdam, and later moved to Aalsmeer, the heart of a flower-growing district, where his father had bought a greenhouse for rose production. He enjoyed the chores among the flowers and decided to follow a career in this field. He spent six years studying horticulture, economics and marketing and, after electing not to work for his father, became a salesman for a French rose breeder. While travelling from greenhouse to greenhouse in Holland and other parts of Europe, he heard enough about all the difficulties and concerns of the industry there to set his sights on a future across the ocean. His tenure at Creekside gave him a good insight into the peculiarities of growing and marketing in North America.

He readily admits that his start in business, although "scary" because of the uncertainties, cannot be compared to the experiences of the immigrants who settled in Niagara in the late 1940s and early 1950s.

"I did not experience the same amount of emotional stress because, to a large extent, the financial resources were taken care of. I didn't come with a large family. The Dutch community and the greenhouse community were already established here. There was a reasonably good market. Yes, a lot of the roads were already paved for us."

Bert and Marjan now have 72,000 square feet of greenhouse area in which Sweet William, stocks, sunflowers and cut mums are grown for the wholesale market. There are outdoor products as well, notably pussy willows and forsythias, which are cut and forced to bloom in early spring.

Bert is obviously satisfied with the area he picked to launch his career.

"We – the growers and wholesalers in Niagara – have a lot of advantages. Most growers here have found their own niche or are specialized. We grow our products in a great climate compared with other parts of this continent. We also have a tremendous distribution system for all our products in this area."

In regards to the future, he says: "In our industry, there are still a lot of great opportunities. We will have our

challenges. But we have to trust and believe in what we are doing because nobody else can do that for us."

Marjan, the mother of six children, adds: "In the daily running of the business, it's just Bert and me, and we have to trust that God will direct us and take care of our needs."

— Bert and Marjan Vrolijk stand among some of their forsythia bushes. In the background are pots with Sweet William to be planted in the greenhouses in December.

CHAPTER NINE

CHANGING CAREERS

'We did a small trial of gerbera in 1992 and were pleased with it.
In five years, it was all gerbera.'
— Kendrick Westerhoff

First-time visitors to Cedarway Floral Inc., a stone's throw from Lake Ontario near Beamsville, invariably blink twice when they come across a large, white tank shaped like a loaf of bread.

Unquestionably, it presents a peculiar sight in a greenhouse setting.

There's a hint of pride in the eyes of Kendrick Westerhoff, owner of the operation, as he offers an explanation. He belongs to the category of growers who won't hesitate to implement new technology, mostly from Europe, and is obviously pleased with what is being achieved.

'The first thing I did was put in an energy curtain to cut down on costs.'

"We're one of the few growers of cut flowers that use the exhaust gases from the boilers to supplement the carbon dioxide levels inside the greenhouses, greatly helping plant growth," he says. "For this process, our boiler is running all the time during the day, even when heat is not needed. The water that passes through the boiler goes into insulated storage tanks – that loaf of bread. If heat is needed at night to drive out humidity or control the temperature, the computer pumps that hot water into the heating system and the greenhouses are heated even though the boiler is off."

Cedarway Floral also recirculates its excess irrigation water and sterilizes it with a computer-controlled system supplied by a company in the Netherlands. This firm also picked the Niagara grower for its first North American installation of a new computer program.

Kendrick's father, Ceus, comments about his son's innovative efforts: "It's a feather in his cap that a company chooses our facilities because they trust that we will give a good evaluation."

Ceus handed over full control of Cedarway to his son in 2001 and officially retired, ending a successful growing career that began in earnest in 1984 after he purchased the property on Merrit Road, then used for the production of roses, and left his job as a high school teacher of chemistry, biology and mathematics.

— Kendrick Westerhoff of Cedarway Floral Inc. checks the gerbera harvest at his new facility on Bartlett Road near Beamsville.

With a rural background – his father was a dairy farmer in Aduard, in the Dutch province of Groningen, before emigrating with his family to Canada in 1949, and also farmed in the Peninsula – his focus during his teaching days was often directed to working with the land. He frequently did chores before and after school on a 400-acre dairy operation near Wellandport in which he was a partner. He later bought a 26-acre fruit farm in Fenwick and harvested cherries and pears. Although he liked teaching – first in St. Catharines, then in Thorold – he felt that he would be happier running his own business. He now says of his career change: "It was the best move I ever made."

The rose business that he took over was a viable concern initially. But a number of factors in the early 1990s effected a drastic change: a slowdown in the economy, increasing imports from Ecuador and Colombia and the collapse of the wholesaler that handled 60 per cent of the firm's output.

"All this came after we had ordered new greenhouses from Holland," says Ceus. "They were already on the boat. Well, we survived all that somehow. On the whole, I was an optimist. There were day-to-day concerns, but no real anxiety. It never got to the point where I said to myself: 'Hey, why did I get myself into this?' "

But the chain of unwelcome events did convince Ceus and his son, who had joined the firm as a partner after his marriage to Elizabeth in 1988, that another product should replace the roses.

Floral Passion

— A few glimpses of Cedarway's gerbera production.

"We did a small trial of gerbera in 1992 and were pleased with it," says Kendrick. "In five years, it was all gerbera, and we added more greenhouse space. We now have 115,000 square feet at this location."

A second greenhouse facility of 50,000 square feet for the production of miniature gerbera was built on Bartlett Road, south of Beamsville, in the spring of 2002.

Sixty per cent of the production of the vividly-coloured cut flower goes to the United States and a good portion of the remainder is sold at the flower auction in Mississauga.

Father and son think alike when it comes to using the latest equipment and growing methods.

"I bought a place with 40,000 square feet," says Ceus. "It had a primitive heating system, no shading, no energy curtain. The first thing I did was put in an energy curtain to cut down on costs. Then, steadily, we took advantage of new technology whenever it became available."

"It's necessary," adds Kendrick. "You have to keep up to date."

— Tim and Irma Gibson at the old farmhouse on the property of Ditsch Greenhouses near Ridgeway.

"They had used the greenhouse for tomatoes and also flowers – bedding plants, geraniums, begonias – which were sold mainly at the wholesale market," says Tim. "For me, it was a new experience; I hardly knew a petunia from a geranium. But there were no big problems because Irma had a feel for the work. And, with my farming background, I could easily put in a 12-hour day. I learned quickly. And then I started taking flowers apart."

Most of the flowers and plants now produced in the 41,000-square-foot facility are sold at the Ditsch garden centre from just before Easter to the first week of July and during the Christmas season.

'Our facility is not fancy, but we grow beautiful things.'

"We've decided to stay small so as to control our own market," says Irma. "As long as it's gorgeous and properly presented, we know where the product is going to go – through our own cash registers. We used to be open year-round, but now we're closed in the summer. It's a lifestyle decision. We go to our cottage on Manitoulin Island to fish, swim, boat and relax." They have two children, Rachel and William.

When the holidays are over, the Gibsons go back to work. In addition to growing plants for their own use, they propagate specialty products for other greenhouse growers.

Tim Gibson likes to describe the small greenhouse operation that he and his wife, Irma, operate near Ridgeway as a laboratory.

"If a flower looks particularly nice, I take it apart to find out why," he explains. "I want to look at it from a scientific angle. It's the only way to get nice stuff."

Equipped with a Bachelor of Science degree from McMaster University in Hamilton, Tim obviously knows what he's doing. His business, Ditsch Greenhouses on Nigh Road, which includes a retail garden centre, has built up a reputation for growing quality flowers.

"Our facility is not fancy, but we grow beautiful things," he says. "That's what sells. We aim for the 'Wow!' factor in our finished product. The biggest reward is the feedback we get from our customers."

Born in 1953, Tim was raised on a beef farm in Caledonia. He started his higher education at the University of Guelph, then worked as lab superintendent in the gypsum division of Domtar in Caledonia and attended night school at McMaster for six years to finish work on his degree. He met Irma, a fellow student, in a university pub. They were married in 1975. Eight years later, they took over the 60-acre mixed farm and greenhouse operation of Irma's parents, Adolph and Anna Ditsch, who were retiring. The Ditsch family, of German origin, had emigrated from Yugoslavia in 1956.

While he's satisfied with the way things are going in Niagara's greenhouse business, particularly in his own operation, Tim admits to occasionally having "scary" thoughts about the future.

"Ninety per cent of the floral products now go to the United States. Greenhouses have been put up just to look after the export. There could be trouble if the dollar changed dramatically. Or some event may come along to affect things. It was an eye-opener when the terrorists struck on September 11, 2001. How many flowers went into the dumpster that week? We at Ditsch are not exposed to developments in the export market, but we would feel the repercussions."

— *Workers at Ditsch Greenhouses take advantage of pleasant autumn weather to clean cuttings outdoors. The business includes a retail garden centre.*

Paul Koornneef had a good job in the research department at Stelco in Hamilton.

He had a regular work week, brought home a fair paycheque and was eligible for many benefits. He should have been happy to continue on in the kind of occupation he had trained for as a student of mechanical technology at Mohawk College. But he had other ambitions.

"My wife, Jean, and I wanted a business of our own," he says. "And when the opportunity came along, I didn't hesitate to abandon all the security I had at Stelco. I quit my job and began a new career."

> *'I had been around greenhouses all my life, but a lot of the work we got into was new to me.'*

With his younger brother, Rick, and his wife, Frances, who were also eager to start on their own, they launched a greenhouse business, Hillside Growers Inc., on a 32-acre former fruit farm on Highway 8 directly below the escarpment in Winona.

— Paul and Rick Koornneef at their flourishing business in Winona.

They had purchased the site in 1987, a huge commitment that necessitated Paul to remortgage his house and Rick to sell his and move into a smaller farmhouse on the property. However, both brothers agree that their dream could not have been realized without the financial and moral support of their parents, John and Joanne.

Buying the property was only a start to the expenses. In their off hours the following year – Paul was still at Stelco and Rick worked with his father, uncle and two cousins at their greenhouse operation down the road – the brothers built a small warehouse, 50 feet by 50 feet, and then started erecting 25,000 square feet of greenhouses which they had purchased, leaving only the electrical work to be done by tradesmen. They needed boilers, benches and a host of other equipment and tools, as well as poinsettia cuttings to start their first crop. Finally, in August, the production could get under way.

"I had been around greenhouses all my life, but a lot of the work we got into was new to me," says Paul, born in 1956, seven years before Rick arrived. "So much of it was self-taught. Rick probably knew as much as I did because at A. Koornneef and Sons Ltd. the main crops were cut flowers and here we used pots and soilless mix and tried totally different crops."

In the first two years, there were some discouraging moments. Rick recalls dumping a fair number of Easter lilies because not enough buyers could be found.

"It hurt. We had paid a dollar for each bulb and had spent so much of our time making sure that the plants were nice. Well, we decided to grow the same amount the next year. By that time, we had more contacts. And we did very well."

In time, Hillside Growers became a vibrant wholesale concern. Its facilities were enlarged in stages to keep pace with the increased production of a variety of potted plants, foliage baskets, hanging baskets, geraniums and other products. The greenhouse area now totals 120,000 square feet, a size that suits Rick fine.

Asked if more expansion is around the corner, he chuckles: "We'll see if our kids are interested in joining us in our business. If so, we'll take it from there."

— A gorgeous sight at Hillside Growers Inc.

IT'S HARD TO STOP

Nick VanGeest took a big leap in 1951 when he emigrated to Canada as an 18-year-old because he wanted to "do a little pioneering."

Nearly 25 years later, he took an even bigger jump, abandoning a long-time career in trucking to become a greenhouse grower.

"The first two years were difficult," he recalls. "We had to learn a lot about the business. But we got better at it with more experience. We've been here over 25 years now, so we must have done a few things right."

With close to 200,000 square feet of greenhouse area, his company, Gregory Greenhouses Inc. in St. Catharines, is a significant component of Niagara's flower industry. It has a weekly program for potted mums and seasonal ones for bedding plants and holiday crops. In addition, it grows 300,000 hydrangeas a year, one of the largest outputs of this product in the Peninsula.

— Nick VanGeest: "I wouldn't know what to do with myself if they told me tomorrow morning not to bother coming in."

The company also has a wholesale arm, Gregory Floral, which was set up after Nick ended his association with Flora Pack, a similar wholesale firm with which he had been involved since its beginning. Products are bought from other growers, mixed with the Gregory material and then sold across the border. The shipping is done with Gregory's four trucks and hired vehicles.

Nick wasn't a total stranger to greenhouse work when he landed in Canada. His father, Peter, ran a small greenhouse operation in Maasland, the Netherlands, and that's where he worked until he was bitten by the pioneering bug. He stayed on a farm in Tweed for a year, carrying out a commitment to his sponsor, and from there made his way to Niagara. He worked at a few different jobs and became involved in welding before buying a dump truck in 1954.

'We've been here over 25 years now, so we must have done a few things right.'

"I had done a bit of trucking in Holland and enjoyed it," he says. "So it was a natural thing for me to get into. I worked out of St. Catharines under the name of Nick's Hauling. Well, the business grew. We got involved in hauling lumber, concrete blocks and different things and eventually had 18 trucks on the road. The name was later changed to Peninsula Equipment Leasing."

As an investment and insurance for the future, Nick purchased a 12-acre farm on Gregory Road. Since the trucking industry had become very competitive, he thought that perhaps he could start a greenhouse operation someday. That day came closer when he met a visitor from Holland who wanted to get into the growing business here.

"I went to Holland to see him and talk about a partnership. In six months, I had greenhouses brought from Holland and he came here to run them. That was in 1975. I was still working in the city. After a year, he decided that he didn't like this part of the country and wanted to move to the States, which he did. So we had to carry on ourselves. Fortunately, I found a person who could run the place for awhile. My son, Fred, was just out of high school and he

— Robert VanGeest checks over hydrangeas growing at Gregory Greenhouses Inc. in St. Catharines.

came on board. I tried to free myself from the trucking business so that I could join too. When the trucks were sold, mostly to the drivers, I became a full-time grower."

The Gregory operation, with 65,000 square feet of greenhouses, initially grew potted mums for Easter, cucumbers and tomatoes after that and then poinsettias in the fall. As the years went on, production increased. Robert, the second son of Nick and Dutch-born Wilhelmina – they had married in 1959 – joined the staff. So did Mike, the husband of their daughter, Joanne.

"Fred and Rob are the main persons in the business now, but I still like to keep an eye on things," says Nick, now in his early 70s. "It's hard to stop after having done this work for so many years. I wouldn't know what to do with myself if they told me tomorrow morning not to bother coming in."

— *This riot of colour at Gregory Greenhouses was captured by our photographer through a fish-eye lens.*

IT BEGAN WITH COWS

John Pieterse isn't trying to kid anyone when he says that his greenhouse business on Highway 3 near Wainfleet grew out of a dairy farm.

"It's true," he laughs. "We had cows here once."

His interesting story begins in 1951 when his parents, Walter and Agetha, emigrated from the Dutch village of Noorden, not far from Aalsmeer. His father, a market gardener, had found Canada alluring because his two younger brothers, John and Art, were there already and he knew about the spaciousness and the opportunities.

'It's been interesting around here ever since my father started milking cows.'

After his arrival, Walter began work for a florist in Oshawa. But the pay wasn't much, so he applied for a job at General Motors and was hired. In 1957, he and his family moved to the Wainfleet area.

"He had bought a 100-acre dairy farm," says John, born in 1952. "He had never milked a cow before, so he had to learn quickly. The idea was to sell off the cows right away and start growing vegetables. But that didn't materialize and he had to milk for five years. When he finally got rid of the cows, he did some market garden stuff – tomatoes, cucumbers and strawberries."

— John Pieterse and his son, Sean, with some of their beautiful flowers.

— Gloxinias are one of the main products of Pieterse Greenhouses Ltd.

This pursuit led to the construction in 1963 of 12,000 square feet of greenhouses for growing hothouse tomatoes. These were sold to wholesalers in St. Catharines and later to Bayshore in Burlington. In the spring, the outdoor production of vegetables resumed. The remaining acreage was rented out. While Dad was kept busy on the farm year-round, Mom worked as a nurse in Port Colborne and Welland. Besides John, they had two daughters.

"My father grew vegetables until 1972, the year I came back," says John, now the owner of the business, Pieterse Greenhouses Ltd. "I had lasted one year at the University of Western Ontario in London. Well, I entered into a partnership and started making a few changes. I had heard that the Farm Credit Corporation was offering financing, especially for younger people. Our greenhouses were not in good shape, so I applied for a loan. When it was approved, we built 20,000 square feet with a new boiler system and also expanded the stuff outside to 20 acres."

Flowers made an appearance in the greenhouses in 1976. Begonias and gloxinias were grown successfully and then marketed at the auction in Mississauga and to a few wholesalers. It took three years before the switch to flowers was completed. Outside vegetable production also came to an end.

The ensuing years at the Pieterse operation have been marked by substantial growth. With the purchase of an adjacent property, the farm has doubled in size. Neighbours look after the cash crops – corn, soybeans and wheat – that are grown on most of the 200 acres. The greenhouses now total 90,000 square feet. The production of begonias and gloxinias, still the main crops, amounts to 600,000 pots of different sizes annually.

"It's been interesting around here ever since my father started milking cows," says John, who bought his parents' share of the business in 1984, the year he and Jeannette were married. They have four children. "I'm sure there will be more to add to our story in the years ahead."

HE STUCK WITH IT

Intent on becoming a greenhouse flower producer, construction contractor Les Van Egmond of St. Anns wasn't dissuaded when his mother told him: "Do you know what you're getting into? You're just buying yourself work."

In the 1970s, he had gone a few times to Rijnsburg, his birthplace in the Netherlands, and observed how many of its residents, including his relatives, were involved in flower growing. As a result, the thought of doing the same in Niagara remained in the back of his mind.

'Then he said: 'That's it.' He sold the construction company and stayed with the greenhouse business and developed it even bigger.'

He decided one day to go ahead, despite the misgivings of others, and built a 20,000-square-foot greenhouse on his eight-acre property, then the headquarters for Les Van Egmond Construction Ltd., a fair-sized firm. He started with carnations and followed with poinsettias and bedding plants.

"He stuck with it and soon built another 20,000 square feet," says his son, Harry, now President of the greenhouse business, Les Van Egmond and Sons Wholesale Florist Ltd. "In the meantime, he kept busy in construction and also did some flying as a hobby. But it all became too much for him and he suffered a bad heart attack. Then he said: 'That's it.' He sold the construction company and stayed with the greenhouse business and developed it even bigger."

Annette was the first of the six children of Les and his wife, Ann, to join the staff. She looked after the cut flower end and remained in the business until she was needed to look after her own growing family. Jerry stayed a few years and then left to start his own business, building greenhouse structures. Harry became a full-time worker when he was 15 and Peter came on after finishing high school. Both are operating the business today. The other children, Leslie and Gordon, spent a few years with the firm and left to find employment elsewhere in the greenhouse industry.

The grandparents, Henk and Anna, emigrated in 1952

from Rijnsburg where they had been in the soil business. They and their children, including Les, arrived in Hamilton and later moved to Fenwick where a job was available at Prudhomme's. Grandpa later started buying and selling manure and also dealt in sand and gravel with a business called Van Egmond Haulage.

Les did some hauling too, then went into landscaping and next formed a construction company in partnership with his younger brother, Andrew. The firm was a contractor for Bell Canada, Ontario Hydro, CN Rail and others. Les later went on his own in construction, operating the business from his property on Regional Road 69.

The greenhouse pursuit that he founded has grown to 155,000 square feet and six full-time employees. At certain times of the year, additional growing space is rented and seasonal staff is hired. The products include poinsettias, hydrangeas, lilies, bedding plants, geraniums, hanging baskets and impatiens cuttings. Ninety per cent of the output is sold directly by the firm to customers throughout Ontario and in parts of the U.S. For delivery, there are two tractor-trailers and two smaller trucks.

Two big fires have struck the place since its inception. The first one, in March, 1985, was of unknown origin and caused $250,000 damage to the barn and equipment. The next one, involving a boiler, occurred in August, 1993, resulting in damage of $500,000.

— Harry and Peter Van Egmond take a break from working in their field of hydrangeas.

"A safety valve malfunctioned and the boiler exploded," says Harry. "A guy came into our driveway around suppertime and yelled: 'Your barn's on fire!' Fortunately, no one was injured. Now we have alarms all over the place. But we're hoping that we'll never have another fire."

— A boiler-related fire struck the Van Egmond firm in August, 1993, causing damage of $500,000.

It was winter and Lawrence Schilstra was bored.

There was little work for his business, Byng Construction, based in the village of that name just south of Dunnville. All he could do was sit at home and fret and wait for the phone to ring.

"It was time to do something different," he says. "I started looking around. There was a chicken farm I liked. But then I settled on this place."

The place was a 75-acre farm with an 80,000-square-foot greenhouse operation on Highway 3 west of Wainfleet. The owner, Ben Vermeer, wanted to retire. Lawrence and his wife, Karen, bought the property in July, 1995.

'I just followed him around and learned something new every day.'

"I knew nothing about greenhouse growing," he says. "Ben agreed to stay on as consultant for two years. He had been growing snapdragons. I just followed him around and learned something new every day. Well, we're still growing snapdragons – quite successfully."

The fact that Lawrence came from a farming background helped him adjust quickly to his new environment. His parents, Jack and Tina, originally from the Sneek area in the Dutch province of Friesland, owned a dairy farm in the Dunnville area. "Basically, greenhouse growers are indoor

— Lawrence and Karen Schilstra and their children, Laura and Jeremy, among the snapdragons at Schilstar Greenhouses Ltd.

— Annie, a basset hound, keeps an eye on things.

farmers," he says. "I felt comfortable after six months."

Lawrence, born in 1958, met Karen while both worked in a fertilizer factory. They have two children, Jeremy and Laura. Besides her household duties, Karen does her share of work for the business, Schilstar Greenhouses Ltd.

"When we started, I worked side by side with the workers, planting, weeding and cutting," she says. "I didn't particularly like the work – it was hard – but it gave me a chance to learn about the basic greenhouse duties and the flowers. It also gave me a chance to get to know the girls here. We have three full-timers and hire more workers for the busy periods. I also had to learn how to do the bookkeeping. I'm now in the greenhouse one day a week. I look after the seeding."

The demand for snapdragons prompted Lawrence and Karen to expand their range by 30,000 square feet in 1998. Their flowers, produced year-round, are sold to wholesalers, including a number from the United States. The acreage not

used for greenhouse production is rented to a neighbouring cash-cropper.

"I love doing what we're doing," says Lawrence, obviously no longer affected by boredom.

Greenhouse Statistics, 2001

	Ontario	Canada
Number of greenhouses	1,120	3,235
Area in square feet:		
Glass and plastic	94,325,000	185,387,500
Glass	24,395,000	56,486,500
Plastic	69,930,000	128,901,000
Greenhouse sales, including ornamentals, plants and vegetables		
	$1,000,326,000	$1,855,983,450

Source: Statistics Canada

GREENHOUSE FEVER

Pete Van Berkel couldn't see himself climbing ladders until his retirement at age 65.

So, in 1996, after more than 20 years of running his siding and window business in St. Catharines, he returned full-time to his first occupation: greenhouse work.

"My business was good for me," he says, "but I guess I always had that greenhouse fever. It was in my blood. I couldn't get it out of my system."

He had worked for his father, John, who owned a greenhouse operation on the lakeshore near Beamsville, growing mostly cut chrysanthemums. When this place was sold in the early 1970s, he was out of a job. It was then that he set up his business, Pete's Siding and Windows, and began going up and down ladders.

'On one of my yearly trips to Holland, I went through a greenhouse with orchids and thought of them as a hobby. Well, this hobby has grown a little bigger now.'

His greenhouse firm on Third Street in St. Catharines, Van Berkel Enterprises Ltd., is a thriving concern, specializing in cut lilies of the Asiatic and Oriental varieties. More than two million bulbs are planted each year, producing a weekly output of 40,000 to 50,000 flowers. In addition, the firm is well on the way to becoming a major producer of orchids. Its greenhouse area has expanded in stages from the original 30,000 square feet to the current 160,000 square feet.

Pete bought the property of nearly five acres, a peach orchard, in 1987. He rented it to someone who looked after the trees and harvested the crop. Deep in the back of his mind was a plan to eventually use it for his own purposes. In 1990, he decided to put up his first greenhouse. He did the work himself with the expert help of a buddy who held a job in greenhouse construction. In March, 1991, he planted his first crop: tomatoes.

"I got Dad to work for me while I kept the siding business going," he says. "Dad had been in trucking before that. It

worked out fine for both of us. I had a good helper."

John had come to Canada in 1949 as a single 19-year-old from Naaldwijk, in Holland's Westland district. He had first worked for a landscaper in Niagara-on-the-Lake. In 1960, when Pete was five years old, he had begun his own business with 45,000 square feet of greenhouses imported from Holland. With such a background, he naturally was tickled pink to be back in a greenhouse environment. He's still there, working only in the mornings.

As his new business expanded, Pete began to realize that holding two jobs was too demanding. In time, he left construction and became a full-time grower. His first major decision was to order lily bulbs from Holland, beginning the process of replacing the entire tomato crop with flowers. The peach soil was ideal for lilies. These are now grown year-round, thanks to a system of storing bulbs below the freezing point and thawing whatever amount is needed for a particular planting. A bulb-planting machine calculates the correct spacing and depth, ensuring the most efficient use of space.

Although he intends to stay with the lilies, Pete is directing considerable attention and resources to the production of orchids.

"On one of my yearly trips to Holland, I went through a greenhouse with orchids and thought of them as a hobby," he says. "Well, this hobby has grown a little bigger now. Our Phalaenopsis orchids occupy 30,000 square feet that were taken out of lily production and we're adding on another 50,000 square feet that will be used strictly for orchids. Our goal is to produce 200,000 to 250,000 pots per year."

Most of Pete's flowers are sold directly to brokers. Seventy-five per cent is marketed in Canada and the rest in the United States.

In his ongoing battle against high heating costs, Pete has installed energy curtains throughout his range.

"I'm convinced this is saving me a bundle – at least 40 per cent. In 2000, for example, I had 30,000 more square feet and spent less on gas. The initial outlay is a big investment but, if it pays back in two or three years, it's well worth it. I

— Pete Van Berkel with some of his orchids. He also produces lilies in his greenhouses in St. Catharines.

also use the curtain for shading."

The firm's books are kept by Pete's wife, Rita, a former employee in the finance department of the Regional Municipality of Niagara. They have three children: Michelle, a teacher; Kevin, an engineering student, and Ryan, who is interested in greenhouse work and is taking a business course at university to prepare himself for a future role.

Dad's entrepreneurship has rubbed off on his sons. At the age of 15, Kevin began growing sunflowers in unused space along the outside walls of the greenhouses. He's now earning enough to pay for his university education as well as a few extras, such as a small truck. Ryan has stepped into the sunflower business too to put himself through university. The brothers' yearly production amounts to 120,000 blooms.

"I take my hat off to these guys," says Pete, beaming with pride.

— *These closeups highlight the delicate beauty of orchids produced by Van Berkel Enterprises Ltd.*

CHAPTER TEN

KEEPING IT IN THE FAMILY

'There might have been tough times, but we pulled through them together.'

— *Cor Van Geest*

The happiest day in Ed Sobkowich's long and successful career in the greenhouse business was in 1984 when his only son, Ed Jr., announced that he would stay on board and earn a living with flowers instead of jumping to a career in the high-tech field.

"When Ed was growing up, going to high school, he was interested in electricity and electronics – computers and things like that," the father recalls. "He liked working in the greenhouses, but I wondered: 'What's he going to do?' So when he said later on that he wanted to stay here, I couldn't have been happier."

'We're in the greenhouses up to 10 hours a day, probably the same as we are in the house, so we decided to make it nice there too.'

Ed Jr. grins.

"I was leaning towards the computer field," he says. "But when I started working in the greenhouses full-time, I really enjoyed the diversity of the job. I always figured that you had to be very patient in the greenhouse business and I was one who wanted to see results quickly. As I got into the work, I learned that things do happen very quickly in a greenhouse. That brought a little more excitement. And then I found that I can use my technical knowledge and experience in electrical and electronic things almost daily. There's always something to repair or operate. So I decided to stay – and have never regretted it."

Father and son run Ed Sobkowich Greenhouses Ltd. in Grimsby, a flourishing operation known in the industry for its expertise in plug production of spring annuals and propagation of spring cuttings. It's the exclusive Canadian propagator/distributor of Kientzler New Guinea impatiens from the Paul Ecke Ranch in Encinitas, California. With the yearly production of seedlings and cuttings numbering in the tens of millions, its greenhouse area of 155,000 square feet is sometimes fondly referred to as the biggest maternity ward in the Peninsula. Of course, with Ed Jr. on board, it's fully equipped with modern devices that lend a great boost to efficiency and growing.

— Ed Sobkowich and his son, Ed Jr., at their beautifully-landscaped office area.

Ed was born in 1940 in Matachewan, in northern Ontario. His father, Walter, had come to Canada by himself from Poland in the early 1930s. He worked in a gold mine. After eight years, he had saved up enough money to pay for the overseas voyage of his wife, Sylvia, and his brother, Stan. The family moved to the Grimsby area when Ed was six months old. His father had bought a small fruit farm with pear, cherry and plum trees. As this business progressed, he acquired an additional farm where he grew mostly grapes for the fresh market and for many people in the Toronto area who made their own wine.

"As a young kid, I worked on the farm after school," says Ed. "I enjoyed it. Dad did not pay. There was no money for that. There was no allowance either. If I needed something

– nothing foolish, that is – it was there. Anything he made went back into the farm so that he could pay it off."

After completing Grade 12 and a year of special commercial study, which covered subjects such as typing, bookkeeping and business law, he began working full-time for his father. In addition to the regular chores, he bought fruit from other farmers and took this, along with his father's harvest, to the wholesale market in Toronto. This kept him busy during the warm seasons for two years.

"The winters were another story," he says. "There was no work other than trimming trees. One year I worked in a grocery store just to have something to do."

An idea then struck the bored young man: he would build a greenhouse and grow tomatoes on recently-acquired property on Maple Avenue in Grimsby. Backed with his father's signature, he obtained a loan from the Bank of Commerce, enabling him to engage Gary Hogenkamp of Holland Construction to erect an 8,000-square-foot greenhouse of steel and glass.

In 1964, two years after launching his business, Ed married Estelle, a registered nurse, and also doubled the size of his greenhouse. When his father died shortly after, he also took over the fruit acreage.

"I grew hothouse tomatoes for 12 years, but couldn't see any money in it," he says. "When I went to the market and saw that some people were also selling bedding plants, I thought: 'Why can't I do that too?' I didn't know at the time what a petunia or any other flower was. I put up some cold frames and started growing spring bedding plants from seed. Then I got into spring annuals, then into Easter lilies, then into poinsettias. When we got into the holiday crops, the tomatoes were phased right out."

As the flower production grew, so did the need for more space. A greenhouse section was added every few years to take care of this problem. These were covered with plastic, instead of glass, because it was cheaper and in vogue. Some locally-manufactured hoop houses were also added.

Whenever new technology came along, Ed took advantage of it. He acquired soil mixing machines, a seeding machine for bedding plants, energy curtains, rolling benches and so on. And, thanks largely to his son's expertise and foresight, he entered the computer age with a system that monitors programmed areas and automatically controls the climate, the watering and the lighting.

An ever-present smile and an aura of joviality show that Ed is proud of his up-to-date enterprise, its success and its reputation for producing quality plugs and cuttings for growers across the continent. The firm is involved with Proven Winners, a coveted designation given to plants selected for promotion after surviving rigorous tests. He's proud, too, of the role of his family members. His wife is Office Manager, his daughter, Debbie, looks after the financial matters and Ed Jr., with the title of Vice-President, is in charge of the day-to-day operations, along with his wife, Diane.

All this pride is reflected in the attractive appearance of the premises, particularly the newly-built office area. Everything seems spotless.

"We've always tried to do things properly, limited to the finances that were available," says Ed. "We're in the greenhouses up to 10 hours a day, probably the same as we are in the house, so we decided to make it nice there too."

There's another reason for keeping everything tidy, adding gorgeous outdoor floral pieces, landscaping the perimeter of the property and paving the driveway to eliminate dust. When Ed first went into business there, growing tomatoes, few neighbours were within sight. Now the place is abutted by residential development. With the improvements, the greenhouse operation blends in nicely.

Not all the memories are happy ones. Ed clearly recalls the day in 1973 when his new boiler exploded due to mechanical failure, resulting in fire that destroyed the boiler room and even crept into a greenhouse where tomatoes were growing.

"It happened at 8 a.m. One of the ladies living down the street saw the smoke coming out of the boiler room when she passed by on her way to pick peaches. I was at the market in Toronto. You can imagine my dismay when I got home. Our other boiler, a used one, was also damaged, but we managed to repair it and put it in operation. We had some losses, but we moved on."

They moved on the point where, already in 1984, a writer for The Grower, a farm trade publication, described the operation as "shining brightly amid all the floricultural treasures to be found in the Niagara Peninsula."

— Ed Jr.: "When I started working in the greenhouses full-time, I really enjoyed the diversity of the job."

— With greenhouses in Grimsby and St. Catharines, Cor Van Geest has plenty of work for his children, Rob, Brian, Colin, Andrea and John.

Only 19 years old and just back from a trip to Europe, John Van Geest was told in 1986: "It's all yours, John."

The young man, who wasn't even sure in his high school days that he wanted to follow a career in growing, had been put in charge of Westdale Greenhouses, then a 120,000-square-foot range on Seventh Street in St. Catharines.

"It was just before Easter," he recalls. "The coolers were loaded. I didn't know the staff, the customers, the products. I was tested – and survived."

Westdale, which has grown to a 180,000-square-foot facility that produces cut mums and alstroemeria for the wholesale market, is now looked after by John and his younger brother, Rob.

Their father, Cor, purchased the seven-acre property knowing that he would not be able to expand at his location on Kerman Avenue in Grimsby. With the two locations, he was able to keep four sons and one daughter employed in the company.

The Grimsby operation, which grows gerbera in a greenhouse area of 120,000 square feet, is run by Brian, Colin and Andrea.

The two other daughters of Cor and his wife, Barbara, are also involved in the floral industry. Sandra's husband, Mark Buys, formerly of Beamsville, is a partner in Northland Floral in Barrie. Jennifer is married to Gerard Schouwenaar, owner of Orchard Park Growers Ltd. on Gregory Road in St. Catharines.

Cor was 15 years old when his family emigrated to Canada in 1951.

His father, Cor Sr., had a successful greenhouse operation in Honselersdijk, the Netherlands, and initially had no desire to leave his parents and friends and move to another country. But the thought of his family splitting up made him take the big step.

"One of my sisters had moved to Canada in 1949, one year after her husband-to-be, Clarence Vanderhout, had moved," says Cor. "Then my brother wanted to go to Canada too. One day, my father went to an information session on Canada. Later that night, he decided to emigrate just to keep his family together, not because he wanted to. It was a big sacrifice for him to leave everything."

The family arrived in Dundas where Ben Veldhuis, Canada's Dutch-born cactus king, provided employment for Cor Sr. and his two sons. The work for Cor Sr. and Adriaan didn't last long; they were laid off. The father then got a job at Stelco in Hamilton. But it wasn't to his liking, especially the Sunday work, so he looked around for something else. One year later, he began growing gladioli in nearby Copetown. For young Cor, the work at the Veldhuis concern lasted eight years.

"Then I bought the Grimsby location with Adriaan," he says. "There were five acres and 30,000 square feet of greenhouse. It was probably the oldest greenhouse businesses in Grimsby.

We found records dating back to 1875."

Son John adds: "The greenhouse was rebuilt once or twice before my father and uncle bought it. When we were building the lunchroom, we dug up an old boiler and kept finding pieces of old greenhouses. Today it has become a modern greenhouse."

Cor and Adriaan started with tomatoes, which were in the greenhouse when they bought it, and quickly changed over to spray and commercial mums, carnations and ferns.

"Our brother-in-law, Clarence Vanderhout, started a wholesale flower operation at the same time," Cor recalls. "In the beginning, he mostly sold everything that we grew. It was a big help for all of us."

The gerbera production started in 1992.

'We look at our blessing every day and thank Him for it.'

In 1969, after 10 years of partnership, the brothers parted ways. Cor stayed on Kerman Ave while Adriaan bought property and built greenhouses on the east side of Grimsby. The new place, Park Avenue Greenhouses Ltd., is now owned by Adriaan's son, Gord.

Barbara is originally from Yorkshire, England. Her father was Dutch and her mother English. She was attending church in Fruitland, while on a visit to a cousin, when Cor first set eyes on her. They were married in England in 1964.

"There might have been tough times, but we pulled through them together," says Cor. "Overall, our family has been richly blessed by our Heavenly Father. We look at our blessing every day and thank Him for it."

— *The colourful gerbera at the Van Geest operations present a breathtaking sight. Andrea displays some of the blooms.*

A Winning Technique

When it comes to the wholesale marketing of his wide variety of potted plants, Ted VanderKaay of Garden City Growers Inc. in St. Davids is not content with doing things in traditional ways.

"We try to be a little different in bringing our products to the market," he says. "We upgrade our displays and sell them for more. This is reflected in the retail price. But the customers look upon their purchase not as an afterthought but as something of value they received for their dollar."

Clients are always looking for something different, he says, and Garden City Growers strives to meet their wishes. As the company explains in a brochure: "By offering upgraded containers, bows and picks, we can transform an ordinary African violet into an on-display gift item."

Ted is employing a technique that works well. The extra touch has contributed substantially to the rapid growth of his production and wholesale business. Sales now total $10 million a year.

He was five years old when his parents, Tony and Elizabeth, moved the family from De Lier, the Netherlands, to Niagara in 1974. His father, who had a greenhouse operation in Holland, set up a similar business here: Garden City Greenhouses Ltd. on Read Road in St. Catharines. "I was walking through flowers already in Holland, so I've been in flowers all my life," he chuckles.

Ted joined his father in 1989 after graduating from the University of Guelph with a diploma in horticulture. He

— An automated packaging line at Garden City Growers Inc. in St. Davids.

— Ted VanderKaay at a potting machine: "Our biggest concern is to cut costs."

did greenhouse work. There was plenty to do because the family then was operating two farms. In 1984, his father had purchased 50 acres of land with an existing 60,000-square-foot greenhouse on Concession 5 in St. Davids. He ended up running this place.

'We try to be a little different in bringing our products to the market.'

"My father had his views and I had mine, so we thought it would be better to operate the property in St. Davids as a separate entity," says Ted, who is single. "I purchased St. Davids when the company was split in 1998. I was now in charge of my own destiny."

Garden City Growers has grown into a large operation. It has 240,000 square feet of greenhouses for production of potted plants, mostly seasonal products. In early 2000, Ted launched a second enterprise, Maple Leaf Greenhouses, on 23rd Street in Vineland. Operated in partnership with Bernie Langendoen, this business has

170,000 square feet of greenhouse area. In addition to the combined production, which is channeled through Ted's sales department, products are purchased from 100 other growers.

"We've become a wholesale company in addition to a production one," says Ted. "Most of our sales are across the border. We have five trucks on the road all the time and also use outside carriers when warranted."

Thirty full-time workers are employed in St. Davids and another five in Vineland.

Ted maintains a close association with the original Garden City firm. His father does a lot of propagating for him and he, in turn, provides his father with warehouse space. Sometimes bulk purchases are made for both companies to effect savings.

"Our biggest concern is to cut costs," he says. "Labour is an expensive item. We already have a modern range, with robotics and so on, but we're always on the lookout for other ways to make our operation more efficient."

A LONG ROAD

Shortly after moving to Niagara-on-the-Lake in 1976, Hank and Riek Postma drove around the area to look for a place where they might start a greenhouse business. They came across a small operation on Concession 6 near Virgil and thought that something like that would be perfect.

"We told a real estate representative what we were looking for and he took us right to the place that had caught our eye," recalls Hank. "That was a surprise because there was no For Sale sign. The business was owned by Mennonites who wanted to move. We didn't hesitate in buying it."

Postma's Greenhouses Inc., a 38,000-square-foot operation that specializes in Persian violets, is now owned by their son and daughter-in-law, Hank Jr. and Annette. But it's still a part of their every-day lives. After all, they live right next to it, in a lovely house built on a lot severed from the four-acre property.

'I always wanted to go into the flower business.'

Hank has been around flowers for as long as he can remember. He was born in Nijmegen, the Netherlands, in 1932, one of seven children of parents who had "the nicest garden in the neighbourhood, with lots of vegetables and beautiful flowers, including dahlias." He likewise developed a deep passion for growing things.

"I always wanted to go into the flower business," he says. "After my horticultural schooling, I wanted to start for myself, but my parents had no money to help me out. The director of my school said the government needed foresters. But that job would require two more years in the classroom. I finished the two years of study and then worked for my uncle's brother on a farm in the province of Overijssel. While there, I seriously began to think about what to do with my life."

When a friend and his family emigrated to Canada, he made up his mind to also move out of Holland. A week before leaving in May, 1953, he got engaged to Riek. They would marry a year later.

"I was sponsored by a farmer in Aylesford, Nova Scotia, and that's where I went," he says. "We later stayed later near Kentville. From the very beginning, I was in contact with a greenhouse business, but they didn't need another worker. Then in 1956, while I was living in Port Williams, a call came and I was offered a job. I got a bedding plant business going and started a garden centre. For five years, I also looked after a rich lady's estate to make extra money. I did this every night after work and hired some people from our church to help me."

In 1964, the dean of the Nova Scotia Agricultural College in Truro became a member of Hank and Riek's congregation. He informed Hank that a carnation grower in Oxford, in the northern part of the province, was seeking a worker. Hank went after the job, seeing it as a "getaway" to Ontario where he and his wife really wanted to go. They had six children then. Their two oldest sons, six and five years old, often went with Dad to his work.

— Hank and Riek Postma maintain an attractive garden, with beautiful lilies, at their home next to greenhouse business near Virgil that is now owned by their son, Hank Jr., and his wife, Annette.

"When the time came to move to Ontario, I went first. I got a job in Brampton and then the family came over. But the job didn't work out, so I found work in Leamington. We lived there 11 years. We had a little hobby farm of 10 acres and grew peaches and asparagus. Our summer holidays were spent picking peaches."

The Postma family moved to the Peninsula after they spotted an advertisement in a church publication in which a builder who owned a large greenhouse operation asked for a grower. Hank applied and was accepted. His desire to once again have a place of his own led him to scout around for property.

The place he and Riek bought on Concession 6 had an old house and an old 18,000-square-foot greenhouse used for tomato and cucumber production. They continued with these crops and moved into flowers the next year, growing hydrangeas from cuttings. Later on, they began concentrating on bedding plants.

Hank Jr. came on board in 1981, one year after graduating from Niagara College's horticultural program.

More greenhouse space was built right away. Two years later, Hank Jr. and Annette were married. When they were expecting their first child – they now have three – Dad figured it was a good time for him to step aside.

"They were renting a small house in Virgil and needed more room with a baby on the way," he says. "So he bought the business in 1985 and we started working for him. When our new house was ready, he and Annette moved into the old one. Everything worked out perfectly."

Hank Jr. began replacing the older greenhouses which were deteriorating rapidly. The house was moved 12 years later and a new one was put in its place. The focus now is on production of Persian violets – 75,000 a year – in addition to mums, pansies, poinsettias and hanging baskets, all for the wholesale market.

"We're quite thankful of what we were able to accomplish, especially since moving to the Peninsula," says Hank. "We feel deeply that we were directed by the Lord in each step that we took."

— Hank Jr. and Annette with their children, Jason, Kristen and Eric, among the exacums at Postma's Greenhouses.

Canada's Largest Grower

If all the plants that Fernlea Flowers Ltd. supplies in a year were planted six inches apart, they would stretch across the United States 13 times.

Or if one person were to grow all these plants, he or she would need a backyard the size of 10,000 football fields or 20,000 hockey rinks.

Fernlea, with 100 acres of greenhouses in six locations, is Canada's largest producer of flowers.

The family-owned company, which ranks among the top 10 growers in North America, is headquartered near the southern Ontario town of Delhi, right in the middle of a tobacco-producing region.

It was founded in 1939 by Lloyd and Mary Veil who opened a little store in Delhi for selling the flowers they grew in their greenhouse. After the Second World War,

stores were opened in Aylmer and Tillsonburg as well. In 1948, the couple experienced a severe setback when fire destroyed their expanded facilities, including the warehouse, the boiler room and most of the greenhouses. But they rebounded and moved ahead, later adding a new display store at the Fernlea operation and retail outlets in St. Thomas, Ingersoll and Simcoe.

— Fernlea's exciting Icicle Pansies.

The company, now owned by Joe and Virginia Howe, has two other greenhouse locations in Ontario, at Campbellville and Ottawa, and three in Florida, at Tallahassee, Apopka and Stuart. It grows a wide range of annual bedding plants and hanging baskets, some two million poinsettias and other holiday specialties, a large percentage of which is sold to retailers throughout the Eastern U.S. and the U.S. Midwest.

Although it seems to have enough on its plate already, Fernlea is not content with the status quo, and continues to search the world for new trends and ideas in gardening. It has introduced Awesome Accents, a line of green foliage plants for container growing, and an exciting product called Icicle Pansies.

"The Icicle Pansies were introduced in September, 2000, after several years of research and testing," says a company spokesperson. "These were bred for fall planting in northern climates. They provide copious blooms through fall into winter, then bloom again in the spring – guaranteed."

Life appears to go on swimmingly for Colin Dodd, owner of Dodd's Greenhouses Ltd. on Concession 2 in Niagara-on-the-Lake.

He operates a neat, modern range, newly expanded and fully equipped with environmental controls, and specializes in year-round production of ivy products, including lovely topiaries. His wife, Maureen, is at his side, looking after sales, and they live in a new house on the premises.

"Yes, everything is going just fine for us," he says. "But getting to this point wasn't easy. In fact, it was a struggle at times."

Colin was born in St. Catharines in 1959 to parents who had emigrated from Gloucestershire County, England, two years earlier. His father was a draftsman. While in Grade 9, he got his first part-time job at Gregory Greenhouses in the area where he lived. A few months later, he went to Pioneer Flower Farms. And after graduating from high school, he worked full-time at Bayview Flowers. His ambition, however, was to become a cabinet maker.

"I was trying to get an apprenticeship even when I worked full-time in the greenhouses," he says. "I was finally accepted into the four-year program in 1980. But I got laid off in the first year and that was the end of that dream. I knew the greenhouse industry well, so that's where I went."

'Yes, everything is going just fine for us. But getting to this point wasn't easy.'

He began work at Vander Hoeven Greenhouses, got married and then was offered a job at yet another operation, Garden City Greenhouses, where he would stay for three years. After the first of his three children was born in 1982, he accepted a suggestion that he put up some greenhouses on the Vander Hoeven property, where he was already renting a house, and earn some extra money growing tomatoes and peppers and hopefully make a solid start on a greenhouse business of his own. He erected two hoop-style houses and planted a crop. But he quickly found out that holding two jobs was "brutal," so he built three more houses, left Garden City and started full-time on his own. The following year, he put up three more houses.

"By 1985, it was time to move," he says. "We looked for property and found this place, a rundown farm of 10 acres. We moved three of the houses over, scrapped three and sold the remaining two to Cornelis Vander Hoeven. When we finished building, we had 15,000 square feet of gutter-

— Colin and Maureen Dodd specialize in year-round production of ivy products.

connected greenhouses and eight single houses for a total of 39,500 square feet. We grew holiday crops and sold at the clock in Mississauga. We added on in 1988, 1989 and 1992. By then, we were growing cut flowers as well."

The hard work and the long hours brought misery to Colin's personal life. "I spent too much time in the business," he confesses. "I was crazy. It was just go, go all the time." His marriage broke up in 1994.

The following year, he met Maureen. "I started working part-time here," she says. "When a sales position came up, Colin hired me. Then we started dating. Two years later, we were married."

As part of her job, she started out for the wholesale market in Toronto at 2:30 a.m., driving the truck herself. Upon arrival in what she describes as "a man's world," she tried to sell her flowers.

Maureen's grandfather, Herbert Gray, an immigrant from England, was a former St. Catharines parks superintendent responsible for his community being called The Garden City. Some of Colin's ancestors also were involved in horticulture. His great-grandfather was a gardener at Hodnet Hall in England, a famous estate with prize-winning gardens, and his grandfather was a chauffeur and handyman at Abbotswood, another English estate widely known for its gorgeous gardens.

Dodd's Greenhouses began specializing in ivy in 1997 while still keeping its spring bedding plant production. Pleased with having found a niche, and filled with confidence, Colin undertook an expansion and modernization program a year later. A 30,000-square-foot facility and a loading dock were built and the rest of the place was updated.

"We put in trough benches for recirculating the water that we use for the plants," says Colin. "It's no longer wasted. One of the benefits is a 40 per cent saving in our fertilizer costs. We're quite happy with how things have turned out. We could have been left in the dust if we hadn't taken certain steps."

— Neil Van Geest grows cut mums at his Kerman Avenue Greenhouses.

similar concerns about energy costs.

"The gas prices have doubled in the last year," he says. "A major concern for us would be the volatility of gas prices and deregulation of hydro."

Like many growers, Neil and Gord have taken steps to improve their efficiency and combat to some extent the rising cost of doing business. For instance, in the winter when his fans are not in use, Gord covers them with plastic both outside and inside to lessen the escape of heat.

"We can't raise our prices because of the competition from imports, so we're looking carefully for ways to save," he says. "That's one of the benefits, if you can call it that, of the high heating costs. We're going to be in this business awhile, so we try to be efficient. So far, we're able to hold our own."

The brothers' father, Adriaan, wanted to be a bus driver when he and his family came to Canada in 1951 from Honselersdijk, in the Westland region of the Netherlands. He enjoyed driving, having transported vegetables to market for a number of growers. But his plan came to an abrupt end when he learned that bus driving lessons were on Sunday mornings, time for him to be in church. For a few months, he drove a truck for cactus grower Ben Veldhuis of Dundas. After being laid off, he jumped from job to job. When settled, he sent for his sweetheart in Holland, Jobje Hanemaayer, to join him in Canada. They were married in Hamilton in 1952.

Adriaan's greenhouse bug resurfaced and, with his younger brother, Cor, he purchased an existing business on Kerman Avenue in Grimsby. In 1969, after 10 years of partnership, he bought five acres alongside the QEW and set up his own operation. This is the place now run by Gord and his wife, Anita. Dad later also bought 10 acres on the other side of the highway, now the location of the business run by Neil and his wife, Mary-Jane.

Neil, born in 1954, remembers well how he "hated" the greenhouse work that he had to do for his father after school and on Saturday mornings. "I loved sports," he says, "but couldn't get involved because I had to work." After completing Grade 12, he held a sales job and then became a carpenter. He went back to greenhouse work for his

Neil Van Geest, owner of Kerman Avenue Greenhouses Ltd., jokes that he's in a good position to keep an eye on his younger brother, Gord, owner of Park Avenue Greenhouses Ltd.

Their cut mum businesses are on opposite sides of the Queen Elizabeth Way on the eastern outskirts of Grimsby, directly across from each other.

But Neil is deadly serious when the talk turns to problems he faces at his 60,000-square-foot operation on South Service Road, such as meeting high energy costs and finding people able and willing to fill jobs.

"People in the greenhouse business, especially the smaller ones, are burning out nowadays," he says.

Across the busy highway, on Lake Street, Gord voices

— Neil: "It was a pretty stressful life."

father after his marriage. A year later, in 1977, he bought an old operation on Kerman Avenue in Grimsby and began growing carnations. When imports started to take over this market, he switched to cut mums.

"It's a rather cheap crop to get into and it's not that difficult to grow," he says. Then he adds with a grin: "Besides, I'm good at it."

In 1987, when more space was needed, he purchased his father's property on South Service Road and relocated his business. His range has grown to 60,000 square feet and his yearly production to nearly a million stems. Mary-Jane, mother of four boys and one girl, is one of his steady workers.

'We're going to be in this business awhile, so we try to be efficient.'

For Neil, stress on the job did not originate with the alarming rise in his gas bills. He had enough bad experiences in his first year of operation to make him wonder whether he should be doing something else for a living.

— Gord Van Geest of Park Avenue Greenhouses with freshly-cut mums.

— Gord took over the business from his father in 1992.

"First there was the blizzard. The strong winds blew the tops off some of the greenhouses. Later, while work was being done on a new greenhouse, the gutter started sagging. We had to redo a lot of stuff in the spring. On top of this, one of our big customers went broke. I lost $28,000 over that. It was a pretty stressful life. I can remember lying on a greenhouse roof in a windstorm, trying to keep down the glass that was flopping. That was scary."

In the winter, he never goes away overnight just in case a severe storm should strike or his equipment should malfunction.

Gord, born in 1961, began working for his father at Park Avenue Greenhouses in 1986 and took over ownership in 1992. The original range of 44,000 square feet was expanded by 22,000 square feet in 1972. Anita, mother of three children, looks after the company's books.

Mums have been their specialty all along. Most of the product is sold in buckets with fresh water. Half of them are picked up by the customer. The rest is delivered locally, within a half-hour radius of the site. Product that goes to customers beyond the Golden Horseshoe is boxed and sent by transport.

Gord is very conscious of the environment. His soil is tested regularly. And he keeps the grass around his place short so as to eliminate a possible harbour for bugs that could enter his greenhouses.

"If you're not on top of the bugs, there could be trouble," he says.

As for his brother's jest about keeping an eye on him, he laughs: "I don't compete with him. There's enough room in the market for everyone."

As the father of four young daughters, Rick Batenburg doesn't know yet whether his family's involvement in the flower business will continue when he and his wife, Linda, decide to retire in the distant future.

All he can do is offer encouragement.

"The eldest, Nicole, is beginning to help a bit in the greenhouses, so maybe that will lead to something," he says. "It'd be nice to keep the place in the family because of all the family connections to it."

Batenburg Greenhouses Ltd., a producer of cut mums, traces its beginnings to 1969 when Rick's grandfather, Arie, a 1947 arrival from Aalsmeer, the Netherlands, moved to the Peninsula. After working on a vegetable farm in Holland Marsh, a reclaimed gardening area north of Toronto, and at a few other jobs, he bought 25 acres of land on Thirty Road above the escarpment near Beamsville and began producing apples, pears, cherries, strawberries, corn and vegetables.

'It'd be nice to keep the place in the family because of all the family connections to it.'

When Arie became too old to manage the farm, his sons took over and split it into two parts. Harry's domain was – and still is – the orchard. On his portion, John built a 25,000-square-foot greenhouse for hothouse tomatoes. Two years later, an addition was already in progress. Eventually, the greenhouse area totalled 80,000 square feet and mums for the wholesale market were the sole crop.

John retired in 1993 and put the business in the hands of his son, Rick, who had been working for him since he was 19 years old. Linda does the books and helps out in the greenhouses when things get extremely busy.

"We have to put up with problems occasionally, such as oversupply and diseases," says Rick. "And the high costs of fuel and labour cause some headaches. But I can't envision another way of life. The best part of the greenhouse business is that the family is together."

— Mum grower Rick Batenburg: "I can't envision another way of life."

IT WORKED

Isaac Van Geest Sr. of Central Greenhouses Grimsby Ltd. needed to hustle to secure clients for his geranium cuttings.

He really had no choice. It was all part of the routine of a small grower who had decided to dabble in something new.

So he left his greenhouses in Grimsby in the care of his twin sons, Peter and Isaac, and motored to the Maritimes, a region where the market presumably was not as saturated as in Ontario.

"He was gone for three weeks or so, knocking on doors in Nova Scotia and Prince Edward Island," recalls Peter. "When he got home, we could see his disappointment. He had not made one sale. We all were pretty sullen after that. But a month or so later, the phone started to ring. Some of the people he had met were placing orders. Well, you can imagine how we felt."

'We're making a good living. What more can we ask for?'

The aggressive sales approach also included exposure through advertising in trade magazines and displays at trade shows. As a result of all the efforts, the demand for Central's geranium cuttings rose 25 per cent a year. The annual production has catapulted from 2,500 cuttings in the mid-1980s to four million today. The biggest customer is Ball Seed Company, a leading wholesale horticultural distributor in the United States.

Isaac Sr. and his new wife, Corrie, emigrated in 1953 from Zwijndrecht, a town between the Dutch cities of Dordrecht and Rotterdam. His first wife, also named Corrie, had died of cancer at age 32. He worked for a number of fruit growers in the Grimsby area before buying a small chicken farm. His sold this business in 1963 and bought a five-acre fruit farm on Central Avenue, intending to set up a greenhouse operation.

"He paid $17,000 for the property and sold part of it for $10,000," says Peter. "It was probably a good deal at the time, but I wish we had it back because we're at the limit; there's no room left to expand. He started with 30,000 square feet and grew tomatoes and cucumbers. Later on, he

— Twin brothers Peter and Isaac Van Geest at work at their Central Greenhouses in Grimsby.

switched to potted mums and carnations."

Peter and Isaac, who were born in 1964, joined the business in 1983. A year or two later, the flood of imports from South America caused the family – there was also one sister, Johanna – to get out of cut flower production and search for a promising replacement. That's when geranium cuttings entered the picture.

The brothers took over control when their father retired in 1992. In addition to cuttings, they and their staff of nine full-timers and up to 20 part-timers grow poinsettias, garden mums and a variety of bedding plants in their range of 72,000 square feet. They also operate a retail garden centre at their premises in the spring and the fall.

"We're making a good living," says Peter. "What more can we ask for?"

One doesn't have to go beyond Morningside Greenhouses on Sobie Road, above the escarpment between Beamsville and Smithville, to find out to what extent the flower industry has mushroomed over the last two decades.

Jan VanderMey and his sons, Peter and John, began dabbling in Oriental and Asiatic lilies in the early 1980s, growing 15,000 in the first year. It was difficult to sell them because the varieties were still relatively unknown in the marketplace. The business now grows lilies exclusively, producing 2.5 million cuts a year, and it has no trouble selling them to wholesalers and at the flower auctions in Mississauga and Montreal.

"The industry in Niagara has seen a lot of growth and we've been part of that," says John. "And it will keep on growing as long as the exporting continues to go up. I've heard of a lot of places that are planning expansions."

His parents, Jan and Petronella, emigrated from Rijnsburg, the Netherlands, two weeks after their marriage in 1951. Dad, who had worked for a vegetable grower, had his sights set on similar work in Canada and eventual ownership of his own business. He began working for Deny de Jong, a flower grower in Beamsville, and later joined the sales staff of Staalduinen Floral Ltd., a wholesale firm. In his spare time, he worked in partnership with his brother-in-law in Beamsville, Geerlof Kralt, who had a business called Lincoln Florist.

"They started out with gladioli and then went into mums," says Peter. "My uncle grew and Dad sold. He left his

— John and Peter VanderMey grow lilies at their Morningside Greenhouses.

full-time salesman's job in 1972 after buying 33 acres to expand Lincoln Florist. He put up 21,000 square feet of greenhouses and grew tulips, irises and daffodils, as well as tomatoes in summer."

John, born in 1952, one of six children in the family, was his father's right-hand man. Peter, born in 1958, came on board in 1976 after graduating from high school. The famous blizzard struck the following year.

'The industry in Niagara has seen a lot of growth and we've been part of that.'

"Our road was blocked for half a mile with drifts six to eight feet high," recalls Peter. "Snowplows were useless. We had to hire a machine to scoop away the snow so the oil truck could get to our place. Then people got mad because we didn't clear the entire road. Well, at $150 an hour, it had already cost us plenty to get the machine as far as our driveway."

His father died on February 14, 1986, after complications from open heart surgery. John and Peter then inherited his half of the business. Morningside was formed in 1992 when they split from their uncle's sons who had taken over his half in the late 1980s. John looks after maintenance and personnel and Peter is in charge of sales and programming. Both are growers. They are assisted by 11 full-timers and a few part-timers in the year-round production of lilies in their range of 120,000 square feet.

There are families to look after too. John and Gerri have three children and Peter and Wilma have four.

"I enjoy what I do," says Peter. "The business supplies me with a decent living and I like being my own boss. And the family is always close by. I couldn't ask for anything better."

— The soil is being prepared for a planting of lily bulbs.

BATTLING RISING COSTS

— Gary Verkade produces cut mums and alstroemeria at his greenhouse operation in Grimsby.

Gary Verkade's hands are caked with dirt. His clothes also show evidence that he's been busily at work. But he's not finished yet with his chores among the cut mums growing in his greenhouses in Grimsby, so his visitors will just have to wait awhile.

Most small growers like Gary have to labour hard, with minimal help, to keep their operation going and put bread on their table. Which is why they wince when the bills come in. The rising costs of running a business, especially for heating, are making life difficult.

"I sometimes wonder if it's possible to make a living anymore," Gary says, having finally made it to his nearby house. "The costs are going up faster than what you're getting for your product. The margin is going down all the time."

Regardless, he is determined to carry on, producing two main crops, alstroemeria and cut mums, in his 50,000 square feet of greenhouse space.

"We got into alstroemeria production in the late 1980s," he says. "It was all cut mums before then. But the imports became a lot cheaper, taking business away from us. So we split up the crop."

'I sometimes wonder if it's possible to make a living anymore.'

His business, Jack Verkade Wholesale Florist, was started on a small property in another part of town in 1969 by his father, Jack, in partnership with an uncle, Simon van Spronsen. It was moved to its present 1.7-acre site on Kerman Avenue in 1970.

Jack, originally from Monster, in the Westland district of the Netherlands, met his wife, Carrie, in Canada. They have four children, including Wendy, who operates a greenhouse business in Grimsby that produces vegetables and spring bedding plants for retail sale.

Gary, born in 1963, worked in his father's greenhouses after school and during the summer when he was a teen. He saved his earnings and enrolled in the two-year agricultural course at the University of Guelph. After his studies were completed, he began taking over more and more of the work at home. He purchased the business a few years after marrying Kim in 1990. She looks after the books and their two children.

Before hurrying back to his greenhouse, Gary comments: "Although I wonder sometimes where the prohibitive price for fuel is leading us, I don't sit back and lament all the time. That gets us nowhere. So I've put new shading cloth in the greenhouse to help us save energy."

CHAPTER ELEVEN

QUALITY OF LIFE

'I would sooner give up the business than compromise what I believe in.'
— *John Broekema*

— Ben Vellekoop relaxes in his garden with his father, Leendert, and his daughter, Tina.

Flower producer Ben Vellekoop was at the top of the world.

He had built up his business, B.V. Greenhouses Ltd. in Vineland Station, from a humble beginning to 85,000 square feet of greenhouse space. He had 12 full-timers besides himself and his wife, Marleen. He was making a handsome profit. In fact, everything was going so swimmingly that his sights were set only on more production and more expansion.

Then one day, as he looked at his three young children romping about the grounds, he asked himself: "What are we doing?"

He quickly resolved to spend more time with his family and also enhance the quality of his own life instead of working in the greenhouses day and night, seldom taking time off for holidays, constantly preoccupied with matters and thoughts related to the business.

So he downsized, selling his greenhouse property next door and reducing his full-time staff to five. Now he has 30,000 square feet left in which he produces ivies, his specialized crop.

He's happier now than he ever was during the growth period. And he's still making good money.

"Bigger is not necessarily better," he says, relaxing on his comfortable patio. A hammock swings invitingly a few steps away. Nearby is a swimming pool.

"I enjoy my time off. Now I do things that I never found time for before. I just love building things – that new garage, for example."

Ben was 12 years old when he emigrated to Canada in 1974 with his parents, Leendert and Cornelia, and three siblings. His father was greenhouse grower in 's-Gravenzande, in the Westland greenhouse district of the Netherlands, initially producing only vegetables and later switching over to flowers.

"My mother had a sister here and she went for a visit. When she came back, she told my father that it's a beautiful country, with lots of room, and that he should take a look. My father went for a week, took a good look, liked what he saw and decided to emigrate."

The family lived in Grimsby for six weeks and in St. Catharines for nine months. Dad had found employment with Paul Boers Greenhouse Construction Ltd. in Vineland Station, figuring that he would stay out of greenhouses and just help to build them. But the growing end of the industry proved to be too much of a pull. He began working for Bill Snoei, who owned Bayview Flowers in Jordan Station.

At about the same time, the family moved to the Vineland area where Dad had bought four acres. He put up a few hoop houses and began growing flowers as a hobby. This developed into a full-time pursuit, producing bedding plants at the outset and later hanging baskets and poinsettias as well. After a few years, it was on to bigger

things: a farm near Beamsville with a 40,000-square-foot greenhouse.

"We bought at the wrong time," says Ben, who had started working for his father after quitting school on his 15th birthday. "That was in the early '80s when interest rates skyrocketed. For 14 months, we were stuck with a mortgage at 22 per cent. Basically, the whole family was working just to make the payments. But we got through it. It was a good thing that our first crop – tomatoes – was a super success."

At age 25 and recently married, he left the farm and went to Holland. He worked in the greenhouse trade there for nine months. Upon his return, he started erecting greenhouses for growers in Niagara – "I was extremely busy and made good money" – and even built two small hoop houses for the benefit of his wife, who also had a greenhouse background. Then he purchased his present property on Martin Road and became a grower of cut flowers, bedding plants and plugs. The demand grew steadily – and so did his greenhouse capacity. The downsizing and the new focus followed.

'I enjoy my time off. Now I do things that I never found time for before.'

Thirty per cent of the ivies Ben produces goes to the wholesale market in Toronto. National Grocers takes 25 per cent for its supermarkets. The rest is exported to the United States through Ontario Flower Growers, a subsidiary of the Mississauga-based co-operative. This sales arm was established in 1997 after Ben, then one of the co-op's directors, had convincingly promoted the merits of such a move.

Vines bearing a variety of Dutch grapes are flourishing in a hobby greenhouse on the Vellekoop property. They are the pride and joy of his father, who lives next door. To Ben, this pastime and the enjoyment it delivers are symbolic of the quality of life that he has sought to etch in his own agenda.

Smiling broadly, he says: "You've got to value life while you have it."

— *Leendert Vellekoop shows some of the grapes that he grows in his hobby greenhouse.*

— Frank Engelage is perfectly happy with his small greenhouse operation.

With only 20,000 square feet of greenhouse space on their 10-acre property near Vineland, Frank and Nelly Engelage are just small players in Niagara's flourishing flower industry.

That suits them fine.

"We are making a living," says Frank. "It's something we'll never get wealthy doing at the size we're at. But we made a choice. We decided that lifestyle is more important than income. Others have made more money and have expanded a lot in the last few years – and more power to them. This was never our intent."

By remaining small growers, he and his wife can continue to spend a great deal of quality time with their young children, David and Stephanie, and be available when called upon for volunteer duties.

"We've had the opportunity over the last 14 years to be with our children," he says. "We were home with them every day. Later, we put them on the bus and we were here when they came home. We were able to spend a lot of time with them and enjoy them. That was an important choice for us, one we don't regret at all. We are able to provide time for volunteer activities. We're involved in the school and the church. If there's a class trip to a museum, for example, we can say: 'If you need volunteers, we are free to come'."

Frank was born in Newmarket in 1960 and moved to Grimsby with his family at age 12. His father, also named Frank, managed poultry farms. He and his wife, Frieda, had emigrated from the Netherlands as children in the early 1950s. After finishing high school, their son had no idea what he wanted to do. Westbrook Greenhouses was hiring, so that's where he applied. He was handed a little hand hoe and put to work weeding roses with a man in his 70s. The co-workers built up a friendship. Naturally, Frank's future was discussed.

"This man's daughter was a nurse at the Mack School of Nursing at Niagara College and she brought me an application form for enrolment at the college," says Frank. "I entered the two-year horticultural technican program. While at school, I continued to work part-time at Westbrook. My first full-time job after graduation was at a greenhouse in Fruitland. That lasted a few months. Then I went to work for Batenburg Greenhouses near Beamsville and stayed there for eight-and-a-half years. Nelly and I were married in 1982. Six years later, we bought our property on Tintern Road – it had a house and a small greenhouse operation – and went into the business of growing flowers."

Tintern Gardens annually produces 12,500 poinsettias, 15,000 hydrangeas and 8,000 potted gerbera. Frank markets his own products. Eighty per cent of the output is sold at the Ontario Food Terminal where he rents a market stall for $800 a year. He's also developing a customer base among charities and other groups who raise funds through flower sales.

'We decided that lifestyle is more important than income.'

Frank and Nelly have experienced a few struggles since they started out on their own. One particularly low point came when they had a stillborn baby, a son, at a time when their business was going through a tough period.

"We were trying to deal with economic struggles and emotional struggles. You know, at times like that, things just become a blur. We really felt the support of our church community, friends and neighbours who stepped in and helped us out tremendously, providing support and labour. Throughout all of that, we got stronger and became more resilient. We learned that we cannot control everything that is around us and to just live with the moment and enjoy it. Well, we're still here and doing the same things."

John Broekema strongly believes he's in the greenhouse business as owner of Hunter Road Greenhouses Ltd. near Virgil because of providence, the benevolent guidance of God, and not a desire on his part to be a grower.

"When I was going to school, I worked part-time for my uncle, Tom Valstar, at his greenhouses on Scott Street in St. Catharines," he says. "I was there also when I finished school. Although I enjoyed the work, I kept on thinking: 'Is this what I want to do for the rest of my life?' "

He decided to do something else. Since photography was his hobby, he applied for a job at a company in Toronto that shot portraits in department stores. The shy 18-year-old was hired and, equipped with camera, tripod and other studio gear, began travelling from store to store in Ontario.

"I was quite successful at the job," he says. "After a time, I could even pick my stores – I chose the ones closest to home. By dealing with people all the time, I also became more outgoing. But after 10 months, I quit. I had married Joanne and didn't want to do any more travelling."

John went back to his uncle's business, only to decide once again that he didn't want to do greenhouse work for the rest of his life. He next joined a firm that installed aluminum siding on new houses. But this work came to an end when his boss decided he wanted to get into the greenhouse business, of all things. The employee contentedly began collecting unemployment insurance.

Joanne worked at Northend Gardens, a greenhouse business then located on Lake Street in St. Catharines. While picking her up one day – it was just before Easter, 1984 – John met a grower, Robert Bierhuizen, and was offered a job. He reluctantly accepted. Then things started happening quickly. Before the year was over, he and Joanne had moved to the five-acre property on Hunter Road where, with borrowed money, he had become an equal partner with Robert and two other Niagara growers, Ton Hanemaayer and Dick Vanderende. The greenhouse area then was 78,000 square feet.

The partnership changed when Robert bought out Dick and again when Ton died.

"The business was doing a little bit better and the share

— After a reluctant start, John Broekema is now enjoying his greenhouse career.

value was going up rather quickly," says John, "but I could never save enough money under the arrangement. I kept thinking: 'I'm doing the work but making it so expensive for me. It was a time of really strong prayer, of questioning what direction the Lord wanted me to take."

'We have great people working for us. You know, good people make you look good.'

In 1996, he decided to seek full ownership. His bank initially turned down a request for the needed money. He had better results when he compiled an ambitious proposal for the coming year, projecting an increase in sales of more than 20 per cent, "to show the bank that I wasn't just the guy who got his fingers dirty." He then presented an offer to Robert.

As the full owner, John didn't waste any time in launching an expansion program. New greenhouses were added and old ones were replaced. More land was bought. The operation now has 145,000 square feet for producing a variety of potted plants, mainly for the holiday seasons, as well as assorted annuals and hanging baskets. All is for the wholesale trade.

"Our focus on wholesale helps to keep me out of the greenhouse on Sundays," says John, a member of Immanuel Orthodox Reformed Church in Jordan. "And I like to be home, to watch my four children growing up. I would sooner give up the business than compromise what I believe in."

He was born in 1960 in St. Catharines. His father, John, a framer, was 18 years old when he emigrated to Canada from Sebaldeburen, a village in the Dutch province of Groningen. His mother, Henny, came with her family from De Lier. The parents have three other children, including Rob, who is one of eight full-time workers at Hunter Road.

"We have great people working for us," says John. "You know, good people make you look good. We truly enjoy what we're doing now. I see the Lord's hand more and more in all that I do."

NOBLE ORIGIN

When Jim Heida, a salesman for Vineland Feed, needed extra income to pay for the education of his six children at a Christian School, which operated without the benefit of tax support, he turned to a field that interested him greatly: greenhouse growing.

With the advice and help of his father-in-law, Louis Dam, a grower for Westbrook Greenhouses, he put up a 25,000-square-foot structure on 13th Street in Jordan Station in 1975 and began growing tomatoes. It was a part-time pursuit, providing him and his wife, Elsie, the means to give their children a schooling based on biblical principles.

'It's working out fine. Our children are enjoying the studies.'

Both had come from the Netherlands with their parents in the early 1950s – he from the province of Friesland and she from the province of Drenthe. They, like many other immigrants from that country, strongly believed that the public school system could not guarantee the wholesome curriculum that they desired.

In 1988, the business with such a noble origin was struck by fire. It started in the barn. A neighbour spotted flames shooting 50 feet into the air at 3 a.m. and immediately alerted Jim. When he got there, he found that the fire was being fed by a natural gas line. He tried desperately to turn off the supply.

In the end, the barn and all the equipment it held were destroyed. Moreover, the fire crept into the greenhouse, ruining the crops. The sight of the mess was depressing. So was the fact that insurance covered only one quarter of the loss.

But Jim and his family pulled themselves together and decided to rebuild, believing that it was more important to look at what they had left than at what they had lost. The business that rose from the ashes, with the clever name of Heida-Way Greenhouses, is now a respected concern, growing 140 potted varieties selected from the European Traditions product line. Sales have increased dramatically.

This achievement is a feather in the cap for Jim's son,

— Louis Heida and his father, Jim, at Heida-Way Greenhouses in Vineland.

Louis, who had started working full-time in the greenhouse when he was out of high school in 1987. He and his wife, Bernadine, took over the ownership after the place went back into production. In the rebuilding, it had been set up for growing tomatoes hydroponically. That went well, but the prices hit rock bottom for two successive years and no profit could be realized. Then things started happening.

"We sold the property and bought four acres with 25,000 square feet of greenhouses on Honsberger Avenue," says Louis. "We added 13,000 square feet and began growing strictly flowers – bedding plants, Easter mums and poinsettias. We also rented 50,000 square feet at a nearby location. Then we bought land on Cherry Avenue in Vineland and built an acre of greenhouses. The next year, we added 20,000 square feet."

The addition of the European varieties in 1995 proved to be an excellent move. Their popularity boosted business to such an extent that Louis had to arrange with six

greenhouse firms to grow close to 150,000 square feet of product for him. All his own production was switched to Vineland and the Honsberger property was put up for sale.

Seventy per cent of the output goes to National Grocers which services 220 stores in Ontario and Quebec. Another big customer is Terra Greenhouses in Waterdown, a retail outlet with three stores. The rest goes to the wholesale market in Toronto.

Like their parents, Louis and Bernadine are proponents of Christian education. A half-hour Bible lesson precedes regular studies for four of their five children who are taught at home by Bernadine from 8:30 a.m. to 12:30 p.m.

"It's working out fine," says Louis. "Our children are enjoying the studies. And they're learning. They know all about work too. In the summer, they spent their afternoons doing piece work in the greenhouses. Sometimes they make $8 an hour."

Chapter Twelve

Exciting Pursuits

*'I said to the boys that I never regretted for one day
that I came here to work.'*

— *Andrew Hendriks, with his wife, Helen*

"She's created a monster."

Rick Hendriks looks fondly at his mother, Helen, who reacts with a broad smile.

Yes, she says, it's true. It was her hobby that directly led the family firm, A. J. Hendriks and Sons Greenhouses Inc., to start producing tropical plant products. Since then, the business has experienced remarkable growth. And there is no letup in sight.

As a young girl in the Netherlands, Helen already grew plants in a corner of her father's greenhouse. This pastime was revived in the early 1970s when she once again claimed a small space, this time among the tomatoes growing in the Hendriks operation on the North Service Road along the QEW near Beamsville, and planted a variety of house plants. She must have looked after them professionally because one visitor after another asked: "Can we buy one?" Of course, they could.

'Before you work at my place, get an education in horticulture and work for someone else to open your horizons to different ways of doing things.'

A little business was born. Different varieties of tropical plants were put in plastic containers, an idea borrowed from the cacti operation of Ben Veldhuis in Dundas. Later on, clay pots and then wicker baskets were used. Right from the outset, the dish gardens were a big hit. They were even delivered to IGA grocery stores in the area.

"One of our first customers was Westbrook in Grimsby," recalls Andy, another son. "We used to deliver the pieces in the back of our station wagon. I remember that when we made 100 pieces in a whole week, Dad said: 'This is crazy. It's getting out of hand. If this keeps up, we've got to hire more people'."

His father, Andrew, doesn't think that way anymore. The firm that developed under his direction now has 65 full-time employees – seasonal work can swell the payroll number to 110 – producing and packaging tropical plants. Their work area consists of 180,000 square feet of

— A colourful display of novelty baskets at A. J. Hendriks and Sons Greenhouses Inc.

greenhouse space, including a 55,000-square-foot section added in 2001, and a spacious warehouse. They also process plant material from other growers in the area. The shipping is done through local and east coast distributors.

Andrew grew up in Loosduinen, a village near the Dutch city of The Hague, where his father grew vegetables, mainly tomatoes, in a greenhouse. After finishing Grade 7, he went to an agricultural school for four years. He attended classes two days a week and spent the other four days – Sunday was a day of rest – working without pay in the family operation.

His parents, John and Clazina, emigrated with their 11 children in 1951. Andrew was 15 years old at the time.

"We were designated to go to a sugarbeet farm in Alberta," he says. "But in Halifax, where we landed, we were told there had been a change and to go to St. Catharines instead to work for Schenck Farms. There was a house available for us on the property. The place grew tomatoes in the greenhouses and also had peach, cherry

and asparagus crops."

At the end of the season, there was no more work for Andrew, his father and two younger brothers. And the family could no longer remain in the house. So they scouted around and found a farmer near Niagara-on-the-Lake who offered the vacant half of a house without washroom facilities. One of the boys, employing carpentry skills learned in Holland, made a shower room out of the wooden crate in which the family's furniture pieces and other belongings had been shipped. Dad did farm labour, Andrew made doughnuts on the night shift and a few others set up pins in a bowling alley. Although the total income was meagre, it was enough to feed the many mouths.

In 1953, Dad took a big step: he bought a 12-acre farm with some fruit trees and a little greenhouse, 18 feet by 100 feet, with the sides a mere two feet high and made of concrete. He was able to make the payments with the support of sons Andrew and Nick, both of whom held factory jobs. Before the end of the year, he had erected another little greenhouse made of plastic and used it to continue growing cut mums, the crop of the previous owner. These were sold mainly to flower stores for use at funerals and weddings.

The limited market for flowers in those days and unfamiliarity with growing mums prompted Dad to switch over to tomato production. This was still the main crop in 1967 when Andrew, a partner, assumed full control. Nick, the other partner, took over a grape farm from his in-laws and left the business.

In addition to tomatoes, Andrew began growing one crop of potted mums strictly for Easter and Mother's Day. This ensured year-round production. Then along came the hobby of Helen, whom he had married in 1960, and the beginning of a venture that would steer his business in a new direction and toward a period of continuous growth.

In the ensuing years, additions were built to handle the increasing production of tropical plants. In the 1980s, sons Rick and Andy came on board after first following their father's sound advice: "Before you work at my place, get an education in horticulture and work for someone else to open your horizons to different ways of doing things." The greenhouse space then totalled 40,000 square feet.

— The Hendriks family: Rick, Andrew, Helen, Dennis, Helen Luey and Andy at their foliage and dish garden operation near Beamsville.

143

Andy is now General Manager and Rick is in charge of growing. Their father, although retired, retains the position of President. Their sister, Helen Luey, who looked after the payroll and other financial matters for many years until that task was taken over by a comptroller, is Purchaser. A brother, Dennis, works in the shipping department.

Andrew, who devotes much of his time to his hobby greenhouse at the back of his nearby residence, remembers a further piece of advice that he gave his sons when they joined him: "In the beginning, I was used to a salary from General Motors. So when I took over my Dad's farm with a junior farmer's loan on condition that I become a full-time farmer, my income was cut in half and my hours were doubled. Yet I enjoyed it more than working in the factory. I said to the boys that I never regretted for one day that I came here to work. What you earn doesn't matter as much as whether you like it."

Obviously, the boys have a profound liking for their work. As visitors are led around the premises, they enthusiastically explain all aspects of the operation.

Their mother, the creator of this "monster," couldn't be more pleased. She says: "I'm happy the boys can make a go of it."

— Delivery trucks are being loaded with finished product.

THE MINISTER'S SON

— Bert de Bolster grows kalanchoes at his greenhouse operation near Vineland.

Bert de Bolster still talks affectionately of his former boss, the late Ton Hanemaayer, after whom his greenhouse operation on 23rd Street near Vineland is named.

"When I started to work for him, he was like a father to me," he says. "He helped me along in many different ways. Whenever I had concerns, he was always there. It became a relationship where I started going to his house twice a week, in the evenings, to chit-chat and learn more about the greenhouse business."

The close personal connection developed into a business partnership as well. It continued until Ton died of cancer in 1986. And when Bert, as full owner, moved the business from its constricted location on Arthur Street in St. Catharines to its present site in 1990, he retained the name Hanemaayer Greenhouses Ltd.

"It's like a big thank-you," he says. "If it hadn't been for him, I wouldn't be where I am."

Bert's father is Rev. Henry de Bolster, a minister of the Christian Reformed Church, who is known widely for his involvement in the founding of Redeemer College in Ancaster. He was the first President of this respected Christian institution. He and his wife, Coby, have five children, including a medical doctor, a psychologist, a teacher and a dental office worker.

"I'm the farmer," says Bert, laughing heartily. He was born in Hamilton in 1955 and later moved to St. Catharines.

With a friend, he worked part-time for Ton Boekestyn at Virgil Greenhouses on Hunter Road before and after high school. He began work at 6 a.m., showered at school, attended classes and then headed for the greenhouses again.

"I always had in mind that I wanted to be self-employed and that I wanted to go into a business that had a future and where some money could be made. I enjoyed working for Mr. Boekestyn and appreciated the way he did things. He told me once: 'Here's a whole greenhouse of geraniums. Take my truck and see what you can sell. I want so much a pot and the rest is yours.' Well, my friend and I made over $600 that day. This encouraged me."

One day, while working in the greenhouses, he was approached by Ton Hanemaayer who said one of his employees was quitting and that the job was available. He accepted the offer and began full-time work after finishing school in 1974. The 32,000-square-foot greenhouse on Arthur Street produced potted mums in a weekly program.

For two winters, Bert went to night school at Niagara College in St. Catharines to increase his knowledge in horticulture. In 1976, when his foreman left to start his own greenhouse business with a partner, he became the man in charge. Then his boss, whose involvement with the Lakeshore Produce wholesale firm was growing rapidly, asked him to become a partner. The offered arrangement was simple: "You keep the place full and I'll sell it." Bert and his bride, Jane, moved into the house on the property.

The bond between the two men grew even closer as the years went on. The four children of Bert and Jane came to regard Ton and his wife, Maria, as family, calling them Opa and Oma.

'I always had in mind that I wanted to be self-employed and that I wanted to go into a business that had a future and where some money could be made.'

Under the partnership agreement, Bert became full owner of the business when Ton died. Two years later, he revived an earlier plan to relocate it to a larger property because the one on Arthur Street was landlocked, preventing expansion. He bought 13.5 acres with some greenhouses on 23rd Street, moved in 1990 and quickly launched an enlargement program. The present range totals 110,000 square feet.

Bert grows kalanchoes exclusively, producing 3,000 six-inch and 5,000 four-inch varieties every week. He buys cuttings from Costa Rica, sticks them in pots and then keeps them in lit areas for four to nine weeks, depending on size. Since 14 hours of darkness are needed for them to take bud, his greenhouses are equipped with a blackout system. Ninety per cent of the output goes to Lakeshore, the company he has continued to deal with since Hanemaayer Greenhouses became his responsibility.

"Mr. Hanemaayer's last words to me were: 'Bert, you'll be OK.' How true they turned out to be."

TOPS IN MUMS

On a summer day in 2001, workers are busily tearing down the old and putting up the new as Peter Vandermeer leads his visitors through the expanse of greenhouses near Virgil that carry his name.

"It's a big project," he says. "They're rebuilding a large section and modernizing everything with automated netlifting systems, growing lights and the like. It's an investment of around $2.5 million. That takes a lot of confidence. I don't know if I would have been able to do it. I take my hat off to them."

The reference is to Peter's son-in-law, John Van Berkel, and his daughter, Angie, his only child, in whose hands he placed ownership of Vandermeer Greenhouses Ltd. on Creek Road in Niagara-on-the-Lake upon his full retirement in 1995. Their business, with 280,000 square feet under glass, is now the largest grower of cut mums in Ontario.

'I put up 25,000 square feet of greenhouses, a barn and a house, all in the summer of 1976.'

"John came here in '78 after working for Stelco," says Peter. "While I did the selling and delivering, he began looking after the growing. This was not unfamiliar to him because his father, John Sr., also used to grow mums. The arrrangement worked out very well. John was a good grower and he was also interested in the other parts of the business. Angie looked after all the paper work. So when I started slowing down in 1990 already, they were well prepared to take over."

Peter, one of 10 children, was born in 1930 in De Lier, the Netherlands, where his father ran a store that sold wine, liquor and tobacco products. His mother's family was involved in the area's vegetable industry and this enticed him and a brother to attend horticultural school. At 19, he started his own operation on rented land by growing onions and tobacco. The following year, he bought some cold frames and grew carrots, lettuce and endive.

"The business grew from there," he recalls. "I built a greenhouse on rented land in 1951. My brother, Hans,

— Peter and Wilhelmina Vandermeer share a light moment among the mums at Vandermeer Greenhouses Ltd.

joined me two years later. By 1955, we had heated greenhouses and grew hothouse tomatoes."

His first visit to Canada was in 1968. His wife, Wilhelmina, had relatives living in Brampton and Hamilton and that's where they went for their 12½ - year wedding anniversary. After returning home, he raved about the "really nice country" they had visited. Soon they went again, and again, and again. Finally, a greenhouse grower in Grimsby said: "Peter, you can live better here than in Holland because you're always here."

That's all the encouragement Peter needed. He sold his part of the business to his brother and emigrated with his wife and daughter in 1974. He worked for a number of growers over the next two years and then decided to start his own greenhouse business again. After looking throughout the Peninsula, he bought five acres near Virgil and started building.

"I put up 25,000 square feet of greenhouses, a barn and a house, all in the summer of 1976. John, who was dating Angie, gave me a hand."

He began with growing commercial mums under contract. When this didn't work out to his satisfaction, he changed over to spray mums. His first customers were Bayview, then run by Bill Snoei, Staalduinen Floral Ltd. and J. Vaar Wholesale. Spray mums have been the specialty of Vandermeer Greenhouses ever since.

"I became a member of the auction in Mississauga, but I preferred dealing with wholesalers because with them we knew exactly what our price was going to be and could figure out our costs."

With business steadily increasing, the greenhouse area was expanded by 12,000 square feet. The growth has never stopped. Over the years, 12 more acres were purchased

— The Vandermeer firm is operated by John Van Berkel and his wife, Angie.

from neighbours. There are now 16 full-time workers, including John and Angie's three sons, Jonathan, Randy and James, all assisting in the production of millions of blooms.

"Ninety per cent of the 15 varieties of mums that we grow is sold in Ontario and Quebec," says John, taking a break from his busy routine. "Once we are in full production, we will be able to cut 15,000 bunches a week. With an average of six stems per bunch, that amounts to a lot of flowers."

He points to all the construction activity. "The boys have really helped out with this massive project," he says. "I'm very thankful that they are involved in our business and loving it as well as I do."

— Peter Vandermeer and Randy Van Berkel at a flower harvester that cuts off roots and trims leaves.

Tom Alkema has chalked up a remarkable record of achievement since he left the family business in 1989 to launch his own greenhouse operation on Read Road on the eastern outskirts of St. Catharines.

He has since set up a second operation, on the South Service Road near Beamsville, increasing his total growing area to 230,000 square feet, and has become one of the biggest growers in Canada of clematis, a perennial vine with bright-coloured flowers that is commonly trained on a trellis.

"We always did a good job with the product," says Tom, owner of Linwell Gardens Ltd., "and someone who was not happy with other producers asked us to start growing it in a big way. We started out with 10,000 square feet. By the third year, we had 30,000 square feet. And now we do 50,000 square feet."

'My faith comes first. My family is next. And then the business.'

He was 12 years old in 1952 when his parents, Hendrik and Ike, and their six children left Harlingen, a town in the Dutch province of Friesland, and sailed to their new homeland. He joined the family firm, Alkema Greenhouses, after it had been relocated to Grimsby from Burlington in 1972. A year after the death of his father, he decided to go on his own, leaving the operation in the sole care of his brother, Clarence.

He bought a property of nearly five acres on Read Road, built a 30,000-square-foot greenhouse and began growing mostly annuals and geraniums and propagating geranium cuttings and other vegetative lines. After a few years, everything was going so well that more space was needed. In 1996, a 17-acre fruit farm along the QEW was purchased and five acres of greenhouses were built.

Tom is General Manager of the St. Catharines location, used mainly for growing mother plants. But he's still very much involved in the entire operation and visits the Beamsville plant four or five times a week. The person in charge there is his eldest son, George, President of the

— Tom Alkema is joined by his son, George, and grandsons, Jacob and Jesse, during a tour of Linwell Gardens near Beamsville.

company. His other son, Neil, is grower. They and their two sisters, Andrea and Edie, all have shares in the business. Their mother, Maria, is actively involved too, responsible for handling all the confidential matters.

Linwell Gardens, which employs 35 people full-time and another 35 part-time in the spring, is a wholesale company. It handles a portion of its poinsettias and cuttings through the broker system and markets the rest itself. The clematis plants – there are more than 70 popular varieties and new releases – go to customers in an area stretching from Saskatchewan to Nova Scotia.

Visitors to the Beamsville plant are greeted by a pleasant sight: a nicely-landscaped area with large stones and a little waterfall near the main entrance.

"We always have a lot of people coming here," says Tom, "so it makes sense to have it look nice."

Obviously, he takes a lot of pride in what he has been able to accomplish in little more than a decade. But the business is not the most important thing in his life.

"My faith comes first," he says. "My family is next. And then the business. You know, there are many Christians in the greenhouse industry. They run their businesses with Christian ethics. That's the aim of our company too. The Lord has blessed us because of that."

— Part of the landscaped area near the main entrance to Linwell Gardens.

EFFICIENCIES

Henk VanLeeuwen is proud that some flower growers from the Netherlands, his former homeland, have come to his greenhouses to view the lighting and cooling systems he installed for his alstroemeria production.

"Holland is ahead in a lot of things," he says, "but we're ahead a little in some areas too."

VanLeeuwen Flower Farms Ltd. on 3rd Avenue in St. Catharines uses Ontario-manufactured generators for producing electricity for its growing lights which are needed for year-round production. The heat from the generators is stored in an underground tank and used when the temperature drops at night. Another system, also made in Ontario, makes the mist that cools the air and raises the humidity to the required levels.

'Sometimes you don't have to spend a lot of money to make things more efficient.'

Henk, who's originally from Voorhout, a village near Leiden, was experienced in greenhouse work when he and his wife, Ria, emigrated to Niagara in 1981. He had worked at a business that produced freesias at first and roses next. He had also gone on the road for a year, selling his boss's products.

He and Ria, then both in their late 20s, packed their belongings and headed for Canada, having concluded that

— The VanLeeuwen operation produces at least 40 varieties of alstroemeria.

— Henk VanLeeuwen on alstroemeria: "They're beautiful flowers and come in many colours."
On the use of bicycles: "It's a lot easier than walking."

it offered better opportunities than Holland for starting up their own business. Henk began working at Creekside Gardens Ltd. in Jordan Station. Two years later, he and Ria were on their own.

"We bought an existing business of five acres with one acre under glass," he says. "It was a cut mum operation and we continued this for two years. We had bugs in the flowers and sprayed every day, but they were hard to get rid off. The market wasn't so good either. So we tried a bit of alstroemeria. There was an opportunity because they were being imported from Holland."

In the first year, Henk and Ria had a difficult time selling their new flowers. But business improved after they joined the flower auction in Mississauga. Alstroemeria became their only product. And the demand for the delightful, multi-flowered stems grew to such a point that they had to double their greenhouse space to 80,000 square feet.

"I like growing alstroemeria," he says. "We don't need to plant often because the plants last four years. We also don't need to spray much and we don't need blackout curtains.

Besides, they're beautiful flowers and come in many colours. We grow at least 40 varieties."

The water that keeps everything growing nicely comes from three sources: the ground, the sky and 16 Mile Creek via a two-inch line that extends 1.5 miles. Even so, it's been necessary to truck in water during periods when rainfall is scarce and the water table is low.

For the first few years, Ria helped in the greenhouses. But then she had to devote her attention to her growing family. There are four sons and one daughter. Ria still does office work, keeping the books up to date and looking after the sales records, bills and paycheques for 12 to 15 workers.

These employees can make use of bicycles that are placed at various points along the long aisle between the alstroemeria plants.

"They can hop on and ride to wherever they need to be," explains Henk. "It's a lot easier than walking. And it's faster too. Sometimes you don't have to spend a lot of money to make things more efficient."

— Brothers Glenn, Bruce and Douglas Van Hoffen are all smiles as they pose among colourful snapdragons at their Maple Crest Farms near Grassie.

Broiler chickens have a special place in the hearts of brothers Glenn, Bruce and Douglas Van Hoffen, growers of snapdragons at their Maple Crest Farms on Mud Street near Grassie.

"Our father started with chickens when he bought the farm in 1969," says Douglas. "He had 35,000 of them. Later on, he also had pigs, but there was no money in them. He wanted something for his sons – there are five boys and two girls in the family – so he built some greenhouses, 18,000 square feet in total, and started growing snaps. He kept the chickens though."

John, their father, emigrated in 1952 from Ridderkerk, the Netherlands. He met his wife, Irene, in Brandon, Manitoba. They married in 1959 and moved to Ontario in 1966.

The wholesale greenhouse operation is now situated on two abutting properties and has 120,000 square feet of indoor growing area. The chicken barn is still there, set back a ways from the other buildings, and serves as temporary home for 55,000 broilers.

"We sell them to different processors," says Douglas. "They provide a good income and they're not a lot of work. Glenn looks after them on a day-to-day basis and we pitch in if he needs a hand. But most of our time is spent in the greenhouses."

'Our father started with chickens when he bought the farm in 1969.'

The brothers produce snapdragons throughout the year. Their annual output is around three million stems. This number will probably rise in the years ahead.

"Every time we say we're not going to build, we end up expanding the next year," says Douglas. "So we'll probably keep on growing."

— Little Kiersten radiates happiness.

CHAPTER THIRTEEN

THE WILL TO SUCCEED

'There was nobody around here who could help out by saying try this or try that with this specific crop. I had to figure out everything myself.'

— John Persoon

DETERMINATION

— John Persoon works among his azelea plants.

John Persoon didn't let setbacks in the early days of his operation interfere with his determination to move on and succeed.

The owner of Ultra Grow Ltd. near Grimsby provokes a few chuckles when he describes his azelea business as "an overnight success in eight or nine years." But smiles were rare, particularly in the first year, when he ran into one problem after another. He doggedly continued on, solving problems on his own, and gradually established himself as a premier azelea grower who now produces half a million of the woody house plants in various sizes annually.

"There was nobody around here who could help out by saying try this or try that with this specific crop," he says. "I had to figure out everything myself. But I always believed in the product and every year it went a little better."

'Since it takes so long to grow the plants, we are always looking at squeezing a few more plants into our space.'

John was raised in a greenhouse environment in the Netherlands. His parents grew tomatoes, cucumbers, cut mums and bedding plants in De Meern, a village near Utrecht.

"As a kid, I always had to help out," he says. "I didn't mind doing it."

He emigrated to Canada in 1976 at age 23 after completing service in the Dutch navy.

"I didn't want to continue working at my Dad's place. I wanted to see something of the world and get some different experiences. The Ontario government was encouraging greenhouse people to come over to help build up the industry here. Jobs were lined up. Well, I applied, was interviewed in The Hague and got accepted."

He worked one year for his sponsor, Waterloo Flowers in Breslau, near Kitchener, and then became a partner in a greenhouse operation near Fenwick. Ten years later, he was ready to start his own business, having purchased a 10-acre field with a little bungalow on Mountain Street. He put up 30,000 square feet of greenhouses and began azelea production.

"No one else around here was growing this product," he says. "It was was being imported from the United States. I thought this was a possibility for me to do something different."

Pots with azelea stock from Holland were placed on the ground in the greenhouses. Since the plants would take at least a year to grow, that was the best place for them. The bench space was used for cyclamen and a few other crops to provide John and his bride, Sheila, with some income in the interim. While he had his hands full with growing, trying to figure out what to do and not to do, a big problem surfaced.

"The ground was terrible – a very heavy clay. The drainage system I put in didn't help because it had been covered with the same soil. Well, the irrigation water never got down through the clay to the tiles. So everything had to be dug up and gravel had to be put in place. That was quite a chore."

In its relatively short history, Ultra Grow has developed into a modern operation of 100,000 square feet. Azelea pots now stand on concrete flood floors with built-in heating lines. With the plants soaking up moisture from the bottom, there is no need for overhead watering. The result is a cleaner greenhouse environment.

Another feature is the raised platforms that have increased the indoor growing area by 30 per cent.

"Since it takes so long to grow the plants, we are always looking at squeezing a few more plants into our space," John explains. "By growing a crop above another, we are getting optimum production out of the same square footage."

The raised plants are fed individually through tubes. The excess water runs into troughs and is collected, along with the runoff from ground level, for recirculation. This closed system prevents any fertilizer and chemical residue from entering the outside environment.

— The growing space at Ultra Grow Ltd. near Grimsby is used to full advantage.

John is continually looking for ways to make his operation more efficient. He has already fashioned a number of labour-saving devices, including a mounted lawnmower that can trim thousands of plants at even height in minutes. He has 10 full-time workers, including Sheila, who has responsibilities in sales, administration and packing. Ninety per cent of his output goes to wholesalers and most of that is sold in the U.S.

Confident that the demand for flowers will continue to increase, he is planning one more expansion. After that, in five to 10 years, he'll probably step aside and let someone younger take over. His successor, he believes, will not be spending too much time at greenhouse work. It's a trend that is already noticeable in the industry.

"The grower will be more of a businessman and environmentalist," he says. "He will be less of a grower and more of everything else."

— A kitten checks up on visitors.

Jim Meyers got hot under the collar when the bank manager to whom he had applied for a loan to build a greenhouse said he wanted to check first with a prominent grower in the Peninsula. Obviously, the banker had no idea what the people who worked in glass and plastic houses were up to.

But Jim felt belittled by the approach. "The idea of asking the grower was not in my book," he says. He promptly withdrew all his money – $17,000 – closed his account and headed for another bank. In no time, he had secured a $40,000 loan and the impetus to move ahead with an expansion.

Jim had shown that he was not to be pushed around. He was a fruit farmer, a fledgling grower and, like many others in his field, a hard-nosed businessman. With foresight, determination, savvy, help from friendly bankers and support of his family and workers, he went on to lead his business through a long period of steady growth.

Meyers Fruit Farms Inc. in Niagara-on-the-Lake is now a huge operation, grossing $5.5 million in sales annually. It consists of 200 acres of peach trees, 100 acres of grape vines for wine production and a greenhouse range of 300,000 square feet, the biggest income generator, in which poinsettias, lilies, potted mums, geraniums, New Guinea impatiens and hanging baskets are produced.

Jim was born in Veere, a small community in the Dutch province of Zeeland. He went to agricultural school, served

— Jim and Clazina Meyers at their home in Niagara-on-the-Lake.

with the Dutch army in Indonesia and then worked at a government-run experimental farm for fruit and vegetables in the Westland region. For three years, he and his financee, Clazina, waited for a house in Naaldwijk. Fed up with failure to get one – their names were on a long list – they decided to head for spacious Canada. They got married three weeks before boarding the boat. That was in 1951 when Jim was 26 years old.

'We thought the trees, the vines and the greenhouses were a good mix.'

He picked fruit for a farmer in Niagara for four summers. In the winters, he pruned grape vines and worked at the drydock on the Welland Canal in St. Catharines. Then he met an elderly fruit farmer of English background who owned a 50-acre orchard in the Niagara-on-the-Lake area. He came to like this man, a veteran of the First World War, and spent hours listening to his gripping tales of wartime adventures. The personal relationship developed into a business one and he and Clazina moved to the farm on Irvine Road in the spring of 1955.

"I sharecropped with him for a year," he says, "but that didn't work out. The machinery he had was outdated and I had to pay for the repairs. He suggested that I rent the farm for, say, a five-year period. But then he became sick and urged me to buy the property. He said I could have the 50 acres, with the house, for $40,000 with $1,000 down and interest of six per cent. I accepted."

Jim's dream had come true. He now was his own boss. But his start in ownership turned out to be inauspicious. Although his first peach crop was abundant, the hot weather caused the fruit to ripen so fast that the processing factory couldn't handle it all. His gross income was only $15,500. The second year was so wet and the peach crop of such poor quality that the gross income plunged to $7,200. To make ends meet, Jim worked in landscaping.

But he stuck with his orchards and soon experienced better times. He even built a greenhouse of about 20,000 square feet for tomato and cucumber production. When his son, Fred, was 18 years old and interested in following a career on the farm, he bought another 50 acres of

peach trees and also built more greenhouses. Other land purchases followed. The switch to flowers began in the early 1980s.

"We thought the trees, the vines and the greenhouses were a good mix," says Jim. "We still think they are a good mix."

This marriage works well in the area of labour. The farm workers, for example, can be taken away from picking peaches for a few hours to assist with certain greenhouse chores. Says Fred, now in charge of the operations: "We've had trailers parked here early in the morning. The men would come in, load them and then go back to the field."

During the busy periods, his workforce consists of 15 full-timers, as many as 50 part-timers and 33 offshore workers – Jamaican men and Mexican women – who are allowed to stay six months.

"We got involved with the offshore labour pool in 1972," says Fred. "It provides us with experienced, reliable farm help. Some of the people have been with us for 25 years. We provide transportation, housing, overalls and a pair of boots. For a long time, we could use the workers only on the farm. But the regulations have been changed and now we can use them in floriculture too."

When he and his sisters, Elly, Sharon and Helen, were in their teens, Mom and Dad made sure that they did their share of work in the business. As they grew older, the chores did not diminish. Their parents paid for their college education on condition that they spent the summer months among the flowers, peaches and grapes. Elly is the only daughter now on the payroll. Another daughter, Irene, died at age five when she was hit by a truck while walking along a road in the neighbourhood.

Clazina often helped her husband with farm and greenhouse work and also looked after the firm's bookkeeping. She's retired now. But Jim remains active, showing up for work every day.

"In peach time, I supervise the picking," he says, grinning. "I make sure the workers never run out of boxes and things like that. When I'm around, everyone's working. They call me the peach police."

154

Michael Konkle is so appreciative of his heritage that he displays the year 1796 on the sign at his greenhouses on Robinson Road near Dunnville.

"My family's been in the Peninsula a long time," he says. "It was in 1796 when my great-great-great-great-grandfather, Adam Konkle, successfully petitioned for a land grant of 200 acres in Clinton Township near what is now Beamsville. So, in effect, the business that I have now goes back to that time."

Konkle Farm and Greenhouses, with a covered growing area of 145,000 square feet, produces flowering annuals, herbs, ferns, ornamental peppers and other products, including the hanging baskets that are used by Hamilton and a few other municipalities to adorn their downtowns.

'You should never get too cocky over success.'

Michael's ancestor credited with starting it all was only one year old when his parents, from the Palatinate region in lower Germany, boarded the ship Patience in Rotterdam, the Netherlands, and sailed to Philadelphia in 1748. The family came to be identified as Pennsylvania Dutch, an English corruption of the German word Deutsch. After the American Revolution, many of the settlers in Pennsylvania who remained loyal to England began to migrate to other areas, including the Peninsula. That's where Adam, a farmer, ended up after trekking hundreds of miles through wooded territory with his wife, Mary, and several small children.

The people who migrated to what was to become Canada generally applied to become United Empire Loyalists, making them eligible to receive large land grants from the British Crown. The Konkles, proud of their new possession near the lake, became respected farmers and staunch defenders of the land. One of the sons, also named Adam, took part in the War of 1812 between the United States and Great Britain and narrowly escaped death in the Battle of Queenston Heights when a bullet tore off a tuft of his long hair and his coat collar.

When Michael was courting Mary, his future wife, they went for a stroll through a bushy tract near her home in the

— Phillip Konkle takes time out from his greenhouse work to admire the flowers at his parents' house near Dunnville.

155

general area of the original Konkle farm, now the location of two well-known greenhouse businesses, A. J. Hendriks & Sons Greenhouses Ltd. and Plant II of Westbrook Greenhouses Ltd.

"We came across a little cemetery with a few old headstones," he says. "When I saw the name Konkle, I was stunned. I didn't know much about the family history then, let alone that there was an old family burial plot. It gave me a weird feeling to stand on the spot where my ancestors used to walk. Vandals later damaged the cemetery. I had the remaining stones refurbished or repaired several years ago."

Mary's family is also linked to the early settlement and agricultural development of the area. Her mother, Beulah Freeman, was a daughter of Leo Martin, a pioneer vegetable grower with Mennonite roots. Her father, Carman, became a vegetable and flower grower a few years after the Second World War. Her brother, Tim, who took over the farm, is now the largest grower of herbs in Canada.

Michael's father, Ronald, began his working life on the family farm. When war broke out, he enlisted. He was injured in 1945 near Apeldoorn, the Netherlands, and, as a result, lost a leg in 1952. He then went to work at TRW, an auto parts manufacturer in St. Catharines.

— Young Phillip plays while his mother is busily at work in 1976.

Michael, born in 1947 and the eldest of six children of Ronald and Alice, was a member of the first graduating class of the horticultural program at Niagara College in St. Catharines.

"Mary's father got me interested in greenhouse work," he says. "I helped him with his tomatoes and really liked the work, although Mary detested it. In fact, she used to tell her family that she would never marry anyone from a greenhouse background so that she could have a normal lifestyle."

They were married in 1969.

Initially, Michael worked as landscape foreman for the University of Toronto while Mary taught elementary school teacher. Then he inherited from his grandparents a three-acre parcel on Lakeshore Road West, across from Jeffery's Greenhouses Inc. This gave him a great opportunity to launch his own greenhouse business. In 1974, he built a small greenhouse, 27 feet by 96 feet, and grew cucumbers while continuing to hold the foreman's job. He often ended up with only two hours of sleep.

When the couple moved to Niagara – Michael had become landscape foreman for the Ontario Housing Corporation in Hamilton – Mary also did double duty, running the greenhouse and looking after their little son, Phillip. They also began growing flowers for a small retail centre set up at their place. The business eventually grew to 25,000 square feet, but that was the limit because the property was landlocked. It was time to move.

"I quit my job in Hamilton in '82 and we moved to Balfour Street near Fenwick where we had bought a 23-acre property with sour cherries and pears," says Michael. "We spent a lot of money improving the orchard and also cleared some of the land for a 40,000-square-foot greenhouse for flower production. Everything looked promising, but we ended up having a difficult time. When the sour cherry market fell apart, everything we had put into the orchard was gone. We were short of money then and I started thinking: 'Do I really want to be doing this?' Then I reminded myself of how our parents and grandparents had struggled through difficulties, and what our former neighbours, the Jeffery family, had experienced, and concluded: 'I don't think we have it so bad after all.' So we resolved to keep going."

The Konkles moved to the Dunnville area in 1993. While living in town, they purchased a 73-acre farm on Robinson Road and put up a 47,000-square-foot greenhouse. In short order, they expanded their growing facilities and built a lovely house in a rustic setting beyond the greenhouse range. But all this didn't happen without another dose of distress.

"On a summer day four years ago," says Michael, "I was kayaking in Toronto – it's my favourite sport – and stayed around for a fireworks display at Ontario Place. It was quite spectacular and I was anxious to tell Mary. I called her and she told me that we had a fire at our place. She didn't give me any details. Well, there I was, trying to rush home and getting stuck in heavy traffic. You can imagine how exasperating that was."

Mary recalls: "We still lived in Dunnville then. Neighbours on Robinson Road phoned to tell me they could see flames at our place. When Phillip and I got there, there was nothing we could do. We just watched everything burn for hours. The barn with the boilers and some adjacent greenhouses were destroyed. It was horrible. I knew Michael would be devastated, so I just told him we had a fire."

Michael: "I got a shock when I saw the extent of the damage. I thought: 'Here we go again. What are we going to do now? If I'm being tested, I hope I pass the test.' My first impulse was to pack it in and do some other line of work. But then I saw how Phillip was digging in and realized that the business was his future. And I again thought of the hardships that others had gone through. So I started digging in too."

Two days after the fire – it is believed to have started behind the boilers – cleanup work was in full swing. Many people – relatives, friends and neighbours – came to lend a hand. When that task was done, the rebuilding got under way. And soon the place was back in full production.

"You should never get too cocky over success," says Michael, "because all it takes is for a hailstorm or some other calamity to come along and change things completely. But no matter how bad things get, you never have to look far to see someone in a much worse situation."

156

Beyond Beamsville

Jake Koornneef must have caused a few eyes to pop when he continued to build acre upon acre of greenhouses, heated ones at that, near the southern Florida city of Delray Beach in the 1970s.

After all, the area on the Atlantic Ocean north of Fort Lauderdale is blessed with a tropical-like climate that suits the growing of foliage plants in the outdoors just fine.

But the former Beamsville grower knew that greenhouses would give him a big advantage over other producers in the Sunshine State, offering more protection, better plants and up to one-third more production.

"The secret is turning over production, and that's what you can do in greenhouses," he told an interviewer after he had been in business for a number of years. "You can also get better utilization of space by hanging baskets overhead. I never have an empty spot. We are in a position where we can offer the customer more. How many growers in south Florida can guarantee plants for the spring?"

Jake's company, Delray Plants, Inc., began as a 14.5-acre operation that specialized in six-inch Dieffenbachia and holiday Poinsettias for the wholesale trade. These crops sold out repeatedly. Jake then became determined to make his farm a one-stop shop and continued to add different varieties to his mix. Of course, this required more and more growing space.

Delray is now a giant in its field with six locations totalling 180 acres in Palm Beach County, in which Delray Beach is located, as well as a new operation in Venus, in inland Highlands County, consisting of 250 acres in full development and an additional 600 acres for future growth.

Jake was born and raised in De Lier, the Netherlands. When his friends, Bram and Bert Boekestyn, were about to head for Canada, he decided to go too. He landed in the Niagara Peninsula in 1954.

Two years later, he and his wife, Mary, bought a farm in Beamsville and began growing tomatoes and cucumbers. Potted mums came next. So did a partnership with Ton Hanemaayer, Andy Olsthoorn and Bill Vermeer in a wholesale venture called Lakeshore Produce.

After 18 years in Beamsville, Jake and Mary moved to Lake Worth, Florida. He would devote his full attention to the foliage plant operation which the partners had set up at nearby Delray Beach. He became full owner of the business when the partnership dissolved a year later and quickly built up a reputation in the industry for aggressive production, honesty, service and quality product.

He's still at work every day, overseeing the growing of a full selection of assorted plants and hanging baskets, as well as new products such as bromeliads, orchids and anthuriums. Other members of the Koornneef family are there too – even grandchildren, some full-time and others when they're not in school – all carrying out their own responsibilities.

— Jake and Mary Koornneef.

Ed, the oldest son, has worked with his father since his teenage years. He now handles all the development, greenhouse and construction needs of the company, looks after farm maintenance and is in charge of the office computer systems. He is instrumental in developing and maintaining the efficiency of the farms. For example, he designed and built the "shine machines" placed at every loading dock.

Jake's daughter, Marian Gilde, manages the personnel and payroll department. The current workforce totals 300.

Her husband, Randy, who joined the company in 1982, is General Manager. He oversees the production at the Venus location, manages the sales department, acts as main communicator with all buying offices and is over-all facilitator of employee and customer relations. Over the years, he has played a large part in increasing and maintaining the firm's shipping facilities.

Bill, the youngest son, works in the delivery end of the local trade.

Jake once said: "The strongest will survive and the weakest will fail – the strongest should survive. My strongest point is my production. If you can grow good quality plants, you can sell them day in and day out."

No wonder he keeps on adding acres upon acres of greenhouses to the Florida landscape.

— Part of the massive greenhouse complex of Delray Plants, Inc., in Venus, Florida.

CHAPTER FOURTEEN
LABOUR OF LOVE

*'You know, it's easy to complain. But when you weigh the
good against the bad, there are a lot of things to be thankful for.'*

— Harry Van Egmond

"I wouldn't be able to run this business without the women."

Dario Grisonich's candid statement elicits appreciative smiles from the two women who are seated with him at a picnic table at his house in Jordan Station: his wife, Maria, and their daughter, Francesca.

Maria has been at his side ever since he launched his business, Grisonich Farms and Greenhouses, in 1966. Although she's not averse to getting her hands caked with soil, her major role over the years has been in sales. She's the one who gets up at 12:30 a.m. three times a week to head for the wholesale market in Toronto with a truck laden with flowers and plants.

'We each have our own expertise. Mine is growing and hers is selling. It works out fine.'

"I've been doing this since 1967," she says. "I used to drive by myself, but now I have a driver. I enjoy going to the market. I know so many people there. Two other women also go there regularly and we're often referred to as 'The Three Marias' even though I'm the only one with that name."

Dario is content to stay at home, nestled in his bed, and rise early to put in a full day's work.

"We each have our own expertise," he says. "Mine is growing and hers is selling. It works out fine."

Francesca and her brothers, Victor and Claudio, are also important members of the team, involved in growing, selling and shipping. Besides serving customers in Toronto, they market and deliver their products across the border, particularly in the area from New York City to Boston.

Dario came to Canada in 1957 from Trieste, a city in northern Italy near the Slovenian border, where his family grew fruit and vegetables. He was 22 years old, married, with two children, and possessed a green thumb, a diploma from a horticultural school and a dream to have his own business. He had made up his mind to "look for a better

— Maria Grisonich and her daughter, Francesca, at their greenhouse operation on 13th Street in Jordan Station.

country – and Canada was it."

After arriving in Beamsville, he worked at a succession of jobs: first at Prudhomme's, then at a brickyard, then in a basket factory and next at Dofasco. In 1966, he finally took a big step toward realizing his dream, buying a 13.5-acre fruit farm on 13th Street in Jordan Station. While holding a full-time job at the Ontario Paper Company, he grew peaches, apples, plums and cherries, as well as gladioli, peas, cabbage, cauliflower, onions and watermelons. Then he bought more land. When he found that he had taken on more than he could handle, he consolidated all the growing on the first property. His first greenhouse was erected two years later.

The Grisonich family moved into flower growing in a serious way in 1989. They now produce an assortment of bedding plants, cut blooms and potted products, including patio planters, as well as vegetable plants, in their range of 43,000 square feet and in their adjoining fields. As a touch of nostalgia and a source of income, they also harvest an abundance of figs from four trees and sell these at markets in Toronto and Sudbury. And they continue to be on the lookout for other ways to gain more customers.

"We're now trying wall bags with mums," says Francesca during a tour of the place. "We're quite excited about this."

MOM TAKES CREDIT

Mary Horbach was fond of reminding her sons, Don and Pete: "Look at what I've gotten you fellows into."

In the early 1970s, she convinced her husband, John, to build a small greenhouse on their farm on Concession 2 in Niagara-on-the-Lake so that she could grow her own vegetable transplants which she would sell, along with home-grown tomatoes and peppers, to local fruit markets and at the public market in Niagara Falls. Her reputation for offering quality products spread. Before long, customers were knocking on the door of her greenhouse.

John, formerly of Ukraine, and Mary, a native of Toronto, had bought their 14 acres in 1950 from relatives on her side. They harvested pears, peaches, plums, grapes and vegetables. John held a job in a foundry in St. Catharines,

and often worked in stifling heat, so switching to the outdoors was a welcome relief. His wife was at his side, especially in the busy periods.

When the flower market began to develop appreciably, the Horbachs gradually shifted their focus away from vegetables. The greenhouse became the nursery for petunias, marigolds and other annuals.

As sales grew, particularly after the business became a member of the clock auction system in Mississauga, so did the need for more indoor growing space. Expansions followed. The latest addition, in 2001, boosted the range to 105,000 square feet.

— Don Horbach with regal pelargoniums at his greenhouses on Concession 2 in Niagara-on-the-Lake.

Don and Pete, the current owners of Horbach's Greenhouses, direct most of their output, including regal pelargoniums, cyclamen and poinsettias, to the wholesale market. But retail sales are not ignored. Every May, they turn a front greenhouse section into a centre where the public can browse and buy.

Don, born in 1955, believes the good times for the flower industry will continue as long as the value of the Canadian dollar remains favourable for export to the United States.

'For us, the dollar is right, and we're happily growing flowers and selling them.'

"Although we're getting to the point where production is a little more saturated now, there's still room for growth," he says. "But if the dollar ever went way up, there could be a change. If a lot of these trucks that go across the border with flowers had to stay in Canada, the greenhouse industry could be facing big problems. But we can't really worry about that. For us, the dollar is right, and we're happily growing flowers and selling them."

— Ton Boekestyn of Trend Floral Inc. demands top quality, saying: "The product has got to sell itself." Some of his efforts are shown below.

Ton Boekestyn of Trend Floral Inc. believes it's time for Ontario's flower producers to start vigorously promoting their product.

"The babyboomers are retiring and they have money," he says at his greenhouse business on Line 8 in Niagara-on-the-Lake. "So there's an opportunity for more business. We should be out there as a group, letting everyone know about the beautiful things we grow and how these can brighten their lives and the world around them."

'We should be out there as a group, letting everyone know about the beautiful things we grow and how these can brighten their lives and the world around them.'

His dream, and the dream of most others in the industry, is to have the per-capita consumption of flowers in North America at the same level as in Europe where full vases and pots embellish living rooms year-round, not just on special occasions, and gardens are ablaze in colours.

Ton's interest in flowers began when he was a young boy growing up in De Lier, the Netherlands, where it's common to see a husband cycling home from work with a bunch of blooms on the back of his bike. He spent hours in the hobby greenhouse of his father, a furniture upholsterer, admiring the development of plants and the gorgeous blooms. He later attended horticultural school, enjoying the subjects immensely. After graduation, he started working for an exporter at an auction centre.

His personal life took a twist when he broke up with his girlfriend. He decided to go to Canada for a year to get away from it all. He had relatives living there, including his brother, Ysbrand. Well, he got hooked on Canada, acquired landed immigrant status and eventually became owner of his own business, producing assorted lilies, hydrangeas and other flowers for sale to wholesalers and at the auction in Mississauga.

After his arrival in 1987 at age 22, he worked two years for Tony VanderKaay, his second cousin, at Garden City Greenhouses in St. Catharines. Meanwhile, he did some

outdoor growing for himself and then with a partner and even built some hoophouses. In time, this became a full-time pursuit.

"We bought 10 acres in 1992 and put up a greenhouse the following year," he says. "We were in business together for awhile and then we split up and he started his own business. Things have been going great. I rented another greenhouse place, doubling the space to 110,000 square feet. I also have close to three acres for outside growing."

Ton married Jackie, a registered nurse, in 1993. They have two children, Alex and Jake. Eight full-timers and six part-timers are on staff, helping Ton maintain the quality of product he demands.

"As a company, we have to offer something what the others can't, especially with all the imports from South America," he says. "That's what keeps us in the market. The product has got to sell itself."

Floral Passion

— *A high camera angle at Trend Floral captures the brilliance of various potted blooms.*

Now that they've built up a greenhouse business that involves nearly every member of their family, Bas and Trudy Slappendel of Fenwick could easily sit back, relax and, well, continue to watch it grow.

But they're not quite ready for retirement yet.

"This work has been my life," says Bas, smiling. "You can't just walk away from it."

With his sons, Edward and James, he operates Slappendel Greenhouses Inc. on Maple Street, an 80,000-square-foot operation. In addition, he has a new 37,000-square-foot facility on Canboro Road, just east of Victoria Avenue, that is managed by his son-in-law, Tim Van Hoffen. Together they produce seasonal crops such as poinsettias, Easter lilies, bedding plants and hanging baskets, as well as hydrangeas and tropical house plants. The year-round foliage production occupies 25,000 square feet.

Bas was 10 years old when he arrived in Stoney Creek in 1951 with his parents, Willem and Cornelia, and three sisters. Dad had been in the greenhouse vegetable business with his brothers in Hazerswoude, a village in the Dutch province of Zuid Holland.

'This work has been my life. You can't just walk away from it.'

After his high school education, Bas worked at a number of greenhouses in Stoney Creek. In 1963, he married Trudy, a 1952 arrival from the Frisian town of Heerenveen. They moved to Fenwick two years later. Bas and his parents had jointly purchased a 25-acre farm there with fruit trees and a few small greenhouses in which carnations and mums were grown.

"We concentrated on the fruit for the first few years and then built more greenhouses," he says. "We sold some of our fruit at the markets in Port Colborne and Welland and later took bedding plants there too. I continued going there until a few years ago. Now we're strictly a wholesale business."

The years in Fenwick were marked by steady progress, the result of hard work by all members of the family, including daughters Kathleen and Elaine.

There was a bit of excitement in the 1970s when a steam boiler ran out of water and overheated, triggering the alarm in the middle of the night. No serious damage resulted, but nerves were frayed.

"Bas slept in the greenhouse all night for a few nights just to keep an eye on things," recalls Trudy. Her husband adds: "I didn't sleep much though."

Now all the excitement emanates from positive developments, among them the expansion of the business in 2000 to the 16-acre property on Canboro Road and the addition of modern systems such as flood floors for potted plants and a cystern under the greenhouses for collecting water.

Of course, there's also the enthusiastic involvement of the family, including daughters-in-law Jacqueline and Bernice and even some of the older grandchildren on Saturdays and during school holidays.

It's a comforting situation that someday may lead Bas and Trudy to think seriously of retirement.

— Bas and Trudy Slappendel obviously are proud of the enthusiastic involvement of their family in the operation of their business, Slappendel Greenhouses Inc.

164

— *Here are a few examples of the magnificence that can be found in the greenhouses of Bas and Trudy Slappendel.*

There's a small community near the Ontario town of Seaforth called Egmondville, named after a swashbuckling Dutchman, Col. Anthony Van Egmond, who played an instrumental role in the settlement of the vast Huron Tract in the early 1800s.

It's too bad that the name is already accounted for because it can be aptly applied, in an entirely informal way, to a cluster of greenhouses on Read Road in east St. Catharines that are owned by members of a family with the same surname.

— A Dutch touch at the Van Egmond residence.

Harry Van Egmond owns Van Egmond Inc., an 85,000-square-foot greenhouse business that produces potted mums, geraniums, violets, tulips, hyacinths and hanging baskets. Next door is Lakeview, a 90,000-square-foot concern owned by his brother, Danny, and across the road from them is Bridgeview, an 80,000-square-foot operation owned by their brother, Gerrit. All three places grow basically the same products and sell to wholesalers and at the auction in Mississauga.

Harry emigrated to Canada in 1952 after completing two years of service in the Dutch army. Twenty-one years old and single, the greenhouse worker from Rijnsburg wanted to get into the flower business in the new land. But it took him a few years to realize that goal.

"My sponsor was a dairy farmer in Moose Creek, north of Cornwall," he says. "I got $50 a month and free room and board. When I asked for a raise, he said no, so I quit even though the understanding was that I had to stay there for a year. I went to Holland Marsh and worked for 60 cents an hour for a farmer who grew onions and carrots. In the fall, after the crops were harvested, there was no more work. I ended up in St. Catharines, worked in construction for awhile and then got a job at General Motors. I made $1.30 an hour, which I thought was pretty good. But I got laid off. After that, I tried a bit of landscaping and then was hired by Alliance Paper Mill. I stayed there 12 years."

'When I asked for a raise, he said no, so I quit even though the understanding was that I had to stay there for a year.'

In 1954, he was joined in Niagara by the rest of the family: mother, father, two brothers and three sisters. With one son already in Canada and another one making noises about going, Dad, a canning factory worker, had suddenly announced one day: "Let's all go." He was 52.

Harry bought a five-acre property on Read Road in 1958 and built his first greenhouse a few years later. His wife, Henda, a 1948 arrival from Holland, looked after the crops, initially tomatoes and cucumbers, while he continued his

— Flower grower Harry Van Egmond: "We've done OK."

shift work. She also had to care for a family that would number five children.

In the meantime, his father and two brothers set up a greenhouse business on a seven-acre property next door. Since coming to Canada, the senior Van Egmond had worked on a farm in Jordan and at a ready-mix concrete firm in St. Catharines. He was no stranger to flower growing, however, having done this work as a sideline in Rijnsburg. Danny later took over his father's business and Gerrit started his own operation across the road.

"We've done OK," says Harry. His son, Gerry, is also in the business. "I was able to get a government loan for adding on to my first greenhouse. Then I quit my job at the paper mill and started working full-time here. Mind you, we've had a few headaches over the years. Our property shrunk when land was expropriated for widening of the Welland Canal, which was never done. You know, it's easy to complain. But when you weigh the good against the bad, there are a lot of things to be thankful for."

Bram Hanemaayer worries about the future of small greenhouse operations like the one he owns on Hutchinson Road near Dunnville.

"I believe some big problems are coming in regards to the economics of trying to sell our product," he says. "A banker told us once: 'The only way to survive is to make an arrangement with a large grower and start growing for him.' The small guys are already suffering. Their profit margin is shrinking all the time with the high cost of fuel and other things. How long can this go on before some start going under?"

'How long can this go on before some start going under?'

Bram and his sons, Arend and John, are continuing to do their own growing and selling. They serve an established customer base and sell whatever is left to buyers at the flower auction in Mississauga. But it's not easy for them to turn their thoughts away from what may develop down the road.

The owner of Hanemaayer Greenhouses was four years old when his parents, Arend and Antoinette, left their greenhouse business in De Lier, the Netherlands, and

— These snapdragons are flourishing at Hanemaayer Greenhouses on Hutchinson Road near Dunnville.

— Maintenance work is one of the routine tasks of small growers like Bram Hanemaayer.

emigrated with their six children to Canada in 1947. Five more children were born later. The family lived first in Blenheim and then moved to Holland Marsh, a vegetable-producing area near Bradford distinguished by its black muckland.

After working for a grower, Arend Sr. set up a greenhouse operation of his own. He began with tomatoes and ended up with roses. The business, Mid Valley Gardens, is now run by his son, Bert. Another son, Jim, was the first one in the family to move to the Dunnville area. He started a greenhouse business on Highway 3 called J and K Growers, a producer of alstroemeria and lilies. As an investment, Arend Sr. bought a 100-acre cash-crop farm on nearby Hutchinson Road. He sold it to Bram in the 1970s.

"I worked for a time at the Bick's Pickles plant in town and then put up some greenhouses," says Bram, who's married to Dini, originally from Georgetown, and has five children. "I started with gerbera and added roses. We still grow these, as well as snapdragons and stocks, in our range of 56,000 square feet."

Most of his land is rented out to a cash-cropper. But at $35 an acre, this is not a great generator of revenue. Which is one more reason why his thoughts often turn back to the days when he was living in the reclaimed swamp often referred to as the salad bowl of Ontario.

"I could never understand how I ended up here," he says. "It must have been the Lord's will. I still think Holland Marsh is the best land around."

GENDER PROBLEM

Jeltje Latour finds it's an uphill battle for her to be accepted as the owner of a greenhouse business.

"I'm often not taken seriously until I get cranky," she says in a tone of disgust. "Some people call, ask for the owner and then won't speak to me when I tell them I'm the owner. I can own a dress shop or a boutique, but not anything that's blue collar."

Jeltje bought Bosma Greenhouses on Dominion Road near Ridgeway in 1982, a year after the death of her father, its founder. For many years, it was widely known in the area for its retail garden centre. Now it's strictly a wholesale operation, growing cyclamen, begonias, hydrangeas and a variety of other plants.

"When we added a new section in the spring of 2000, we decided to change," she says. "We didn't want to invest in tables that we would need to display everything for the public. We were leaning toward wholesale anyway. Retail around here is a cut-throat business, and I can't make a living with price wars. Besides all that, it's nicer to sell by the truckload than plant by plant."

The Bosma family – Abel and Ali and their two daughters, Jeltje and Ellie – emigrated in 1950 from Heerhugowaard in the Dutch province of Noord Holland and arrived in Oakville where their sponsors lived. Abel worked as a groundskeeper while Ali cleaned houses. The next move was to Port Colborne where Abel had found work at the Maple Leaf Flour Mill near the entrance to the harbour. In the late 1950s, he purchased 50 acres on Dominion Road – the site of his future greenhouse business – and grew corn, peppers, tomatoes and other produce as a part-time pursuit. There was even a gladiolus field. In 1963, he built a house and a greenhouse on the property.

"He sold a lot of vegetables at our roadside stand, including stuff he picked up from other farmers," says Jeltje. "He also went to the market in Toronto. And he had a full-time job in maintenance at the Peace Bridge. He was a busy man. He certainly didn't have time for any cycling. He raced bikes in his younger years in Holland and even took part in the Tour de France."

'I can own a dress shop or a boutique, but not anything that's blue-collar.'

As the years went on, the focus at Bosma Greenhouses shifted to flowers. That's now Jeltje's forte. In fact, much of the former vegetable acreage lies fallow. Her son, Eric, is in charge of growing in the 30,000-square-foot range. She also has a daughter, Danielle.

"I prefer greenhouse work," she says. "The office is punishment."

— Jeltje Latour, owner of Bosma Greenhouses near Ridgeway: "I can't make a living with price wars."

BASIC STANDARD

— Daniel Emmons and his father, John, with some of the products grown at Barron's Flowers.

the Barron name, kept the shop open and used the 10,000-square-foot greenhouse exclusively for growing clematis and geraniums cuttings. These products were shipped to nurseries and retailers throughout Canada and the U.S. In 1983, the business was relocated to Hurricane Lane.

'I just want to run a good business that serves my customers well.'

"My parents didn't have room to expand in Fonthill, so they bought a larger property," says Daniel, born in 1951. "We dropped the retail and went strictly into growing. The first five years were difficult because of the debt load. Upgrading costs money. But once we got over the hump, everything was fine."

With the help of his younger sister, Reta, his parents and as many as 40 workers in the busy periods, he now chalks up impressive yearly production figures, such as 500,000 clematis plants and 250,000 geranium cuttings.

As the operator of one of Niagara's oldest flower-growing businesses, Daniel Emmons prefers to stick to the basic standard of his predecessors.

"I just want to run a good business that serves my customers well," he says. "That's my main interest. Big doesn't excite me."

Not that his place is small. Barron's Flowers, a family business, operates on a 12-acre site on Hurricane Road in Pelham and has 200,000 square feet of glass greenhouses and poly hoophouses for growing clematis, geranium cuttings and ground covers.

But the all-important emphasis on quality of product and service is what has kept the concern going ever since it was founded in Fonthill around a century ago by Charles Fisher and his son-in-law, William Barron, both experienced

nurserymen from the northeastern United States.

While working as a propagator with Jackson and Perkins of Newark, New Jersey, Charles learned the ins and outs of growing clematis. This product became the mainstay of the business in its early years, although climbing roses were also popular. Interestingly, clematis has remained the specialty of Barron's right up to the present.

As the local community grew, a retail florist shop was added to the operations. It turned out to be a sound move. The store became a popular place, offering cut flowers, plants, arrangements, bouquets, corsages and tributes. In 1938, the Barron family moved everything to a 1.5-acre site on Highway 20.

John and Elinor Emmons, greenhouse growers from Port Colborne, became the new owners in 1960. They retained

Depressed, desperate and ready to try something other than growing, George and Betty VanderMeer put their small greenhouse place up for sale in 1991. The bottom had fallen out of the tomato market and they had lost $30,000, more than what they could bear.

Now they're glad that no one came around with a firm offer for their Larkin Road Farms in Niagara-on-the-Lake and that they plodded on, eventually easing out of tomatoes and concentrating solely on bedding plants and cut mums.

"We did a lot of praying," says George. "And with the support of our families and others, including a greenhouse grower in our area, we were able to stay in business. We couldn't pay our mortgage for four months, but we paid double and caught up the following year."

He was born in 1962 in Hagersville where his parents, Bert and Clara, both postwar arrivals from the Dutch province of Friesland, lived on a farm. The family later moved to a chicken operation on the Niagara Parkway. Betty's parents, Henry and Tilly Hoekstra, who also left Friesland after the war, lived in Whitby initially and then moved to Niagara Falls. Her father, who delivered produce, had a little hobby greenhouse for his garden transplants. This was the only greenhouse connection in both families.

— George VanderMeer relaxes with his friend, Max, at Larkin Road Farms.

"When I was a teen, a friend got a part-time job in a greenhouse, and that's when I became interested in growing," says George. "I started working after school at Niagara Greenhouses and enjoyed it. In Grade 11, I had a summer job at Vandermeer Greenhouses and was offered a full-time position. I quit school and worked there three years. Then there were a few other greenhouse jobs. Both Betty and I were working at the same greenhouse business before we were married in '84."

After the wedding, George started working at Port Colborne Poultry. Then an opportunity came along for him and Betty to move into the greenhouse business. In 1987, they purchased a six-acre farm on Larkin Road with fruit trees, grapes, a house, a 26,000-square-foot greenhouse in which tomatoes and cucumbers were grown and two hoop houses for bedding plants and hanging baskets.

'We did a lot of praying. And with the support of our families and others, including a greenhouse grower in our area, we were able to stay in business.'

"I worked in the greenhouses during the day," says George, "and at night I went to my job in Port Colborne. That was exhausting. I often had no more than four hours of sleep."

When he was away in the evening, Betty went to the greenhouses as soon as her baby fell asleep. She worked among the plants for hours on end, sometimes until 11 or 12 at night, while constantly keeping a close ear to the baby monitor.

After eight months, George couldn't handle two jobs anymore, so he quit his work in Port Colborne. He still put in a long day at home, trying to minimize labour costs as much as possible, but felt much better. Betty continued to give him a hand, even after the second child was born. In fact, Jenica and Stephanie were raised in the greenhouses – well, almost – and began working for Mom and Dad in a limited way when they were only four.

— Jenica VanderMeer, shown at eight months of age, often sat in a tomato box while her mother, Betty, was packing. Betty recalls: "She could sit there for hours without complaining and occasionally eating a tomato."

The couple even expanded their facilities, buying a used greenhouse in Tillsonburg, disassembling it with the help of family members and putting it back together again on their property. When extra money was needed for improvements to the house, George got a chance to work for Frank Jonkman and Sons Ltd. of Bradford, helping to build the Butterfly Conservatory of the Niagara Parks Commission. However, the earnings went into the business because of the poor tomato prices.

Later, as a sideline, George and Betty reared hedgehogs and sold them as breeding pairs or as pets. Their basement once held 103 of the spiny critters which roll themselves into a ball for defence. The venture ended after three years because it demanded too much time during the busy periods.

The couple got over the humps – the financial loss and the later collapse of a greenhouse under the weight of snow – and developed a viable business. They took a big step in 2002, expanding their greenhouse area by 38,000 square feet for growing mums on a weekly basis.

"We're not making big bucks," says Betty. "But after 15 years, we're obviously still enjoying the work."

— George VanderMeer has decked out his motorcycle with some of the products of his greenhouse operation in Niagara-on-the-Lake.

A WONDERFUL PLACE

— Peter van Beurden of Westland Greenhouses: "To me, it's very important to do it right."

Peter van Beurden couldn't have found a better mentor when he arrived in the Niagara Peninsula in 1968 after leaving his home in Schipluiden, south of the Dutch city of Delft.

His cousin, Rita, was married to Andy Olsthoorn, one of the founders of Lakeshore Produce and a major builder of Niagara's greenhouse industry, and it was in their house in St. Catharines that he lived for five years while learning almost from scratch the elements of flower growing and marketing.

"Before I came, I didn't know anything about the flower business," he says. "My father was very musical and would have liked to make a living in music as a conductor, but that was not possible after the war. He became a mailman. I did work in cold frames for a time and was familiar with vegetables – cucumbers, lettuce and tomatoes. But flowers were entirely new to me."

Peter worked until 1976 in Andy's greenhouses on Scott Street. Then, with plenty of experience and knowledge and a desire to move up in the world, he became a junior partner with Andy in a new operation, Westland Greenhouses (Jordan) Ltd., on 15th Street in Jordan Station, abutting the Lakeshore place. In time, he became the full owner.

Westland grew into a sizable business. It now has a fully-computerized greenhouse area of 210,000 square feet, producing potted plants such as cyclamen, chrysanthemums, poinsettias and Christmas cacti, as well as assorted bedding plants. An eight-and-a-half-acre parcel of adjacent land has been acquired for future expansion.

As he talks about his business, particularly its growth, Peter acknowledges some pride in what he has accomplished since the day Andy picked him up at the Toronto airport. But he adds: "To me, it's very important to do it right. It gives me a good living, but I like doing it too."

Like on any road leading to success, there were a few bumps to endure. Peter came across the first one in January, 1977, soon after Westland had been put in production. A big blizzard roared across the Peninsula, sending glass flying, caving in structures and creating widespread panic. At Westland, the vicious wind ripped away a side wall, causing the loss of 3,000 lilies and some mums. By the next day, a repair crew had closed off the damaged section. There were also some rough years early on when the flower business was a far cry from where it's at today.

Peter, like many others, persevered and moved ahead. The climate gradually improved, due largely to new markets, better availability, increased variety and growing consumer demand, and the greenhouse people began to reap the benefits. Peter says: "I've never been sorry for one minute that I left Holland."

He had wanted to go to Canada already at age 17, but his father wouldn't let him. He served his compulsory stint in the Dutch army, worked for a few years after that and then headed for Niagara as a 23-year-old bachelor. While under Andy's wing, he was eager to learn all he could about the flower business and even took evening courses at Niagara College to grasp the basics.

Sometimes, when he was not working or studying, there were moments of loneliness. After all, he had left his parents and nine siblings behind. He also missed playing the oboe. In Holland, he had been a member of a drum band, a small orchestra, a carnival band and an army band.

But life didn't stand still and any shortcomings, real or perceived, were overcome in time. Peter met Marianne, his future wife, at a social function at the Club the Netherlands in St. Catharines. They have two sons and a daughter. Neil, the eldest, works in the business. One of Peter's sisters, Marian, emigrated in 1981 and now lives in nearby Jordan. Her husband, Aloys, is involved in the horticultural computer field. And in his spare time, Peter now sings in choirs and golfs avidly. And, yes, he has picked up the oboe again.

As he relaxes in his house, reliving memories, business is never far away. His phone rings constantly. Between calls, he reveals his admiration for Andy, his former partner, whom he describes as having been the "big motor" of Niagara's greenhouse industry, always on the lookout for more effective ways of selling flowers and plants, such as putting them in supermarkets. At Westland, Peter looked after the growing end and Andy, through his Lakeshore company, did the selling and shipping.

'I've never been sorry for one minute that I left Holland.'

He also talks with a degree of awe about all the technology that growers now have at their fingertips. From his desk in the house, at a push of a button on his computer, he can control all aspects of growing: ventilation, heating, carbon dioxide levels, shading, watering and fertilization. Alarm settings can alert him immediately to any malfunctions. All this gives him great peace of mind.

But there's one problem: despite being close to Lake Ontario, well water is virtually non-existent on his property. As a result, all of the water used throughout the greenhouses is recycled. It is collected from the roofs and stored in three cisterns for use as necessary. But when it doesn't rain for weeks and the supply runs low, water trucks have to come to the rescue.

"All in all though, this area is wonderful place to be," says Peter. "Everything is close by for the growers. If we need something repaired or whatever, there's always someone we can call. We have a great infrastructure."

CHAPTER FIFTEEN

GARDEN BEAUTIES

'We've had our ups and downs, but when we see what has been accomplished, we can only say that Canada has been good to us.'
— Peter Van Capelle Sr.

Tears glisten in Nell Vermeer's eyes as she looks back to the days in the early 1960s when she and her husband, Gerrit, struggled to put food on their table after buying a small greenhouse business in Welland.

"One year we made no money at all," she says. "So I picked some pears from our tree, sold them at the road for $18 and could finally get some groceries. We were dirt poor then. I made a dress for myself out of a curtain I had once bought for $1.98."

'I don't have to go to Florida. I have Florida right here.'

But Nell's eyes light up when she talks about the turnaround after a retail store was built in 1974 to complement the greenhouse operation and how the total business has grown and diversified to become a popular stop for floral shoppers from the Niagara Peninsula and beyond.

"I don't have to go to Florida," her late husband once said. "I have Florida right here."

— Nell Vermeer and members of her family – Cynthia, Gerry, Margaret, Karin, Stephanie, Shannon, Jessica and Gerrit – are surrounded by Yuletide beauty.

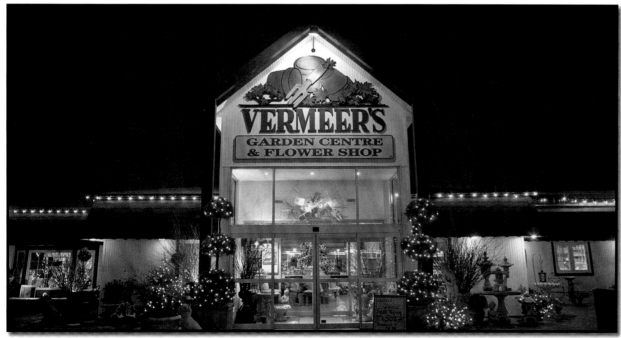

— A night-time view of the attractive Vermeer's garden centre in Welland.

He was from 's-Gravenzande and she from Honselersdijk, both in Holland's Westland region. They were married on February 14, 1952, and sailed for Canada a few weeks later, heavy-hearted over leaving behind their families – she had 11 siblings and he nine – but nonetheless eager to start a life together in the new land. They settled in St. Thomas with Gerrit's two brothers and their families.

Gerrit worked in fruit storage at the Elgin Co-operative. He next went to a factory that made Coca-Cola signs. Then he became a landscaper at the St. Thomas-Elgin General Hospital, putting in lawns and planting trees. This type of work was more to his liking because he had been brought up in a horticultural environment. After five years at the hospital, he set up his own landscaping business.

"This was a big mistake," says Nell. "The winter was so long and there was nothing to do. I did sell Christmas trees at the house. We used the profits to pay for a trip to Holland in 1958 with our two girls, Margaret and Irene. It was so nice to see the family again. For a time, we didn't know

— A touch of winter enhances Vermeer's postcard-like setting.

regularly at the greenhouses to pick up fresh potted flowers. As the business grew stronger, the couple decided to build a store in 1974. From that point, their pursuit really started to take off.

Karin and Gerry have combined as a brother-and-sister team in the ownership of Vermeer's. Dad passed away in 1999 at age 74, but Mom is still very active in the business. Sister Irene lost her life to breast cancer at age 37. Gerry, who runs the wholesale operation, grows bedding plants and various seasonal potted plants, including primulas, shamrocks, Easter lilies and poinsettias, and forces spring bulbs imported from Holland. The greenhouse area totals 55,000 square feet. Karin and Margaret manage the retail flower shop and garden centre where customers can buy

— Fall flowers can extend the enjoyment of the gardening season.

whether we wanted to go back to Canada. But we did."

Three more children – Karin, Gerry (pronounced Gary) and Lorraine – came on the scene later.

In December, 1961, the Vermeers took a big jump, buying a 3.5-acre property with an old greenhouse and a house on South Pelham Street in Welland. The former owner, Walter Emmons, had grown plants for his store in town. Gerrit started with Easter lilies, which he sold to a wholesaler, and then worked on a crop of snapdragons. His surroundings were far from ideal. He sat up many nights to keep a wary eye on his coal-fired boiler which leaked.

During this tough time, when the income barely covered the expenses, there was never any thought of giving up. Gerrit and Nell knew that there would be a brighter tomorrow and put their trust in the Lord. Their perseverance and hard work – even young Margaret shovelled coal after school – eventually began to pay dividends. A number of wholesalers took their products. Customers stopped

flowers, potted plants, nursery stock, garden accessories and a wide assortment of gift items. Vermeer's employs 15 people full-time and its staff can swell to 50 at peak periods.

"In December, 1997, we had our first preview gala evening for our annual Christmas open house," says Karin. "At that time we started our mailing list with our customer base of roughly 1,000 people. We now have well over 4,000 people on our list. That shows how busy this place has become."

— It's spring! With the help of her son, a customer checks over an alluring display.

The operators of Van Noort Florists Inc. at Four Mile Creek and Hunter Roads near Virgil like to promote one main quality to their retail customers: freshness.

"We grow most of what we sell," says Robert Van Noort, the President. "This is a great selling point. People want flowers that are fresh, especially for weddings and other special occasions, and we can certainly look after that."

In his greenhouses, which total 38,000 square feet, he produces mainly cut flowers such as gerbera, alstroemeria and Asiatic and Oriental lilies for both retail and wholesale use.

His father, Harry, purchased the business in 1961, 12 years after leaving his family's bulb-growing operation in Warmond, in western Holland. The 23-year-old headed for Canada in search of adventure and opportunities. He found plenty of the former before even setting foot in the new land.

"I went with a small freighter, the Prins Maurits, and it took 17 days to go across the ocean," he says. "We ran into a terrible storm. For four days and four nights, the captain never left the bridge."

After arriving, he went to an uncle in Markham, a resident of Canada since 1928, who owned a bulb-stock operation that shipped from coast to coast. He was put on the payroll. The uncle had lost five children in a house fire in 1942. Because of the war, none of his relatives in Holland knew about this tragedy until after peace was restored.

'People want flowers that are fresh, especially for weddings and other special occasions, and we can certainly look after that.'

After a few years in Markham, Harry met Rita, who had come to Canada from a polder near Amsterdam in 1952, and they were married in 1954. They would become parents of four children.

While on the lookout for an opportunity to start his own business in the floricultural field, Harry toured Niagara and

— Robert Van Noort works among gerbera, one of the main cut flower varieties he produces at his greenhouse business near Virgil.

came across a one-acre property with a small greenhouse whose owner wanted to retire. He bought it and began his own business, growing carnations, mums and freesias. Within two years, he had expanded. More land was purchased later.

Robert, born in 1957, graduated from The Niagara Parks School of Horticulture and then spent five years in Saskatoon, Saskatchewan, as greenhouse foreman of the city's parks and recreation department. He returned to the family business in February, 1985.

"I was going to sell the place, but Rob said he was interested," says Harry. "He bought it in 1987. So it has remained a family operation." Robert's wife, Sharon, mother of five children, looks after retail and payroll matters. Mom

is still in the office, in charge of accounting. Dad shows up when general maintenance needs attention.

Not everything has gone smoothly over the years. In 1986, a hailstorm that swept through the area shattered half the glass, causing $15,000 damage, just after the Van Noort family had cancelled their insurance because of the high cost. And in 1994, their main operating building was destroyed in a fire caused by an electrical fault in a cold-storage compressor. The loss was in excess of $200,000.

"The Mennonites in this area are just great when it comes to such situations," says Harry. "They were here in no time to offer their assistance. Greenhouse growers around here were very helpful too. We're living in a nice community, really."

He's Satisfied

For a small operation, R. Jordan Greenhouses Ltd. on Main Street West in Grimsby grows an incredible number of different flowers and plants – some 2,000 varieties, including from 600 to 700 perennials.

"This makes my work interesting," says Jeff Jordan, the owner, who looks after the production in glass and poly greenhouses totalling 31,000 square feet and an outdoor area of 50,000 square feet. Many of his products are sold to florists in the Hamilton area and at the wholesale market in Toronto. His property also has a retail centre, Jordan's Country Garden, which is open year-round.

"I don't want to grow larger," he says. "I would have to move then. I can't imagine being like some of my friends who just hold management jobs and are not involved in growing. I'm a hands-on person and like to fine-tune things."

His grandfather, Rene Jordan, founded the business in 1932, three years after emigrating from Messiers, Switzerland. As an experienced grower, having worked at a number of operations in his homeland, he first worked for a florist in Hamilton, producing potted plants. He spotted the Grimsby property, then four acres with a 4,000-square-foot greenhouse, while travelling on the electric trolley that ran along Highway 8 from Hamilton to Beamsville. He and his wife, Mildred, whom he had met in Hamilton, began growing flowers such as geraniums, African violets, cut mums and varieties of hydrangeas from Switzerland and sold these to flower shops.

> *'I can't imagine being like some of my friends who just hold management jobs and are not involved in growing.'*

Jeff's parents, Allan and Judy, took over the business in the early 1960s and continued it as strictly a wholesale operation. The retail part was developed after Jeff came on the scene as a full-time employee. He had worked at a botanical garden in Hawaii for a year after graduating from the four-year horticultural program at the University of Guelph in 1985. He's been the owner since his father retired in 1999. Dad, who also has twin daughters, is still a regular at the place.

Jeff has his hands full producing his huge variety of products, including hydrangeas, Easter lilies, geraniums, begonias, bedding plants, hanging baskets and perennials. He has other responsibilities too: he's married to Rebecca and they have a young daughter, Olivia.

He's particularly fond of his tropical house, a carryover from his Hawaiian days, featuring a banana tree and other plants. It's a display area, and sometimes also a growing area, where people can relax and enjoy and "get some idea of what the inside of a greenhouse looks like."

With aged greenhouses, limited space and many different requirements, Jeff prefers to stick to traditional growing methods that work well. But he's modern all the way when it comes to disease and pest control. For example, instead of spraying pesticides, which could be disastrous because of many different plants in one area, he releases insect-eating ladybugs and wasps.

"Biological control," he says, "is the way of the future."

— Jeff Jordan displays some of the lovely lilies he grows at his greenhouse business in Grimsby.

— Peter Van Capelle Sr. looks after 30 to 40 birds, including exotic ones, in a private aviary and enclosed pens at his house near Welland.

Having a miniature zoo at a greenhouse business is not every grower's cup of tea.

But for Peter Van Capelle Sr. of Rice Road Greenhouses in Pelham, near Welland, the mix worked fabulously until spiralling insurance costs convinced him to disperse his beloved animals to good homes in the area.

"For me, it was a hobby," he says. "It started already in Holland with chickens, rabbits and even a goat. I continued it at my garden centre, putting up one cage, then another, then another, and soon I had a petting zoo which I opened up free of charge to the public. It proved to be a great attraction and brought in many people. And that, of course, was good for my business."

At its peak in the early 1990s, his menagerie held 75 animals, including a camel named Mack, llamas, deer, monkeys, donkeys, a mule, a baboon, ferrets, seven kinds of sheep and five kinds of goats, a groundhog, a skunk and rabbits, as well as emus and a large number of tropical birds. It was a great place for children. One spring, 62 busloads of students stopped by during their end-of-the-year class outing.

The animals were tenderly cared for by Peter and a semi-retired fellow who put in 24 hours a week. To offset the costs, feed cones were sold at 50 cents apiece and eight coin-fed feed dispensers, similar to bubblegum machines, were also installed. On an average weekend, the feed sales brought in $500.

While Peter was having the time of his life, enjoying the laughter and banter of his visitors, sinister minds were at work. Vandals struck a number of times, quickly taking away the fun. Cages were damaged and some of the feed machines were ripped out even though they were emptied daily of their cash. In the darkness of night, thieves broke through plastic and grabbed a pair of talking parrots worth $1,500 each.

As if all this wasn't bad enough, Peter's insurance company raised his premium for liability insurance from $1,000 a year to $48,000. That's when he decided to give up the petting zoo and send his animals, including a pony that had lived at his place for 15 years, to the farms

— A pleasant view at Rice Road Greenhouses.

— One of Peter's exotic charges checks out a visitor.

of friends. One night in August, 1994, when he was still winding down his hobby, thieves scaled the seven-foot fence surrounding the area where his remaining animals were housed and took off with two rheas, delicate ostrich-like birds valued at $6,000.

"I felt terrible," he says. "There were feathers on both sides of the fence. The birds were probably killed on the way out."

Peter, who turned over the operation of Rice Road Greenhouses to his son, Peter Jr., in 1991, continues to look after 30 to 40 birds, including exotic ones, in a private aviary and enclosed pens at the rear of his house next to the garden centre. There's also a little pond for ducks and a coop for chickens. As a nostalgic touch, a number of tropical birds are displayed in cages throughout the garden centre.

Peter and his wife, Rita, emigrated in 1960 with their five children – two more were born in Canada – from Wateringen, a community south of The Hague. He had been a bricklayer and small contractor. Ever since his return from service as an infantryman in the Dutch East Indies, now Indonesia, where he got a taste of spacious living, he had been anxious to move away from his congested homeland.

"I ended up milking cows for our sponsor, a farmer near St. Catharines," he says. "I didn't know much about that type of work. The night before leaving Holland, I had gone to a farmer who showed me how to milk. We stayed on the farm one year, as per agreement, and then we moved to Oakville where I worked as a blocklayer for a Danish man. After three months, I was out of a job. Then we went back to St. Catharines where I was hired by General Motors. I stayed there three years."

'For me, it was a hobby. It started already in Holland with chickens, rabbits and even a goat.'

In the meantime, he acquired a five-acre property near Niagara-on-the-Lake and put up a 20,000-square-foot greenhouse for tomato production. This became a full-time pursuit, later branching into flower growing as well. But the business went downhill rapidly when he spent most of his time with his son, Christopher, who was dying of cancer in a St. Catharines hospital. Later, he decided to open a garden centre with Peter Jr.

"I bought 10 acres on Rice Road in 1976," he says. "There were 120 old apple trees on it. I rented a bulldozer, put everything in a pile and burned it. Then we built 30,000 square feet of greenhouses. We put a counter in part of a greenhouse, bought an old till for $35 and opened for business. We grew poinsettias, bedding plants and Easter lilies."

Rice Road Greenhouses, open year-round, is now one of the largest garden centres in Niagara, offering a huge selection of flowers, plants, concrete ornaments and gardening products, including different soils and gravel. Its property, expanded to 18 acres, has 70,000 square feet of greenhouse area. There are nine full-time workers and as many as 45 seasonal ones in the spring.

The business once had three trucks for delivering products to 140 florists. When Peter Jr. took over, the wholesale arm was abandoned and all efforts were directed to the retail side. His brother, Johnny, also worked for the concern initially but left to start a trucking firm and become owner of a hay farm. Another brother, Gerry, is a contractor in Bracebridge.

"We've had our ups and downs," says their father, "but when we see what has been accomplished, we can only say that Canada has been good to us."

— The founder of Rice Road Greenhouses says hello to some of his birds.

Paul and Pam Bongers are resolutely pursuing a long-term goal: to be the owners of the largest garden centre in the Niagara Peninsula.

They've already made giant strides toward that end, turning The Country Basket Garden Centre on Lundy's Lane in Niagara Falls into a flourishing and expanding enterprise that resembles a beehive in springtime with customers swarming in and out.

"There are a few centres ahead of us," says Pam, who looks after the retail sales. "But we're growing every year. It will happen."

'People like dealing with the actual grower to get advice on how to correct problems.'

The business was founded in the early 1970s by her husband's parents, Harry and Mary. They had come to Canada in the 1950s from separate villages in the Dutch province of Noord Brabant – he from Boekel and she from Oeffelt – met here, tied the knot in Holland and then returned to Niagara. While he managed a lumber store, they bought close to five acres of land on Lundy's Lane, one of the busiest tourist routes in the region, and began growing sweet corn, field tomatoes and other vegetables to supplement their income.

"We started by selling the products off a picnic table placed at the road," says Paul, born in 1964. "All three children – Carol, Andrew and I – helped out. As we got busier and busier, offering fruit as well, the picnic table was replaced with a little Dutch barn like the ones people have in their backyards. It was custom-made so that the front would open up. When this became too small, we built a fruit stand, and it wasn't long before we had to extend it on both ends."

His father became more ambitious.

"He saw all those Dutch guys with greenhouses and thought there must be money in that business. So he started building his own greenhouse, 30 feet by 150 feet. He got

— Paul Bongers with some of the gorgeous products of The Country Basket Garden Centre in Niagara Falls.

some used steel, bent it and placed it in old railway ties that he had lined up on the ground. An old wood furnace looked after the heating. He began growing hothouse tomatoes and soon got into geraniums as well."

After attending the University of Western Ontario in London for a year – "I thought it was a waste of time" – Paul sold real estate for five years. His father and Andrew ran the greenhouse business, then 70 per cent wholesale and 30 per cent retail. In 1995, when his father wanted to retire, he and Pam bought the place, intending to expand the retail side. Andrew set up his own wholesale greenhouse operation next door.

"In the first year, we put up a 20,000-square-foot greenhouse for retail," says Paul. "We've had an expansion in almost every year since then. It's nice to hear people say: 'You guys just keep on growing.' That's why we use the slogan 'We keep growing.' It has different connotations: that the business is getting bigger every year and that we grow a

lot of our own product. People like dealing with the actual grower to get advice on how to correct problems."

He and Pam changed the focus to retail for a number of reasons. Both liked to deal with people; Pam was associated for a long time with social services in Niagara. They found that the margins in wholesale were so tight that an increasingly higher volume would be needed to make a decent living. And they saw that wholesale and retail were overlapping – "we would be growing wholesale product in the retail greenhouse and people would come in and say: 'Why can't I have any of these?' "

Now they can. Eighty per cent of the output in the 40,000 square feet of production greenhouses is destined for retail customers. The centre opens a few weeks before Easter and closes at the end of June, a period when Pam works from 8 a.m. to 8 p.m. "with no time to think about sitting down."

Geraniums are the centre's specialty, generating nearly $500,000 in sales. There are also bedding plants, potted plants and more than 5,000 hanging baskets. The latest addition, a 15,000-square-foot retail greenhouse, houses nursery stock and perennials and provides shade protection and housing from the outdoor elements.

The centre reopens in the fall for the sale of more than 10,000 garden mums.

Paul goes to the public market in Port Colborne every Friday with a load of flowers. He also travels occasionally to the wholesale market in Toronto. But the selling at the centre is the exclusive responsibility of Pam. Her brother, Wayne Collins, is Manager of the operations.

"Our goal is to be number one," says Paul. "With that in mind, we've adopted a no-hassle guarantee. If a plant dies, no matter who is to blame, we will replace it. We figure that from three to four per cent comes back. But instead of fretting about our costs, we decided to focus on running our place well so that we will have good stock and fewer losses. The replacement policy is a good one. People expect it nowadays."

'IT WAS A BIT SCARY'

Martin Langbroek admits to having a few sleepless nights after he and his brother-in-law used their savings for a downpayment on a mortgage that gave them ownership of Regal Greenhouses Inc. on Niagara Stone Road in the heart of Virgil.

"It was a bit scary," he says. "It takes a pile of money to buy one of these places. And when you use up all your eggs, you tend to start chewing your nails for awhile."

He was chewing them for at least two years.

"I kept on thinking: 'What if we lost a crop? That would set us back five years'."

But when he didn't lose anything, and the business actually grew, he got over his uneasiness.

Regal is now a flourishing concern, producing bedding plants, hanging baskets, four-inch potted plants, seasonal crops and ivy hoops, all mostly for the wholesale trade, and operating an attractive retail store and garden centre that offers the company's products as well as many others.

Martin, who's married to Michelle and has four children, looks after the greenhouse operation and his partner, Darrell Boer, is in charge all retail operations.

Martin's father, George, emigrated with his family from the Netherlands in 1952 and settled in St. Catharines. He

—Cheryl, a Regal employee, adds colour to an already vivid setting.

worked initially at a Loblaws grocery store and next worked a flower shop route for Creekside Gardens Ltd. while working part-time on art. After that, he started doing his art full-time. With two other artists, he now owns an art studio in Jordan called Nivanik Native Arts.

Martin's mother, Joanna, also born in Holland, is a 30+-year employee of her brother-in-law and her nephew, Tom and Gord Valstar, at Scott Street Greenhouses Ltd. She looks after most of the seedling production.

"After school, I used to monkey around in my uncle's greenhouse with my sister, Diana, while we waited for our mother to finish work," says Martin, born in 1967. "I got a summer job there when I was 12. My mother or father never pushed greenhouse work on me; I just seemed to enjoy it for the most part. By the time I finished my schooling, I knew that this is what I wanted to do. I spurned a job at General Motors that would have given me a fairly good wage and started working in the greenhouse full-time. I was only 18 or 19 when I was made foreman. I didn't know how to deal with so many employees, but learned quickly."

'I was only 18 or 19 when I was made foreman. I didn't know how to deal with so many employees, but learned quickly.'

He stayed in this job until September, 1997, when he and Darrell purchased Regal, an existing business on 3.5 acres, from Lakeshore.

"I had been looking at it for a few years, but chickened out because of the finances. The retail portion of the business was a big unknown because I had no experience in that end of the business. Then Darrell lost his job at Duthler Textiles because of the store closing down. That gave us both a good opportunity to start our own business. It was a great match because he was very experienced in retailing and merchandising and I could concentrate on the growing and the wholesale part of the business. It has worked out marvellously."

— Martin Langbroek of Regal Greenhouses Inc. in Virgil: "I love the business."

In the nail-biting period, Martin and Darrell were encouraged by the number of tourists who stopped at the store, located on the main road from the QEW to the old town of Niagara-on-the-Lake. Sales increased steadily. On the wholesale side, Martin kept a good working relationship with Lakeshore. This firm continues to handle most of the greenhouse products.

Two years after taking over, the partners expanded their range by 25,000 square feet. The total area, including the retail garden centre, is now 76,000 square feet. Altogether, there are 15 employees.

"I love the business," says Martin. "It's very challenging. The people involved in the industry are great. There always seems to be help just around the corner when someone needs it. For the most part, there is a sense of community, which keeps the work very interesting and fun."

CHAPTER SIXTEEN

THERE'S ROOM FOR MORE

'Customers are the most important thing.
We treat people like we want to be treated ourselves.'
— Jan Prins, with his wife, Fabiola, and their children, Fay and Sarah

One of Niagara's newest greenhouse operations can trace its beginnings back to 1978 when four sons began helping their father earn extra money to pay for their education at the privately-funded Calvin Memorial Christian School in St. Catharines.

In his spare time, Peter Dykstra, a delivery person for Avondale Dairy, looked after two acres of lawns at a home for senior citizens across the street from the school. For seven years, he was ably and willingly assisted by Rick, Randy, Ray and Larry who knew that the work was solely for their benefit.

With all this experience in lawn maintenance under their belts, Rick, Randy and Larry set up their own landscaping business, Dykstra Landscaping, in 1989 and did mostly residential work in the St. Catharines area. There wasn't much to do in winter. So, after a number of years, they began thinking of venturing into greenhouse work as well.

'Without good people, you can't make it go.'

"We saved up money and looked around for land," recalls Larry. "We found a 15-acre piece on Seventh Street that had seven acres of grapes on it. We negotiated for a year and then bought it. We could now grow nursery stock for our landscaping. And we could put up a greenhouse for flowers. The grape production would be rented out."

A range of 52,440 square feet, with a height of 16 feet under the gutter, was built and Dykstra Greenhouses went into production on February 1, 2001, with a crop of Easter mums for another grower. A variety of bedding plants and more seasonal crops, sold mostly to wholesalers, completed the successful year.

Larry, who's in charge of the greenhouse side of the business, was born in Grimsby in 1967. He moved to St. Catharines in 1975 with his Dutch-born parents, Peter and Jane, and five siblings. Prior to going into landscaping with Randy and Rick, he had worked at Virgil Greenhouses on Hunter Road near Virgil. But he still had a few things to learn about flower growing when he started on his own. A

— Larry Dykstra is one of the newcomers to Niagara's floriculture industry.

retired grower made things easier by happily volunteering advice during his regular visits.

The landscaping-greenhouse mix works well, particularly for staffing.

"We have 12 people between the two businesses," says Larry, "and we sometimes do some switching, depending on which part is busier. In that way, we don't lose any good landscaping people in the winter. Without good people, you can't make it go."

His wife, Mariam, the mother of four children, does the bookkeeping for both businesses.

As for the future, he aims to expand the greenhouse operation until he has reached age 40, some five years from now.

"We'll probably double the place -- we have enough boiler and generator power for that -- and then we'll sit back and have another look," he says.

A Young Couple On The Go

Since they left the Netherlands in 1999, eager to find more elbow room, Jan and Fabiola Prins have not wasted any time fitting into the fabric of life and work in spacious Canada and positioning themselves for what they and many others believe will be a bright future in the business of growing and marketing flowers.

They've erected a state-of-the-art greenhouse on newly-acquired land adjacent to their original operation on Fairlane Road in Jordan Station, where statice is grown exclusively, and have developed a long-range plan to replace the older structures and, in accordance with the Dutch way of doing things, make maximum use of every square foot of space.

'I know the rules in Holland and expect these to be adopted here someday, so I'm prepared.'

185

— Sarah Prins enjoys a ride among the beauty in her parents' statice operation.

Jan, born in Maasdijk, in the Westland greenhouse district, was first introduced to Canada in 1990 when he was an 18-year-old horticultural student. As part of his schooling, he worked as an intern for seven weeks at a greenhouse operation in Niagara.

"I wasn't too serious then," he says, displaying a big grin. "I made sure I worked not more than eight hours a day and had Saturdays off so that I would have lots of time for fun stuff. I had relatives in the Niagara-on-the-Lake area, which was nice for me, but I never thought of moving to Canada someday. When the seven weeks were up, I went back to Holland for another year of school."

Greenhouse work was not new to him. He was often required to help his father, a grower of freesias, and at an early age decided that he would follow a similar career. While still in school, he rented and farmed his own plot. After graduation in 1991, he bought land with his father's help and began growing statice, a flower used in bouquets, and carnations.

Three years after their marriage in 1994, Jan and Fabiola travelled to Canada for a vacation. Actually, it was more of a scouting trip to inspect the possibilities of emigrating and going into business here. At this time, they owned land in two different places and rented a house in another, a situation that was awkward, inefficient and not conducive to expansion.

"I was impressed with what I saw here," Fabiola recalls. "The biggest thing was all the space. The nature was also wonderful. When we were back in Holland, we prayed for guidance. Two weeks later, someone came along and offered to buy our farm. Well, that settled things for us."

The couple applied for landed immigrant status. That's usually not a big hurdle for self-employed people with resources and good health, although Jan found all the necessary paper work frustratingly complex and slow. While he waited, his two uncles in Virgil, Pim and Ton Boekestyn, arranged the purchase of a three-acre property on Fairlane Road with 55,000 square feet of greenhouse space that had been used for producing potted plants. Hired help was lined up. Statice plants from Holland were brought onto the site. And in the spring of 1999, shortly after landing in Canada, Jan and Fabiola could start production.

"The Boekestyn family gave us a jump start," says Fabiola. "They provided us with knowledge of sales and the way of living in Canada."

Within a short time, Prins Grow Inc. has become a going concern, specializing in a singular product that is sold mostly to wholesalers and also at the flower auctions in Mississauga and Montreal. Its new 25,000-square-foot greenhouse, the first phase of the modernization program, incorporates some of the latest techniques involving rainwater runoff and light exposure. Says Jan: "I know the rules in Holland and expect these to be adopted here someday, so I'm prepared."

The family is growing too. Fabiola now has two children to look after -- Sarah and Fay -- in addition to all the paper work.

Besides quality and efficiency, Jan believes a key ingredient for success in business is a good name.

"Customers are the most important thing," he says. "We treat people like we want to be treated ourselves."

The good name applies to neighbourly relations as well. In the new greenhouse, dark curtains are drawn at night to prevent the growing lights from causing sleeplessness -- and perhaps bouts of high blood pressure -- among nearby residents.

— *The Prins family – Fabiola, Fay, Sarah and Jan – with some of the gorgeous blooms produced at their business in Jordan Station.*

FROM PAINTBALL TO FLOWERS

It was a giant leap into the unknown when David Craig left the paintball business in 1992 to join Niagara's greenhouse community.

Neither he nor his wife, Susan, knew anything about growing flowers commercially.

"All I knew was that there were a lot of greenhouses in this area," he says. "And I thought: if there are that many greenhouses, something must be working for them. It seemed like a good business to get into even though I knew nothing about it."

David, born in Stoney Creek in 1960, wanted a career change after eight years of making a living with a popular recreation in which people run through the woods and shoot paintballs at each other in pretend war games. His involvement had included ownership of a paintball facility in Niagara, buying and selling of paintball products and, in a partnership arrangement, a business in California for wholesale manufacturing, distribution and mail order.

'It seemed like a good business to get into even though I knew nothing about it.'

After deciding that flower production would be their next pursuit, he and Susan bought a five-acre property in Jordan Station with an existing greenhouse area of 23,000 square feet. Their first crop consisted of bedding plants. These turned out to be mediocre at best.

"The first two years were a real struggle because we didn't know what we were doing," he says. "In retrospect, I first should have worked for somebody else for a year. But I wanted to get going. We did a lot of learning as we went along. In the third year, our bedding plants started to look better. They wouldn't have won any awards at the fall fair, but they were OK. Everything became less of a struggle. We even added outdoor garden mums to our product line."

David sold some of his flowers to a few small retail outlets across the border. The bulk of the output went to the market at the Ontario Food Terminal where he found the selling tough because of competition from experienced growers. A big break came after the third year when, with improved

products in hand, he was able to make arrangements with a large garden centre in the U.S. to supply it with flowers. He also hooked up with Mel Sawaya, a consultant, who "put together a lot of pieces of the puzzle in regards to watering, fertilizing, growth regulating, chemical use, and so on."

After five years in the flower business, it was time for David and Susan to make a decision: stay or leave. They had given themselves this time frame to make their operation viable. They were making enough money to keep their heads above water, and the future of the business looked promising, so they elected to stay -- and to expand. They sold their property and bought a 22-acre field, with no buildings, directly below the escarpment on Main Street West in Grimsby. In the winter of 1999, they built 42,000 square feet of greenhouse space and began growing basically the same crops as before. The greenhouses have since been expanded to 54,000 square feet. There's also a retail garden centre.

The work at Trillium Hill Greenhouses is now done by David and a staff of four. Up to 18 workers are employed in the busy spring season. Susan has her hands full with other things: she teaches English in high school and looks after a family of four young children, including a set of twins.

187

— A symbol of happiness at Trilliam Hill Greenhouses.

"It's a good business and I enjoy it," says David, who has a BA degree in economics from McMaster University in Hamilton. "It pays the bills. But I think there's potential in me beyond this. If I get an itch or if something comes along, I may want to change. I can see myself pursuing something else and having someone run this place for me."

— Workers are applying some tender loving care to the outdoor plants at the Trillium Hill operation below the Niagara Escarpment.

Bill MacDonald became hooked on greenhouse work when he was a 15-year-old student working part-time for a grower just down the road from his house in London in 1975.

Now he has a greenhouse operation of his own, in a picturesque area on Welland Road near Fenwick, and he couldn't be happier.

"I'm having the time of my life," he says during a break from overseeing the production of ivies, his specialty crop, and the construction of a 16,000-square-foot addition to his greenhouse space.

He and his wife, Linda, have owned the business, Anmar Greenhouses Ltd., since 1997. Their property includes a comfortable house, a spacious garden in which their two children can romp and a swimming pool. The greenhouses are barely visible beyond a screen of tall trees.

Young Bill's first job for the London business, Davis Greenhouses, was reglazing the glass. After that, he did inside work with carnations and bedding plants. Other than the fact that his older brother also was working part-time for the grower, there was no family connection to flower and plant production. Their father, Graham, was Superintendent for the local board of education.

— Bill MacDonald with some of the ivy hoops he produces at Anmar Greenhouses Ltd.

'I'm having the time of life.'

Enjoying the work tremendously, Bill was in the greenhouses after school, on weekends and during the summers until he completed his four-year agricultural program, majoring in soil science, at the University of Guelph in 1983. He then began working full-time for the London grower, on a profit-sharing basis, taking up an offer that he had received while in his third year of study. He stayed at the business until 1990, marrying Linda in the meantime, and then returned to the university to work on his master's degree in floriculture, studying nitrogen, nutrients and chrysanthemums.

In February, 1992, after labouring all night in the lab, he went to the cafeteria for breakfast and was greeted by his floriculture extension person who informed him that the

new owner of Gordon's Greenhouses, a 450,000-square-foot operation in Oxford, Nova Scotia, needed a production manager. Recognizing this as a great opportunity, he applied right away. The owner invited him down for an interview and a tour of the place and practically hired him on the spot.

"I was pleased," he says. "So was Linda, who's originally from the east coast -- Prince Edward Island. The fact that I had not written my thesis didn't matter to me. For six weeks, though, I commuted to Guelph because I was teaching a class there. Gordon's was a big place, growing a little bit of everything. As big a headache as the job was, it turned out to be the best learning experience I could have had."

In 1965, he met Tony and Mary Alkemade, then owners of Anmar Greenhouses, who visited Gordon's while on vacation. He had bought ivy cuttings from them, so there

were a few things to talk about. During the conversation, he learned that Tony and Mary were thinking of selling their place. His interest was kindled because he was ready for another change, having become dissatisfied with spending more and more time behind a desk instead of in a greenhouse. He travelled to Niagara in the summer of 1996 and looked around. His wife made a separate visit later. Both were impressed with the Anmar operation, which had a greenhouse area of 38,000 square feet, and ended up as the new owners.

Bill chuckles: "I tell people that I liked the cuttings so much, I bought the business."

He's been on cloud nine ever since, producing various ivies and ivy products with the help of eight full-time workers, selling these through brokers, at garden centres and on the wholesale market in Toronto, and facing the future with confidence, savvy and an ever-present smile.

CHAPTER SEVENTEEN

GREENHOUSE DELIGHTS

'We carefully control what we feed the plants and make adjustments as they grow. We end up with a clean, healthy product.'

— *Toine van der Knaap*

With people generally becoming more conscious of what they eat, turning to salads and other healthy fare, the bell pepper business is a great one to be in.

And when the peppers themselves are grown in an almost perfect environment, biologically controlled, and then promoted as a wholesome product of superior calibre, colour and size, their producers happily accept the challenges of meeting the ever-increasing demand.

Welcome to St. David's Hydroponics Ltd., a relatively young company that has grown into a giant, producing 10 million peppers a year in two plants in Niagara with a total growing area of nearly one million square feet.

"We grow our peppers hydroponically – that is, we grow them in rockwool instead of soil," says Toine van der Knaap, the General Manager. "The key reason is we can perfect the circumstances we grow them in. We carefully control what we feed the plants and make adjustments as they grow. We end up with a clean, healthy product."

> *'Niagara is a nice area in which to work and live . . . It's a good place to be in charge of a business that has an excellent future.'*

St. David's was the brainchild of Andy Olsthoorn of Lakeshore Produce. In the early 1980s, his wholesale company was importing a tremendous number of hydroponically-grown peppers from the Netherlands to fill the vacuum in the market when there were no field peppers. But it was always a major hassle to get the peppers off airplanes and into trucks, ship them to border points such as Detroit, get them across the border with the foreign paper work and then continue on to supermarkets. Besides, it was a costly business.

After telling his family that "I can do this myself," Andy teamed up with two men who shared his belief that a pepper production facility in Niagara would work: Tony VanderKaay of Garden City Greenhouses Ltd. in St. Catharines, who had land available on Concession 5 in St. Davids, and Jack Vink, a specialist in the bulb business,

— A worker at St. David's Hydroponics Ltd. needs some help to reach the top of the tall bell pepper plants.

who had formed a close relationship with Andy and his wife, Rita.

The trio formed a company, built a large greenhouse in St. Davids and began growing red, yellow and orange peppers with hydroponics technology in 1985. There were a few problems initially with achieving the desired quality. But these were fixed after Martin Bos, a pepper expert from Holland, joined the partnership. The peppers became so popular that Lakeshore had to continue importing them so that St. David's could meet the demand. In time, a second plant was put on the drawing board.

The site, along the QEW in Vineland Station, needed to be raised considerably before construction could begin. Andy, a master at making deals, arranged for the crews who were tearing up and rebuilding the highway to dump all the dirt onto the property. Five thousand dump-truck loads were needed. The new facility, including the head office, was completed in 1996. It was expanded two years later.

Lakeshore discontinued selling and shipping for St. David's after the new plant was built. The pepper company now does its own marketing and shipping. It has three trucks for local deliveries and uses transport firms to reach other points.

According to Toine, the Vineland Station location is more suitable for pepper growing than the one in St. Davids. It's closer to Lake Ontario, where the temperature is usually a few degrees cooler than in other parts of the Peninsula, which makes all the difference for a product that doesn't like hot weather. Most of the peppers are harvested from mid-March to the end of November.

"Winter production is limited because of the reduced hours of daylight and sunshine," he says. "Extending the season through the use of artificial lighting would not be practicable for us financially. There is a tremendous amount of imported peppers from Mexico, Florida, Israel and Spain on the market in the winter and the prices are not in our favour."

Toine, born in 1965 in the Dutch town of Wateringen, is pleased that he was able to work with the soil before hydroponics growing came into vogue. Now, when it comes to comparing the two methods, he can join the discussion with knowledge based on experience. In his boyhood, he helped his father, a greenhouse grower of eggplants, tomatoes, plums and grapes. Later, he and his brother ran their own pepper-growing business. He left this after three years and, in 1990, went to the United States, the country of birth of his wife, Maura. He spent three years at a large greenhouse in Pennsylvania where tomatoes, cucumbers and bell peppers were grown. He then worked with a producer of tomatoes in Colorado for three years. In 1996, he joined St. David's.

"Niagara is a nice area in which to work and live," he says. "The people here are very sociable, and intellectual, and the climate is very moderate. It's a good place to be in charge of a business that has an excellent future."

— Hundreds of thousands of hydroponically-grown bell peppers are sorted and packaged for shipment to customers in Canada and the United States.

— Tim Freeman annually grows 1.5 million potted herb plants in 70 varieties and supplies 450 independent garden centres.

Tim Freeman remains awestruck over the phenomenal rise of his business to its current status as the top producer of herbs in Canada.

"Every time I say we're the largest," he says, "I have to pinch myself because I can't believe it."

At its greenhouse facility on Lincoln Avenue North near Beamsville, Freeman Herbs Ltd. annually grows 1.5 million potted herb plants, in 70 varieties, which are supplied to 450 independent garden centres in Ontario, Quebec, New York and Michigan and distributed to many other places in North America via a number of wholesalers.

Tim remembers well the day in the late 1970s when he went to the market at the Ontario Food Terminal in Toronto with hopes of selling 50 dozen geraniums left over from the garden centre which his parents, Carman and Beulah, had set up on their property years earlier for marketing the spring flower and vegetable plants from their greenhouse.

"I was trying to get $5 for a dozen geraniums and some bedding plant fellows were asking $3 to $4 for their stuff. And here was this herb guy beside me getting $12. No one was questioning his price. Later, while sitting on the back of the pickup truck, I told my girlfriend: 'That's what I am going to grow.' I didn't even know what a herb was. But I had never felt so confident and positive in my life."

Back home, Tim dumped the geraniums he had not sold, looked at a spice rack to get a few names, such as basil and parsley, and went to Grimsby to buy four packages of seed. He grew the plants successfully. With three trays of herbs, he went to garden centres and tried to convince the owners to take him on as a supplier. But no one was interested.

"I didn't give up and grew 300 trays the next year. I decided to take them to the market in Toronto because I needed connections and that was the place to get them. I again sat next to the herb guy and was shaking like a leaf.

Well, within two weeks, I had sold all the trays. I even received an order for 40 trays from a representative of Plant World in Toronto. I was walking on air."

Tim went to the market for 10 years and built up a solid clientele. He began selling to stores when a strike prevented buyers' trucks from entering the grounds of the terminal. After that, his herb business mushroomed. He phased out his seedless cucumbers, his last non-herb crop, and turned his entire range over to herb production.

The original Freeman family in Canada came from Yorkshire, England, and settled in Amherst, Nova Scotia, in 1759. The Freemans later spread to the Burlington area where a small settlement was named after them. Tim's grandfather was a dentist in Beamsville and his father was born there in 1914.

"Dad had a nice garden," recalls Carman. "He liked growing. There was always a competition among the neighbours as to who would have the first corn or tomatoes, and Dad was always good at it."

The father must have passed on the growing bug to his son. After wartime service with the Royal Canadian Air Force, in the radar field, Carman began working for Leo Martin, his father-in-law, who grew flowers and vegetables in a greenhouse operation in Vineland Station. He stayed there for a year, learning the ins and outs of the business. Then, in 1947, he bought a five-acre farm with a house, outdoor fields and a small greenhouse in which spring flowers and vegetables were produced. He continued the work of the previous owner and sold his products at a garden centre he built beside his house and also at the Martin place.

'Every time I say we're the largest, I have to pinch myself because I can't believe it.'

Tim, born in 1951 and the only son among four children, completed high school and was accepted for early admittance to the bachelor of agriculture program at the University of Guelph. But his higher schooling didn't last long. He quit suddenly one Friday afternoon after being totally turned off by a session in the zoology lab at which fetal frogs were being dissected.

"I told the instructor that I didn't know the inside parts of a frog and didn't want to know. Other people needed the education to get a job, but I didn't. My job was waiting; they needed me at home. When I told my Dad that I wasn't going back to university, he said: `That's fine. We better build some more greenhouses'."

Father and son did most of the work themselves, using pipes and other material obtained from scrapyards. The property also was enlarged to 12 acres with the acquisition of an adjacent peach orchard.

The greenhouse area has doubled since the start of herb production and now totals 130,000 square feet. When the herbs are growing, Tim finds there are not enough hours in the day. His wife, Anne, who has retired from her job as a public school principal, is "right beside me, no matter what has to be done." But when the yearly crop is out the door, and life is not so hectic, Tim finds time to pursue in earnest the study of guitar playing as a student of the Ontario Conservatory of Music. It's a trait he inherited from his father.

"When Dad was 71, he got a $1,500 bill from the accountant. He said: 'Hey, that's way too much money. I can do that work myself.' So he went to night school to learn how to do it. He did our books until he ran into a health problem four years ago. He still uses a computer regularly to search for things on the Internet."

Tim publishes a full-colour newsletter with tips and information on growing herbs and using these in cooking. He also travels widely to speak about herbs to garden clubs, trade shows and conventions. In 2001, he was named winner of the CIBC Enterprise Award at the eighth annual Niagara Entrepreneur of the Year Awards. Amid all this attention, he often thinks back to the days when success was still a dream.

"I remember when Dad came to the peach orchard where I was working and said the oil was going up two cents a gallon. The price was 12 to 14 cents a gallon then. He said: 'I think we better fill the tank.' I just looked at him and said: 'Where are we going to get the money for that?' "

— A concrete wall of Carman Freeman's original boiler room remains in use.

Floral Passion

'I KNEW I COULD DO IT'

In the early 1980s, a report in a Dutch trade magazine about seedless cucumbers being grown above the soil on material called rockwool caught Gerard Haakman's attention.

At his greenhouses on Foss Road in Fenwick, where cucumbers were being produced in large numbers, he had already progressed from soil to straw bales, so the new method of growing in rockwool seemed to be a logical step for him.

"I discussed this with my sons, Robert and Peter, who were working with me in the business, and they said: 'Let's try it out.' I then flew to Holland to see what was going on and find out what would be needed to do that here."

'At one time, I was growing 28 different varieties. It was like a research station here.'

He invested a few hundred thousand dollars in new equipment, applied for a government grant to partly offset the cost and went into growing on rockwool in 1985. "I was looking forward to it. I knew it worked in Holland and I knew I could do it too."

As far as he knows, Haakman Greenhouses Ltd. was the first operation in Canada, and possibly North America, to grow seedless cucumbers hydroponically on a commercial basis. One grower in British Columbia was already using the method, but it was only for tomatoes.

"The first year we were in rockwool, a lot of people came over for a look," says Gerard. "The industry started to change over soon after that. Now 85 per cent of the producers are growing in soilless culture."

His pioneering efforts caught the attention of seed companies in Holland. He ended up testing their new varieties to determine if these would do well in Ontario. "At one time, I was growing 28 different varieties," he says. "It was like a research station here."

He and his wife, Helen, a long-time teacher in Welland and Niagara Falls, are now living in retirement in a lovely house a short distance from the 285,600-square-foot

— Gerard Haakman pioneered hydroponic production of seedless cucumbers in Canada.

range where their son, Peter, is in charge of the cucumber production. Robert, the elder son, left at the time of the changeover to start his own nursery stock business. There is also a daughter, Audrey.

Gerard didn't know anything about cucumbers when he arrived in Canada in 1953 as a single, 20-year-old immigrant. Nor did he need to know. In fact, it wouldn't be until 1978 that he grew his first crop of cucumbers after first learning a few basic things from other growers.

He had worked for his father's fruit tree nursery in Nibbixwoud, a village in the Dutch province of Noord Holland. In Canada, there was a succession of jobs. He began at a dairy farm near Montreal and soon moved to Niagara Falls where a friend from his village lived. He worked in a winery, laid sidewalks for a construction firm, did landscaping, spent time at a grocery store and then was hired by the Ontario Paper Company mill at Thorold where he would stay until the early '70s. He met Helen, a teacher in Volendam, while on a visit to Holland and they were married in Canada in 1956. Twelve years later, he bought 30 acres in

Fenwick with intentions of planting an apple orchard.

"I bought the root stock in Holland," he says, "and started off with five acres. I planted late, but all the trees survived. In the second year, we had a late frost and everything was frozen out. The same thing happened in the third year. When we froze out again in the fourth year, I said: 'Forget it. I'm going to do something else'."

He turned his attention to an ever-bearing strawberry variety he had heard about while in Holland. He planted some, and more the next year, and they grew and produced well. But he couldn't find enough pickers, even though unemployment was high.

"Here I had these beautiful strawberries and they were rotting in the fields because I couldn't get help. I became so upset, I got ulcers. So I took a disc and ran over 60,000 plants I had put in for the following year. Then I switched to sweet corn."

Later on, while still working in Thorold, Gerard decided to try his hand at indoor growing. In 1972, he built a greenhouse with only 1,000 square feet of space and put in a tomato crop. Before long, some hoop houses and a used greenhouse came on the scene. When he wanted to build more greenhouses, he applied to the Ontario Farm Credit Corporation for a loan. It was approved on condition that he become a full-time grower, which he did.

"We did very well in tomatoes," he says. "We sold them all to Bayshore Vegetable Shippers in Burlington. But then I heard that cucumbers could provide a faster return and a better cash flow. So, in 1978, I decided to put in a fall crop of cucumbers. This worked out well. The cucumber business grew from there."

In the ensuing years, Gerard undertook an active role in the affairs of his industry. He helped to set up the Centario Greenhouse Vegetable Co-operative and was its treasurer for 13 years. He was also a director of the Ontario Greenhouse Vegetable Growers' Marketing Board for 17 years and a director of the F&V Energby Co-op for 12 years.

Of his achievements and contributions, he simply says: "We tried to put our two cents' worth in the industry for the benefit of the next generation."

— *Peter Haakman and his son, Bryan, among the cucumber plants at the Haakman greenhouses in Fenwick.*

CHAPTER EIGHTEEN

FOR THE GREEN THUMBS

'People from all over come here to look at our production techniques.'
— Dave Bakker Sr.

A LEADER

Dave Bakker Sr. of St. Catharines took on quite a battle in the 1960s when he tried to persuade obstinate local politicians to grant operations such as his nursery the right to tap into the municipal water supply for their irrigation needs.

"We argued that if industries such as General Motors could get city water, why couldn't the same apply to growers, who also provide jobs and pay taxes," he says. "But the politicians in those days didn't have enough foresight to accommodate the horticultural industry other than the fruit people. It took eight years to win the fight. The bylaws were finally changed, allowing growers to get city water if they had access to it and the supply to households wouldn't be endangered."

The operators of J. C. Bakker and Sons Ltd. on Third Street installed a private main and got the quality water that they sorely needed for the healthy growth of their nursery stock. The water from ponds was unsatisfactory because it was laced with herbicides washed from farmers' fields. The water from Lake Ontario, especially if pumped from close to shore, also was far from ideal.

"Since the city water is regionalized, many growers have benefited from our fight," says Dave.

The region has benefited too. Over the years, the Bakker nursery gained a solid reputation for producing products of top quality, grew by leaps and bounds and became a leader in its field.

It now farms 370 acres of owned and rented land, including 30 acres for more than 100 varieties of roses, and employs up to 130 workers in the busy periods.

"We've become known across North America for our innovation in nursery machinery," says Dave. "We're always searching for ways to become more efficient by adapting equipment for our particular needs and developing new machinery. People from all over come here to look at our production techniques."

He's particularly proud of the propagation greenhouse whose roof can be opened, allowing plants to adjust gradually to the outdoor light and thus eliminating the shock when they are placed outside.

"It saves us a pile of money because we don't need all the outside shading anymore," he says. "I saw the concept at a trade show in Holland – it was actually an idea from Italy – and we contracted Westbrook Greenhouse Systems to design and manufacture such a greenhouse for us, keeping in mind winter's snowload."

The greenhouse's mist system is activitated by light sensors, instead of a clock, following an idea developed by Dave's nephew, John Bakker III, the General Manager and person in charge.

— Workers tend to acres upon acres of nursery stock at J. C. Bakker and Sons Ltd. in St. Catharines.

Floral Passion

Dave and his brother, John II, who ran the business as a partnership for many years, retired from the day-to-day-operations a few years ago, leaving their responsibilities in the hands of the younger set: John III and his brother, Ken, the nursery's technical wizard who constructed the handsome office building on Third Street; Dave's son, Dave Jr., who looks after the propagating, and his son-in-law, Gerry de Haan, who's responsible for shipping, soil analysis and seasonal workers from Mexico.

The Bakker family – John, Helena and their five children, ranging in age from three to 18 – came to Niagara in 1948 from Scherpenzeel, a small community in the Dutch province of Gelderland. The father's first job was at a nursery, Prudhomme's, which suited him fine. After all, he had been a nurseryman and market gardener for most of his 48 years. But he had something else in mind: a business of his own.

He soon rented six acres of land on the western outskirts of St. Catharines and planted tomatoes, having secured a contract with a canning factory. In time, there were other crops as well, including pansies and garden mums. Then, in a little greenhouse, he began growing evergreen cuttings. Garden roses were also added to the production even though he had vowed, after destroying his worthless crop during the Depression, never to grow them again.

> *'We try to get our message across that we're better at it, have better products and are better located.'*

"Roses were not being brought in from the States or Holland, so he saw this as an opportunity," says Dave. "But it was a tough thing because he had to buy the plants in

— The principals of the Bakker firm: Gerry de Haan, Dave Bakker Jr., Dave Bakker Sr., John Bakker III, John Bakker II and Ken Bakker.

Holland and there was no spray material. My father's first few years in business were difficult. I worked at General Motors and my brother somewhere else and everything we earned went into the family pot. But then everything started to come into place. Home gardens and landscaping were becoming trendy and that, of course, was good news for the nurseries."

Dad and sons Dave and John entered into a partnership – the other children pursued different careers – and eventually established a family corporation with a three-way split of shares. Dave and John bought out their father when he reached 67. The company was poised to enter a period of growth, with more acreage and more production of evergreens, shade trees and roses. Then city water began to flow, causing container growing to take off.

— Another view showing the vastness of the production at the Bakker nursery.

Floral Passion

The Bakker catalogue now lists more than 110 rose varieties and from 300 to 400 different plants. These products are shipped to chain stores, including all the Walmart outlets from Newfoundland to Saskatchewan. They also go to many areas of the United States and even to Holland and Germany. The goal is to develop a sustained export market much like that of the flower producers.

"In the States, we are competing with people who have better climate, cheaper labour and cheaper land," says Dave. "We try to get our message across that we're better at it, have better products and are better located. But what really opens the door is the price. By staying competitive, we find our exports are increasing every year."

Promotion is a big part of the business.

"We don't have a government agency proclaiming the quality of our stuff," says Dave. "We have to do that ourselves. As a nursery, we have to promote the plant material in different ways, in different areas, and get paid for it with royalties or whatever."

— A field of flowering rosebushes near Lakeshore Road West presents a breathtaking sight.

— The Bakker firm uses the latest in nursery machinery, such as this sprayer.

The firm produces a full-colour catalogue that features the Niagara-grown products, large posters that advance new varieties such as the rose bearing the name of famous Quebec singer Celine Dion and informative labels that retailers can pass on to their customers.

Dave and the other family members involved in the nursery are obviously proud of what has been accomplished since 1948. Their office building resembles a mini-museum, with displays of old photographs and other memorabilia. But they are also thankful that their success has enabled them over the years to assist in building churches and Christian schools and fund other causes as well.

"We came to Canada for economic reasons," says Dave. "But much deeper and broader things motivated us in the years that followed. And that's been a blessing."

THE WORK ETHIC

When they took their first steps into the nursery business in the 1970s, John and Jocelyn Langendoen didn't mind holding a few extra jobs to earn the money they needed to plant their feet firmly on the ground.

"We did what we had to do," says Jocelyn, "although there were many times that we felt our feet weren't too firmly placed."

The couple's determination and hard work eventually began to pay dividends. Their business, Willowbrook Nurseries Inc. near Fenwick, now covers 102 acres over four properties.

John, born in 1952, was the first of seven children of Bas and Jane Langendoen who had come to Canada the previous year from Brielle, the Netherlands. He went to school in St. Catharines and then attended Niagara College Horticultural School. He enjoyed working for his father, who owned Windmill Landscaping in St. Catharines, and also got one year of experience in the garden centre of Central Nurseries. He then moved to Dundas and worked at Connon Nurseries.

'You've got to love what you're doing and have a passion for growing plants.'

In 1975, John and Jocelyn were married and lived in Hamilton. A year later, they purchased an apple orchard in the hope of getting a nursery started at the same time. John still worked at Connon Nurseries and Jocelyn was a secretary at McMaster University. Apples were very labour intensive, and although they worked the orchard with another couple, they decided after two years to sell it. They moved to a small apartment in Grimsby and stored their nursery supplies at the place of John's father for a year.

John next worked at Baycoat, a steel factory, doing the night and afternoon shifts as much as possible so that he could work at his nursery during the day. Other than for six hours of sleep, his day consisted of work, work, work. Jocelyn worked too – for Calvinist Contact (now Christian Courier), a weekly church paper issued in St. Catharines. At night, she was a typesetter for Paideia Press, a book publisher in Jordan Station. The typesetter was later moved to the mobile home she and her husband lived in.

In May, 1979, the couple's first child was born, and they rented some land with an option to buy on Balfour Street near Fenwick. In 1982, after five years in the factory, John decided to follow another pursuit while still trying to get his nursery on a firm footing. He and his wife purchased a lawn-spraying franchise for the St. Catharines-Welland area. They operated this for four years and then sold it, along with a list of 1,200 customers, and went into nursery work full-time.

Rob Bouwers, who also ran the spraying business, later became – and still is – Willowbrook's Canadian sales representative.

"Our wholesale nursery business grew from rented land," says John. "After a five-year lease, we purchased 10 acres in 1984. We now grow in four locations: 18 acres on Balfour, 50 acres on Farr Road and two properties on Victoria Ave. We have a workforce of 50 full-time to 125 seasonal, including students."

Willowbrook started with field stock and then moved on to container stock.

"Container stock was expensive to get into," says Jocelyn, "and when we did the math, we really didn't think we could afford it. But we went ahead anyway. Willowbrook now produces container-grown evergreens, vines, flowering shrubs, perennials, groundcovers, dwarf trees and, for a number of years, decorated living Christmas trees. Most of our products are sold to garden centres in Canada and the U.S., as well as to landscapers and rewholesalers."

Increasing attention is being directed to marketing. Willowbrook produces an annual catalogue, picture-tags its products and supplies flyers and posters to its customers. Its products are trademarked Medallion Perennials and Garden Pride.

"Research is an important part of the job," says John. "I like to study the market carefully. I'm a faithful reader of trade magazines and retail garden magazines to keep up with the trends."

— An impressive view of one of Willowbrook's nursery production areas.

Progressiveness is shown in the development of the office/greenhouse shipping area on Victoria Ave. There are four huge ponds on the property – John calls them "our lifeblood" – in which rainwater and surface runoff are collected for irrigation purposes.

Jocelyn remains at John's side and works in the administration of the company. Their eldest son, Chris, is a section manager on the Farr Road location. There are two

— John and Jocelyn Langendoen and their son, Chris, stand among some of the beautiful products they produce at their nursery near Fenwick.

other sons: Darryl, who is studying social work at Calvin College in Grand Rapids, Michigan, and Brad, a high school student interested in meteorology. In the past year, the family has been enlarged by a daughter-in-law and granddaughter.

Operating a business that seems to grow bigger year after year is a demanding task. But John takes it in stride, saying "you've got to love what you're doing and have a passion for growing plants."

Jocelyn adds: "We are thankful to the Lord for His many blessings and for always being with us through the struggles and challenges of our business. We continually pray for God's guidance in our day-to-day lives."

Floral Passion

On a spring day a few years ago, a pail of ornamental branches called snowballs caught the eye of Karl Vahrmeyer when he made his regular trip to the Ontario Food Terminal in Toronto with a selection of his nursery stock.

"The fellow was selling 40 stems for $50," he recalls. "I thought: 'I can do that too.' And so I did."

Karl and his wife, Wilma, produced and cut stems off two rows of bushes they had planted at their farm on Metler Road near Ridgeville. Well, their snowball venture snowballed to such an extent that Green Park Nurseries is now producing many other ornamental branches, including hydrangeas, dogwood, curly willow and pussy willow.

The grower with the entrepreneurial touch began his life dream of farming in 1977 while still in high school in St. Catharines. He rented 17 acres of land and grew 1,000 tomato plants, as well as some peppers and onions. With a partner, he also began propagating and growing nursery stock. In 1983, three years after marrying Wilma, he bought out his partner. The couple then launched their nursery on rented land near Fenwick. Ten years later, they finally bought their own farm, keeping the rented land for cold-frame hoophouses and some growing.

"We came across an abandoned fruit farm," says Karl. "We put in an offer in July, 1993, and then waited for the courts to go through a long process to give us clear title to the 33-acre property. It literally had been used as a garbage dump. There was junk all over the place. The house, built in the 1860s, was in terrible shape and had water in the basement. I'm sure our parents wondered what we were doing. I thought of bulldozing the house, but then we decided to fix it up and even built an addition a number of years later."

'Family was always important, but now we are more aware of how important it is.'

It took most of the year to clean up the place. In the meantime, Karl and Wilma had to do some growing too.

"It was difficult at times to do both," he says, "but I

203

— Karl and Wilma Vahrmeyer at their Green Park Nurseries near Ridgeville.

had just turned 35 and was eager to start. Because of a downturn in the economy shortly after moving, we once again turned to vegetables to generate cash flow."

A new barn was built with lumber cut from a wooded area on the property and shaped by a sawmill brought onto the site. Trusses and concrete were the only items purchased. Hoophouses, some of them heated for vine growing and propagation, were also erected.

Production and sales continued and the business stayed on the path of steady growth. Soon the need for more land was apparent as Karl and Wilma decided to grow fall decorative crops. Corn stalks, straw bales, pumpkins and gourds were grown on rented land nearby, giving them income year-round. There are now approximately 8,000 square feet of heated polyhouses and 25,000 square feet of cold frames.

Amid all the clearing, fixing, building and getting a business up and running, family life remained the top priority for Karl and Wilma, the parents of five children. In the first years on Metler Road, while nursery stock sales were in a bit of a slump, Karl took his vegetables to the Farmer's Market in Welland and used the earnings to pay for the children's education at the local Christian school.

— A barn is being built with lumber cut from a wooded area on the farm.

— *This scenic view of the Green Park operation on Metler Road is an example of the many picturesque spots that be found throughout the Niagara Peninsula.*

The couple's parents came from the Netherlands at a young age in the early 1950s.

The family went through an agonizing period in 1995 when the youngest daughter was diagnosed with a brain tumour. Surgery followed.

"Our relatives and church community gave us tremendous support, but I don't think we would have been able to deal with this without our faith," says Wilma. "When you have a faith life and are happily married, that becomes the bottom line no matter what happens. Our daughter has done very well and is fine."

"An experience like this made us focus on what is important in life," says Karl. "Family was always important, but now we are more aware of how important it is. We put in a swimming pool and take the time to do things with our family. Even when it gets very busy on the farm, family comes first."

Floral Passion

CHAPTER NINETEEN
HELPING HANDS

'After discussing the situation with local growers, we decided to focus our efforts on the Netherlands, knowing that immigrants would quickly and easily be assimilated into the relatively large population of Dutch origin in Niagara.'

— Tony Thompson

— Lawyer Thomas A. Richardson in
his St. Catharines office.

Niagara's greenhouse growers are already fully aware of public sensitivity to matters such as noise, light, drainage and traffic insofar as these relate to their operations. They need to add another concern to the list: air flow.

"It's an issue that's been raised peripherally and it's likely to come up again," says Thomas A. Richardson, a St. Catharines lawyer who specializes in administrative, environmental and municipal law and knows intimately the nature of complaints commonly directed at the greenhouse industry. "I think you'll see it being used as one of the weapons in the conflict that seems to have developed between the tender fruit growers, the grape growers and the greenhouse growers."

Grape growers, he explains, have become extremely conscious of their microclimate, including the critical south-to-north air flow down the escarpment toward Lake Ontario. When air flows through their vineyards, the likelihood of damaging pockets of frost developing is lessened.

"What we're now hearing is that grape growers are beginning to express concern about the flow being impeded. If you build a greenhouse in that current, you back it up and you're likely to affect, so they say at least, the vineyard to the south of you."

So what can greenhouse growers with expansion plans do to address this issue? Tom leans back in his chair, thinks for a moment and answers: "To some extent, it may be a matter of the manner in which they locate their buildings on the property or where they locate them on the property. It may also affect the locations where they acquire their properties in the future. I'm aware that several growers in the Town of Lincoln have acquired land immediately north of the railway right-of-way so now there can't be any allegations they're impeding air flow there because of the embankment the railway sits on."

Much of the ongoing discord in Niagara centres on the use of the land. There's concern, especially among the wineries, about greenhouse expansion reducing the acreage that could be used for grape production. There's concern that the growth, reflected in recent mega projects, is driving up the price of land. There's even concern that greenhouses are spoiling the traditionally serene and picturesque landscape of orchards and vineyards admired by millions of visitors from around the world.

Individual complaints often arise when a greenhouse owner proposes to expand his facilities or build a new one in an area close to residential development. If an amendment is required to the planning document, usually the zoning bylaw, the municipality holds a hearing at which people have an opportunity to state their concerns. These sometimes stray beyond the planning area into environmental matters. When it's not possible for both sides to come to an agreement, the application can be referred to the Ontario Municipal Board for a decision.

There are increasing pressures in the Niagara Region to force new greenhouse operations to locate to the poorer soils south of the escarpment, thus avoiding the conflict between the grape growers, the tender fruit growers and the greenhouse operators. The proposed mid-Peninsula corridor from Burlington to Fort Erie, a new highway intended to ease the congestion on the QEW, would provide another transportation route for greenhouse operators locating south of the escarpment.

Tom is often engaged by greenhouse growers to handle matters involving land use, particularly ones that could lead to the Municipal Board, the Environmental Assessment Board or the Niagara Escarpment Commission. He's uniquely experienced to advise clients in their contacts with officialdom, particularly in the Niagara Peninsula where he's well known by municipal councils and municipal and governmental staff. After his admittance to the Law Society of Upper Canada in 1972, he served as City Solicitor for St. Catharines for 12 years. He's one of 26 lawyers, each with their own specialties, who are associates of Sullivan Mahoney, the largest law firm in Niagara with offices in St. Catharines and Niagara Falls.

In his many years of public and private practice, he has gained wide knowledge and thorough understanding of the issues that involve greenhouse growers, municipalities and the public. So when he talks about where the relationship stands today, ears are perked. His assessment is not entirely rosy.

"The Planning Director in St. Catharines in the '70s, now long deceased, said that in his view greenhouses are not an agricultural use. They are an industrial use. They are high users of gas, electricity and the transportation system and therefore they should be located in industrial parks. That was his view then, and I think you are going to see some of that thinking resurface."

Several years ago, he says, Lincoln proclaimed itself to be greenhouse friendly and actually sought to encourage the industry to locate there. But nowadays not everyone is welcoming new development with open arms. In fact, the current attitude can best be described as "mixed." There's recognition that the greenhouse industry represents a much higher volume in gross dollars than the grape and wine industry. There's also concern that the large growth in the greenhouse industry is resulting in less land being available for tender fruit and grape production.

"My view is that a backlash has been created over the last few years because no one, including the town council, ever conceived of developments as large as the ones on Fourth Avenue. I believe Lakeshore has approval to go to a million square feet when finished. Such developments have brought with them issues of compatibility with their neighbours."

Municipalities like Lincoln now impose site plan control – a stronger measure than a zoning bylaw – to address the impact of large greenhouse projects on nearby residents.

The first alleged impact that Tom recalls hearing emerged when a greenhouse operator sought approval to build a facility in west St. Catharines larger than 15 per cent of the lot coverage, the limit then specified in the zoning bylaw.

"The allegation was that the greenhouse, by being built on farmland, would impede the drainage of the fruit farm next door," he says. "The farmer next door said – it was the first time I heard that expression – 'peaches do not like wet feet.' He said if you build a greenhouse, you'll impede my surface flow. It will cause the water to pond on my property and drown my peaches. That was the first issue that had to be addressed in allowing the project to proceed. The site plan agreement was then utilized in order to provide drainage requirements, ensuring that the farmer next door wasn't affected. There's an irony in this: the farmer is now in the greenhouse business."

Drainage continues to be a matter of great concern to properties, both agricultural and non-agricultural, that surround the location of proposed greenhouse development. It's one that has to be addressed each time through the site plan process.

"My view is that the industry has now learned that it can use the water," says Tom, "so it's capturing it and directing it into cisterns. They bring their own answer to their neighbours' problem. And they're solving a problem of their own – water supply – as well."

Other concerns involve noise from trucks starting at 4 a.m. to take supplies to market and from large fans that are used to control greenhouse environment, growing lights that burn through the night and traffic-related matters. Again, many issues can be dealt with through the site plan procedure. At the new plant of Bayview Flowers Ltd., for example, huge berms were installed along the west and north sides to screen the entire development from the houses on the west side of Haynes Avenue and address to a large extent issues raised by residents. And in the design of the new Lakeshore plant, the trucking area was moved to the middle of the greenhouses, and set back a ways, so that when the project is fully completed, the greenhouses will screen any noise from vehicles.

'Greenhouse growers have to be smart in the sense of locating their sites away from residential dwellings and taking into account some of the issues, such as air flow, that they are likely to face.'

The issue of growing lights illuminating a neighbourhood at night, disturbing the sleep of residents, is one that falls within the control of greenhouse operators. Blackout curtains are already commonplace. Most growers realize that light escaping into the night sky is lost energy.

Tom says one of the weapons used by ratepayers to oppose greenhouse development is to allege environmental impacts.

"In one case, there were allegations of a greenhouse dumping a chemical into an adjacent stream. It's a chemical that is used in small amounts in the greenhouse but it's also used in orchards. What we concluded as likely happening was that when tender fruit growers to the west were spraying, some of this drift was condensing on the greenhouse and being washed down the greenhouse and into the stream. The greenhouse was being tagged as the polluter. Because it was a chemical they use in their own process, there was a devil of a time trying to determine that the greenhouse chemical couldn't be on the outside of the glass."

Obviously, life is not easy for the owner of a greenhouse business who wants to expand to keep up with the growing demand for his products. The municipal zoning bylaws impose restrictions on what can be done. In the agricultural area of west St. Catharines, for example, a farm is required to have a minimum lot frontage of 16 metres, the maximum lot coverage is 25 per cent, greenhouses must be located within at least 15 metres from all property lines and any fans should be at least 25 metres back from these lines. Of course, there's also site plan control to contend with.

Even tapping into the municipal water supply can be difficult. On Fourth Avenue, for example, a hookup is permitted only if the property fronts on the road. The connection is limited to a three-quarter-inch line, hardly big enough to supply water to the large operations. The restrictions were imposed before the arrival of the greenhouses as a measure to limit non-farm development such as houses.

According to Tom, the greenhouse industry can take steps to improve its image in the local communities.

"Greenhouse growers have to be smart in the sense of locating their sites away from residential dwellings and taking into account some of the issues, such as air flow, that they are likely to face. I think that now all of the bigger operators are acutely aware that they have to preserve their water and not allow it to run off site, that they need to know the drainage patterns in their area and that they need to block the escape of light. Technologies are available that allow them to address some of the concerns, including noisy fans. From my point of view, if they acquire the land, they need to have some regard for the difficulties they are likely to get into."

He smiles affectionately as he describes the greenhouse operators of Niagara as "fine people" who work hard, know their business and always stand ready to help each other even though they're competitors. "All the ones I've worked with when they had difficulties were willing to find a way around the mountain."

207

— As Executive Director of Flowers Canada,
Dr. Garry Watson is often called upon to deal with
many different and often difficult issues.

Flowers Canada, the 1,100-member national trade organization of the Canadian floral industry, has been around in one form or another for more than a century.

Its beginnings can be traced to 1897 when 50 gardeners, florists, nurserymen and seedsmen gathered in Toronto and decided to form and support a national group. The Canadian Horticultural Association came into being the following year.

The industry in that period was small. In Toronto, for example, there were only 13 florists – jacks of all trades, growing vegetables in season, flowers and plants for special events and nursery stock as the market demanded. But they could foresee tremendous potential for growth through promoting their industry and addressing common concerns.

In 1905, when its membership stood at 122, the association listed four issues that needed particular attention:

1. The need for some standards of excellence in the industry.

2. Central registration of newly-introduced plants so a neutral authority could test and evaluate them.

3. Changes in tariff schedules to reduce duties on those floral goods, plants and insecticides needed in Canada but not produced in the country.

4. The need for properly trained staff in both the retail and production sectors.

Interestingly, these issues remain important matters affecting Canada's $1.27 billion-a-year floriculture industry even though some have taken a slightly different form.

Over the years, the national association changed names several times. There were even two groups once: the Allied Florists and Growers of Canada and the United Florists of Canada. These merged in the mid-1960s at a meeting in Barrie to form what would become known as Flowers Canada. Its mission was – and still is – to improve the strength and unity of Canadian floriculture through communication, education, marketing, member services and representation.

Education has been one of the priorities of Flowers Canada since its beginning. In addition to assisting in the development of floral courses at schools across the country, it has instituted an accreditation program that rewards successful candidates with the recognized titles of Canadian Accredited Floral Designer, Canadian Accredited Floral Manager or Canadian Accredited Master Florist.

For its members, 28 per cent of whom are growers, the association offers significant savings on the costs of fuel, insurance, long-distance telephone calls, business forms and supplies, vehicle lease or purchase and credit-debit card processing.

Floral Passion

There are areas of focus specifically affecting retailers, distributors and growers. For the growers, these are listed as follows: Flowers Canada works to keep greenhouse operations defined as farms with all agricultural tax advantages to save growers money; it annually leverages $100,000 of voluntary grower contributions into $2.2-million worth of floriculture research for better products; it lobbied for plant breeders' rights legislation to apply to all species and to ensure fair access to new varieties; it enabled many pesticides to be registered for use in Canadian greenhouses; it negotiated relaxed quarantine regulations, and fights trade irritants to keep the U.S. border open to flower growers.

'It helps to have everyone on board and working together from a position of strength.'

Border issues have the close attention of Dr. Garry Watson, Executive Director of Flowers Canada. From the association's offices on Fifth Line South near Milton, he works hand in hand with various federal government departments to resolve problems that arise now and then. Since exports play such a big part in the well-being and growth of the Canadian industry, his message to members, is basic: "Follow the rules."

News Vine, an informative bi-monthly publication of Flowers Canada, listed two examples of border matters in its spring 2001 issue.

"U.S. Customs and Department of Agriculture officials have stepped up their inspections of potted plants and cut flower bouquets exported to the U.S.A.," the first article stated. "Many truckloads have been turned back from the border with large losses for some of our members. The focus is country of origin labelling and pest inspections . . . All products must be clearly marked with the country where they were made or grown. Even wrappers, sleeves, care tags, picks, photo labels etc. must indicate where they were printed and the source of the material . . . It is not acceptable to label a bouquet or arrangement Product of Canada if some flowers are imported from off-shore even if the majority of flowers are grown in Canada . . ."

Canada has rules too, of course. The second item concerned an announcement by the Plant Health and Production Division of the Canadian Food Inspection Agency of a complete prohibition on the importation into Canada of live decorative branches of quince, apple, plum, cherry, pear and willow from all countries. "These branches are potential high-risk hosts to an array of quarantine insects and diseases."

The border issues came up again in 2002. News Vine reported in June:

"Phytosanitary (pest inspection) and customs problems at the U.S. border increased in frequency again during the heavy export shipping around the recent floral holidays. Flowers Canada reminds all exporters to ensure their paperwork is in order and their plant material is free from pests. Several member companies have experienced prolonged periods of inspection scrutiny by U.S. officials, increased costs, and loss of expedited clearing privileges as a result of what most would consider single minor infractions. These are very difficult to overcome given the high degrees of freedom in decision-making enjoyed by most border officials."

Once more, Flowers Canada jumped into action on the diplomatic front, bringing the irritants to the attention of senior government officials in the U.S. and Canada.

Garry grew up and attended school in Toronto and received his doctorate in plant biochemistry and physiology from the University of Toronto. His research interests involved lipid metabolism and ultrastructure in plant chloroplast membranes.

He worked initially as Registrar, Division of Sciences at the Erindale College Mississauga campus of the University of Toronto. At the George Brown College of Applied Arts and Technology, Canada's largest community college, he was Registrar, Director of Student Services, and Director of Computer and Audio/Visual Services.

Garry's interest in plants took him next to be the Director of the Royal Botanical Gardens in Hamilton, the third largest botanical garden in the world. As Adjunct Professor at McMaster University in Hamilton, he was responsible for the scientific and research program at the premiere

attraction. He joined Flowers Canada in 1996.

"It's a big challenge," he says of his current position. "We – the board of directors and the staff – represent members from across Canada and have to deal with many different and often difficult matters. It helps to have everyone on board and working together from a position of strength."

THEIR RIGHT-HAND MAN

— Dr. Irwin Smith of Flowers Canada (Ontario) Inc.
presents the 2001 award for research excellence
to Jorge Guiterez, a student from Mexico
at the University of Guelph.

Dr. Irwin Smith has a lot on his plate in his capacity as chief promoter of the floral industry in Ontario and its spokesman on many serious issues affecting greenhouse production, wholesaling/distribution and retailing.

Yet the jovial and outspoken Executive Director of Flowers Canada (Ontario) Inc., based in an office unit in a business mall on Elmira Road North in the western outskirts of Guelph, asserts that he can handle more, particularly in the area of promotion and image-building.

"We already do a fair amount of marketing to educate the public about flowers," he says. "For example, we have in the past published a six-page, full-colour brochure called Fresh Flowers Speak. But we can't do as much as we want in this area because of budget restrictions."

The growers, who make up the bulk of the organization's membership, say they are more concerned about border issues than promotion. This attitude, says Irwin, is legitimate. If hassle-free access to the vast U.S. market isn't maintained, Ontario flower producers and distributors could face severe difficulties. Already some U.S. politicians have made noises about the province "dumping" cheap flowers onto their market.

Even with those concerns aside, says Irwin, the growers seem disinclined to focus on promotion because they usually sell everything they produce and figure increased efforts and expenditures to spread the good news about flowers are unnecessary – at least for now.

Flowers Canada (Ontario) was formed on March 10, 1966, as the latest of a number of associations that have represented the floral industry since 1898. It was first known as United and Allied Florists of Canada (Ontario) Inc. The present name was adopted in April, 1986. Guelph has always been its home base – first in a warehouse, then in the downtown and now in the mall – because of the location of many other agricultural commodity groups in the area. There has also been a long-time involvement of the University of Guelph in horticultural research and education.

The national Flowers Canada group, based near Milton and directed by Dr. Garry Watson, deals with any issues that may arise on the border or on matters affecting the industry from coast to coast and often involving federal authorities. "If a truck is stopped at the border, they'll phone Garry first," says Irwin. The Ontario association and its regional chapters, including one in Niagara, follow their own active agenda.

Eighty per cent of the annual membership fees of Irwin's group is paid by 175 growers from across the province. Retail florists also belong to it, and a lot of time is spent on issues directly affecting their part of the industry. In fact, one of the main programs is the School of Floral Design held at the University of Guelph every July.

"It operates on an annual $120,000 budget," says Irwin, "and accommodates 120 students who pay fees ranging from $600 to $1,000, depending on which one of the seven courses they take. Each one runs a maximum of 10 days. We use successful business people as instructors. The certificate that is awarded is recognized throughout the industry."

Flowers Canada (Ontario) also is deeply involved in ongoing efforts to ease some of the anxieties among growers over the energy situation. The F&V Energby Co-op was set up in 1988, with its own board, to purchase gas in bulk, and now two years in advance, giving its 330 members security in a fluctuating market. The Ontario Greenhouse Vegetable Growers' Marketing Board, located in Leamington, is also an active supporter of the co-op. Indeed, half of the $100-a-year annual memberships are paid by vegetable growers.

"The energy market is a complicated one," says Irwin. "By being a member of the co-op, you don't have to worry about it. We can provide stable gas prices, not necessarily the cheapest. The advantage is the security and knowing your costs of operation."

There's also a telephone co-operative, FFVTEL, set up in 1995. By pooling long-distance calls, cheaper rates are available.

"It's run out of our office and is working well," says Irwin. "It's saving money for our members."

Research is another area of extreme interest for Flowers Canada (Ontario). Support for government efforts in this field is made possible by having growers pay voluntary levies according to square footage.

— Instructor Kathy Mustard shows some of the finer
points of working with flowers at the
School of Floral Design in Guelph.

Proceeds from the group's annual golf tournament go to the Cecil Delworth Foundation which was set up in 1966 to encourage and support research on the culture, marketing and handling of floriculture crops and to encourage and support floriculture education programs. Cecil Delworth was a former director of Flowers Canada who travelled across the country to hold grower education clinics and preach the need for scientific flower production.

Some research money is also realized from the Canadian Greenhouse Conference, a big trade show that has moved from the University of Guelph to Toronto. As a member of the board of directors, Irwin is involved in managing the event.

'We need to do more to get people interested in greenhouse work.'

His other responsibilities include lobbying the provincial government on specific issues affecting growers, such as ones dealing with pesticides. He often works hand in hand with the fruit and vegetable growers who have similar interests. In fact, he sits in on the meetings of the Ontario Fruit and Vegetable Growers Association.

Flowers Canada (Ontario) is also involved with F.A.R.M.S., the organization that operates the foreign labour pool in Ontario. Thirty-five flower producers used offshore help in 2001.

"Many flower growers are finding it difficult to get good labour from the local market," says Irwin. "In Niagara, there's a lot of competition from the tourism industry. It's pretty aggressive. We haven't been as good at it. We need to do more to get people interested in greenhouse work."

The man with the growers' interests at heart was born in 1947 in Salisbury, Rhodesia, renamed Zimbabwe in 1980. His grandparents had emigrated from Ireland to South Africa in the days of the Boer War. His father, born in Capetown, was two years old when the family moved to Rhodesia. Grandpa and his son ran a men's clothing business, importing fine goods from England.

Irwin, one of four children, enrolled at the University

of Natal in Durban, South Africa, in 1966 and spent four years there, specializing in horticultural science. After his graduation, he returned to Rhodesia and began work at a government research station. He also married Zofja, a teacher of Polish background. But life in his strife-torn native land was fraught with anxieties and dangers, prompting him to go back to South Africa.

After a sojourn on a pineapple farm, he accepted a lectureship at his alma mater. He lectured for 15 years, in the meantime earning a doctorate degree with his thesis on growing greenhouse crops in soilless media such as sawdust and developing bark as a growing medium.

His life was suddenly turned upside down in 1990 when

Zofja was killed in an auto accident. He was left to care for three sons, aged 11, 10 and 8.

"After my wife died," he says, "I went on sabbatical leave to Canada with my sons. A friend of mine lived in Edmonton. I soon needed some work and ended up at Lakehead University in Thunder Bay. I met a Canadian woman, Katharine, and knew then that I was in Canada to stay."

He's been with Flowers Canada (Ontario) since January, 1998, working diligently on behalf of the people whose colourful and variegated blooms brighten the lives of so many North Americans.

Tony Thompson reflects on a birth announcement he received from a couple in the Netherlands who had earlier sent him a notice with the words Wij gaan naar Canada (We are going to Canada) emblazoned near the top.

"It shows the really good relationship we've established with Dutch greenhouse growers who are thinking of moving to Canada," the energetic Horticultural Business Consultant to the Niagara Economic and Tourism Corporation says. "They appreciate our efforts on their behalf."

The idea of going overseas to make direct contact with growers was conceived in 1998 after the release of a report that stated North America needed 500 more acres of greenhouse vegetable production to meet the demands of a rising consumer base.

"After discussing the situation with local growers, we decided to focus our efforts on the Netherlands, knowing that immigrants would quickly and easily be assimilated into the relatively large population of Dutch origin in Niagara," says Tony.

"A consultant in Holland advised us on where to have our open house meetings," says Tony. "We had four of them – in Naaldwijk, Sassenheim, Zoetermeer and Grubbenvorst – attended by a total of 145 people. Many of them stayed after the meetings and talked and talked. They were very interested. Sometimes we didn't get to our rooms until one in the morning. We also made contact with Dutch banks, legal and accounting companies and greenhouse manufacturers. It was a very busy week."

As a result of the presentations and discussions, more than 45 people, mostly vegetable growers, but also some flower growers and even a group of poultry farmers, travelled to Canada for a first-hand look. The Corporation arranged a full agenda for everyone who wanted to learn and explore. A two-man team, including Tony, then made a follow-up visit to Holland to meet individually with a number of growers who had shown a strong inclination to move to Niagara.

— Tony Thompson meets with J. G. (Como) van Hellenberg Hubar, the Netherlands Ambassador to Canada, in Niagara-on-the-Lake in October, 2002.

'We can't dictate where they will go. But we can show them Niagara's many advantages.'

"Basically, the people who came here really liked what they saw. The biggest reaction concerned the amount of space. In fact, one man walked into this office – I had never met him before – and, before saying 'Good morning,' his first words were: 'I can't believe all the space you have here.' That's so important to them because there is no room to expand in Holland."

He organized a one-week mission to Holland in 1999 as part of an aggressive effort by the Corporation to convince restless growers, particularly ones involved in vegetable production, to set up business in Niagara Region. A number of them have already decided to head for Ontario, although not necessarily to Niagara. The couple with the baby, for instance, picked a place in Courtland, near Tillsonburg.

"We can't dictate where they will go," says Tony. "But we can show them Niagara's many advantages." He believes that as many as 10 families may be on the move eventually.

The Niagara team that flew to Europe to hang out the big welcome sign was made up of two local mayors, Ralph Beamer of the Town of Pelham and Ray Konkle of the Town of Lincoln; William Connor, Chief Executive Officer of the Corporation, and Tony; Bram Radix, Lincoln's Economic Development Officer; Morris Looby of the Royal Bank of Canada's Niagara Agri Business Centre, plus a member of the Business Immigration Section of the Ontario Ministry of Economic Development, Trade and Tourism.

Co-operation with the Netherlands continues to be one of the highlights on Tony's program. On October 11, 2002, on behalf of the Corporation, he welcomed to Niagara the Netherlands Ambassador to Canada, J. G. (Como) van Hellenberg Hubar, the Netherlands Consul General in Toronto, Jan Hesseling, Consul Rudolf Wagener, Consul Napoleon Winia and their wives. The group visited a greenhouse operation and a winery, attended a round-table meeting with local corporate and academic representatives, continued with a reception attended by many of Niagara's Dutch floral community and ended the day with a dinner hosted by the Netherlands Consulate General.

Tony was born in England on New Year's Eve in 1932. He married a Canadian girl, Libby Cameron, in 1970 and for five years they lived in Cambridge, England, where their two children, Cara and Graham, were born. After moving to St. Catharines in 1975, he worked 16 years for JVK, a wholesale supplier of seed, plant material, plant labels and greenhouse supplies to commercial growers. In 1992, he became Horticultural Business Consultant for the Niagara Region Development Corporation, which later amalgamated with the Region Niagara Tourist Council to become the Niagara Economic and Tourism Corporation.

In addition to its Dutch project, the Corporation actively promotes the export of Niagara floral products to the United States.

"We co-operate with Canadian and American wholesale florists," says Tony, "and in 2001 we were invited to exhibit Niagara products at a U.S. trade show. After the show, a number of wholesalers came to tour greenhouses and inspect the crops. They are now buying from Niagara growers. We also produced a brochure, Advantage Niagara, and distributed it to wholesale florists in America, some of them selling in excess of $20 million U.S. a year. We support the greenhouse industry in this way because we believe it is a vital and important part of the Niagara Region scene and economy."

Since 1993, the Niagara Economic and Tourism Corporation has produced the Ontario Greenhouse Growers' Directory and Buyers' Guide. This definitive publication, listing greenhouse growers, wholesale florists and suppliers, is distributed in Canada, the U.S., Asia, Australia and Europe. The number of copies printed annually has risen to 6,500, an increase of 30 per cent from the 5,000 printed for the first issue.

The success of the directory has enabled the Corporation to invest $120,000 in floricultural research in Ontario through the Cecil Delworth Foundation. The Foundation has given something fitting in return: recognition to the Corporation for its ongoing support and the 2000 Cecil Delworth Award to Tony for his significant contribution to the floriculture industry.

213

— Greenhouse operations, such as these on Fairlane Road in Jordan Station, contribute significantly to the local economy. Efforts are continuing to lure more greenhouse growers to Niagara.

Floral Passion

Wayne Brown stands ready to offer free expert advice to any greenhouse grower in Niagara who is struggling with an annoying and potentially costly problem related to a production, plant disease or insect matter.

"Growers are worried about these things all the time," says the Greenhouse Floricultural Specialist at the Horticultural Research Institute of Ontario on Victoria Avenue North near Vineland. "I can get 15 calls a day about problems, particularly in the production and disease management area, and a visit is usually required with the complex ones. If this sounds like a lot, it isn't. There was much more one-on-one contact when I started in this job in 1979."

Instead of spending a big part of his day visiting individual growers and dealing with their unique production problems, which he did after taking over the position from Dr. Theo J. Blom, Wayne now devotes most of his time to developing programs for the industry as a whole and doing applied research as well.

'No one has to tell them that they have to stay on top of diseases.'

— Wayne Brown examines the root system of a problem plant at the Horticultural Research Institute of Ontario.

It's not that diseases and bugs are going the way of the dodo. They're always lurking, ready to pounce and do harm. In fact, Wayne finds that a big industry-wide disease problem arises every four or five years. But growers, he says, have become more observant and knowledgeable and in most cases are quite capable of handling matters effectively without involving the Research Institute directly.

"No one has to tell them that they have to stay on top of diseases. If they get a quarantinable one in their operation, the government inspection agency can close their greenhouses. The quarantine material could be destroyed and a fungicide program would have to be applied. An operation could be out of production for an extended period, which translates into a lot of lost money and market."

The Institute was founded by the Ontario government in 1906 on 90 acres of land, part of which had been donated by M. F. Rittenhouse of Chicago, a former resident of the Niagara area. Called the Horticultural Experiment Station, it gradually absorbed the work of the 15 fruit experiment stations that had been established in the province in the 1890s.

The Vineland facility originally functioned to determine varieties of fruit best adapted to growing on the tender fruit belt of Ontario and for the production of new and more valuable varieties. Other duties came along: investigation of cultural problems, pollination, soil management, pruning, propagation and weed control. The program was expanded to include vegetable crops and ornamentals. In 1947, a horticultural products laboratory and a grape substation were established. When the greenhouse industry started to blossom in Niagara, the research station was ideally located for handling work related to floriculture.

The current name was adopted in 1966. At that time, the 442-acre facility was administered as a branch of the Ontario Ministry of Agriculture, Food and Rural Affairs. On April 1, 1997, it became part of the University of Guelph which, through the Ontario Agricultural College, had enjoyed a long and close association. It is currently a division within the Department of Plant Agriculture.

Wayne, born in 1952 to John and Evelyn, was raised on a dairy farm near Meaford, Ontario. He remembers spending time in his early years with his grandmother, Sarah, an avid gardener who lived next door, and helping her with her geranium cuttings on the sunporch.

He went to the University of Guelph, intending to study dairy science. But he changed his mind and took horticulture instead. He had a love for trees and plants. He earned his Bachelor's degree, taught for a year at Olds College, Alberta, and returned to Guelph to complete his Master's studies.

After graduation, he became greenhouse floriculturist and mushroom specialist based at Vineland.

"I had a counterpart, John Hughes, who worked out of Brampton and covered the rest of the province," he says. "His office was later transferred to the university. As mushroom specialist, I was responsible for the entire province."

Besides being on call for advice, Wayne and the Institute devote resources to educating growers. There are publications on what to do in production management and what to use in case of diseases or pests like thrips and white flies. Pest management workshops and production night schools are held annually to train new employees and growers how to identify and control insects and diseases. The role of the environment and nutrition on crop growth and quality is also taught. Monthly newsletters are inserted in trade magazines. Furthermore, the Institute sponsors and assists in organizing the Canadian Greenhouse Conference, an annual event that features the latest approved methods and tools available on the market.

Wayne also does some applied research on flowers, using the Institute's extensive greenhouse facilities.

"Growers like this," he says. "They can see things growing under Ontario conditions. We provide them with an unbiased evaluation. For them, this is more reassuring than just to have something that's promoted by salesmen."

His predecessor and colleague, Theo Blom, emigrated from the Netherlands in 1973, two months after being told a job was available. His plan was to set up his own business. But he eventually ended up in the employment of the provincial government instead.

Theo, born in 1949, came from Aalsmeer where his parents, Theodorus and Marie, grew cut roses. Their operation was next door to the one of Frank Bulk, father of the Bulk brothers who emigrated and became respected rose growers in Ontario. But Theo's association with the Bulk name doesn't end there.

"While I was at the greenhouses of rose grower Peter van Wees in Princeton," he says, "I met a lady, Anneke, whose father, a grower in Holland, had bought the operation that Frank Bulk owned before he became our neighbour. She was a teacher who was visiting an uncle in the West and then visited the van Wees family where I met her for the

first time. She became my wife. There's a further twist to this: Jake, one of Frank Bulk's sons, is now the owner of the business in Princeton."

Theo was well educated, having obtained his Master's degree in Wageningen, Holland, with soil science as his specialty. Encouraged by Peter van Wees to continue his university studies, he enrolled at the University of Guelph and started working on his doctorate.

"While still studying, I was told of a job opening in Vineland in floriculture," he recalls. "I applied for it and was accepted even after I laid down one condition: that I start work a half year later so that I could finish my PhD. I started on March 1, 1976."

He had no trouble handling the job of greenhouse floriculturist. His thorough knowledge and sharp mind quickly earned him the respect of growers.

"My biggest problem was a talk on soil nutrition in Woodstock organized by Flowers Canada," he chuckles. "I didn't know the language too well and was very nervous after only a couple of months on the job."

Stamina, not nerves, was his main concern when he took part once in a 100-mile cross-country skiing race between Montreal and Ottawa.

"We raced 50 miles a day," he says. "I was dead tired but barely slept as it was minus 25 Celsius in the woods where I stayed overnight with 20 to 25 other skiers."

In 1979, his responsibilities changed. The director of the Institute phoned, saying he wanted to start a floricultural program. After answering a few questions, Theo was told: "You can start." No formal interview was necessary.

The focus of the new program initially was on energy conservation and crop production. A solar greenhouse was built. And energy curtains were tested. At the end of the 1980s, the focus changed to applied production research. A lot of time was spent on sub-irrigation, determining such basic questions as: "How long does it take for a pot to get soaked if it is watered from the bottom instead from above?"

When the Institute became part of the University of Guelph in 1997, Theo became an Associate Professor of Greenhouse Floriculture. He does research and teaches greenhouse production to third-year students.

"Teaching is something I enjoy," he says. "For 12 years, I taught night school for the Niagara Parks Commission. And I also taught a 10-night course for local growers on plant nutrition, organized through Flowers Canada and held in Vineland. As you can see, I got over my nervousness about standing in front of an audience a long time ago."

— An experiment in lighting draws the interest of Dr. Theo J. Blom.

GLENDALE'S VISION

With terraced gardens and other beautifully landscaped areas on its 68-acre site just below the Niagara Escarpment, the new Glendale Campus of Niagara College is already one of the most attractive educational institutions in the country.

Busloads of tourists visiting Niagara stop by to admire it all, especially the gorgeous blooms in the 25,000-square-foot, state-of-the-art greenhouse complex.

'We want Glendale to be the best showcase of horticulture in Canada.'

But today's amenities of Glendale's living laboratory concept are just a drop in the bucket compared to what is in store for the property at Glendale Avenue and Taylor Road, just off the QEW in Niagara-on-the-Lake. An ambitious 25-year plan includes an arboretum, formal gardens, interpretive gardens, nurseries and vineyards. Moreover, nature trails, gazebos, seating areas, community gardens and display areas will encourage the public to explore and learn along with the students.

"We have a vision," says Jon Ogryzlo, director of the college's Environment, Horticulture and Agribusiness Division. "We want Glendale to be the best showcase of horticulture in Canada."

The horticulture program has been around for nearly 35 years. It was started in 1968, a year after the college was founded as part of a new post-secondary school system in Ontario geared to serving the needs of the local communities, and for many years was located in a building on Niagara Street in St. Catharines that was part of an Agriculture Canada research station.

"Our aim right from the outset was to create a general horticulturist," says Jon. "There was, and is, a definite need in Niagara for such training because of all that we have here: the vineyards, the orchards, the parks and, of course, the greenhouses. On Niagara Street, we graduated from 20 to 25 students a year. After the evolution of our present program began in 1995, the enrolment for the two-year diploma course has ranged from 100 to 164."

In the first year of general horticulture education, the emphasis is placed on practical horticulture, greenhouse operations, nursery production, grounds maintenance and landscape planning. In the second year, students have the option of specializing in one of three areas: greenhouse technician, landscape technician or horticulture technician. Practical work experience is included.

"We want all our students to be horticulturists first and specialists next," says Jon. "With that solid background, they could easily switch careers if the one they had picked turned out to be not to their liking."

He and others involved in the college's School of Horticulture and Agribusiness were deeply disappointed when the greenhouse course was first offered a few years ago and only four students applied, 20 short of

— Horticultural students at the Glendale Campus of Niagara College have access to a state-of-the-art greenhouse.

Floral Passion

217

— Here are some examples of what makes Glendale one of the most atractive educational institutions in the country.

the minimum needed to get it operational. They had not expected this because of the known demand in the greenhouse industry for qualified workers.

"We have some work to do in this area," says Jim Thomson, manager of campus development in the Environment, Horticulture and Agribusiness Division. "The challenge is to get young people interested in the subject. As one step, we have invited high schools to send students here to see what we have to offer to get them ready for a career in greenhouse growing. There's a perception among many of them that greenhouse work is just a part-time job. We need to show there is a future for them in the industry."

And the industry, he adds, can do its part by directing young people, even new employees, to the program.

"The industry is making strides in attracting young people," says Jon. "Progressive companies are adopting apprenticeship programs to train their workers and implementing higher pay scales for skilled graduates of our diploma programs. These types of changes will definitely help to attract young people to make career choices that include the greenhouse and horticulture industries."

Challenges aside, the Glendale officials are pleased with the success of their general program – they are now training third-generation horticulturists – and are laying the groundwork for even more exciting times. For example, discussions are under way with the Niagara Parks Commission and the University of Guelph to set up a four-year degree program in horticulture technology.

The superb greenhouse facility to which horticulture students have access has put Glendale well on the road to reaching the status of best Canadian showcase. It is equipped with computerized climate controls, rolling benches, shade and energy curtains and a propagation mist bench. The complex includes a teaching lab and classroom designed for subject areas such as practical horticulture, floral design and ecosystem restoration. For encouraging first-hand contact with the public, there is also a retail area for the sale of bedding stock, nursery stock and seasonal potted plants.

Of course, lots more is planned. And the goal of it all, according to Jon, is "an opportunity to raise the bar – to promote a professional attitude in the industry."

— *The greenhouse's growing lights create a spectacular night-time view at the college at Glendale Avenue and Taylor Road in Niagara-on-the-Lake.*

— As part of their training, students of The Niagara Parks Botanical Gardens and School of Horticulture are responsible for maintaining and developing the beautifully landscaped Niagara Parks Botanical Gardens.

The story of the school goes back to 1885 when The Niagara Parks Commission was formed for the purpose of preserving the scenic lands adjacent to the Niagara Falls. These lands were to be self-sustaining and free to public access. In the 1920s, the parks system had expanded to the point where there was a dire need for qualified gardeners.

In 1908, the Chief Horticulturist, Henry Moore, had already recommended that a training program be started to fill the need of trained gardeners in Canada at that time. But it wasn't until 1936 that the school was established.

'And while we're training people so that they can excel in their fields, we're also providing enjoyment and education for many thousands of others.'

The Niagara Parks Commission Training School for Apprentice Gardeners, as it was initially called, was patterned after the British apprenticeship style of training. Students were required to attend school year-round, starting with the growing season in April. There were eight male students in the first year. They were required to sign an indentured servitude to The Niagara Parks Commission.

In the 1970s, enrolment included female students and the admission was increased to 12 students a year. The school was then known as The Niagara Parks Commission School of Horticulture. It was changed in the early 1990s to The Niagara Parks Botanical Gardens and School of Horticulture, although most people, thinking this is quite a mouthful, refer to it simply as Niagara Parks School of Horticulture. The school now admits up to 15 students a year, selected from among as many as 100 applicants. There are plans to slightly increase enrolment at some point as the gardens develop.

Applicants must provide an Ontario Secondary School Diploma or its equivalent and an official transcript showing a mininum of 60 per cent in each of the mandatory courses at the advanced level – mathematics, English, biology and chemistry – or 70 per cent at the general level. They must also have practical experience amounting to at least two or three summers of work in a parks department, nursery,

Tourists come by the hundreds of thousands every year to walk, free of charge, through the manicured gardens of The Niagara Parks Botanical Gardens and School of Horticulture located on the Niagara Parkway, a short drive from the Canadian Horseshoe Falls.

The many features include the rose garden with its 2,300 colourful and fragant roses, complemented by seasonal annual displays, the herb garden, the vegetable garden, the rock garden, the parterre garden with its breathtaking displays of annuals, the perennial collection and the arboretum.

For a reasonable admission fee, visitors can can also explore a fascinating bit of the world of fauna: the Butterfly Conservatory, a tropical paradise with exotic plants that

is home to more than 2,000 free-flying butterflies from butterfly farmers around the world.

While on tour of the 100-acre gardens or just relaxing with a light lunch or snack in the Butterfly Cafe, visitors will probably spot young men and women busily at work, pruning, planting, raking or weeding. They're students of The Niagara Parks School of Horticulture, situated on the property, responsible for maintaining and developing the botanical gardens as part of their horticulture training under the direction of instructional staff.

Some of the graduates of the three-year program are now owners of successful greenhouse operations in the Peninsula.

greenhouse or other horticultural operation under the supervision of a professional horticulturist.

Tuition is $875 a year. In the on-site student residence, room and board is provided free of charge as a taxable benefit for first and second-year students. Third-year students are required to obtain off-campus accommodation at their expense.

Besides the beautifully landscaped botanical gardens, the students have a state-of-the-art greenhouse available for instructional purposes. Thousands of different flowers are propagated in the 10,000-square-foot facility for later transfer to the gardens. It was built in 1996 as part of a $34-million enhancement program that included construction of the 11,000-square-foot Butterfly Conservatory, the largest glass-enclosed one in the world. The lecture hall, built in 1961, houses a library, a laboratory and the administrative and instructors' offices.

The faculty consists of five full-time instructors and other professionals in the industry who teach some courses in the academic program. The key administrators are Liz Klose, Superintendent, School of Horticulture, Tom Laviolette, Superindent, Botanical Gardens, and Melvin Dell, Curator of the Butterfly Conservatory. Tom and Melvin are graduates of the school.

Deborah Whitehouse, Senior Director of Parks for The Niagara Parks Commission, is in overall charge. She was born in Flushing, Michigan, grew up in that state and obtained a Bachelor's degree in biology from the University of Michigan and a Master's degree in forest science from the University of Missouri. She became an instructor at the school in 1980 and served as acting Director of Horticulture and School Superintendent before being appointed Senior Director of Parks in early 2001.

"Some of the graduates stay with us," she says, "but most of them go on to other organizations or develop their own businesses. They've ended up in responsible positions in the horticultural industry across Canada. Some have gone into the greenhouse business in Niagara. And while we're training people so that they can excel in their fields, we're also providing enjoyment and education for many thousands of others. That's our mission."

221

— Horticulture students are busily at work, planting another showcase for the public's enjoyment.

Floral Passion

222

— Liz Klose, Superintendent, School of Horticulture, and Tom Laviolette, Superintendent, Botanical Gardens.

— Deborah Whitehouse is Senior Director of Parks for The Niagara Parks Commission.

— Hundreds of thousands of tourists visit The Niagara Parks Botanical Gardens every year to enjoy the flowers, plants, trees and other delights, including the colourful inhabitants of the Butterfly Conservatory.

NIAGARA PARKS

— *There's always something to see or do at the world-famous parklands that run the length of the Canadian side of the Niagara River.*

A TRUSTING FRIEND

— Niagara Credit Union's striking head office building in St. Catharines.

The European immigrants who settled in rural Niagara shortly before and after the Second World War possessed farming skills, good work ethics and a determination to buy a piece of land and move ahead.

But these qualities rarely were taken into consideration when they applied at a bank for a loan to make a start on a business of their own or to purchase a truck, a piece of machinery or whatever. New farmers with no assets to speak of were often deemed too risky to be trusted with money that had to be repaid.

Fortunately for them, and the community as a whole, a small group of kind people with an entirely different attitude stood ready to lend a helping hand. They were the officers of the Niagara Credit Union, mostly farmers themselves, who understood the aspirations and plight of the applicants and were ready to do business with a key ingredient in mind: trust.

"The credit union's losses after 16 years of operation – it went into business in 1945 – were only $2,264, which is miniscule when measured against the gains," comments Bill Goertz, who retired from his Chief Executive Officer's position in 1993 after 38 years with the institution. "It shows the honesty and integrity of these people. They would rather not eat than not pay back on a loan."

Stacks of papers documenting the history of Niagara Credit Union from its beginnings to the present are in front of him. He's researching it all for a book he is writing with the capable assistance of another retiree, Bill Steinman, formerly with the credit union's human resources department.

"In the early days, a lot of business was done on trust," says the former boss. "For example, a half-ton truck could be offered as security, but it was strictly a formality because the registration number and other identification weren't even recorded. The mere mention that his father was so and so could give a member a loan. Then there was the advice offered by the credit union's founder: 'An applicant should be invited to bring his wife along. If you see dirt under her fingernails, give him a loan'."

With its roots deeply imbedded in the soil of Niagara, the credit union grew in pace with the gradual development of the region's rural areas, including the greenhouse sector. It branched out, offering higher dividends and more financial services, and attracted the attention of people in the urban areas as well. Its growth never stopped. It now is the largest credit union in Ontario and the fifth largest in Canada, with a handsome head office along the QEW in St. Catharines, 15 branch offices, more than 80,000 members and assets well over $1 billion.

The history of Niagara Credit Union actually goes back to 1937 when the Niagara Township Fruit Co-operative came into being in the village of Virgil. It had 100 members, mostly Mennonite cashcroppers growing asparagus, field tomatoes, strawberries and so on. Ears perked up when, in 1943, the provincial government's Department of Agriculture organized a seminar at the University of Guelph on the formation of credit unions. Since the co-op was in need of money, some of its members figured that a credit union could become a useful financial arm and take care of this problem.

"A. P. Regier, the miller at the co-op, thought otherwise," says Bill, the ex-CEO. "He felt that a credit union should be open to everyone. He was a Mennonite from Ukraine who had lost everything, went to Alberta where he homesteaded, buying 160 acres from the government for $10, and then came to Niagara. He was a firm believer in co-ops and credit unions, knowing from experience that they could be of invaluable help, and became the leader in setting up the credit union."

A charter written on a scrap piece of paper was signed by 24 persons in July, 1944, and the credit union began operations in Virgil the following year with 63 members and assets of $2,421. The first loan – $300 listed as account No. 3 – was granted to John A. Willms, a member of the co-op board and a director of the credit union. "He didn't need the money," says Bill. "He merely wanted to show how a credit union works and get the ball rolling."

'In the early days, a lot of business was done on trust.'

The ball never stopped rolling. Along the way, the credit union helped many people get their feet planted on solid ground and, through hard work, a bit of savvy and wise investments, advance to success. For example, a 1952 arrival from Germany, an upholsterer by trade, got a $300 loan to buy a sewing machine and then built up his young

— Bill Goertz: "We always stood ready to help."

business into a large enterprise and branched out to other endeavours as well. Similar stories can be told about some of the greenhouse growers.

"When these people arrived here," says Bill, "they began growing vegetables or fruit. They later moved into flowers when that industry showed promise of taking off. Of course, availability of money was a critical factor. We always stood ready to help. And we're still here, ready to help. Our membership includes 18 firms that are involved with greenhouses in some way."

— Niagara Credit Union's constant growth is reflected in the construction of a new branch facility in Virgil.

'In Toronto, if something broke down, you'd call a repairman. But if a greenhouse grower could fix something himself, he would. This exited me and I saw the business as one I would enjoy.'

— *Leigh Harrison*

— Bob Murch of JVK in St. Catharines: "Keeping on top of everything requires a lot of research and time involvement." At right, some of his firm's catalogues.

As a boy in Stayner, a town near Collingwood, Bob Murch was aware of the flower bulb business that an enterprising Dutchman named Jack van Klaveren ran out of an old barn in nearby Creemore.

But this meant absolutely nothing to him until many years later when, by sheer coincidence, he joined the staff of JVK, the St. Catharines-based greenhouse supplier that had evolved from the pursuit set up by the super salesman from the land of the tulips. He's now co-owner and president, managing a widely respected company that handles no fewer than 70,000 line items.

"Van Klaveren had a typical old-style Dutch bulb import business," says Bob. "He made his rounds of greenhouse growers and others in Ontario and took the train to Pennsylvania and British Columbia to do the same thing there. Then he went back to Holland – he was from Sassenheim – to pack all his orders and send them on the boat to Canada. He came over again to deliver it all. It was like a one-man show."

Bob's father was a high school principal in Stayner and taught Jack's son, Cor, who lived in the area during the months when the bulb undertaking was in progress.

After Jack became ill in the early 1970s, the business was taken over by Jack Vink, a bulb specialist in Holland, who moved it to his 18-acre peach and grape farm on Seventh Street. It continued as a bulb importer with Jack supplying the bulbs and Keith Grey of St. Catharines, formerly with Stokes Seeds, looking after the business end. Gradually, they added other products such as seeds and plant material. Over the years, other principals came and went and the company developed into what it is today.

Bob, born in 1954, always had a love for horticulture. He grew up in a rural environment. He even had a little landscaping business while in high school. Later on, when his father taught at a Canadian Forces school in Baden-Baden, in Germany's Black Forest region, he had opportunities to visit nurseries and greenhouses in several European countries. Back in Canada, he became a student at the Niagara Parks School of Horticulture.

'We go wherever we need to go in the world to buy the best quality products which we bring here and resell.'

"This school taught me how to work and how to survive," he says. "We physically had to work seven or eight hours a day and then go to classes at night. And the bills had to be paid somehow, so most students worked all weekend long at their own jobs."

While at the school, he became acquainted with Jim Dennington, instructor of the greenhouse course, who was employed at JVK. After graduation, while working in a municipal parks position in Calgary and looking around for other opportunities, he came across the JVK name again. He applied for a sales job that was open and was hired. Ten years later, in 1988, he was President.

JVK is a wholesale supplier to the North American greenhouse industry. It has its own line of flower seeds which are grown primarily in the southern hemisphere where two crops a year are possible. The other product areas are supplies (chemicals, fertilizers, containers, etc.), plants (cuttings and bulbs) and tags.

"We go wherever we need to go in the world to buy the best quality products which we bring here and resell," says Bob. "Our staff, which can rise to 90 people in the busy periods, includes key buyers in each of the four product areas and 16 sales people located from coast to coast in Canada. In the U.S., we deal through agents."

In the summer, the company has trial gardens for new seed and plant varieties at its St. Catharines location and at the Niagara Parks School of Horticulture near the Falls. These are also the venues for a Growers' Day in July at which appreciation is shown to customers amid a bit of promotion. Guests can tour the facilities: the warehouse, the coolers for the bulbs and the atmospherically-controlled storage areas for seeds. There are new things to see each year.

"We add from 100 to 500 new varieties and colours a year, depending on how prolific the breeders are," says Bob. "At the same time, we remove some of the older ones. Keeping on top of everything requires a lot of research and time involvement. The difficult part is that the results are extremely unpredictable. We can work on something for three or four years and it can turn out to be a dud in the end."

His interests go beyond the Canadian border in more than a business sense. He and his wife, Lezlie, have adopted two children from Bolivia. In addition, they have sponsored visits of 20 other South American children, not officially adopted, so that they too could get a taste of life in North America.

— Nick Blokker, as a small child in 1899, takes a ride on a wagon with bulbs that are in transit to the docks for shipment overseas.

233

Robert de Jager's eyes shine as he tells one fascinating anecdote after another about the people who shaped his family firm, Vanhof & Blokker, a leading importer of Dutch flower bulbs and plants.

Obviously, he is proud and appreciative of what they managed to achieve many years ago in the fields of their family business in Akersloot, a small village south of Alkmaar, and in the wide open marketplace of North America.

"They had a lot of foresight," says Robert, the firm's Vice-President, Sales and Marketing. "They worked hard and they knew how to sell. When all that's combined with a good product – the Dutch have the expertise and the right soil conditions to produce quality bulbs – then it's just a matter of time before success is reached."

Today's Vanhof & Blokker is something to be proud of too. It's now exclusively a Canadian wholesale company, serving growers across the country out of its handsome building on Pacific Circle in Mississauga, close to the auction of Ontario Flower Growers Inc. Its sales representatives offer a wide range of material, including bulbs, perennial plugs and rose bushes, all imported from the Netherlands.

'Our strength lies in our ability to offer new products.'

"I go to Holland twice a year to see what's new," says Robert. "Our strength lies in our ability to offer new products."

The firm's history dates back to 1868 when Nicolaas Blokker, a mixed farmer in Akersloot, turned to bulb and flower growing. He was quite successful at it, cultivating 82 varieties of tulips and Frittilaria imperialis. Alas, he died unexpectedly at the early age of 45.

His widow, Lena, courageously carried on the operation for a number of years even though she already had her hands full with eight children. Her burden was eased somewhat when she married her foreman, the much younger Jan van 't Hof.

Her eldest son, also named Jan, had the foresight, ability and energy to steer the business in an exciting new direction: to the vast market beyond the Dutch borders. While working as a trainee at a nursery in England, he had seen the possibilities for exporting bulbs for both dry sale and forcing. He had also learned how to converse in English, a prerequisite for engaging in such business.

In 1898, at the age of 30, he issued his first bulb catalogue in English and then boarded a steamboat to New York City with ambitious plans to line up customers for his bulbs and plants in the United States and Canada. The results were encouraging. For the next 30 years, he would continue to visit North America annually.

Jan's only son, Nick, joined the company just before the outbreak of the First World War. Since Holland remained neutral, a noncombatant, the young man could make his first transatlantic crossing with his father in 1916, the year the firm's catalogue listed 225 varieties of tulips. In the Irish Sea, their ship struck a mine and sank. Fortunately, most of the passengers, including the Blokkers, were rescued and were able to be accommodated on another ship heading for New York.

Nick would make that crossing for more than 45 years. This doesn't include the five years that the Germans occupied Holland during the Second World War. Exports

— Hyacinths are in full bloom in this old photograph taken at the Vanhof & Blokker bulb operation in Akersloot.

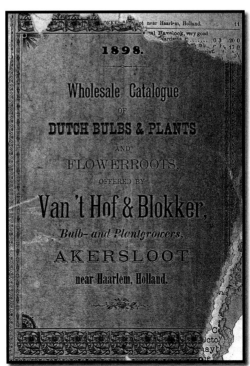

— Vanhof & Blokker's 1898 English catalogue.

were halted then and the company stayed afloat by producing much-needed food – that is, pulp from ground tulip and crocus bulbs. After the war, when the export business started up again, Nick and other Dutch bulb salesmen would spend most of their winters in North America, promoting and selling their products to the greenhouse trade, seed stores, mail order companies, public parks, schools, horticultural societies, private estates, and so on.

Vanhof & Blokker was at the forefront in making Ottawa a tulip showcase. It supplied many of the bulbs that were gifts from the grateful Dutch people and their royal family for the significant role of the Canadian military in the liberation of Holland and the hospitality extended to Princess Juliana and her daughters during their years of exile in the Canadian capital. It continues to supply the bulbs that set the grounds at Government House, the official residence of Canada's Governor General, ablaze each May.

"There are some interesting sidelights," says Robert. "One of our former general managers in Canada was Arie van Rijn who used to be one of Princess Juliana's bodyguards in

Ottawa. And our present building was officially opened in 1985 by Malak Karsh, a famous Ottawa photographer who, through his work, was one of the top promoters of Dutch bulbs in Canada."

The offices and warehouses of Vanhof & Blokker have been at a number of locations in the Toronto area since the first facilities were opened in 1926 on King Street West. In Holland, too, the firm has not stood still. In 1921, it moved its operations from Akersloot to the nearby village of Limmen. That's where Nick was instrumental in setting up Hortus Bulborum, a bulb garden featuring many old varieties. In 1978, new offices and warehouses were built at the firm's nurseries in Heiloo, in the same region.

Robert's father, R. David de Jager, was appointed President of Vanhof & Blokker in 1959, two years after Nick had a severe heart attack and could no longer travel to North America. David was married to Nick's only child, Kay, and was the youngest of four sons who had joined P. de Jager and Sons, a family-owned bulb company established in 1869. Now it was up to him to make the annual trips.

— Robert de Jager: "They worked hard
and knew how to sell."

The Niagara area is serviced by Dick Veerman of Beamsville, a freelance salesman, who has been involved in growing and selling ever since he emigrated from Boskoop, the Netherlands, in 1949 because he didn't want to serve in the Dutch military.

"I started at a nursery because my father had a nursery in Boskoop and I was familiar with the work," he says. "In 1951, I began selling nursery stock for a friend. This was for only two months of the year, so I started selling fall bulbs door to door at a commission of 30 per cent. I decided to take a course to get better at it. They said: 'Set a goal, normally $20 to $30 a day, and work towards it.' Well, I set $50 as my goal, and the following weekend I made close to $100. So it worked."

Dick held sales positions with Superior Bulb Company and Deny de Jong, a grower of mum cuttings in Beamsville, before becoming a representative for Vanhof & Blokker in 1968.

"I now look after 40 customers in the Peninsula," he says. "Their requirements are steady – Easter lily bulbs make up the biggest orders. But the job is never boring. Maybe that's why I like it so much. Some of that enjoyment must have been passed to my family because I have two sons, Brian and Ron, who sell flowers to the States."

235

David and Kay ended up living in Toronto several months of the year. The close ties they established with Canadians, on both personal and business levels, were reflected in David's active participation in the Netherlands Canada Chamber of Commerce in the Hague and his service as treasurer of the National Committee "Thank You Canada," the Dutch volunteer organization that brings over Canadian war veterans for special occasions.

Vanhof & Blokker sold its operations in Holland in 1991 and concentrated solely on supplying the Canadian market from its location in Mississauga.

"We buy high-quality products from selected and dependable growers and then sell and distribute these," says Robert, who left Holland in 1985 after finishing his studies. "We gave up our business in the United States and now focus all our efforts on Canada, from coast to coast, with a team of sales representatives."

—The Vanhof & Blokker building on Pacific Circle in Mississauga.

Greenhouse growers are a demanding lot.

The people of Ball Superior, a Brampton-based producer and distributor of flower seeds, plants and other supplies, can attest to that.

"With plugs, or starter seedlings, growers want to maximize the number per square foot," says Paul Philp, the company's sales representative for Niagara. "As a result of this, they have put a lot of pressure on seed companies to deliver high quality seeds. Ten years ago, if growers got 65 to 75 per cent germination, they were satisfied. Today, if they don't get at least 90 per cent, they are unhappy."

Ball Superior, of course, wants to keep its clients happy. It is heavily involved in seed research, mostly in Central America, to continually improve the products that it offers to growers from coast to coast in Canada. In Niagara alone, it has more than 100 customers.

'It's remarkable how much business is being done with just a handshake.'

The firm is part of the family-owned Ball Seed Company of Chicago which was started in 1908 primarily as a seed breeder and distributor. In 1974, Ball Seed purchased Superior Bulb Company in Mississauga, founded by Max O'Brien in the 1960s as a supplier of Dutch bulbs for the Canadian flower industry, and changed the name to Ball Superior. The business grew from there.

The parent company has facilities in Costa Rica and Guatemala where seeds are grown and harvested and plant cuttings are produced. Seeds are first shipped to Chicago and then sent directly to greenhouses. Cuttings, which are live material, go to growers directly from Central America.

Paul, who joined Ball Superior in 1989, offers an interesting insight into the life of a cutting produced by his company.

"It starts in Costa Rica and is shipped to a grower in Niagara as an unrooted cutting. In the greenhouse, it is rooted in a three to four-week period. Then it is shipped to another one of our customers who finishes it in 10 weeks.

The finished product goes to, say, the Home Depot in St. Catharines which then sells it to the consumer. This is a long process and we're involved most of the way."

Some of the larger growers who have the required facilities are now rooting cuttings themselves, thereby eliminating the middleman. In an effort to ensure top quality, there's also a trend to using new raw material every year instead of propagating from the old.

Paul, one of eight Ball Superior sales people across Canada, visits his major clients once a week during the busy periods.

"This keeps me on the hop," he says.

He feels at home in the greenhouse environment. Born in 1953, he grew up on a mixed-agriculture farm in the Kitchener area. He earned his Bachelor's degree in soil science from the University of British Columbia in Vancouver, worked for a tree nursery in Mississauga and then joined the Ball Superior staff as a sales representative. He and his wife, Sue, and their three children live near Fenwick, in the heart of Niagara.

Paul also admires greatly the traits of the greenhouse people, including their work ethic, their knowledge, their business sense and particularly their trust.

WHY TULIPS BLOOM IN OTTAWA

A dark curtain descended upon the Netherlands in May, 1940, after Nazi Germany's war machine had successfully carried out Adolf Hitler's orders to invade and conquer.

That curtain would not be lifted until after five long years of often brutal occupation.

The royal family – Queen Wilhelmina, Crown Princess Juliana, her husband, Prince Bernhard, and their small children, Princess Beatrix and Princess Irene – had escaped

—Princess Juliana visits Dutch troops at the Juliana Barracks in Stratford, Ontario, during the Second World War.

capture by fleeing to England before the Dutch defenders laid down their weapons.

Since the Germans were threatening to add England to their list of conquests, Juliana and her children would soon be on their way to the safer shores of Canada.

The princesses lived in Rockcliffe, an upscale suburb of

Ottawa, for the duration of Holland's occupation.

Juliana tried to live a normal, quiet life, just like any other mother in the neighbourhood. Sometimes she did have to break away to attend to official business on behalf of her country. One of her favourite stops was the Juliana Barracks in the Ontario city of Stratford, and later in nearby Guelph, where Dutch nationals were being recruited and trained for service with a Dutch freedom brigade in England.

In January, 1943, the Dutch flag flew alone atop the Peace Tower of the Canadian Parliament Buildings to herald the birth of her third child, Princess Margriet, in the Ottawa Civic Hospital. The ward had been declared extra-territorial by the Canadian government so that there would be no dispute about the newborn's Dutch nationality.

Some 5,712 Canadian servicemen sacrificed their lives

in the great and heroic effort that succeeded in ousting the Germans from Dutch soil.

"It makes me sad to leave," Juliana said when she was about to return to her liberated country in 1945. "Five years is a long time, and one becomes attached. We have made so many friends. We shall leave such happy memories."

Later that year, the grateful people of Holland sent a gift of 100,000 tulip bulbs to Ottawa as a token of their appreciation for all that Canada had done for them and their royal family. These were planted in front of Parliament Hill and in other prominent places. In 1946, Juliana sent a personal gift of 20,000 bulbs as part of a lifetime bequest. Shipments would arrive each year after that.

'We have made so many friends. We shall leave such happy memories.'

Tulip beds began to replace the Victorian-style displays as the focus of the capital's floral showcase, attracting many visitors during the blooming time in May. Then an idea was born: let's use all that beauty as the centrepoint for an annual celebration, with various events, to mark the arrival of spring. The Canadian Tulip Festival came into being in 1953.

The National Capital Commission, which takes care of the beds, began regular purchases of Dutch bulbs for planting in the fall. The colourful displays were expanded to such an extent that Ottawa could rightfully promote itself as the Tulip Capital of North America.

The popular festival celebrated its 50th anniversary in 2002. Among the guests of honour were Princess Margriet and her husband, Pieter van Vollenhoven. The princess unveiled a monument, Man With Two Hats, that commemorates Canada's role in the liberation of her homeland. For many people, her presence served as a touching reminder of why millions of tulips bloom in Ottawa each spring.

Floral Passion

— *Hundreds of thousands of tulips turn Ottawa into a sea of colour each spring, forming the setting for the*

Canadian Tulip Festival, a celebration that includes flower boat flotillas, concerts, theatre performances and fireworks.

—The building of Priva Computers Inc. houses offices and manufacturing space.

Greenhouses do not foul the air with gases. Instead of merely taking up valuable land that could be used for other purposes, such as tender fruit production, they have become one of the big players – surpassed only by tourism – in the region's economy, providing and generating thousands of jobs.

As General Manager of Priva's North American operations, based in a two-storey building on the South Service Road in Vineland Station, Joep has a direct interest in the future of the greenhouse industry in Niagara and the rest of North America. If flower and vegetable production continues to thrive and grow, his company stands to benefit greatly.

He arrived here from De Lier, in the Netherlands, where Priva was founded in 1959 by two men named Prins and Valk and where its headquarters are located. He's been with the company since 1987, holding a number of positions and travelling across the globe to wherever horticulture is practised. In the process, he has observed a lot.

"I haven't seen the use of technology as diverse as it is here," he says. "There are high-tech growers who are on the highest level and, amazingly, there are growers who still do everything by hand. On the Canadian side, the level of technology is much higher than on the American side. When you look at these differences, you see a gigantic potential for all those growers who don't have high-tech equipment to progress."

After arriving in the Niagara Peninsula in March, 2001, it didn't take long for Joep van den Bosch of Priva Computers Inc. to observe that a huge potential exists for enormous growth in the area's greenhouse industry.

"Compared to people in other countries such as the Netherlands, England, France and Germany, Canadians and Americans use very few flowers in their gardens," he says. "Ninety-five per cent is grass. If people can be educated to use more of their free time in the garden, to make it look better, imagine the opportunity for Niagara growers to provide the garden plants that will be needed."

A great opportunity for tremendous growth also faces greenhouse vegetable growers who are able to produce, without the use of pesticides, cleaner and better-looking products than the ones that come from open fields. They are in a good position to look after the needs of consumers who are becoming very picky about what they eat.

But Joep stresses that all this growth is not going to happen without vigorous promotion and increased co-operation among growers in developing and stimulating their markets. Moreover, he says, the greenhouse business needs to overcome a big image problem.

"It's a clean, high-tech industry, yet most Canadians and Americans don't look at it that way," he says. "They see greenhouses as polluters of air and water. They don't like how they look, especially when there is no landscaping, and therefore regard them also as polluters of land."

It's obvious to Joep and many others that an extensive and ongoing effort will be needed to correct misconceptions.

'It's a clean, high-tech industry, yet most Canadians and Americans don't look at it that way.'

In all of North America, only 20 per cent of the greenhouses are fully computerized. The Niagara region does a lot better than that – between 60 and 70 per cent of the greenhouses have some form of automation. Even so, says Joep, there is room for a lot of improvement. As a target, he points to Holland, where 96 per cent of the greenhouses are controlled by computers.

OPPORTUNITIES

Priva arrived in North America in the early 1980s. It set up an office in Vancouver because of the concentration of greenhouse vegetable producers in that area and their demand for higher technology. After a few years, it became apparent that a more central location was needed. Niagara was selected because of its expanding greenhouse industry and its close proximity to the United States.

The company's building, opened in 1987, contains offices and a manufacturing facility. Priva does not sell its products directly; other firms, re-sellers, look after that. But it does assemble a complete product line, using components shipped from Holland as well as ones purchased here, which entitles it to use the important CSA-approved label. Many of the staff of 24 are highly-skilled technicians.

Priva manufactures products such as Integro, an advanced greenhouse control system for ventilation and temperature; Maximizer, a climate control system with a complete weather station for monitoring greenhouse environment; Supervision, the latest graphic user interface for the Integro and Maximizer computers; PrivAssist, which makes it possible to find out who has been processing what, when and in which quantities; custom-designed interface panels to integrate all circuitry and controls into common modules, and a variety of sensors.

For the average grower, the cost of a complete system, including hardware, software and installation, amounts to $10,000 an acre. The price tag for the smallest system, which can operate in four zones, is $4,000.

"Really, considering the benefits, it's not expensive for a grower to computerize his operation," says Joep. "But it depends on how people look at their business. Some growers are not willing to make long-term investments. They just look at what they earned today and how much they spent today."

So there's work to be done – on convincing these growers to adopt modern control and assist methods, on urging the entire industry to work hard on developing even greater markets than the ones that now exist and on educating the public that greenhouse growing is important to them and their community.

— Joep van den Bosch with Priva sensing equipment.

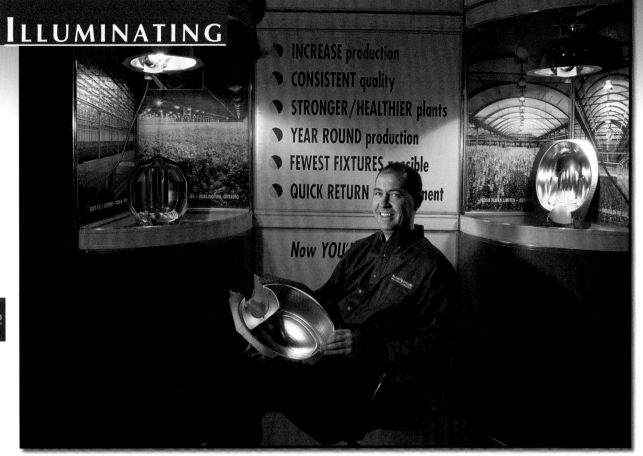

INCREASE production

CONSISTENT quality

STRONGER/HEALTHIER plants

YEAR ROUND production

FEWEST FIXTURES possible

QUICK RETURN

Now YOU'...

242

—Johan de Leeuw with some of the grow light equipment produced at P.L. Light Systems Canada Inc.

One of Toronto's leading newspapers asked in its commercials: "Do you stand, or do you stand out? Do you see, or do you have vision?"

This is exactly the kind of difference that P. L. Light Systems Canada Inc. in Beamsville intends to make.

Owner Teun van den Dool is buoyant when he talks about the opportunities for his company, manufacturer of high-intensity lights for the greenhouse industry.

"The future looks bright for us," he says. "Word is spreading fast about the benefits of grow lights. More and more flower growers decide to use our lights to improve quality, increase yield and control the growing process. They no longer depend on sunlight. When they plant their seeds and seedlings, they know exactly when to expect the finished product because we eliminate the weather as the deciding factor."

Grow lights are also catching the attention of vegetable growers who are looking at year-round production of specific crops to meet consumer demands. If P. L. Light Systems can illuminate this segment of the greenhouse industry, the growers stand to benefit immensely.

South America has a promising market as well and the company is determined to establish itself there. Throughout the Americas, distributors are carrying its torch.

The HID grow lights, ranging from 150 watts to 1,000 watts, are manufactured in a two-storey building on Beamsville's Hinan Drive. The developed reflectors are imported from Belgium and all the electrical components such as ballasts, capacitors and lamps are provided through North American markets to facilitate differences in voltage and frequency.

The firm was established in Canada in 1981. Initially located in St. Catharines, it later moved to Grimsby and in

1997 to a new plant in Beamsville. In 2002, it expanded the warehouse space and added 1,500 square feet to set up a full research lab for providing growers with improved service for their older fixtures.

"We now have the ability to perform light bulb measurement tests as well as component tests," explains Johan de Leeuw, the General Manager. "This helps us advise growers when replacement is necessary. We advocate having a preventive maintenance program in place before major damage occurs. We are also able to measure the output of reflectors and determine when reanodizing may be necessary for older fixtures to regain maximum output. Furthermore, our lab supports us in our drive to find new products that are more efficient to run and have better light spectrums for plant growth."

'It's going to get exciting around here.'

Johan, who has extensive experience in marketing, as well as financing greenhouses, was appointed to his position in 2002.

"We know we have a good product and now it's a matter of spreading the word," says Teun. "Promotion is an important part of our work and we are present at many trade shows across North America every year. We've also contributed to a 180-page technical book, Supplemental Lighting for Greenhouse Crops, which is available in English and Dutch."

Johan adds: "We are preparing ourselves for a big jump forward. It's going to get exciting around here."

Both men stress that their company's mission is to provide the industry with the highest quality products, the newest of innovation and the best possible customer service.

— *HID grow lights supplied by P. L. Light Systems Canada Inc. are a great assist to the mum production at Vandermeer Greenhouses Ltd. in Niagara-on-the-Lake.*

THE IMPROVERS

Leigh Harrison leads an exciting life as General Manager of a humming business that manufactures greenhouses and supplies many of the growers in Niagara and beyond with products such as shades, benches and irrigation systems.

But nothing that happens on the factory floor, in the yard or in an office can compare to the exhilaration she felt when a potential distributor in Japan asked her to come over for an important meeting within a matter of days.

"I quickly packed a few things, including an English-Japanese language guide, and took along a book on business culture in Japan which I read on the plane," she recalls during a break in her busy world.

The Japanese must have been as much impressed with the woman facing them – young, energetic, obviously well educated – as they were with the product she was promoting on behalf of her company, GGS (Growers Greenhouse Supplies Inc.), located on the North Service Road in Vineland Station. A deal was sealed almost on the spot, a rare occurrence. It was learned later that the closest competitor had been trying for 10 years to secure a contract.

'We may not be the first one out of the block, but we build a better mousetrap.'

Leigh's business acumen is partly an inherited quality. Her grandfather, Patrick Harrison, was an innovator in the mining industry – his specialty was shaft sinking – and through his work was responsible for putting towns such as Elliott Lake and Sioux Lookout on the northern Ontario map. He employed his expertise in many other notable endeavours, including a tunnel through a volcano in Peru and a hydro project under the Niagara Falls. Leigh's father, Gerry, was involved in mining, too, but he left it in the early 1980s to try something else: manufacturing greenhouses.

"GGS was started in 1979 by Ron Vidal with two other partners – it was an instant success – and my family got involved when my father bought out the partners," says Leigh. "He saw a tremendous growth potential. So he changed from working under the ground to working above the ground. He learned from employees and customers and

—GGS General Manager Leigh Harrison discusses a greenhouse construction project with John Dreyer, her Plant Manager.

became very knowledgeable about flowers. He worked hard at the business and believed in getting his children involved."

While growing up in Toronto, Leigh knew that she wanted to run her own business someday, probably in the computer field. At that time, she wasn't the least bit interested in greenhouses. In fact, she had never stepped inside one. But all this changed after her father, on his way to a number of greenhouses in the Leamington area, picked her up at the University of Western Ontario in London where she was studying for her business degree.

The trip was an eye-opener. She discovered an industry that was innovative and exciting, with hard-working people receptive to new concepts and eager to find better ways to produce vegetables and flowers.

"The growers I met typically talked about how to modify equipment themselves for their own individual needs. They were resourceful. In Toronto, if something broke down, you'd call a repairman. But if a greenhouse grower could fix something himself, he would. This excited me and I saw the business as one I would enjoy."

Equipped with a degree, Leigh joined GGS in 1993. She began as an inside sales person – "I had to learn the ropes" – and soon worked herself up to sales manager and then general manager. She now has her hands full looking after a company that has grown to become one of the country's largest full-line greenhouse manufacturers with a workforce of 60 that rises to as high as 140 during peak times.

For the nearby Niagara Under Glass project, the firm designed and manufactured the 228,600-square-foot production greenhouse and the adjoining Discovery Centre, complete with the raised walkway for the visiting public. There have been other big projects over the years. At all times, Leigh and her staff are keeping their eyes open for improvements. They sometimes hit upon an idea, such as the gutter vent devised by John Dreyer, GGS's Plant Manager.

"But we're not innovators," says Leigh. "We're better known as the improvers. We may not be the first one out of the block, but we build a better mousetrap."

Leigh's work at GGS has profoundly increased her admiration of the greenhouse people, first developed during the visit to Leamington with her father.

"In the greenhouse industry," she says, "a person's word is their bond. Million-dollar deals are sealed with a handshake. They're straightforward, honest and forthcoming. It's a nice culture to work in."

Niagara Under Glass

A noble idea struck greenhouse grower John Albers in 1994.

Niagara, which draws 18 million tourists a year, should have a new year-round attraction that would raise public awareness of the fast-growing greenhouse industry, particularly its significant impact on the economy and the opportunities it offers young people for a rewarding career.

"I saw what the wineries were doing to link themselves to tourism and began thinking of what the possibilities were for people going into a greenhouse. When you visit places such as the Royal Botanical Gardens in Hamilton or the Epcot Centre in Florida, where there's a hydroponics display, you see people having a good time. I thought that if we had something unique enough and exciting enough, people would pay to get in the door."

The idea emerged when John was faced with deciding whether to expand the growing capacity of his Can-Gro Greenhouses Niagara Ltd. operation in Lincoln or move to new facilities on another site. More space was required because of the phenomenal growth in the demand for calla lilies, his main crop.

Over the next two years, he worked out a business plan for a multi-million-dollar agri-tourism complex consisting of a large greenhouse for his lily production and a connected Discovery Centre where visitors could view and explore.

A Toronto consulting firm was hired to examine the scheme. When the reaction was overwhelmingly positive, financing was arranged for the first phase: acquisition of a 60-acre site just off the QEW between Beamsville and Vineland and construction of a 228,600-square-foot greenhouse featuring the latest in proven design and automation.

John had taken on a partner, Mike Duffy, who had recently retired as general manager of the Niagara Region Development Corporation. A professional engineer, Mike was a business promoter well-known for his love of Niagara and efforts to expand economic growth and tourism in the area. Sadly, he never saw the completed project; he died unexpectedly on Boxing Day, 1999, shortly before the first phase was put into production.

When Bob Tytaneck, formerly with the Niagara Parks Commission, came on board as General Manager of Tourism, work on the second phase, the Discovery Centre, got under way.

There was a lot of enthusiasm among the staff of Niagara Under Glass, as the place was called, when the doors were opened to the public in the summer of 2001. With projections calling for 200,000 people to visit the site each year, they were ready to welcome the crowds and show them the attractions.

Visitors could walk along an elevated walkway for a bird's eye view of the massive growing area for calla lilies and hybridized miniature roses. In the Discovery Centre itself there were interactive displays, plantscapes, hydroponics, a potting experience, a garden gift shop, a luncheon area and meeting/banquet facilities.

Visitors could also wander outside to a number of ponds, an artificially-created wetland, where runoff and waste water was filtered by nature and recirculated into the operation. Even the sewage from the washrooms was not wasted.

"This is the first site in Ontario to be licensed to treat sewage with constructed wetlands," John told us shortly after the opening. "Within two days, it's sparkling drinking water. The process is simple, relatively inexpensive, maintenance-free and without chemicals. It's amazing. We are a pioneer in this field."

Alas, the number of people who came to experience the wonderful world of flower growing was disappointingly small. As the summer progressed, the number continued to fall far short of the projections. Then terrorists attacked the United States with hijacked jetliners on Sept. 11, causing a steep decline in international travel and bus tours and severely impacting tourism in Niagara.

The news in late November came as a shock to many people in Niagara who had been hoping that John's vision and big investment would ultimately meet with success. Niagara Under Glass had been placed in receivership, throwing many people out of work.

While the receiver looked for a buyer, or buyers, the lily production continued and the doors were kept open to visitors. But the excitement that had marked the centre's opening was no longer there.

—Alex van Zijl has been involved with the greenhouse industry since age 18.

Alex van Zijl took along a wealth of international experience in the greenhouse industry when he and his wife, Pascalle, left the Netherlands in April, 2001, and headed for their new home in the Niagara Peninsula.

He had accepted an invitation to join the senior staff of Paul Boers, the respected Niagara greenhouse manufacturer located on the South Service Road in Vineland Station.

It didn't take long before Alex was advanced to the position of General Manager, giving him the opportunity to fully apply the knowledge and leadership that he had gained from involvement in some of the largest greenhouse construction and turn-key projects globally.

"I began building greenhouses after leaving school at age 18," he says. "After six years in construction, I moved up to sales and sold greenhouse projects in Holland, Belgium and Germany. I then accepted a position as an Export Manager with P.L.J. Blom BV Kassenbouw in Naaldwijk. This position

required that I travel through Europe and North America frequently, and we developed many innovative projects. During these trips, I also began to enjoy Canada and appreciate the quality of life that exists here."

No arm-twisting was needed after one of the owners of Paul Boers, whom he had met on his travels, invited him and Pascalle to move to Niagara.

'During these trips, I also began to enjoy Canada and appreciate the quality of life that exists here.'

Paul Boers, a Dutch immigrant, launched the company in 1958. Then known as Paul Boers Greenhouse Construction Ltd. and located on York Road in St. Davids, it manufactured NuGro gutter-connected greenhouses, a design that met with huge acceptance due to its simplicity. As technology evolved and the market demanded more elaborate systems, the firm kept pace. It began importing the popular Venlo greenhouses from Holland in 1983.

The present partners took over the company in 1995 from Roelie Boers, widow of the founder, and continued to manufacture free-standing and gutter-connected greenhouses of various designs, as well as cold frames, growing benches and ventilation and irrigation systems. The following year, heating systems were added to the list.

With the volume of business consistently growing, the time soon arrived for Paul Boers to move to larger quarters. A 30,000-square-foot office and manufacturing facility was built on an 18-acre site along the QEW and officially opened in 1998.

Alex speaks proudly of how his company, with a workforce of 45, can design and supply a complete greenhouse system for a grower.

"If required," he says, "construction is done with the use of sub-contractors. Fueltec Combustion Inc., an affiliated company, provides service for Dutch and North American boilers and burners, commissioning and refurbishes used boilers. I'm confident that customers will be left with a sense of satisfaction from dealing with both Paul Boers and Fueltec."

—The Paul Boers facility along the Queen Elizabeth Way.

—These photos capture some of the activity at Paul Boers, a greenhouse manufacturer.

— ITML makes horticultural containers for the wholesale greenhouse and nursery growers.

Remember the days before the age of plastic when growers cultivated their plants in red clay pots?

These containers are now largely nostalgia items found in flea markets and specialty stores.

Initially, many flower producers were reluctant to part with the traditional pots. But when some of the larger operations began using plastic ones, finding them durable, easy to handle and cost-effective, the days of the clay ones were numbered. Now most of the pots are plastic, made from polypropylene resin, and come in all shapes and colours, depending on particular marketing initiatives.

One of the key persons responsible for this transformation is Kees Hensen of Brantford, Ontario, the co-founder and Chairman of ITML Horticultural Products Inc., a leading

manufacturer of plastic containers in North America with a number of production facilities in Ontario and the United States.

Born in 1929, he emigrated to Canada in 1952 with his bride, Joanna. They came from Lisse, a small community in the centre of Holland's famous flower bulb-producing region and the site of Keukenhof, the world's premiere showcase of spring-blooming bulbs. But the young man had chosen a line of work far removed from flowers; he was a tool and die maker.

He worked himself up into a management position at a company in Brantford and by 1963 felt confident enough to leave it and start on his own with the help of a $5,000 loan from the Federal Business Development Bank for machinery. With his cousin, John Vaandering, and five employees,

he launched a tool and die operation, Impact Tool and Manufacturing Ltd., in a double car garage in downtown Brantford. This business, serving the automotive, appliance, farm and aircraft industries in Ontario, grew steadily and it had to relocate to larger facilities within two years.

Discerning new market opportunities in 1970, the company shifted its focus from specializing in tool and die work to include custom plastic injection molding.

"When we started to develop injection molds to make plastic pots, it took some time to find acceptance for the new products," Kees recalls. "It was a big expense and risk for us at the time and we had no guarantee of success. But once there was acceptance for our containers, particularly from the large growers, it started us toward the company we are today."

ITML became a leading manufacturer for horticultural products in the North American market. In 1988, the company relocated to a new 80,000-square-foot plant. Twelve years later, it completed the second phase of a three-phase expansion project, doubling the manufacturing capacity and adding a 40,000-square-foot warehouse, 50 feet high, where electronically-guided, high-level forklifts operate between racking systems that contain thousands of pallets of finished horticultural products. The warehouse computer system is inter-phased to the logistics department within the company.

'We use recycled material in our manufacturing processes and everything we don't use gets recycled.'

In 1990, ITML expanded its manufacturing to the United States, establishing a grassroots manufacturing plant in Waco, Texas. In 1999, it bought out the assets of one of its biggest competitors, Kord Products. In addition to the operations in Brantford and Waco, ITML currently has manufacturing, processing and warehousing facilities in Brampton, Burlington and Lugoff, South Carolina.

Although he retains the position of Chairman and is involved in certain projects, Kees no longer participates in the day-to-day running of the company. The management

AN INNOVATIVE MANUFACTURER

is in the hands of two of his five sons – Ed, Chief Executive Officer and General Manager, and Kleis, Vice-president, Sales and Marketing – along with a strong management team.

The Brantford plant, which operates 24 hours a day, six days a week, and employs a staff of more than 200, remains the company's flagship. In addition to manufacturing and distribution – 75 per cent of the company's sales is exported – it is the location for the corporate head offices and product design, engineering and research and development staffs. There is also an on-site facility for job training in such areas as computers, sales, packing and maintenance, and even instruction in English as a second language is provided.

As Kleis leads his visitor on a tour through the manufacturing facility on Plant Farm Blvd., row upon row of automated molding equipment produces a variety of flower pots, hanging baskets, nursery containers, bedding flats and inserts for the wholesale greenhouse and nursery industry. A number of manufacturing processes are used: injection molding using plyproplyene resins, blow molding using polyethylene resin, thermo-forming all using primarily polystyrene resin and fiber molding using recycled paper products.

"We design all our products with growers' input," he says. "We average about 10 new products a year, all to meet the specific marketing or automation needs of our customers. It's hard to imagine, but we make 725 different horticultural products and over 7,000 skus (specific products within product lines)."

This extensive range of products requires many new and replacement molds. Indeed, ITML has its own mold-building department and contracts with some of the best mold builders in the industry to build high quality molds, using special steels acquired from all over the world. This material has to be 100 per cent pure because the slightest imperfection could cause premature mold failure, resulting in a breakdown and loss of production.

"We even make some of our material handling pallets out of steel," says Kleis. "Our philosophy is recycle, reduce and re-use. This is constantly going on. We use recycled material in our manufacturing processes and everything we don't use gets recycled. Instead of waste bins on the floor, we have actual recycling blue boxes. We want to get everyone in a recycling mindset."

The company regards cleanliness and housekeeping of utmost importance, and this is evident throughout the facilities. Sophisticated equipment even vacuums dust particles from the resin materials as it flows though the different stages of the factory, helping to create an exceptionally pleasant and safe work environment. Other than for earplugs, safety shoes and glasses, the workers need no special equipment. Even outside, where nursery products are stored near rows of steel silos holding millions of pounds of recycled material, everything appears spotless.

All of ITML's products are quality tested during production in a rigorous quality-control program. The firm uses its own or other local labs for checking material, colour, strength and opacity.

"Our engineers have designed the products so that, even when stacked, they do not jam together," says Kleis. "It is very annoying for a grower to pry products apart. Nothing jams, not even products that are packaged on bulk pallets."

ITML has specialized automated equipment to provide a cost-effective process that can apply durable adhesive plastic labels with UPC bar codes, plant information and the grower's name or logos to containers. Even with bedding flats and inserts, each cell pack can be labeled.

The products are shipped in cardboard boxes that display the firm's catchy mascot, a PotMan made from green pots, and the words "Thank you for growing with ITML." Each carton has two hand holes for safe handling by greenhouse and nursery workers.

In 2000, the Ontario Chamber of Commerce recognized Kees Hensen's entrepreneurship by presenting him with its Business Excellence Award of Merit. "This has been such an honour," he said at the presentation. "Mostly I have to thank my wife who supported me through the difficult years. She should be beside me."

He and his family are also grateful to the many staff who are part of the steady growth of the company. A profit-sharing program was introduced in 1994. There is active community participation with ongoing financial support to local organizations and programs that encourage stronger family relationships. Many of the charitable organizations are prominently displayed in the firm's lobby.

The Hensen family also use their Christian convictions as guiding principles in their relations with employees, customers and suppliers. In listing significant factors that have impacted the success of ITML, they identify "a spirit of gratefulness and thanks to God for the opportunity to provide meaningful employment to our staff, to manufacture a quality product and provide excellent service to our customers and the opportunity to work with others to realize and develop our God-given talents and abilities."

— A view of high-speed injection mold equipment at the Brantford plant.

Floral Passion

— Wim Vander Windt with some of the piping that his company, Niagrow, imports from the Netherlands.

The Dutch connection to North Amerca's greenhouse industry is conspiciously present in the large warehouse of Niagrow Systems Inc. on Stanley Avenue in Niagara Falls, Ontario.

"All this comes from Holland," says Wim Vander Windt, the firm's Manager, pointing to stacks upon stacks of steel piping used for greenhouse mechanical systems. "This particular piping is not manufactured in North America, so we have to import it, along with some other components."

Wim is not lamenting. In fact, he looks forward to his visits to suppliers in the Netherlands because he can then also consult with growers there who are using the materials and equipment. The comments and advice he receives are passed on to his customers in North America, resulting in optimum performance and satisfaction.

His aggressive company designs greenhouse systems for heating, cooling, carbon dioxide generation and irrigation, including flood floors, and supplies all the required materials. If requested, it can also arrange for installation.

Niagrow was created in the mid-1980s as a subsidiary of Niagara Plumbing Supply Company Ltd. This wholesale firm, founded in 1926, had already been doing business with the local greenhouse industry for many years, initially supplying valves, pipes and fittings. But when more and more growers were looking at retrofitting their heating systems, changing from steam and hot air to hot water, it was time to start up a separate company.

As Manager of J&A Verbakel BV in Honselersdijk, the Netherlands, Wim had been involved with designing and supplying projects on behalf of Niagara Plumbing Supply.

"I was coming over all the time, but it got to be too much for me," he says. "So I divested my financial interests in the Dutch company, set up Niagrow with Niagara Plumbing Supply – we are partners – and in 1984 moved to St.Catharines with my wife, Tini, and our sons, Walter and Jean Paul."

With all the refurbishing and new construction taking place in Niagara's greenhouse industry, the new firm entered a period of solid growth. In recent years, it has greatly expanded its horizons, securing work from growers throughout North America. It has 10 full-time employees. A number of other workers, in administration and materials handling, as well as the building, are shared with Niagara Plumbing Supply.

Wim was born in 1943 to Dutch parents in the Dutch East Indies (now Indonesia) three months before the Japanese occupiers placed all the Dutch nationals there in concentration camps. His father worked as an inspector for Rotterdam Lloyd, a shipping company.

"My mother and I were taken to a women's camp," says Wim. "My sister was born there seven months later. My father and brother were interned in a camp for males, and we were separated until the end of the war. In 1947, when Indonesia was trying to gain independence, my brother died tragically. He was only 14. A Jeep with Merdekka fighters plowed into him while he was walking home from school."

In 1956, at age 13, Wim was sent to Holland to attend school in Aerdenhout. The rest of the family joined him the following year, relieved to be far away from a political climate where they had felt uncomfortable. They settled in Hoek van Holland, close to the Westland greenhouse district.

Wim has been around greenhouses all his working life. He launched his career in 1967 with Voskamp and Vrijland in 's-Gravenzande. In 1971, he started his own heating consulting firm, Van der Windt-Advies. He worked for another company, Neka in Wateringen, for a year before joining the Verbakel firm in 1973. He continued his global travels – he had already engineered and supervised erections and installations in England, Ireland, Romania, Bulgaria, the Soviet Union and the United States – and eventually became a partner with the two owners. Just before he moved to Canada, the firm's name was changed to Verbakel Bomkas.

'The industry here is still a little ways behind, but in the near future you won't see any difference anymore.'

As a close observer of the flower-producing industry in Ontario, particularly Niagara, he is amazed at the big strides that have been made in modernizing production and boosting sales.

"When I came here," he says, "the flower industry was 20 years behind Holland's in terms of greenhouse growing and marketing. Everything seemed to be geared to producing for special days, such as Easter, and the rest of the year was forgotten. Well, now there is more focus on making sure there is a year-round supply. The industry here is still a little ways behind, but in the near future you won't see any difference anymore."

— One of the Langendoen workers welds a pipe.

Mechanical tradesman Andy Langendoen has been kept on the hop since greenhouses that thrifty growers put together with material bought from scrapyards and other sources started showing their age.

"There was a time when a greenhouse owner wouldn't think twice about grabbing a tool or welding torch to make repairs," he says. "He probably figured that he could do the work quicker than anyone else. And there was the cost factor. But things have changed. Although some growers still like to do repairs themselves, most of them don't have the time for that anymore."

His company, Andy Langendoen Greenhouse Mechanical Inc. on Seventh Street in St. Catharines, is part of the extensive support structure that has developed in Niagara to service the many needs of the greenhouse industry. In addition to welding, he and his 10 workers are licensed to install heating systems, including boilers and tubing, as well as water pumps and irrigation systems.

"The work's been steady," says Andy. "But in the spring, it's always slow. Greenhouses then are full of flowers and, unless there's a serious problem, growers don't want to see you."

His parents, Bas and Jane, emigrated in 1951 from Brielle, an old fortified town in the Netherlands. Bas wanted to set up a greenhouse concern – his father in Holland had one – but ended up in landscaping instead, operating a business in St. Catharines called Windmill Landscaping.

Andy, born in 1954 and one of seven children, worked for Dad until a problem with allergies forced him to look for a different job. He was hired by Frank Jonkman, a greenhouse builder in Holland Marsh, north of Toronto. After two years, he struck out on his own.

He enjoyed the work, but eventually grew tired of all the travel that was involved. So he began to concentrate on work closer to home, offering welding and mechanical services. He soon found out that there was enough demand in this field to enable him to forsake greenhouse construction.

'Although some growers still like to do repairs themselves, most of them don't have the time for that anymore.'

Andy and his Dutch-born wife, Rhea, have five sons, one of whom, Dan, works in the business. Another one, Scott, seems headed for a horticultural career.

"He has a little greenhouse in which he grows flowers," says Andy. "When you look at my family history, it must be in his blood."

— Andy Langendoen checks out a newly-installed boiler at the Cedarway Floral Inc. plant on Bartlett Road near Beamsville.

CHAPTER TWENTY-ONE

GARDEN OF THE WORLD

'We've been quite successful in making people aware of what we have to offer.
Sixty-five per cent of our visitors now are from abroad.'
— *Karin E. Hoogland of Keukenhof*

The Netherlands, the country of origin of many of Niagara's greenhouse growers, is extremely small, extending only 175 miles north to south and 110 miles east to west.

Its total area of 16,034 square miles is occupied by 16 million inhabitants, making it one of the most congested areas on Earth.

No wonder that the Dutch, anxious to use every square inch to maximum advantage, are involved in greenhouse horticulture – the production of food and ornamental crops – in a big way.

The floriculture sector, including 16,873 cut flower and plant nurseries, accounts for only a small percentage of agricultural land use. However, its production is intensive, generating billions of euros a year and contributing significantly to the country's balance of trade. Close to 75 per cent of the huge output is exported.

*'I'm never satistified with the status quo,
no matter how well I'm doing.'*

The Netherlands justifiably revels in its status as a world-class player in the production of cut flowers, potted and garden plants, propagation material and flower bulbs. At every opportunity, it vigorously promotes itself as the garden centre of the world. But there's an underlying realization that the hard work and know-how that developed and sustained the industry in the past will be needed more than ever to ensure continued success.

The competition is growing. There are key players in Africa, South America and the Far East, all striving to capture a significant share of the market with quality products and excellent distribution systems.

To stay ahead of the challengers, the Dutch are heavily committed to ongoing research for upgrading products and seeking more efficient and less environmentally harmful cultivation methods.

— This is a partial view of Westland, one of the main flower-growing areas in the Netherlands and the former home of some of Niagara's growers.

In addition to the institutes and experimental stations that carry on this work, there are scores of breeding establishments engaged in developing new flowers and plants. The most advanced techniques are used to improve cultivars and find varieties with new colours.

The progressive attitude of many growers is another important factor. They have invested heavily in modernizing their greenhouses with leading-edge technology and use the most advanced equipment, invariably manufactured in Holland, for working their crops. This confidence in a robust future bodes well for the other links in the floriculture chain that are responsible for selling and distributing the products and developing new markets.

"I'm never satisfied with the status quo, no matter how well I'm doing," says Joop van der Nouweland, one of Holland's biggest growers of cut roses, the flower that heads the sales list at the auction centres. "I'm always looking for ways to improve things, especially quality. When you can offer the best quality, you don't have to worry about competition."

He annually produces 40 million roses in four colours in 360,000 square feet of greenhouses in three locations at Bleiswijk and Waddinxveen. He's a hands-on owner who prefers to spend his working day under glass.

"Regardless of what you grow," he says, "you constantly have to keep an alertful eye on your plants and take care of them with knowledge and love. When you do that, everything will be OK."

Marjoland, his newest greenhouse named after his Polish-born wife, Mariola, and himself, is a state-of-the-art facility with all the latest techniques to effect optimum growing with as few human hands as possible.

It also has five large, gas-fired generators that produce electricity for the growing lights and other equipment. The water that cools the motors is also used for heating the greenhouse. Nothing goes to waste: a power company buys the excess electricity and five neighbouring growers buy the excess warm water and carbon dioxide.

Such enterprise and resourcefulness can be found throughout the industry in Holland.

In Rijnsburg, for example, lily grower Jan Paauw has a huge steaming facility in which he sterilizes his soil for re-use in his operation. The cleansed soil is removed from large storage areas and placed in small crates. An assembly line crew plants these with bulbs. The filled crates stay in cool cells until they're ready to be placed in the greenhouse by an automatic planter. While in the greenhouse, they can be raised automatically so that the bulbs are evenly balanced during the growing process.

In Holland, like in Niagara, flowers and plants are largely produced by family firms in which the owner plays an active role. So it was not surprising that Aat Imanse, a lily grower in nearby Lisserbroek, was busily bunching flowers when we dropped by. He continued working, anxious to keep pace with a conveyor belt that was bringing him freshly-cut stems from the growing areas.

"I began here in '74 with nothing and gradually built it up," he says, tying another bunch of 10. "We now cut three million stems a year. That figure will go up quite a bit when we've completed our expansion. We have only 10 people working for us. I have two sons in the business and sometimes there are just the three of us looking after everything. That's no problem because we're fully automated."

It's not uncommon to walk into a large greenhouse during business hours and spot no one tending to the crops. Technology has taken over many of the jobs formerly done by labourers. Now there's a demand for people with training in computer work and other specialized areas.

Even with changes in labour requirements, the flower industry in Holland continues to be a big employer. There are 40,000 jobs in production, 7,600 in auctions/distribution, 6,000 in supply industry, 17,500 in wholesaling/exporting and 22,500 in retailing.

Top 10 Cut Flowers In Holland In 2001

(Auction turnover in one million euros)

1. Rosa	653.0
2. Chrysanthemum (raceme)	289.1
3. Tulipa	177.3
4. Lilium	155.9
5. Gerbera	103.8
6. Cymbidium	66.6
7. Freesia	61.7
8. Dianthus	56.2
9. Alstroemeria	44.6
10. Gypsophila	42.0

Top 10 Potted Plants In Holland In 2001

(Auction turnover in one million euros)

1. Phalaenopsis	49.2
2. Ficus	41.5
3. Kalanchoe	35.4
4. Dracaena	34.7
5. Chrysanthemum	26.8
6. Anthurium	26.7
7. Spathiphyllum	24.0
8. Hedera	23.3
9. Hydrangea	22.5
10. Rosa	19.0

Four times a week, at 4:30 a.m. or so, the low ring of the alarm clock prompts Jan de Koning of Rijnsburg to climb out of bed.

After a quick breakfast, he hops into his pride and joy, a Lexus brought over from California, and drives the short distance to FloraHolland, one of the great flower auction centres in the Netherlands strategically located along the busy A44 freeway between The Hague and Amsterdam.

Jan, spry at 70, finds a seat in the buyers' gallery facing the six auction clocks, dons his earphones, adjusts his papers and is ready for the flower-laden trolleys to start rolling by and for the bidding to begin. His son, Dirk, is also there, similarly wired and with his laptop computer turned on. With all the clocks operating simultaneously, and at a lightning pace, it's nearly impossible for any buyer to keep on top of everything.

'On any given day, from 3,000 to 4,000 people are working under the roof.'

"Someday I'll have to stop going here," Jan chuckles when his job is finished a few hours later. "I'm supposed to be retired, but I just love doing this work. And Dirk can certainly use an extra hand."

His son owns and operates the D. de Koning export firm that supplies flowers and plants on a weekly basis to 120 floral outlets in England. It's one of 300 similar concerns in Rijnsburg, a village known as a handelsdorp, a business centre, where the flower trade has been a way of life for generations. It's estimated that the industry directly and indirectly provides work for 10,000 people in the community and surrounding area. This is a remarkable figure, considering Rijnsburg itself has only 15,000 residents.

FloraHolland is the economic heart of this bustling and thriving region. The co-operative dates back to 1914 when a handful of local growers met in a cafe and decided it would be advantageous for them to join forces to market their products. For many years, it was known as just Flora. The new designation came into effect in January, 2002,

when the organization merged with the huge Holland floral auction in Naaldwijk which serves Westland, the glass city. FloraHolland also has auctions in Bleiswijk and Eelde, as well as a vigorous sales office that operates in all four locations and in Boskoop.

With 5,000 members, a workforce of 2,500 and auction sales totalling 1.82 billion euros annually, FloraHolland is the world's largest co-operative auction organization, exceeding the numbers of the massive, 13-clock Aalsmeer operation.

A tour of the facilities in Rijnsburg – or any of the other auctions, for that matter – leaves a visitor awe-struck. There's an immediate awareness of the immensity of the Dutch flower business when the eye beholds the endless stream of trolleys in the cavernous halls. The built area covers 2.7 million square feet and is still growing. It's like a village within a village with its own policing personnel and amenities such as hair salons.

"Here in Rijnsburg, we have 600 people on our payroll," says Bastiaan de Leeuw, the auction's Account Manager, responsible for sales and marketing to the buyers. "But on any given day, from 3,000 to 4,000 people are working under the roof. That includes buyers, employees of companies that rent space for bunching and packaging their purchases and the people responsible for transport to and from the centre."

Up to 2,000 trucks could be parked around the complex, waiting for the next load to be driven to somewhere in Europe. Ninety-five per cent of the turnover is exported.

Apart from flowers and plants supplied by local growers, and since the 1970s by growers in other areas of the Netherlands as well, the Rijnsburg centre handles products from foreign producers. This helps to ensure a wide range, particularly during periods when the choice of the Dutch offering is less varied.

"We operate a large department for imports," says Bastiaan. "From 20 to 30 per cent of our turnover comes from other countries such as Israel, Kenya and Spain. We import roses, carnations, summer flowers, gerbera and so on."

— Jan de Koning: "I'm supposed to be retired, but I just love doing this work."

The Dutch growers have found that the co-operative system, as opposed to independent selling, is the best way to handle their product, enabling them to concentrate on production and arrive at a high degree of specialization.

As a member of a co-op such as FloraHolland, a grower is obliged to market his entire output through the auction centre and to pay it a small percentage of the proceeds. He takes his flowers and plants to the centre where they are stored in the cold room until their turn to be placed on the trolleys and paraded in front of the clocks.

The auctioneer sets a higher-than-expected price, whereupon the clock descends to a lower price. As soon as a prospective buyer causes the indicator to stop at a given price, he becomes the owner of the batch on sale.

Another sales method is known as mediation. Growers let the auction know in advance what price they wish to receive for their products. The centre then approaches traders who either accept or reject this price. Thus it is sometimes necessary for a grower to make adjustments. In Rijnsburg, direct sales without the clock now account for eight to nine per cent of the total volume and the figure is steadily rising.

Computers control most aspects of the operations, accounting for the fast and efficient way the trading proceeds day after day. The clocks are linked to administration systems and invoices are produced immediately after a trader has finished buying. No time is wasted in sending the purchases to either the rented processing areas or the loading platforms.

Tele-auctioning and information auctioning are new developments. With tele-auctioning, it is no longer necessary for all the trolleys to pass before the clocks. Via a large vido screen, the batch being auctioned is displayed to the buyers' gallery. Information auctioning is an electronic system that allows customers at home and abroad an insight of the supply a day prior to selling. This is effected via computer line connections between auction, exporter and customer. All batches to be sold are first recorded on video tape.

One of the tasks of the auction is to make sure that the products passing through its facilities meet the nation-wide quality standards. Inspectors carefully check the material on arrival, and their classifications are made known at the time of auctioning. It's the same principle that was followed in earlier days when an auctioneer didn't hesitate to bellow his opinion about a particular offering in no uncertain terms.

Jan de Koning has observed the growth and development of the Rijnsburg operation for more than half a century. His father, Dirk, began growing flowers in an open field on the outskirts of the village in 1925 and advanced to a small greenhouse a few years later. Jan took over the business in 1960 after having worked in it for 10 years. The greenhouse then was 25,000 square feet. Of course, the selling was done through Flora.

"I began to specialize in lilies in 1970," he says, "and developed a real liking for them. In fact, I'm still very much involved with lilies. I was with a group of six people – there are now 10 – who bought the rights to a variety called Pompei. We paid 550,000 guilders (the Dutch currency before the adoption of the euro) for a stock of 750 bulbs. Our production takes place in France."

Jan's switch from growing to buying began in 1986 with a small, rented truck that serviced 28 customers in

— FloraHolland is the world's largest co-operative auction organization.

— The impressive lobby at the A. Heemskerk B.V. wholesale firm in Rijnsburg.

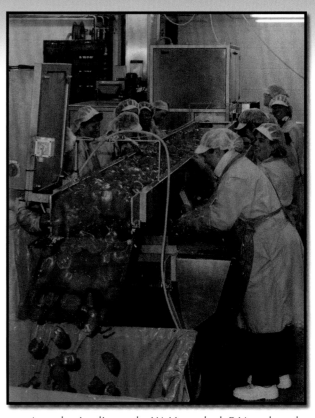

— A production line at the W. Heemskerk B.V. packaged vegetable plant.

England. The fledgling export business grew steadily. Son Dirk, who took over completely five years ago, now sends four large, climate-controlled transports, each laden with 30,000 stems, to England every week to supply the needs of his 120 customers. These florists and others can enter the compartments to make a selection from the tightly-stacked supplies. The purchases are transmitted via computer to the office in Rijnsburg.

The D. de Koning firm, located in a portion of a spacious, neighbouring building acquired in 2000 and employing 20 workers, has a turnover amounting to five million euros a year. The success of the business reflects the vitality of Holland's flower industry, brought about to a large extent by the penchant of the Dutch to seek business outside their narrow borders. But the firm is a minor player compared to some of the other operations in the village, including A. Heemskerk B.V., a 30-year-old wholesale company that has grown into one of the country's biggest flower exporters.

"I always said that if I ever moved, I would want lots of space and lots of height," says Bert Heemskerk, the owner, as he leads his visitors through his new, 130,000-square-foot plant in Florapark, a commercial area developed on the property of the flower auction. "We were feeling a bit cramped in our old place. Now we've created a pleasant and practical environment in which to carry on with our expanding business."

The impressive lobby, with a stylish staircase leading to second-floor offices, could fit well into the design of a luxury hotel. The plant even has a large restaurant, called Bon Vivant, which offers anything from a snack to a full meal.

The company buys its huge requirement of flowers and plants from auctions and directly from selected growers. It supplements its product range by organizing its own imports from selected countries. A fleet of more than 40 trucks services thousands of florists, wholesalers and garden

centres throughout Europe. Regular patronage has been secured from customers as discerning as the organizers of the Wimbledon tennis championships, the Ascot race meetings and the Oscar ceremony in Los Angeles.

The Heemskerk facilities include a popular cash and carry department where customers can see products up close before they buy, a plant hall with an enormous selection of green, flowering and garden plants, a bouquet division where designers prepare tailor-made arrangements to customers' specifications, and a dye department to meet the increasing demand for artificially-coloured flowers.

Bert's grandfather, Albertus Heemskerk, was a market gardener and vegetable merchant in Rijnsburg, and many of his offspring, like so many other people in the village, followed similar careers. Throughout the Netherlands and beyond, Heemskerk is now a leading name in both flower and vegetable production and distribution.

A WAY OF LIFE

Wim, Bert's cousin, has contributed his fair share to this recognition. He's the founder of W. Heemskerk B.V., the largest producer of sliced and packaged vegetables for the free market in Holland. The firm, employing 500 people, turns out five million packages a week at its sophisticated processing facilities in Rijnsburg. Its 24 transports deliver the products to customers throughout the Netherlands and in other European countries.

"I began in 1960 with a pair of washtubs, a stapler and a loan of 600 guilders from my father," Wim recalls. "I still remember that we started at three in the afternoon and when we finished at 10 o'clock in the evening we had 60 packages of soup vegetables. That's 60 packages in one day. Now we produce 120 packages in one minute."

The company's phenomenal growth rate of 40 per cent annually is expected to continue, perhaps even at a higher level, given the trend of women to spend less and less time on preparing meals and a vigorous effort to increase exports to neighbouring Germany, a huge potential market.

"We're looking across the border," says Cor, Wim's son, who took over ownership in 1989. "Ten years ago, we used one truck with four pallets to service Germany. Now we go there with four trailers every day. We want to develop that market even further."

This is good news for the growers in Holland and some other countries, notably Spain, who have contracts with Heemskerk to supply the vegetables needed for its line of 250 different products. It's also encouraging for the community leaders who are responsible for helping to keep the local economy in its robust state.

On the occasion of the company's 40th anniversary, the mayor of Rijnsburg, A. P. van der Lee, said:

"Heemskerk is a terrific business, an example of a Rijnsburg enterprise that expanded in an impressive manner and became a world concern. There are many more examples in Rijnsburg. People who started with practically nothing. People with an entrepreneurial spirit without equal. They remind me of the stories about American boys who began with a newspaper route and built an empire. I have respect and appreciation for such people."

FROM HOLLAND WITH LOVE

Here's a peek inside the beautiful world at the D. de Koning flower export firm in Rijnsburg, the Netherlands.

– *Flowers purchased at the FloraHolland auction in Rijnsburg are neatly arranged, cut to desired length and bunched for shipment by truck to retail florists in England.*

– *These racks, stacked with a wide assortment of colourful blooms, are kept in the cool cells until it's time to load them into the climate-controlled transport trucks.*

– *A breathtaking view of the interior of one the trucks. Florists in England can walk the aisle and pick out what they need for their customers.*

– *Dirk de Koning sends four large transports, each laden with 30,000 stems, across the English Channel once a week.*

— *In western parts of the Netherlands, especially near the North Sea dunes, rectangular fields of tulips, daffodils and hyacinths present a glorious sight in springtime.*

THE TOURISTS COME

Ottawa-born Princess Margriet, smiling radiantly, stole the show when she visited the ultra-modern greenhouses of the Van Klaveren brothers in Rijnsburg in early April, 2002.

She was there to officially open the 25th edition of Kom in de Kas (Come into the Greenhouse), a yearly event in which more than 350 flower, plant and vegetable growers throughout the Netherlands open their doors to the public.

After the princess had done her official duties, the attention at the Van Klaveren operation focussed on the intended stars of the show: rows upon rows of lilies growing in soil that hasn't been steamed for 15 years.

"We use the same soil over and over and even grind up all the old bulbs in it," Arie, one of the brothers, tells us. "We treat it biologically with micro-organisms. It is tested every year in the lab and we are advised on what to add. We've had no problems at all. When we built the greenhouses, we spent a lot of money putting in steam lines. We've never used them. We could have left the money in the bank."

Besides tours of greenhouses, the Kom in de Kas weekend offers related activities such as auctions, cooking shows, flower arranging courses, bicycle trips and bridal bouquet demonstrations. With over 200,000 visitors and participants, the event is unquestionably a huge public relations success.

— Keukenhof, one of Holland's top flower attractions, attracts hundreds of thousands of visitors from around the world every year.

The Dutch horticultural industry is directly involved in other public events as well, all intended to promote awareness, understanding and, of course, business. Some of these have developed into popular tourist attractions, pumping millions upon millions of euros into local economies. In effect, a whole new industry has grown out of the field and greenhouse production.

From early March to late May, when brilliant carpets of tulips, narcissi, hyacinths and crocusses transform the countryside between Leiden and Haarlem into a breathtaking display of colour, the stream of tourists is endless. People come from all over Europe and beyond to enjoy the dazzling sights and pleasant aromas.

The growers want the bulbs, not the flowers, and chop off the heads to retain strength for other flowerings. Alas,

most of the blooms end up in compost piles. But some are rescued by local children who string them into garlands that are offered for sale to passing motorists and cyclists.

The presence of so many blooms and visitors provides local organizers with a great opportunity to present a springtime extravaganza: the annual Bloemencorso, a parade of flowers, which starts in Noordwijk, winds through the bulb region and ends in Haarlem.

Three days before the pageant, hundreds of volunteers begin the painstaking job of pinning more than a million flowers onto the specially-constructed floats. A number of the entries are further enhanced with stunning floral centrepieces. There's a different theme each year; in 2002, it was Art and Nature, portraying works of Vincent van Gogh and other masters.

The first flower parade took place more than 50 years ago as a presentation of the bulb-growing industry. Over the years, it has grown into a vital component of the flower-related tourism business, attracting legions of onlookers and helping to inject more than 100 million euros a year into the regional economy.

Another significant component, also originated by bulb growers, is a 70-acre wooded park near Lisse, right in the heart of the bulb region, which is described without exaggeration as the greatest bulb-flower show on earth. It's called Keukenhof, or kitchen garden, part of the former estate of Countess Jacoba van Beieren of Bavaria (1401-1436), and attracts 750,000 visitors during the seven or eight weeks in spring when its seven million flowers, including more than 1,000 different varieties of tulips, are in full bloom.

— One of the many colourful entries in
the annual Bloemencorso.

The attraction came into being in 1949 after a group of 40 prominent bulb growers had decided to annually display the splendour of their industry, particularly new varieties, in a park-like setting. Beds were laid out masterfully among Keukenhof's majestic oaks and beeches.

The show garden was a hit right from the start. Flower lovers and gardening enthusiasts came from all over the Netherlands and neighbouring countries to admire the blooms. As news of the beauty spread, through vigorous promotion, media attention and word of mouth, the attraction gained world-wide recognition. More and more people put a tour of the place in their travel plans. Even members of European royalty became regular guests.

"We've been quite successful in making people aware of what we have to offer," says Karin E. Hoogland, Keukenhof's Sales Manager. "Sixty-five per cent of our visitors now are from abroad. Even so, promotion remains a big thing. We work closely with the Netherlands Board of Tourism and are visible at trade fairs for tourism and international flower functions. Our embassies also promote us. And we are involved in a joint promotion with KLM, the Dutch airline."

Keukenhof, operated by a board of directors, undergoes change almost yearly. There are new designs and themes. New areas are developed. And perennials and shrubs are made part of the scene. All this is aimed at motivating people to return year after year. Thirty full-time gardeners are employed throughout the year to plant the bulbs in the beds, as well as in a number of pavilions bearing the names of royalty, and to maintain the extensive grounds.

One hundred growers are now involved in Keukenhof, all supplying the bulbs needed to complete the displays. They are identified by a small plaque placed among their plants. A number of them have the right to take orders at kiosks in the park.

Then there's Floriade, a world horticultural exhibition that is organized every 10 years in a different area of the Netherlands and pulls in three million visitors during its run from early April to October.

The 2002 version, held on a 160-acre site in the Haarlemmermeer, was a virtual paradise for plant lovers, featuring the masterpieces of Dutch and foreign growers. For example, in a wooded area with a lake in its centre, 20 diverse international gardens nestled at water's edge. There was even a waterlily pond.

The many attractions included a look at a futuristic community called the Green City, where the focus was on the latest green trends in, on and around the house, and a tall greenhouse that featured the latest technological advances available to growers.

'We've been quite successful in making people aware of what we have to offer.'

Holland has many more flower-related showpieces and events, all contributing to the country's well-deserved reputation as the garden centre of the world. One of our favourites is a relatively new tourist magnet, Panorama Tulip Land, housed in a century-old flower bulb complex in Voorhout, a village in the bulb region. Besides viewing displays of the past, present and future, visitors can have a drink and something to eat on a cosy indoor terrace while watching artist Leo van den Ende work on what will become the world's largest panorama of the bulb fields and local landmarks: a canvas 206.5 feet long and 16.5 feet high.

— A waterlily pond was one of the attractions of Floriade in 2002.

THE TOURISTS COME

He began work on the painting on March 22, 1997, at the age of 58. Since he works only when Panorama Tulip Land is open for two months in the spring, he doesn't expect to complete his masterwork until he is past 70.

There's a definite purpose to this huge undertaking.

"Each spring I am struck by the flamboyant beauty of the bulb-growing region," he says. "But I am also concerned about the destructive process that is taking place. Some of the old buildings that were typical of the area have disappeared. In addition, because of expanding villages, a considerable number of bulb fields have been sacrificed. I believe that we have to be very careful with our heritage, that this process has to come to a stop and that what is left over has to be preserved. This can be achieved by making people aware of the beauty and uniqueness of this area."

— A segment of the panorama of Holland's famous tulip fields painted by Leo van den Ende.

— Jack Vink: "They're competing too much with each other."

Former bulb exporter Jack Vink of Sassenheim retains a soft spot in his heart for Canada, particularly the Niagara area where he used to live for a few months of the year.

"It's a place of tremendous opportunities," he says.

He should know, having taken advantage of those opportunities himself. He's the former owner of JVK, a greenhouse supply firm in St. Catharines, and one of the founders of St. David's Hydroponics Ltd., a bell pepper grower with two production facilities in the Peninsula.

"I first visited Canada in 1952," he says. "It was just a trip. I went there again in 1968 for business reasons. I enjoyed it the first time and I enjoyed the second time even more. I don't know why. It could have been the weather. It could have been some of the people I met."

Perhaps it was the remarkable set of circumstances in 1968 that enabled Jack to become a member of Niagara's business community. At the time, he was the owner of G. B. de Vroomen and Sons, a firm that grew flower bulbs on 110 acres in Holland and exported to Scandinavia, Great Britain, Germany and the United States. The Sassenheim company is now owned by Klaas Oudshoorn and called Deleeuw Flowerbulb Group B.V.

"We didn't do any business in Canada in '68," says Jack. "I was ready to go to the United States, to the Buffalo area, when an aunt in Holland asked me to bring a personal gift to her daughter who was living in St. Catharines. I did that. While there, I decided to drive around St. Catharines on my own. Somehow I hit Seventh Street, which was then a gravel road, and came across a sign reading Farm for Sale. It was an 18-acre fruit farm with peaches and grapes and a nice English-style house. When I approached the owner, he asked: 'Where are you from?' When I said Holland, he asked: 'Can you come over and buy a farm here?' I replied: 'If the money is the right colour, there will never be a problem.' After his real estate broker arrived, we settled on a price within 10 minutes. The owner almost fell out of his chair."

'There are still lots of opportunities for those who have determination, not fantasies.'

Why did you want the farm?

"I had become enchanted with Canada in the short time I had been there. I could smell opportunities. In fact, I was almost ready to migrate immediately, but I had a wife and four daughters in Holland who probably wouldn't be so inclined to move to another country."

What happened next?

"I decided to look around St. Catharines to find out who was importing Dutch bulbs. I went downtown, delivered some dirty laundry and then spotted Stokes Seeds. I walked in and met the managing director, Keith Grey, a perfect gentleman, who answered all my questions on importing, wholesaling and other matters related to the business in Canada. In the end, he gave me a big order for bulbs. Just when I was leaving, Jack van Klaveren walked in. He was a bulb and azalea importer from my village who had set up a business in Creemore, way out in the sticks, because he didn't want to be near industrial centres which he felt could be targets of Russian bombs. He was deadly afraid of the Russians. I accepted his invitation to go to Creemore for the weekend to talk business. It was a wonderful experience. He said he was dissatisfied with his supplier, knew of my company's reputation and wanted to start buying bulbs from me. So here I was, 24 hours in Canada, and I owned a farm and a house, had an order from Stokes and just landed another big order. I thought: 'This must be Heaven'."

How did you take over ownership?

"Jack said he wanted to retire in a few years and asked me if I could make preparations to take over his business. I was agreeable to that because I had suitable property. It would be very easy to move everything to St. Catharines, to the heart of the industry, when that time rolled around. Jack had a heart attack two or three years later and I took over soon after that. It was already a sizeable business then, grossing $575,000 a year. Everything seemed to fall into place. One more interesting twist: Keith Grey from Stokes became my manager. If you had to draw up a plan, would you be able to improve on that?"

How did it go in the first years?

"We continued the company as Jack van Klaveren Ltd., or JVK for short. When a seed company in Burlington went bankrupt, I said to Keith: 'We have to contact the best sales people in that company and offer them a job.' We recruited the sales manager and he brought with him four good men with experience and a trade. That proved to be a big asset for us. JVK grew so fast that we were actually getting into a cash problem. In the industry, orders are booked a year in advance and you get paid only after you have shipped. That can be a wait of from 12 to 15 months. In the meantime, you have to pay your overhead. We had around 20 people on the payroll then. But we got over the hump and kept on growing."

Did you live in Canada?

"I lived in St. Catharines four or five years. That is, I visited at least six times a year and stayed three to four months to keep the business going. I've divested my interests in JVK and St. David's because I'm not getting any younger. But I still love going back to Niagara whenever I get the chance."

Any views on doing business in Canada?

"There are still lots of opportunities for those who have determination, not fantasies. But there are two areas that can present problems: the distances are too great and the population isn't there to support large quantities. That's why it is so essential for the flower industry in Niagara to continue to develop business in the vast U.S. market. If everything is done right, the industry is in a tremendous position."

Can the greenhouse industry improve itself?

"It needs certain guidelines so the growers don't end up killing each other price-wise. They're competing too much with each other."

Is the marketing system employed by the Dutch the answer?

"That's not easy to say. You've got to study the industry in Canada and the marketplace in the U.S. and that has to be done by experts, not someone picked up on the street. It has to be determined how many openings there are in the U.S. and whether a better understanding can be reached with growers in Canada, on an industry-wide basis, on arriving at a price that is rewarding."

In marketing and technology, can Canadians learn from what's happening in Holland?

"Even here in Holland, we can't even keep up with advances in technology. Changes are taking place so fast. But let's face it, the heart of the industry is in Holland, and most of the Canadian growers of Dutch origin are coming over to see what they need to improve their operations. Unfortunately, from my observations, the second generation is not too interested in Holland. They don't want to know what's here. They don't even want to speak the language. It almost seems as if they are ashamed of their parents. This is ridiculous."

How can growers in Niagara do better?

"In this country, if a greenhouse is 10 years old, it is old. They say tear it down, build a new one and put in new technologies so that instead of working with three people, you need only one. That's the name of the game. Canadians have to modernize in their business undertakings. They have to bring the latest technology into their places in order to be competitive world-wide. They would want to spend some of the money they have made in the past to ensure their future."

How can the education system help?

"Well, places like the University of Guelph should be putting a lot of emphasis on teaching expertise in technology. As part of their program, they should arrange visits to Holland so that students can see what is being done here. I believe that would be a great thing to do."

By Lucas Gerrits - Horriculturalist, Ede, the Netherlands

How times have changed!

Fifty years ago, the typical grower in the Netherlands had a small greenhouse. He worked by himself, sometimes helped by members of his family. And he controlled his greenhouse environment by cranking a handle to open up a window.

The average grower nowadays needs a certain size of operation to maximize his economies of scale. He employs staff. And he uses very complex systems to control his climate and operate his automated equipment.

The knowledge of plant physiology and the interaction of the control systems in a modern greenhouse are as complex as what a fighter pilot in a modern jet has to master. The difference between a flower grower and a fighter pilot is that the latter will have gone through a government-paid training program costing millions.

However, even with the lack of taxpayer support for the training of growers and their staffs, there are a few similarities in modern-day training methods.

Historically, say also 50 years ago, knowledge came from lectures and textbooks. After a few years at a school desk, the student would be granted a diploma and be ready to work. Usually, a skill was learned later.

When mechanization was used more and more in agriculture, an important change was introduced in the agricultural education system. It was recognized that students would not be able to perform in the field without practical knowledge. As schools could not afford to buy mechanized equipment, several practical training centres were set up where this equipment would be available and be updated regularly. At these centres, students could master the use of tractors, learn how to plow at correct depths, and so on.

Over the years, the fundamentals have not changed; students from horticultural and agricultural colleges are still trained in practice. Even growers need to refresh their skills regularly.

In the last decade or so, different approaches have been used in describing the needs of students.

Around 1990, a description of qualifications was produced, listing the required theoretical and practical skills. The practical part consisted of one-day-a-week work at approved companies, where students would be coached by trained staff, and one to two weeks of in-house training at a practical training centre.

In 1998, there was a turning point from required qualifications to the description of competencies. For example, a grower needing his licence for crop protection would have to prove his competency at an exam with a practical test.

The principle of earlier acquired competencies gained importance for growers in 2002. Experience shows that many workers in horticulture do not have an agri-horticultural background or study. The measuring of earlier acquired competencies gives an indication of what knowledge someone has acquired in his or her career and where a gap needs to be filled. Employers are able to provide the right training for their workers and add the required skills to their portfolio of competencies.

The fighter pilot needs practice to operate his sophisticated machine with skill and efficiency. But when will the student pilot be allowed to fly solo? This question is no different for the growers when they employ staff.

An example is a typical climate control computer that provides 200 to 400 variables. Growers aim for the highest production at the lowest energy use. An experienced one has a feeling for what happens in his greenhouse and will allow this to be part of the decision-making at his climate computer. Acquiring this experience takes years of daily greenhouse work. Allowing students to play around in a greenhouse to experience the effects of changes in settings on climate and production is too expensive and impractical. Today students gain experience by practising on simulation programs. The operators can experience the effects of changes in control settings on the equipment until they are ready to be "released" into real-life situations where their decisions mean either profit or loss.

Nothing beats hands-on training and practice to be a meaningful addition to a professional team. Simulation programs and practice at training centres make that happen.

Aspiring fighter pilots and growers train their skills in similar ways.

Lucas Gerrits MSc is Account Manager Horticulture at PTC+, a practical training centre in Ede, the Netherlands.

As a close observer of Niagara's flower industry, Piet Borst* has some advice for the growers: shed your desire for independent marketing and work more closely together for the common good, just in case the boom times should be affected by a drastic change in the exchange rate or other developments.

"If Canadian growers don't allow their neighbours to come over for business, they are leaving themselves susceptible to problems in the future," he says. "They should organize themselves into grower groups, whether it be for roses, tulips, alstroemeria and so on. By talking with each other and sharing information, they can solve or prevent a lot of problems. I realize it's not easy to do this in a competitive climate. But the growers in the Netherlands managed to work together, and look at how strong their industry has become."

'We became good growers and we became big in flower growing because we allowed each other to learn.'

Piet has been in the flower bulb business all his working life. He's Commercial Manager of Royal Van Zanten, a large firm based in Hillegom that exports 90 per cent of its huge output of bulbs and plant material to growers around the world, including Ontario. In the course of his work, he's visited the Niagara Peninsula at least 40 times. In fact, we caught up with him just after he had returned to Holland from a convention in Niagara Falls of the International Cut Flowers Association, of which he is a board member.

"We meet twice a year," he says. "We were in St. Catharines six years ago and next year we'll be in Vancouver. It's interesting that our meetings in Canada are the best attended. People have a chance to meet each other and learn from each other. This is something that was encouraged in the Netherlands. We became good growers and we became big in flower growing because we allowed each other to learn."

Over the years, what changes have you observed in Niagara?

"The strong economic growth in the flower industry in Niagara began 10 years ago. Of course, the exchange rate was a contributing factor. But I believe another important reason was that growers were visiting the Netherlands

—Piet Borst: "Flowers come with emotion."

more and more to see what was being done. Some of these people had emigrated because they wanted to be more independent in their business dealings, to do their own thing. But once they saw what was going on in Holland, and how successful the industry had become, they realized that they could still learn a few things. Generally speaking, as far as new technology is concerned, Niagara is still a few years behind the Netherlands. But the gap is growing smaller and smaller."

There's a belief that extensive promotional efforts are needed to raise the per-capita consumption of flowers in North America to the level of that in Holland and some other countries. Do you agree?

"Well, it's easier said than done. We are talking about different cultures. Maybe it's different in the Peninsula, but in the United States people love going out of the home.

They go out for breakfast, for example. They have breakfast appointments and breakfast meetings. In the Netherlands, you'd have a hard time finding a breakfast restaurant. Even on Sundays, no one will think about going out for breakfast. The Dutch people spend more of their time at home. And I think they are more emotional than the American people. Flowers come with emotion. Americans prefer to give a box of chocolates. If you go to an American flower show – because of my profession, I look around a lot – you see teddy bears and that sort of stuff."

You're saying then that it will never be the same?

"It will never be the same no matter what is done. There's another problem to consider. The American consumer might be buying more flowers, but most of this business is done through supermarkets which have a totally different approach to selling than the flower shops in the Netherlands. They always go for cheaper, not particularly for quality. If you try to produce something the cheapest way possible, you can never provide the quality that is so important. Then bad things can happen. If people buy expensive flowers for Valentine's Day that are two to three weeks old already, and a big disappointment is the result, they are likely to switch to chocolates, perfume, lingerie or whatever the following year."

Some growers in Niagara complain that not enough is being done on an industry-wide basis to promote their products. Do you have any views on this?

"Here in the Netherlands, growers and others in the industry pay a percentage of their turnover – 2.1 per cent – for marketing. It's law. This money goes to an organization that is regulated by the government. So if you don't pay, it's like not paying your taxes, and you're in trouble. In the U.S. and Canada, there is no such thing. In California, it was suggested that everyone growing or producing over $100,000 pay half a per cent of his turnover for marketing, but nothing developed because no one wanted to pay. It's the same in Canada. People are not willing to pay an extra tax – that's what they call it – because they feel they can do a better job themselves."

Is this shortsighted?

"It's very shortsighted. Twenty-five years ago, when I first visited Niagara, many of the growers there were dying because they were not able to sell. The exchange rate was not like what it is now and they had to market everything

Horticultural Research

By Prof. Dr. Olaf van Kooten

Research in greenhouse horticulture in the Netherlands is concentrated in two areas:

Product quality management in greenhouse cultivation

In contrast to field agriculture, crop production in greenhouses allows accurate control of most of the environmental factors that affect plant growth and development.

Being able to control crop production in this way also permits the quality of the final, harvested product to be controlled.

We are developing production systems that optimize specific quality traits, such as the content of health-promoting components, taste or storage life.

The environmental factors that we can currently control easily are in both the aerial environment and the rhizosphere. These factors act upon the plant in a complex way. In the long term, they influence plant development in ways that depend upon the genotype, age and planting density.

The history of these developmental effects determines the physiological potential of the plant – for example, the response of photosynthesis to light intensity, and morphological changes, such as flower initiation.

The environment also has a short-term effect that, together with the physiological potential of the plant, determines the instantaneous rate of each of the numerous processes that together determine the physiological activity of the whole plant.

This complex plant-environment interaction is the production system. Ideally, it can be operated as a market-driven system that generates the input for the supply chain and should finally result in satisfying the consumer demand.

Internal product quality and measuring methodologies

The total quality of a product is determined both by components accessible to our senses, such as colour, smell or texture, and by components to which we are insensible, such as storage life or nutritional quality.

The latter components are collectively referred to as the internal quality of the product.

Our other research goal is the development and application of assessment and measuring methodologies for components of internal quality.

Ideally, these methodologies should be generic, which means that though we may develop them initially for one product, they can subsequently be applied to another product with the minimum of modification. This flexibility allows us to develop measurement procedures to determine product quality for a whole range of products at a reasonable cost. The measured quality must also be capable of being expressed quantitatively.

By studying the product quality behaviour in relation to external conditions, it becomes possible to model the quality changes that occur in the supply chain from the greenhouse to the consumer.

And by describing the quality development as a continuous dynamic system, it becomes possible to determine the sensitivity of the entire chain to quality-deteriorating events.

This will permit a more complete separation of the product and information about the product (quantity, cultivar, quality) as it moves through the supply chain.

This separation is a basic requirement for the introduction of quality-based information and communication technology in horticultural supply chains.

The aim is to minimize transport and waste in the whole supply chain and create the possibility of supply chain management with quality guarantees on a global scale.

This research will enable us to develop an efficient consumer response on all levels of the supply chain and implement a certified production and handling protocol to meet the consumer wishes within the fast-changing constraints.

Prof. Dr. Olaf van Kooten is a professor of academic education in greenhouse horticulture, specializing in horticultural production chains. He is on the staff of the University of Wageningen in the Netherlands.

---

locally. Now things are a bit better because of the exports to the U.S. But the system still seems awkward compared to what we have in the Netherlands. The Flower Council of Holland, based in Leiden, analyzes the markets, maintains contact with domestic and foreign market players and does all the promotion work. And all this is being done with levies assessed to all growers."

Holland has developed an international market for its flower bulbs. For example, they're sold everywhere in Canada. Will the good times last?

"Well, Canadians are always going to need flower bulbs from the Netherlands. Our country has the right conditions for growing bulbs. But we're producing bulbs in other places too, primarily Chile and New Zealand. I started a project in Chile in 1987. After 15 years, so many bulbs are being produced in these countries that some Dutch exporters are regarding this as a threat to their business. These bulbs are as good as the ones from the Netherlands – and eventually they can be produced a bit cheaper. But what is more important is that these bulbs give flower growers the opportunity to extend the production season with a better quality flower."

* We received the sad news of Piet Borst's death from cancer while this book was in production.

— *The Dutch spare no effort and money to decorate entries for their annual flower parades. Lilies, roses and other varieties adorn this restored 1932 Ford owned by Jan de Koning and Jan de Ruiter. The showpiece was awarded a gold medallion in the flower parade that wound through Rijnsburg, Katwijk and Noordwijk in August, 2002.*

CHAPTER TWENTY-TWO

PEOPLE WITH VALUES

'They are a people who stand behind their products. But they are also a people who gladly help the poor and are deeply religious. Their generosity and that of many others can be seen in the picture of our beautiful worship centre that was just recently built.'

— Rev. Jerry J. Hoytema

THE MENNONITE JOURNEY

By **Rev. Marv Friesen**
Vineland United Mennonite Church

They came with virtually nothing – yet they came with all they needed.

Mennonites first came to North America following the aftermath of severe religious persecution during the 16th century Protestant Reformation. They came to escape the ongoing oppression, discrimination and intolerance. They came to escape the pressure of rising militarism. They came to seek economic opportunity and adventure. They came to preserve the faith that sustained them through their most difficult days. They came to plant seeds of a New Testament church that reflected Jesus Christ as the foundation for faith and practice. And they came to fulfill the vision for which their fathers and mothers had suffered so much. God was providing them another refuge – a new "promised land."

Those who came were part of two broadly related yet culturally unique streams, the Swiss-South German and the Dutch-Prussian-Russian, with the latter coming first but the former soon dominating the scene until well into the 19th century. At the invitation of William Penn, six men of the 1883 Swiss-South German group were granted 18,000 acres on condition they establish a colony in what is now part of Lancaster County, Pennsylvania.

Following the Revolutionary War of 1776, some Pennsylvania Mennonites began moving north into Canada. By 1800, about 60 persons had settled at Vineland, site of the first Mennonite church in Canada. Another settlement had begun that year in Waterloo County. In 1807, Benjamin Eby founded Ebytown, now Kitchener. From 1873 to 1884, approximately 18,000 immigrants came from Russia and settled in the Midwest of Canada and the United States. Fifty years later, in the decade of the 1920s, some 21,000 from the Soviet Union entered Canada as they escaped the carnage of the Russian Revolution which decimated their rural enclaves in southern Russia and Ukraine.

The most recent mass exodus out of Russia occurred following the Second World War when approximately 35,000 Russian Mennonites of German descent were evacuated to Poland and Western Europe by the retreating German army following the Battle of Stalingrad. Of these, some 7,000 made their way to Canada and were soon

— Rev. Marv Friesen at Vineland United Mennonite Church where he serves as minister.

scattered across the land with friends and relatives.

Mennonites are historically a people of the land, a rural folk who have embraced the Protestant work ethic. They are a people who have suffered great persecution through the generations but have seen the future through eyes of faith. They have persevered with the understanding that God would lead them to a better place and time. Members of the Mennonite Church have a strong historical consciousness. They are keenly aware that their spiritual forbearers suffered and died for the faith and fled from one land to another in search of religious liberty. They identify their pilgrimage in many ways with that of the Old Testament Israelis, in search of that place where they could live and worship in freedom, peace and prosperity – a symbol of God's blessing.

Due in part to their own experiences, Mennonites have developed a deep social concern for those who suffer from ethnic, religious and racial discrimination. They are eager to see all citizens everywhere enjoy the full benefits of acceptance. Many are concerned for social and economic justice in a world that is reflecting an ever-increasing gap between rich and poor, haves and have-nots. As members of the historic peace church movement, Mennonites are grappling with issues of faith related to the biblical call to be peacemakers and peacekeepers in a world of ever-increasing violence and use of military force.

'They are eager to see all citizens everywhere enjoy the full benefits of acceptance.'

Today Mennonites are a valued part of the social and cultural fabric of our great land, Canada. They are now more urban than rural; they are now more acculturated, more wealthy, more established, and have a stronger social and political voice than at any other time in their history. This is both a blessing and a burden as this immigrant group of modest beginnings strives to discern the will of their God who brought them to this land of hope and opportunity.

"For no other foundation can any one lay than that which is laid, which is Jesus Christ." – 1 Corinthians 3:11.

Marvin Friesen is the grandson of Russian Mennonite immigrants who came to Canada in the 1920s' exodus. He grew up on a fruit farm in Jordan. His faith was shaped and nurtured by his family and church, the Vineland United Mennonite Church. After spending the past 10 years abroad with his family, he has resettled in Vineland is the minister of his home church. He is married to Brenda and they have four daughters, Sherrie, Teresa, Melissa and Grace. Historical information for the article was taken from An Introduction to Mennonite History, Cornelius J. Dyck, editor, Herald Press, Scottdale, Pennsylvania, Kitchener, Ontario, 1981.

Floral Passion

By **Clarence Alkema**
Alkema Greenhouses, Grimsby

The immigrant flower growers came to Canada because the Netherlands lacked space and opportunities as most of the nation's resources were tied up in recovering from the devastation of the Second World War.

Canada, on the other hand, had many of the resources that the immigrants needed to build a new life and thrive in their adoptive homeland. Canada had plentiful land, a wealth of natural resources and an expanding economy that offered numerous marketing opportunities. As a country, Canada also had other qualities: it offered civil freedom, free enterprise and democratic tradition, and it was a Christian nation. My family and many other immigrant families needed new opportunities to make a living in their chosen profession of flower growing, and Canada offered them a chance to use the expertise they had developed to make a living through work they enjoyed. Moreover, the immigrants knew that with hard work and perseverance, they could thrive in Canada both economically and personally.

The immigrants also knew that Canada was a tolerant society in which they could live as equals and be accepted by the community. Many of the immigrants took Canadian citizenship with great pride. They added to their respective communities by building Christian churches and schools. Many even joined the mainstream of Canadian life by participating in organizations like the local Chamber of Commerce and the major political parties. Overall, the immigrants were motivated to live and work in Canada by a strong sense that they had chosen one of the finest nations in the world as their new home.

'Immigrant flower growers were known as hard workers who were experts in their field.'

However, starting over in a strange new country was not always easy and the immigrants had many virtues that sustained them through the daily challenges they faced in building a life in Canada. Ultimately, their faith and fortitude were the qualities that helped them to fulfil their hopes and aspirations.

—Clarence Alkema: "Ultimately, their faith and fortitude were the qualities that helped them to fulfil their hopes and aspirations.'

In business and family affairs, the immigrants conducted themselves with the utmost honesty. When a Dutch-Canadian grower offered his or hand in a business deal, everyone knew that he or she was bound by their word. In addition, all the honest effort that was expended to build businesses was for the benefit of the family. Parents often laboured long hours so that their children could go to school and enjoy all the benefits that Canada had to offer.

Immigrant flower growers were known as hard workers who were experts in their field. Often they would do the hard physical work of building heating systems and the rest of the necessary greenhouse infrastructure themselves. They also used their talents in growing and marketing flowers to good effect, and by the 1980s and '90s, the industry enjoyed a boom that allowed many immigrants to prosper and expand their businesses.

But life in Canada was not always so comfortable for the immigrant flower growers as it has been in the last 20 years. Life in Canada produced many challenges that were not foreseen by the flower growers and their families. There was a degree of culture shock when they first arrived. Most immigrants arrived in Canada with very few material possessions, and they had to invest much of their time and energy in order to build their first small greenhouse businesses. Then, as their businesses grew, they had to deal with the difficulties of building and organizing the newly-restructured farms. Through all of the struggles they faced, the immigrant growers realized that they could not overcome the challenges they faced by their own strength. Instead, they relied on their faith in God to sustain them through the passing struggles of this life. Their commitment to their faith and faith communities was shown by the fact that the little free time they had was dedicated to personal devotions, group Bible studies and church consistory and Christian school board meetings.

Throughout the experience of immigration, the work that had to be done was difficult and it took many decades. However, it seems to me that the things that were achieved were not only the work of human effort but a result of the sustaining grace of God. Our parents received many blessings from the Lord and today we still know that we are allowed to work in this great country and this fine industry only because God has allowed us these privileges.

Clarence Alkema is President and General Manager of Alkema Greenhouses on Central Avenue in Grimsby. He has served as Vice-president (1995-97) and President (1997-99) of the Canadian Ornamental Plant Foundation. He attends Forestview Community Church in Grimsby.

273

By **Fr. Philip English**
St. Ann's Roman Catholic Church, Fenwick

The ethnic makeup of most Catholic churches in Niagara varies with each new wave of immigration. Each generation of migrants bring with them a religious faith and spirituality steeped in their own culture and tradition.

When I was first appointed as pastor to St. Ann's Roman Catholic Church in Fenwick, I was pleased to discover a parish community rich in ethnic diversity, a veritable patchwork of nationalities, with representatives from ever corner of the European quilt.

'They are tireless in their industry, strong in their faith and devoted to their families.'

Originally, the fertile, sandy soil of the Fenwick area attracted Polish immigrants. They bought farms in the locality and built, in the hamlet of Boyle, a little chapel dedicated to St. Ann, about half a mile from the present location of the new St. Ann's Church on Canboro Road.

The new church was built to accommodate the ever-growing Catholic community whose ranks were augmented by the recent arrival of a new breed of farmer from the Netherlands. The new Dutch farmers brought with them an innovative approach to agriculture, and thus the era of greenhouse farming was established in both Fenwick and the Niagara Region.

Today, many of the most productive farmers in the Fenwick area are both first and second-generation Dutch-Canadians. Much of their productivity is generated by a tireless work ethic, a "can do" approach to the evolving technology surrounding greenhouse agriculture, and a strong religious faith supporting their family values.

The Dutch community of St. Ann's Church bring to their faith the same qualities which have made them successful in business: energy, intelligence and a certain strength of personality.

St. Ann's Church is enriched by the presence of so many Dutch Catholic farmers. They are tireless in their industry, strong in their faith and devoted to their families. May God bless them and keep them this way for many years to come.

— St. Ann's Roman Catholic Church in Fenwick.

Father Philip English, the pastor of St. Ann's Roman Catholic Church in Fenwick, was born in the United Kingdom and educated mostly in Ireland. For the past 11 years, he has ministered to the needs of the Catholic community in the Diocese of St. Catharines, in Fort Erie, St. Catharines and Fenwick.

Floral Passion

THE WESTLANDERS

By **Rev. Jerry J. Hoytema**
Mountainview Christian Reformed Church, Grimsby

Westlanders are their own kind of people, which in itself is neither good nor bad. As a teenager, I lived in the town of Monster, which is part of the Netherlands commonly known as Westland, and learned some things about them then.

My father, Rev. George J. Hoytema, came to Monster shortly after the Second World War as the pastor of one of the Reformed churches there. It was a large congregation with well over 1,000 people attending worship every Sunday. My family was not from that area, both my father and mother being Friesians. As children, we soon learned that the Westlanders were a hard-working and generous people, though at times a little rough in language.

The annual service of Thanksgiving would have a special offering of thanksgiving for the Lord's blessings for church and work, crops and industry. I keenly remember my Dad coming home after that service and waiting for the result of the offering. Those who counted the offering immediately following the service would come to the parsonage with the result – it would be in the thousands of guilders – and they would celebrate the great generosity of the people with a good cigar and a glass of gin.

It was custom that on the birthdays of my parents our home would be flooded with tokens of love and appreciation. Greenhouse growers would stand at the door of the parsonage with baskets of peaches, boxes of grapes and all sorts of vegetables which we took to Friesland to share with our relatives because we could not eat it all.

Westland was known as the Glass City because of its greenhouses. The greenhouse growers would be up at 2 or 3 a.m. most mornings to bring their wares, often by boat, to the market. With some anxiety, they would wait for the price that would be offered for their produce. When there was too much produce and the price dropped precipitously low, all the produce would be thrown on a heap and sprayed with some substance that made it inedible and illegal for sale.

> *'They know that they are fully dependent on God for a blessing but at the same time need to work hard.'*

Many of the children of these growers would put in several hours of work before school and often also after school. One axiom often offered by parents was that when children would work, they could not get into any trouble, and they would also learn to work hard and be frugal.

I emigrated with my parents to Canada in 1952 and became a pastor in 1964 in the Christian Reformed Church. Interestingly enough, my second pastorate was at Mountainview Christian Reformed Church in the town of Grimsby where our family lived from 1968 to 1973. And then in 1996 I became the pastor of Mountainview for the second time.

My observations about the Westlanders being a hardy, hard-working people, as well as generous and deeply religious, were once again confirmed. In the 1960s, these were immigrant families seeking to establish themselves. Many of them did so very successfully. But they had to work hard. And so did their children. Oftentimes work was waiting for them before they went to school and after they came home. Grades were not as important as work. Some teenagers did not always appreciate that they had to work when other children were playing, and the question might be raised if the next generation will have the same work ethic as their parents.

Westlanders help each other when they are in trouble. But you have to be worthy of help. If you don't work hard yourself or prove to be incompetent, you may be helped once but not again. You would be saved, if possible, from

Rev. Jerry J. Hoytema: "Those early years of the '50s and '60s, when the first greenhouses were built, were tough."

bankruptcy the first time, but not a second time. To be helped, you need to be hard-working and deserving as well as be one of them.

The Westlanders I know today are deeply religious as well as generous, just like they were during my childhood. They know that they are fully dependent on God for a blessing but at the same time need to work hard. I came once to a person who was blessed financially and said to him: "God has richly blessed you." Whereupon he replied: "Yes, but I work hard." The next time I saw him, I said it a little differently: "You really work hard." And his reply was: "Yes, but God is blessing me."

Let me illustrate with another anecdote how their dependence on hard work as well as God's blessing is interrelated. In the early days, plastic was often used instead of glass to cover the greenhouses. These large pieces of plastic were very difficult to handle on windy days. One day, while a greenhouse was being covered with plastic,

a strong wind came and the farmer said: "Boys, pray like mad, and hold onto the plastic with all your might."

Those early years of the '50s and '60s, when the first greenhouses were built, were tough. The Niagara Peninsula is known for its hard, red clay. I remember seeing the farmers on their hands and knees, breaking down the clay and planting tomatoes, tulips and other flowers. But even then, as today, they continued to have a deep faith and a generous spirit. One man who had just started his greenhouse business confided in me that church and Christian school had to be paid. If he could not pay for them, the business was not worth having. A Westlander knows how to spell "shoestring."

The Westlanders whom I am familiar with as their pastor are in some sense hard-nosed and they have a mind of their own as well as not being easily swayed. They are a people who stand behind their products. But they are also a people who gladly help the poor and are deeply

religious. Their generosity and that of many others can be seen in the picture of our beautiful worship centre that was just recently built. It can hold as many as a thousand worshippers and has a gym and classroom facilities. When there is an offering for a special need at home or in the world, thousands of dollars are gladly given for a worthy cause.

In some of these things, the Westlanders have not changed much from the memories I have of them from my childhood. I am not sure, but I would hope that the next generation will know something of that same work ethic, generosity and faith in God.

Rev. Jerry J. Hoytema, pastor of Mountainview Christian Reformed Church in Grimsby, and his wife, Winnie, have four children: George, married to Iris; Judy, married to Bill Vander Lingen; Bert; and Michelle, married to Joel Ezinga. They also have 12 grandchildren.

'Who doesn't love flowers? They enable people to enjoy life better.
They're revitalizing. They relieve stress.'
— *Si Wai Lai*

'THE BEST IN THE WORLD'

The people of Niagara-on-the-Lake take a lot of pride in their historic community, the prettiest little town in Canada.

In the warm seasons, they welcome the hordes of visitors with a profusion of exquisitely-designed floral delights in public places and in private gardens, spreading an infectious feeling of enjoyment and bliss.

Perhaps no one is more happy to observe the smiling faces amid all the natural beauty than John Vandenberg, Parks and Recreation Supervisor for Niagara-on-the-Lake, who has been involved since the beginning with the efforts to beautify the town, especially its Queen Street Heritage District.

He and his expert staff provide and maintain the stunning floral displays along the boulevards on the quaint main street where thousands of tourists come daily to browse, buy and enjoy. The large hanging baskets, with their drooping blooms and foliage, are particularly breathtaking.

"They're the best in the world," enthuses John, formerly of Baarn, in the Netherlands. "We receive complimentary calls from all over. People want to know how we make them so beautiful."

The secret amounts to a lot of tender loving care which John explains as follows: "It's a combination of picking the right plants and colour, using good soil, applying fertilizer once a week – don't skip even once – and watering every day."

There always has been something special about the pretty community at the mouth of the Niagara River.

— Niagara-on-the-Lake, the prettiest little town in Canada, is a premier tourist attraction.

First settled by United Empire Loyalists who had migrated to the area following the American Revolutionary War, it was named Newark in 1792 by Lieutenant-Governor John Graves Simcoe when he selected it as the capital of Upper Canada. The first five sessions of the legislature were held there. In 1796, the capital was moved farther away from the American border, to York, now Toronto.

The frontier place suffered greatly in the War of 1812. Much of it was burned to the ground by retreating American soldiers. But it rose from the ashes and later prospered as an active commercial centre. The stately old homes lining the tree-shaded streets attest to the affluence of the citizens of that period.

A start on floral beautification was made in 1972 when the community merged with the villages of St. Davids, Virgil and Queenston in the Regional Municipality of Niagara. The effort was limited to a few flower pots placed on the main street. When the Shaw Festival arrived, substantially increasing the number of visitors, the feeling grew that more should be done to make the old town more attractive.

In 1982, as a project for the town's bicentennial, a small heritage park was created in Simcoe Park.

"We planted some pansies in the spring and later put in different annuals for the summer," recalls John. "It was nothing spectacular. But we had made a start and could only grow from there."

The big turning point came in 1992 when the town developed a streetscape plan for Queen Street and spent more than $55,000 to enhance the area. This was a shot in the arm, raising the level of enthusiasm a notch throughout the community. It had already been high, especially among members of the local Horticultural Society who had been supportive of the beautification program from the start and helped it along with financial contributions and many hours of volunteer work.

Some merchants offered to pay $1,000 for flower beds in front of their businesses. But the biggest boost from the private sector came in 1997 when Si Wai Lai, the enterpreneurial owner/operator of Niagara-on-the-Lake Vintage Inns, offered to donate $20,000 a year for the purchase of more flowers. In the same year, she also contributed $200,000 for major improvements to Simcoe Park, including the installation of flower beds, trellisses, walkways and a wading pool.

'We receive complimentary calls from all over. People want to know how we make them so beautiful.'

"Who doesn't love flowers?" she says. "They enable people to enjoy life better. They're revitalizing. They relieve stress. I want people to be happy and stress-free, so I'm not shy in using flowers at my own properties and contributing to the beautification of the town."

Indeed, her elegant Vintage Inn properties – The Pillar and Post Inn, Queen's Landing Inn and Conference Resort, The Prince of Wales Hotel, The Oban Inn and Shaw Cafe and Wine Bar – are exquisitely landscaped and adorned.

Alderman Terry Flynn, Niagara-on-the-Lake's Deputy Lord Mayor, says the corporate assistance and involvement is greatly appreciated by the municipality.

"Our program is a good example of how the public and private sectors can work together for the benefit of the community," he says. "On our part, we are using the revenue from the parking meters solely to keep our downtown beautiful. We have already been judged the prettiest town in Canada, in our population category of 15,000 and under, and we are committed to keeping it that way."

Niagara-on-the-Lake entered the Communities in Bloom and Nations in Bloom contests for three years. In 1995, it won the provincial title, in its category, and it triumphed at

— Five people who take deep pride in beautifying Niagara-on-the-Lake with flowers: Chris Allen, John Vandenberg, Si Wai Lai, Terry Flynn and Randy Andres.

the national level the following year. In 1997, it competed at the international level.

The floral displays that bring so much pride and appreciation are the result of a lot of careful planning by John. Each year he visits flower growers in the area to find new material that his department can select for planting the following season.

Si Wai's passion for flowers developed when she was a child in China. She was the youngest of six children raised by her mother. Her father had fled to Hong Kong, then a British colony, to preserve his considerable assets from Communist takeover.

"My mother held two jobs and she taught me all about work," she says. "She also instilled in me a deep love for flowers. Every Wednesday and Saturday, she took me to the market to pick up unsold flowers that had been discarded. We took these home and made beautiful arrangements. So I was able to enjoy fresh flowers right up to the time I left China in 1968 at the age of 16."

Floral Passion

— *A striking view of The Prince of Wales Hotel.*

281

— Niagara-on-the-Lake enhances its attractiveness as an architectural and historical treasure with lavish displays of floral delights.
At right is the Preservation Gallery which features works by artist Trisha Romance.

At the beginning of the Chinese Cultural Revolution, all schools were closed and students were sent to communes to learn how to farm. Si Wai's dreams of pursuing higher education were shattered. With determination, she bicycled to the ocean, and then endured a 36-hour swim to Hong Kong and her first taste of freedom.

After living in Hong Kong, Africa and San Francisco, she arrived with her family in Niagara in 1981 and began her career in the hospitality industry while continuing to invest in real estate. In 1994, she purchased her first hotel in Niagara-on-the-Lake, The Pillar and Post Inn, and immediately launched a major renovation and expansion

project that transformed it into one of the world's most luxurious country inns. There were more acquisitions and renovations of grand properties over the next five years. Of course, flowers and plants became fixtures, adding to the town's prettiness and encouraging others to follow.

The gorgeous exterior arrangements at the Shaw Cafe, part of the Queen Street display, are a floral lover's delight. They are the handiwork of Christopher Allen, who also looks after all of Vintage Inns' interior plants.

"The mass of colour at the Shaw Cafe is spreading all over," says Randy Andres of Green Scenes Groundskeeping

Inc., responsible for installing and maintaining flower beds at all Vintage Inns properties, as well as at some private residential estates. "We are seeing a lot more residents sprucing up their gardens. The local paper helps this along by featuring a Yard of the Week. It's great to see such a large and growing involvement."

Si Wai doesn't want to take too much credit for her community's attractiveness.

"John started it all," she says. "I'm just trying to give him the support he deserves. The entire community benefits."

Floral Passion

NIAGARA HAS BLOSSOMED

© THIES BOGNER, MPA.

— The scenic Niagara River, 35 miles long, is part of the boundary between Ontario and New York.

By *George Bailey*

Niagara Falls, the natural wonder that has lent its world-famous name to the area where so many beautiful flowers are grown for the enjoyment of millions of North Americans, first roared upon this earth some 12,000 years ago. It was created out of melting glaciers that formed the Great Lakes during the last Ice Age.

The origin of the Falls – the Canadian Horseshoe Falls and the American Falls, divided by Goat Island – lies in the pre-historic creation of the Niagara Escarpment. This 600-mile-long shelf of rock cutting across central Ontario once formed the shoreline of a gigantic inland sea that covered much of North America millions of years ago. The Falls we know today began as a trickle over this escarpment at Queenston/Lewiston and grew into a thunderous cataract, gradually carving the Niagara Gorge.

This 6.8 miles of erosion occurred as a result of the undercutting of a top layer of dolomite limestone which forms the cap of the bottom of the Niagara River. The swift-moving water eroded the softer layers of sandstone and shale found below the dolomite. Once sufficiently undermined, the edge of the Falls collapsed into the gorge, resulting in the backward movement.

Floral Passion

— The awesome Niagara Falls has been a source of inspiration to visitors for centuries.

Until the early 1950s, the Falls receded at the average rate of 3.3 feet per year. Since then, major water diversion above the Falls for hydro-electric purposes and the Canada-U.S. Niagara Remedial Works Project, which spread the flow of water more evenly over the Horseshoe Falls, have dramatically reduced erosion. It's now estimated the rate is about one foot every 10 years or about three per cent of what it was previously.

Interestingly enough, without this slowing, the Falls would have disappeared into Lake Erie in about 200 years!

Niagara is not only powerful, it is also beautiful. The water that pours down more than 160 feet at the rate of 12 million cubic feet every minute fills the air with a silvery mist that displays many rainbows in sunlight. The water also sends out a never-ending roar as it strikes bottom. For this reason, the

Iroquois Indians who had settled in the region christened the phenomenon Niagara, meaning "thunder of waters."

Nomadic native hunters camped in the area almost 12,000 years ago, around the time of the birth of the Falls, and they were probably the first humans to set eyes upon the plunging water. Etienne Brule, the first European to see Lakes Ontario, Erie, Huron and Superior, may also have been the first to view the Falls, in 1615.

Floral Passion

The retreating of glaciers below the escarpment left a carpet of rich soil, widely regarded as one of the most fertile areas of Canada. Wonderful vineyards, orchards, nurseries and parks are found here. Lake Ontario and the Niagara River provide lots of moisture to nourish the rich lands and foster the growth of a tremendous variety of plants, including close to 1,000 flowering and fern-like ones near the Falls. There are also over 70 species of trees. Queen Victoria Park, which overlooks the Falls, is one of the finest arboretums in the world.

Many people consider the Niagara Park Commission's 4,250-acre parkland between Lake Erie and Lake Ontario, parallel to the Niagara River on the Canadian side of the border, as the jewel of the Niagara area. When he visited Niagara in 1944, Sir Winston Churchill called the scenic route "the prettiest drive in the world."

The beautifully-landscaped parkland comes complete with natural and person-made attractions, formal and informal gardens, nature areas, golf courses, including the New Legends of Niagara course on the Upper Niagara Parkway, and historic sites. Within the parks system, there are approximately 100 historical plaques, monuments and markers commemorating various people, places and events, many of them related to battles of the War of 1812 between the U.S. and Canada. Numerous areas along the scenic Niagara Parkway provide excellent facilities for picnicking, with sturdy tables and benches. They are usually found under beautiful tree canopies overlooking the river.

Queen Victoria Park is a great place for a leisurely stroll in all seasons. Viewing of the coloured night-lights on the Falls is ideal from this location. A quarter-mile walk south of the Falls will take you to the Niagara Parks Greenhouse. Admission here is free and you will enjoy floral displays at any time of year.

The Niagara area, a mecca for millions of tourists from around the world, has many, many more attractions, ranging from fun parks to museums to fine restaurants to a butterfly conservatory to festivals to casino gambling. A new casino/hotel complex will be opened on the escarpment just above the Falls in the mid-2010s.

— The rising sun casts a mysterious glow over the rushing water.

Niagara has blossomed over the years and it won't end here. You can expect more growth, more life in the years to come.

George Bailey of Niagara Falls was the Director of Communications for the Niagara Parks Commission for 23 years before taking early retirement in 1999. He is the author of three published books, two on Niagara Falls and one on Marilyn Monroe. He is also an avid photographer – many of his photos have been featured on postcards and in newspapers and magazines – a freelance travel writer/ photographer and a member of the board of the Travel Media Association of Canada.

287

© THIES BOGNER, MPA.

— *The attractions, special events and natural beauty in the Niagara area draw millions of visitors every year.*

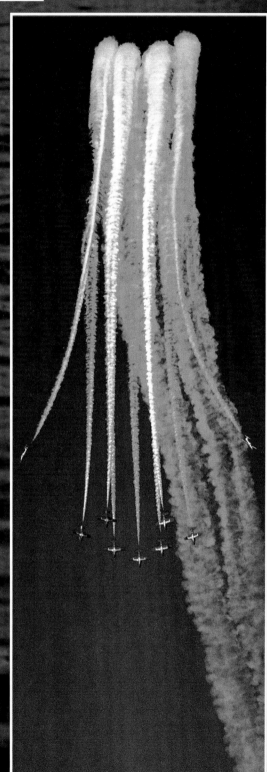

— *Originally constructed in 1829, the Welland Canal between Lakes Erie and Ontario offers a detour around the Falls. The photo shows the Flight Locks at Thorold.*

GOLDEN HONEYMOON MEMORIES

Niagara Falls, Ontario, the world's honeymoon capital, has attracted newlyweds for more than two centuries. In 1803, even Napoleon Bonaparte's younger brother, Jerome, stayed there with his bride. Some say the place became a honeymoon mecca because of the sexual powers of the negative ions generated by the Falls. Others say the sheer majesty of the natural wonder was enough to create the romantic magnetism. Whatever the reason, millions of people from near and far retain happy memories of their honeymoon in Niagara Falls. In 1992, newspaper readers throughout North America were invited through a local initiative chaired by John Van Kooten to participate in a Golden Honeymoon Memories contest. The winning essay is reprinted below.

— Bill and Elly Ryan during their honeymoon in Niagara Falls in 1957.

By *Bill Ryan*

It was a beautiful sunny day in Winnipeg when Elly and I tied the knot on Saturday, May 4, 1957.

The wedding was small, celebrated by relatives and close friends. Dinner was catered at my new in-laws' residence with the reception being held in their unfinished basement, among preserves and clotheslines. It was fun though, with serious tippling, dancing and toasting the bride throughout the evening. Elly's kid brother entertained us with his accordion virtuosity. "Lady of Spain" was his forte.

We had to leave the reception early, as our train was due to depart Union Station at 8:30 p.m. Elly changed, grabbed her suitcase and kissed all of her weeping relatives and friends goodbye. I had to run the gauntlet of well-wishers too. They all had to shake my hand and hug my skinny frame, as we tried to break loose. El's father grabbed me by the shoulders and stuffed a new $100 bill into my wedding-suit pocket and said: "Take good care of my little girl Bill, and have a great time." I said I would and thanked him for everything. The extra hundred bucks would give us $500 for our trip. Our best man, Billy, had his '52 Chevy all revved up and ready to go, as we dashed to the safety of the back seat. A couple of cars followed, honking their horns noisily, as we sped towards the CN station.

We were married on a shoestring and I was lucky, I suppose, as having worked for the CNR over the past eight years as a telegrapher and train dispatcher, I received a free pass for our honeymoon to Niagara Falls. Employees were only entitled to an upper berth in those days, but the chief ticket clerk, having a kind heart, had made certain we would travel in style by providing a drawing room for our round trip. Boy, what luxury! First class all the way! The drawing room contained a chesterfield-bed, carpets, tables and chairs, and a much-needed private bathroom. Just the ticket for shy, young newlyweds!

We boarded the train and headed for the lounge car, followed by our laughing and boisterous entourage. Unknown to us, a trail of confetti was dropping from our clothing, making everyone aware we were just married. The conductor informed us that our train, the Super Continental, would be delayed several hours because of a derailment at Malachi, just down the line. Upon hearing this, our

pals shouted with devilish glee: "Hurrah! We can party all night!" We looked at each other in our plight and silently wished that we could be alone.

After fond farewells to our jubilant friends, we headed for the privacy of our luxurious drawing room. Alone at last, happily we opened the door, and immediately knew why our pals were smirking as they left the train. Rolls of toilet paper were strewn about the room and rubber condoms, blown up with painted smiling faces resembling Li'l Abner's "schmoos" were everywhere. Our suitcases were open and our nightclothes were tied in knots. We laughed until tears were streaming down our faces. Just then, the porter, with a wide knowing grim, probably because he was a co-conspirator, showed up with a chilled bottle of champagne. Our magic moment had finally arrived.

We lay exhausted in our berth, wrapped in each other's arms, watching the moon-bathed wilderness flash by our window. Lakes and streams, pines and distant hills, silhouetted in shadows, cast a spell that enveloped our thoughts. The clickity-clack rhythm of the train gently lulled us into peaceful slumber.

Our three-day train trip was enhanced by tantalizing meals in the dining car. Years before, while working on the northern Hudson Bay Line, I had befriended a cook by the name of Brownie, and lo and behold there he was – the chef on the Super Continental. He treated us royally; making certain that we didn't go hungry, he provided midnight snacks in our private Shangri-la. Some great times were spent in the elegant club car, sipping Manhattans and enjoying the friendliness of our fellow travellers.

We spent a couple of days in Toronto, visiting old friends and sightseeing, then travelled to London, Ontario, where my uncle and aunt welcomed us with open arms. After too short a visit, they loaned us their Pontiac for our honeymoon trip to Niagara.

The scenery was magnificent as we drove along the Welland Canal, stopping every time we saw a ship, and our excitement was growing as we approached one of the great wonders of the world.

It was late afternoon when we arrived at the Clifton Motel and hurriedly unpacked our suitcases. We could hear the

— Bill and Elly Ryan today.

distant roar of the Falls, and see the mist rising over the treetops.

Eager to view the great chasm, we ran hand-in-hand through beautiful Queen Victoria Park. Cherry blossoms were in full bloom and their fragrance was sweet and overpowering. As we approached the railing, the mist washed over our faces and the roar was deafening. We stood arm-in-arm in wonderment of the Falls, admiring its grandeur and its power, as the earth trembled from the force of the cascading water. I could not help but think of the daredevils who had tried to conquer its precipice through the boiling cauldron below. One could almost hear the vows of lovers past who had witnessed this awe – inspiring sight. We were transfixed – one might say hypnotized – by the mighty Falls. It was a long time before we could tear ourselves away to explore the other wonders of this honeymooners' haven.

After purchasing souvenirs and postcards, we reserved a table at the Sheraton Brock Hotel and dressed for dinner. The view from the dining room was exhilarating. While we ate and sipped our wine, we planned our next day's adventure. That evening we danced the night away with

our fellow honeymooners. A special moment was shared as we took one last look at the Falls before retiring. Great coloured spotlights lit the Falls, enhancing the awesome spectacle. We would remember this day all of our lives.

We arose early the next day, showered and dressed in a hurry, gulped down some orange juice and headed out, eager to explore the many exciting sights around the escarpment. Queen Victoria Park, resplendent in her blossomed veil, the Burling Spring, where we peered down through darkness at the flame and wished silent hope for our future together. Then on to Table Rock House where we donned rainsuits and ventured down to the base of Observation Plaza, under the Falls. We laughed at how we looked, drenched in the showers of spray from the Horsehoe Falls. This was the best vantage point for a magnificent and unobstructed view beneath the frothy basin.

'We stood arm-in-arm in wonderment of the Falls, admiring its grandeur and its power, as the earth trembled from the force of the cascading water.'

In our excitement, we had forgotten to eat, so we decided to brunch at the Park Restaurant. A chance to dry off and clean our Pentax, which was clouded with condensation from our picture-taking under the Falls. Our ravenous appetites satisfied, we headed off to Clifton Gate House, Whirlpool House and finally the famous Niagara Spanish Cable Car. We lined up with other sightseeing honeymooners and gingerly stepped onto the swaying trolley. The cable car moved slowly out over the edge of the gorge. Everyone seemed a bit hesitant as the car moved further out over the churning water. Suddenly, the car lurched, shuddered and stopped. Young brides screamed in fright – the rest of us held on for dear life. The car swung slightly on its cable in the wind and, after a short pause, it reversed and trolleyed back to terra firma. That was all the excitement we needed that day.

The flowers were gorgeous at the famous Hydro Floral Clock; more picture-taking, then lunch at the Queenston Heights Restaurant. A visit back in history was next on

our agenda, as we climbed the narrow staircase to the top of the Brock Monument. Whew! That was quite a climb, but the view of the park far below us was well worth it. It was late afternoon when we stopped at the Museum of Indians and Daredevils. The legend of the Maid of the Mist, the escapades of Mrs. Taylor, Blondin, the Hill brothers, among others, and their crude daredevil equipment kept us engrossed for hours in total fascination.

The next day, after a romp through the park for an early morning look at the Horseshoe Falls, we decided to venture to the American side. Through Customs and crossing Rainbow Bridge to Prospect Park, we had an outstanding view of the American Falls. We toured Whirlpool Park, Devil's Hole, Lewiston and Old Fort Niagara before having a picnic lunch at Youngstown. On our return, the trip through Goat Island to Buffalo was scenic and leisurely.

It was late afternoon when we arrived at the famous Chez Ami Restaurant. We were early for dinner and found ourselves to be the only diners there. We were a bit embarrassed, as an army of waiters catered to our every wish. As the orchestra played Shuffle Off to Buffalo, we danced until we were exhausted, then headed back to Niagara Falls and the Clifton Motel.

Time was running out, so the next morning, after a leisurely breakfast, we took one last stroll amid the park's fragrant blossoms. Walking slowly, embracing each other, we strolled to Table Rock for a last, long and lingering look at this great wonder. We were still entranced by this magnificent sight and tried to store its total grandeur in our memory for our long trip home.

The only regret we had is that we didn't have enough time to see everything and especially to ride on The Maid of the Mist. Maybe someday . . .

If marriages are blessed in heaven, then honeymooners must be blessed by their stay in Niagara Falls. I know we were blessed, as we have two great children and three wonderful grandchildren as proof.

Bill Ryan is a resident of Saskatoon, Saskatchewan.

— *Niagara Falls, the honeymoon capital of the world, ushered in the new millennium in 2000 by hosting a mass wedding near the Falls.*

INDEX

INDEX

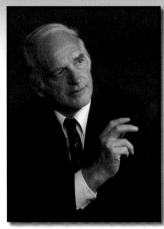

Albert van der Mey

Albert van der Mey is no stranger to the world of books.

In the last 20 years, he has been involved with 24 literary projects in Canada and the Netherlands in several capacities, including authorship.

His first book, Beatrix in Ballingschap, the story of the stay of the Dutch princesses in Ottawa during the Second World War, was published in the Netherlands. The text, written in Dutch, was richly illustrated with about 150 photos, including 29 from the private albums of Princess Juliana and Prince Bernhard. The next project was To All Our Children, a 512-page chronicle of experiences of postwar Dutch immigrants in Canada. The book, published in Ontario, was a tremendous success.

Others followed, including When A Neighbour Came Calling, a collection of stories about the Nazi occupation of Holland; Oranje in Ballingschap, a further look at the exile of the royal family; When Canada Was Home, a pictorial account of the life in Canada of Ottawa-born Princess Margriet; And The Swamp Flourished, an insightful look at the role of the Dutch in the development of Holland Marsh, north of Toronto, and The Dutch Touch in Ontario, a full-colour review of the energy and enterprise that have given the Dutch a solid reputation as hard workers and good citizens.

Albert began his book-writing hobby in the early 1980s while pursuing his full-time work in the daily newspaper business in Ontario. He has been reporter, city editor, news editor and senior editor.

In addition to being an author, he has collaborated on a number of book projects in Holland and has even translated a 115-page genealogy – from Dutch to English – at the request of a businessman in Dusseldorf, Germany. He is currently ghost-writing the autobiography of a resident of Ontario.

Albert has completed manuscripts on the Dutch army's wartime recruitment and training program in Canada; the efforts to prevent the whooping crane, North America's largest indigenous bird, from becoming extinct; the elusive search for treasure on Nova Scotia's Oak Island; the Canadian connection of inventor Alexander Graham Bell, and the two-month stay of Queen Wilhelmina of Holland in Lee, Massachusetts, in the summer of 1942.

And he is passionately continuing the research that he began a number of years ago for what he expects will be a highly successful book: an illustrated history of the Dutch in North America, from the 1600s to the present.

John Van Kooten

During his 25 years in Niagara, John Van Kooten has chalked up an impressive list of achievements in his passionate pursuit of helping his community and promoting the area he so deeply admires and appreciates. He has headed up dozens of causes and projects, recruiting hundreds of talented and enthusiastic volunteers, raising millions and often generating invaluable publicity on a grand scale.

His imagination and leadership brought world-wide attention to his home community of Welland in 1981 when a huge wedding card, signed by 50,000 people, was sent to Buckingham Palace to congratulate Prince Charles and his bride, Lady Diana.

In 1993, five North American television networks and hundreds of newspapers showcased the Champagne Valentine's Day extravaganza which he hosted at the Canadian Horseshoe Falls. Similar attention was focused on Niagara in 1998 when he organized another spectacular celebration: a Marilyn Monroe Look-A-Like Contest.

One of his proudest accomplishments was the founding of the Niagara Film Festival. He managed to raise $1.5 million in funding from 244 tourist-related businesses and four levels of government and attract such big-name stars from the movie world as James Cameron and Christopher Reeve. The exciting event was suspended after two years when John and his wife, Marjie, were seriously injured in a fire at their home.

He also played a major part in raising $1 million for a program that enhanced Welland with 28 massive murals. Moreover, he has served as president of the Welland Rotary Club, as a director of the Chamber of Commerce, as a member of the Welland County Hospital Executive Board and as a marketing director for Niagara's Winter Festival of Lights, the Ontario Winter Games and the region's bid to host the Canada Games.

His unrelenting commitment to community service has brought him a number of honours, including being named Welland's Citizen of the Year by the Chamber of Commerce. He is a recipient of the Murie Misty Award, presented by Niagara's tourism industry for diligent promotional work, and Rotary's prestigious Paul Harris Award for community involvement and contribution.

In his professional career, John has served as Publisher and General Manager of the Niagara Falls Review, the Welland Tribune and the North York and Scarborough Weekly, and as a marketing executive with the Globe and Mail in Toronto and the Charlotte News and Observer in North Carolina.

Thies Bogner

Thies Bogner was born in Celle, Germany, in 1946 and emigrated with his family to Canada in 1953, settling in Welland.

He began his professional career in photography at age 18, studying under the direction of his father, Nikolai, a master photographer specializing in black and white images of superb quality and creativity. Nikolai's work with 35mm Leica cameras made him a pioneer of 35mm photography in Canada since most professional photographers in North America in that period were still using the large plate cameras.

In 1967 Thies became a member of the Professional Photographers of Canada Association and by 1980 received his Masters of Photographic Arts degree. He and his wife, Audrey, also a Master Photographer, own and operate a 10,000 sq. ft. studio and gallery next to the Main St. Bridge in the heart of Welland. In a career spanning 40 years, Thies has taken millions of photographs, including many that have gained him world-wide recognition. He has won many awards for his commercial, portrait, wedding and scenic images. In 1985, he was honoured as Ontario Photographer of the Year. And in 2002, both he and his son, Kristian, who operates a commercial studio in Calgary, Alberta, were included among the top five commercial photographers in Canada. Sixteen of his photographs are in the National Archives of Canada's Loan Collection in Ottawa.

Thies has travelled extensively through Canada, photographing the east and west coasts and the Yukon. He has also been to China three times, capturing the beauty of the country's mountainous regions and teaching his portrait photography style in Beijing, Shanghai, Guilin and Changsha. A collection of his images from China have been exhibited in major cities across Canada.

Closer to home, he is widely known for his remarkable photographs of the Niagara area, including its scenery and its people, shipping on the Welland Canal, the steel, wine and greenhouse industries and sporting events. He has extensive collections of these subjects, particularly Niagara Falls. He also has an impressive collection of black and white portraits of Canada's top authors.

Thies and Audrey have two other children, daughter Arysta and son Andreas, both students at the University of Western Ontario in London.

Floral Passion has started a new chapter in Thies' photographic career. Getting in close and seeing the beauty of flowers through macro photography has taken Thies on an exciting, spiritual journey. Floral Passions has allowed him to showcase the variety of his masterful photographic work.

ACKNOWLEDGMENTS

Kristian Bogner / Sybil Johnson - Team Extreme Media
www.extreme-media.net

Combine world class photography with exceptional design and you have a team … a talented, passionate, high end, energetic team named after their willingness to go to the edge… Extreme Media!!!

The Extreme team at EM has witnessed Floral Passion emerge from a single page to a full scale masterpiece. Each page was crafted with attention to the finest of details. Each photograph was scanned and imaged using a special process to capture every essence and detail. Countless hours were put into the planning, designing, and perfection of Floral Passion.

The Extreme team has the passion to create – Kristian Bogner and Sybil Johnson are the brains and the creative hands behind the Floral Passion book design along with several other members of the EM support team.

Kristian Bogner, president of Extreme Media has had his photography and design business since he was sixteen years old. Kristian learned photography and composition from his parents and Master Photographers Thies and Audrey Bogner and is one of the youngest photographers in his class. Over the past few years he has consistently placed among the top commercial photographers in the country. This year Kristian received the prestigious Commercial Photographer of the Year for Alberta Award as well as numerous other awards. Kristian was also runner up for Commercial Photographer of the Year for Canada for the past two years and has had many of his images accepted into a collection in the National Archives. He inspires others with his passion for his art and his vast technical eXpertise in photography, digital imaging, and design combined with his marketing and print background.

Sybil Johnson, an integral part of the Extreme Media team, graduated from a Package and Graphic Design program in Toronto with distinction. She has made her mark with Extreme Media and more than proven her commitment to the team. Sybil has always had a natural gift – an eye for design and an eXtraordinary perspective.

Extreme Media's award-winning photography and design work can be seen in magazines, billboards, brochures, ads, campaigns, books and web sites across Canada and internationally.

We would like to express our greatest thanks to Thies Bogner who went above all expectations and flew out to Calgary numerous times to ensure that the project was a success. A special thanks to Mr. John VanKooten for his undying support and patience throughout all the grueling stages of this project.

Floral Passion is a reality.

It has taken three joyous years to complete. The task has been difficult and sometimes exhausting, but always rewarding.

On our own, **Floral Passion** would have remained no more than a dream. Fortunately, we were able to assemble a supportive team of talented people who were carefully selected for their proven track records in their specific areas of expertise. In addition, they share a superior sense of creativity, entrepreneurship, social conscience and intellectual integrity. Their support, advice and constructive criticism have played a key role in the development and production of this book.

We first of all want to thank our life partners, Marjorie Van Kooten, Marianne van der Mey and Audrey Bogner, and our families for their patience, understanding, encouragement and enthusiastic support for the project.

We gratefully acknowledge and express deep appreciation to the following people who made it all possible:

Frank Campion, Brad Clements, Brian Leydon and Jim Dohn who created and developed the business and marketing plans for **Floral Passion**.

Jerry Dupas, Don Johnstone and Dennis O'Neill whose input and critical analysis added greatly to the high quality of the project.

Joe Barkovich, Chris Bonfoco, Jack Berkhout, Fran Dekker, Rob Neill of Durward, Jones and Barkwell & Company, Mel Groom, Ben Kooter of Vanwell Publishing, Steve Latinovich of Flett Beccario Barristers, Marten A. Mol, Jan de Koning, Napolean A. P. Winia of the Consulate General of the Netherlands in Toronto as well as a number of his colleagues at the Royal Netherlands Embassies in Ottawa and Washington, D.C., Jevonne Nicolas, Tony Thompson, Theresa Yaeger, Bill Vermeer, Julie Noris, Debi Rosati and Anthony Valeriote for their expert advice, their willingness to take on any task and their never-ending enthusiasm.

Finally, a big thank-you to hundreds of other individuals, many of them named within these covers, who went out of their way to accommodate us as we criss-crossed the beautiful Niagara Peninsula, exploring the wonderful world that exists under all the glass and plastic.

WORKING TOGETHER FOR A BETTER TOMORROW

This mesmerizing story of Niagara's greenhouse industry is made possible through the generous financial support of the sponsors listed below. As good corporate citizens, they realize their privilege and responsibility to support and enrich the communities in which they do business. We wish to express our sincerest gratitude and appreciation for their vision. By endorsing Floral Passion, they have expressed a genuine commitment to the floral industry. With their assistance, the Floral Passion dream has become a reality.

Durward Jones Barkwell & Company	Agro Dynamics
Niagara Credit Union	Berco Greenhouse Mechanical Systems
Niagara Economic Tourism Corporation	Gary's Electric Motor Shop
De Cloet Greenhouse Mfg. Ltd.	Gintec Shade Technologies
Horta-Craft Limited	J. B. Controls & Automation Inc.
Hydro-Agri Canada L. P.	Priva Computers Inc.
Consul Economic Affairs Netherlands	Specialties Robert Legault Inc.
Campion Marketing Services Ltd.	Timbro Design Build Contractors
D'Angelo Printing Co.	Zwart Systems
Agri-Food Laboratories	

– The Netherlands Ambassador to Canada, J. G. (Como) van Hellenberg Hubar (seated), meets with John Van Kooten, publisher of Floral Passion, Albert van der Mey, the author, Thies Bogner, the photographer, and Debbie Zimmerman, chair of the Regional Municipality of Niagara, during his visit to Niagara-on-the-Lake in 2002.

Floriculture's value worldwide is more than $22 billion
annually. This huge industry involves many thousands
of growers around the globe, in countries such as the
United States, Japan, the Netherlands, Germany, Italy,
France, Ecuador, Colombia and Canada. Although this
book deals primarily with the growers in Niagara, one of
the prettiest and best-known spots in the world, it is with
deep admiration and appreciation that we dedicate it to
everyone who is involved in some way in the wonderful
business of growing happiness.

Distributed by Vanwell Publishing Ltd.,
1 Northrup Crescent, PO Box 2131,
St. Catharines, Ontario L2R 7S2
1-800-661-6136   sales@vanwell.com

National Library of Canada Cataloguing in Publication

Van der Mey, Albert
  Floral passion / Albert van der Mey, Thies Bogner, John Van Kooten.

Includes index.
ISBN: 0-9733100-0-6   First Edition

  1.Floriculture–Ontario–Niagara Peninsula–History. 2.Floriculturists–
Ontario–Niagara Peninsula–Interviews. 3.Greenhouse management–
Ontario–Niagara Peninsula–History. 4.Niagara Peninsula (Ont.)–History.
I.Bogner, Thies II.VanKooten, John III. Title.

SB443.4   C3V35 2003   655.9'09713'38   C2003-903996-X